# Information Storage and Management

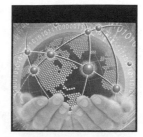

# Information Storage and Management

## Storing, Managing, and Protecting Digital Information in Classic, Virtualized, and Cloud Environments

## 2nd Edition

Edited by
Somasundaram Gnanasundaram
Alok Shrivastava

John Wiley & Sons, Inc.

Information Storage and Management: Storing, Managing, and Protecting Digital Information in Classic, Virtualized, and Cloud Environments 2nd Edition

Published by
John Wiley & Sons, Inc.
10475 Crosspoint Boulevard
Indianapolis, IN 46256
www.wiley.com

Copyright © 2012 by EMC Corporation
Published by John Wiley & Sons, Inc., Indianapolis, Indiana

Published simultaneously in Canada

ISBN: 978-1-118-09483-9
ISBN: 978-1-118-22347-5 (ebk)
ISBN: 978-1-118-23696-3 (ebk)
ISBN: 978-1-118-26187-3 (ebk)

Manufactured in the United States of America

10 9 8 7 6 5 4 3

For general information on our other products and services please contact our Customer Care Department within the United States at (877) 762-2974, outside the United States at (317) 572-3993 or fax (317) 572-4002.

Wiley publishes in a variety of print and electronic formats and by print-on-demand. Some material included with standard print versions of this book may not be included in e-books or in print-on-demand. If this book refers to media such as a CD or DVD that is not included in the version you purchased, you may download this material at http://booksupport.wiley.com. For more information about Wiley products, visit www.wiley.com.

**Library of Congress Control Number:** 2012936405

# About the Editors

**Somasundaram Gnanasundaram (Somu)** is the director at EMC Education Services, leading worldwide industry readiness initiatives. Somu is the architect of EMC's open curriculum, aimed at addressing the knowledge gap that exists in the IT industry in the area of information storage and emerging technologies such as cloud computing. Under his leadership and direction, industry readiness initiatives such as the EMC Academic Alliance program continue to experience significant growth, educating thousands of students worldwide on information storage and management technologies. Key areas of Somu's responsibility include guiding a global team of professionals, identifying and partnering with global IT education providers, and setting the overall direction for EMC's industry readiness initiatives. Prior to his current role, Somu held various managerial and leadership roles within EMC as well as with other leading IT service providers. He holds an undergraduate technology degree from Anna University Chennai, and a Master of Technology degree from the Indian Institute of Technology, Mumbai, India. Somu has been in the IT industry for more than 25 years.

**Alok Shrivastava** is the senior director at EMC Education Services. Alok is the architect of several of EMC's successful education initiatives, including the industry leading EMC Proven Professional program, industry readiness programs such as EMC's Academic Alliance, and this unique and valuable book on information storage technology. Alok provides vision and leadership to a team of highly talented experts, practitioners, and professionals that develops world-class technical education for EMC's employees, partners, customers, students, and other industry professionals covering technologies such as storage, virtualization, cloud, and big data. Prior to his success in education, Alok built and led a highly successful team of EMC presales engineers in Asia-Pacific and Japan. Earlier in his career, Alok was a systems manager, storage manager, and backup/restore/disaster recovery consultant working with some of the world's largest data centers and IT installations. He holds dual Master's degrees from the Indian Institute of Technology in Mumbai, India, and the University of Sagar in India. Alok has worked in information storage technology and has held a unique passion for this field for most of his 30-year career in IT.

# Credits

**Executive Editor**
Carol Long

**Project Editor**
Tom Dinse

**Senior Production Editor**
Debra Banninger

**Copy Editor**
San Dee Phillips

**Editorial Manager**
Mary Beth Wakefield

**Freelancer Editorial Manager**
Rosemarie Graham

**Associate Director of Marketing**
David Mayhew

**Marketing Manager**
Ashley Zurcher

**Business Manager**
Amy Knies

**Production Manager**
Tim Tate

**Vice President and Executive Group Publisher**
Richard Swadley

**Vice President and Executive Publisher**
Neil Edde

**Associate Publisher**
Jim Minatel

**Project Coordinator, Cover**
Katie Crocker

**Proofreader**
Nancy Carrasco

**Indexer**
Robert Swanson

**Cover Designer**
Mallesh Gurram, EMC

# Acknowledgments

When we embarked upon the project to develop this book in 2008, the first challenge was to identify a team of subject matter experts covering the vast range of technologies that form the modern information storage infrastructure.

A key factor that continues to work in our favor is that at EMC we have the technologies, the know-how, and many of the best talents in the industry. When we reached out to individual experts, they were as excited as we were about the prospect of publishing a comprehensive book on information storage technology. This was an opportunity to share their expertise with professionals and students worldwide.

This book is the result of efforts and contributions from a number of key EMC organizations led by EMC Education Services and supported by the office of CTO, Global Marketing, and EMC Engineering.

The first edition of the book was published in 2009, and the effort was led by **Ganesh Rajaratnam** of EMC Education Services and **Dr. David Black** of the EMC CTO office. The book continues to be the most popular storage technology book around the world among professionals and students. In addition to its English and e-book editions, it is available in Mandarin, Portuguese, and Russian.

With the emergence of cloud computing and the broad adoption of virtualization technologies by the organizations, we felt it is time to update the content to include information storage in those emerging technologies and also the new developments in the field of information storage. **Ashish Garg** of Education Services led the effort to update content for the second edition of this book. In addition to reviewing the content, **Joe Milardo** and **Nancy Gessler** led the effort of content review with their team of subject matter experts.

We are grateful to the following experts from EMC for their support in developing and reviewing the content for various chapters of this book:

Content contributors:

| | |
|---|---|
| Rodrigo Alves | Sagar Kotekar Patil |
| Charlie Brooks | Andre Rossouw |
| Debasish Chakrabarty | Tony Santamaria |
| Diana Davis | Saravanaraj Sridharan |
| Amit Deshmukh | Ganesh Sundaresan |
| Michael Dulavitz | Jim Tracy |
| Dr. Vanchi Gurumoorthy | Anand Varkar |
| Simon Hawkshaw | Dr. Viswanth VS |
| Anbuselvi Jeyakumar | |

Content reviewers:

| | |
|---|---|
| Ronen Artzi | Manoj Kumar |
| Eric Baize | Arthur Johnson |
| Greg Baltazar | Michelle Lavoie |
| Edward Bell | Tom McGowan |
| Ed Belliveau | Jeffery Moore |
| Paul Brant | Toby Morral |
| Juergen Busch | Wayne Pauley |
| Christopher Chaulk | Peter Popieniuck |
| Brian Collins | Ira Schild |
| Juan Cubillos | Shashikanth, Punuru |
| John Dowd | Murugeson Purushothaman |
| Roger Dupuis | Shekhar Sengupta |
| Deborah Filer | Kevin Sheridan |
| Bala Ganeshan | Ed VanSickle |
| Jason Gervickas | Mike Warner |
| Jody Goncalves | Ronnie Zubi |
| Jack Harwood | Evan Burleigh |

We also thank **Mallik Motilal** of EMC for his support in creating all illustrations; **Mallesh Gurram** of EMC for the cover design; and the publisher, **John Wiley & Sons**, for its timely support in bringing this book to the industry.

— **Somasundaram Gnanasundaram**
*Director, Education Services, EMC Corporation*

— **Alok Shrivastava**
*Senior Director, Education Services, EMC Corporation*
March 2012

# Contents

# Icons Used In This Book

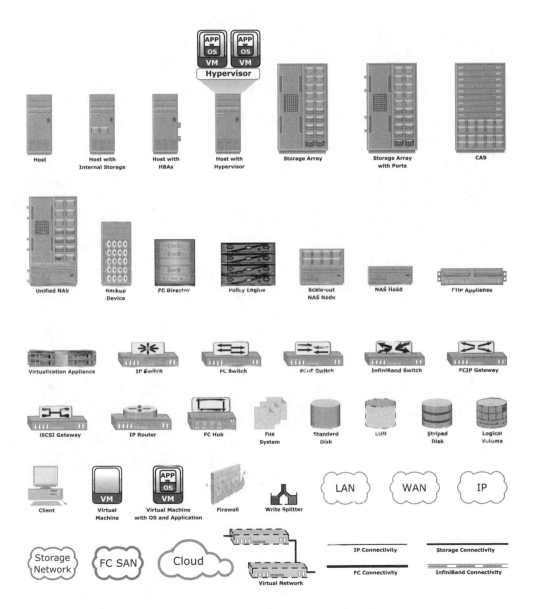

# Foreword

In the two short years since we originally published this book, the world as we've known it has undergone a change of unprecedented magnitude. We are now in a digital era in which the world's information is more than doubling every two years, and in the next decade alone IT departments globally will need to manage 50 times more information while the number of IT professionals available will grow only 1.5 times (IDC Digital Universe Study, sponsored by EMC, June 2011). Virtualization and cloud computing are no longer an option for enterprises but an imperative for survival. And Big Data is creating significant new opportunity for organizations to analyze, act on, and drive new value from their most valuable asset — information — and create competitive advantage.

The Information Technology industry is undergoing a tremendous transformation as a result. The Cloud has introduced radically new technologies, computing models, and disciplines, dramatically changing the way IT is built, run, governed, and consumed. It has created new roles such as cloud technologists and cloud architects to lead this transformation. And it is transforming the IT organization from a back office overseer of infrastructure — with the task of keeping it running — into a key strategic contributor of the business with a focus on delivering IT as a service.

All of these changes demand new core competencies within the IT organization and a new way of thinking about technology in the context of business requirements and strategic objectives — even a new organizational structure within the data center. Information storage and management professionals must build on their existing knowledge and develop additional skills in the technologies most critical to successfully undertaking the complex, multi-year journey to the cloud: virtualization, converged networking, information security, data protection, and data warehousing and analytics, to name a few.

We have revised *Information Storage and Management* to give you an updated perspective and behind-the-scenes view of the new technologies and skills required today to design, implement, manage, optimize, and leverage virtualized infrastructures to achieve the business benefits of the cloud. You will learn from EMC subject matter experts with the most advanced training, certification, and practical experience in the industry.

If you are a storage and information management professional in the midst of virtualizing your data center, or building a robust cloud infrastructure — or if you are simply interested in learning the concept and principles of these new paradigms — transforming your IT skills has never been more critical. And by accelerating your transformation with this book and by taking advantage of the new training and certifications now available to you, you can help close a critical skills gap in the industry, advance your career, and become a valued contributor to your company's growth, sustainability, and profitability.

The challenges in this industry are many — but so are the rewards. Nelson Mandela said, "Education is the most powerful weapon which you can use to change the world." I hope you will make this book a key part of your IT education and professional development — regardless of your current role — and that you will seize this opportunity to help transform yourself and change the world.

*Thomas P. Clancy*
*Vice President, Education Services, EMC Corporation*
*May 2012*

# Introduction

Information storage is a central pillar of information technology. A large amount of digital information is created every moment by individuals and organizations. This information needs to be stored, protected, optimized, and managed in classic, virtualized, and rapidly evolving cloud environments.

Not long ago, information storage was seen as only a bunch of disks or tapes attached to the back of the computer to store data. Even today, primarily those in the storage industry understand the critical role that information storage technology plays in the availability, performance, integration, and optimization of the entire IT infrastructure. During the last decade, information storage has developed into a highly sophisticated technology, providing a variety of solutions for storing, managing, connecting, protecting, securing, sharing, and optimizing digital information.

The wide adoption of virtualization, emergence of cloud computing, multifold increase in the volume of data year over year and various types and sources of data — all these factors make modern storage technologies more important and relevant for the success of business and other organizations. More than ever, IT managers are challenged with employing and developing highly skilled technical professionals with storage technology expertise across the classic, virtualized, and cloud environments.

Many leading universities and colleges now include storage technology courses in their regular computer technology or IT curriculum, yet many of today's IT professionals, even those with years of experience, have not benefited from this formal education. Therefore, many seasoned professionals -- including application, system, database, and network administrators — do not share a common foundation about how storage technology affects their areas of expertise.

This book is designed and developed to enable professionals and students to achieve a comprehensive understanding of all segments of storage technology. Although the product examples used in the book are from the EMC Corporation, an understanding of the technology concepts and principles prepare you to easily understand products from various technology vendors.

This book has 15 chapters, organized in five sections. Advanced topics build upon the topics learned in previous chapters. Section I introduces the concepts of virtualization and cloud infrastructure, which carry throughout the book to ensure that storage technologies are discussed in the context of traditional or classic, virtualized, and rapidly evolving cloud environments.

**Section I, "Storage System":** The four chapters in this section cover information growth and challenges, define a storage system and data center environment, review the evolution of storage technology, and introduce intelligent storage systems. This section also introduces concepts of virtualization and cloud computing.

**Section II, "Storage Networking Technologies":** These four chapters cover Fibre Channel storage area network (FC-SAN), Internet Protocol SAN (IP SAN), Network-attached storage (NAS), Object-based storage, and Unified storage. Concepts of storage federation and converged networking (FCoE) are also discussed in this section.

**Section III, "Backup, Archive, and Replication":** These four chapters cover business continuity, backup and recovery, deduplication, data archiving, local and remote data replication, in both classic and virtualized environments.

**Section IV, "Cloud Computing":** The chapter in this section introduces cloud computing, including infrastructure framework, service models, deployment options, and considerations for migration to the cloud.

**Section V, "Securing and Managing Storage Infrastructure":** These two chapters cover storage security, and storage infrastructure monitoring and management, including security and management considerations in virtualized and cloud environments

This book has a supplementary website that provides additional up-to-date learning aids and reading material. Visit `http://education.EMC.com/ismbook` for details.

# EMC Academic Alliance

University and college faculties are invited to join the Academic Alliance program to access unique "open" curriculum-based education on the following topics:

- Information Storage and Management
- Cloud Infrastructure and Services

- Data Science and Big Data Analytics
- Backup Recovery Systems and Architecture

The program provides faculty with course resources to prepare students for opportunities that exist in today's evolving IT industry at no cost. For more information, visit http://education.EMC.com/academicalliance.

## EMC Proven Professional Certification

 EMC Proven Professional is a leading education and certification program in the IT industry, providing comprehensive coverage of information storage technologies, virtualization, cloud computing, data science/big data analytics, and more.

Being proven means investing in yourself and formally validating your expertise!

This book prepares you for Information Storage and Management exam E10-001, leading to EMC Proven Professional Information Storage Associate v2 certification.

Visit http://education.EMC.com for details.

# Information Storage and Management

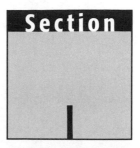

# Section

# I

# Storage System

## In This Section

# Chapter 1
# Introduction to
# Information Storage

Information is increasingly important in our daily lives. We have become information-dependent in the 21st century, living in an on-command, on-demand world, which means, we need information when and where it is required. We access the Internet every day to perform searches, participate in social networking, send and receive e-mails, share pictures and videos, and use scores of other applications. Equipped with a growing number of content-generating devices, more information is created by individuals than by organizations (including business, governments, non-profits and so on). Information created by individuals gains value when shared with others. When created, information resides locally on devices, such as cell phones, smartphones, tablets, cameras, and laptops. To be shared, this information needs to be uploaded to central data repositories (data centers) via networks. Although the majority of information is created by individuals, it is stored and managed by a relatively small number of organizations.

The importance, dependency, and volume of information for the business world also continue to grow at astounding rates. Businesses depend on fast and reliable access to information critical to their success. Examples of business processes or systems that rely on digital information include airline reservations, telecommunications billing, Internet commerce, electronic banking, credit card transaction processing, capital/stock trading, health care claims processing, life science research, and so on. The increasing dependence of businesses on information has amplified the challenges in storing, protecting, and managing data. Legal, regulatory, and contractual obligations regarding the availability and protection of data further add to these challenges.

Organizations usually maintain one or more data centers to store and manage information. A *data center* is a facility that contains information storage and other physical information technology (IT) resources for computing, networking, and storing information. In traditional data centers, the storage resources are typically dedicated for each of the business units or applications. The proliferation of new applications and increasing data growth have resulted in islands of discrete information storage infrastructures in these data centers. This leads to complex information management and underutilization of storage resources. Virtualization optimizes resource utilization and eases resource management. Organizations incorporate virtualization in their data centers to transform them into *virtualized data centers* (VDCs). Cloud computing, which represents a fundamental shift in how IT is built, managed, and provided, further reduces information storage and management complexity and IT resource provisioning time. Cloud computing brings in a fully automated request-fulfillment process that enables users to rapidly obtain storage and other IT resources on demand. Through cloud computing, an organization can rapidly deploy applications where the underlying storage capability can scale-up and scale-down, based on the business requirements.

This chapter describes the evolution of information storage architecture from a server-centric model to an information-centric model. It also provides an overview of virtualization and cloud computing.

# 1.1 Information Storage

Organizations process data to derive the information required for their day-to-day operations. Storage is a repository that enables users to persistently store and retrieve this digital data.

## 1.1.1 Data

*Data* is a collection of raw facts from which conclusions might be drawn. Handwritten letters, a printed book, a family photograph, printed and duly signed copies of mortgage papers, a bank's ledgers, and an airline ticket are all examples that contain data.

Before the advent of computers, the methods adopted for data creation and sharing were limited to fewer forms, such as paper and film. Today, the same data can be converted into more convenient forms, such as an e-mail message, an e-book, a digital image, or a digital movie. This data can be generated using a computer and stored as strings of binary numbers (0s and 1s), as shown in Figure 1-1. Data in this form is called *digital data* and is accessible by the user only after a computer processes it.

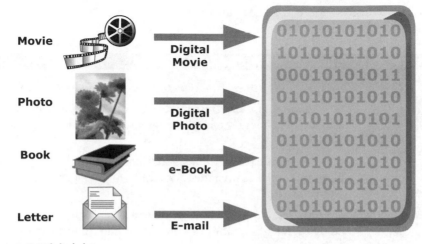

**Figure 1-1:** Digital data

With the advancement of computer and communication technologies, the rate of data generation and sharing has increased exponentially. The following is a list of some of the factors that have contributed to the growth of digital data:

- **Increase in data-processing capabilities:** Modern computers provide a significant increase in processing and storage capabilities. This enables the conversion of various types of content and media from conventional forms to digital formats.

- **Lower cost of digital storage:** Technological advances and the decrease in the cost of storage devices have provided low-cost storage solutions. This cost benefit has increased the rate at which digital data is generated and stored.

- **Affordable and faster communication technology:** The rate of sharing digital data is now much faster than traditional approaches. A handwritten letter might take a week to reach its destination, whereas it typically takes only a few seconds for an e-mail message to reach its recipient.

- **Proliferation of applications and smart devices:** Smartphones, tablets, and newer digital devices, along with smart applications, have significantly contributed to the generation of digital content.

Inexpensive and easier ways to create, collect, and store all types of data, coupled with increasing individual and business needs, have led to accelerated data growth, popularly termed *data explosion*. Both individuals and businesses have contributed in varied proportions to this data explosion.

The importance and value of data vary with time. Most of the data created holds significance for a short term but becomes less valuable over time. This governs the type of data storage solutions used. Typically, recent data which has higher usage is stored on faster and more expensive storage. As it ages, it may be moved to slower, less expensive but reliable storage.

---

**EXAMPLES OF RESEARCH AND BUSINESS DATA**

Following are some examples of research and business data:

■     **Customer data:** Data related to a company's customers, such as order details, shipping addresses, and purchase history.

■     **Product data:** Includes data related to various aspects of a product, such as inventory, description, pricing, availability, and sales.

■ **Medical data:** Data related to the healthcare industry, such as patient history, radiological images, details of medication and other treatment, and insurance information.

■ **Seismic data:** Seismology is a scientific study of earthquakes. It involves collecting data and processes to derive information that helps determine the location and magnitude of earthquakes.

---

Businesses generate vast amounts of data and then extract meaningful information from this data to derive economic benefits. Therefore, businesses need to maintain data and ensure its availability over a longer period. Furthermore, the data can vary in criticality and might require special handling. For example, legal and regulatory requirements mandate that banks maintain account information for their customers accurately and securely. Some businesses handle data for millions of customers and ensure the security and integrity of data over a long period of time. This requires high-performance and high-capacity storage devices with enhanced security and compliance that can retain data for a long period.

## 1.1.2 Types of Data

Data can be classified as structured or unstructured (see Figure 1-2) based on how it is stored and managed. Structured data is organized in rows and columns in a rigidly defined format so that applications can retrieve and process it efficiently. Structured data is typically stored using a database management system (DBMS).

Data is unstructured if its elements cannot be stored in rows and columns, which makes it difficult to query and retrieve by applications. For example, customer contacts that are stored in various forms such as sticky notes, e-mail messages, business cards, or even digital format files, such as .doc, .txt, and .pdf. Due to its unstructured nature, it is difficult to retrieve this data using a traditional customer relationship management application. A vast majority of new data being created today is unstructured. The industry is challenged with with new architectures, technologies, techniques, and skills to store, manage, analyze, and derive value from unstructured data from numerous sources.

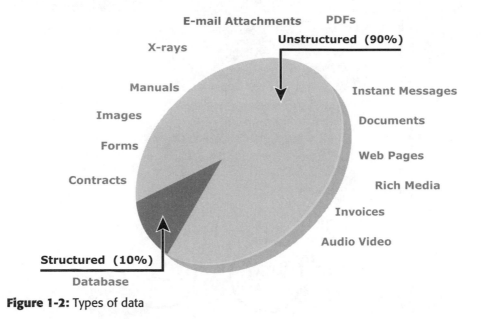

**Figure 1-2:** Types of data

## 1.1.3 Big Data

*Big data* is a new and evolving concept, which refers to data sets whose sizes are beyond the capability of commonly used software tools to capture, store, manage, and process within acceptable time limits. It includes both structured and unstructured data generated by a variety of sources, including business application transactions, web pages, videos, images, e-mails, social media, and so on. These data sets typically require real-time capture or updates for analysis, predictive modeling, and decision making.

Significant opportunities exist to extract value from big data. The big data ecosystem (see Figure 1-3) consists of the following:

1. Devices that collect data from multiple locations and also generate new data about this data (metadata).

2. Data collectors who gather data from devices and users.

3. Data aggregators that compile the collected data to extract meaningful information.

4. Data users and buyers who benefit from the information collected and aggregated by others in the data value chain.

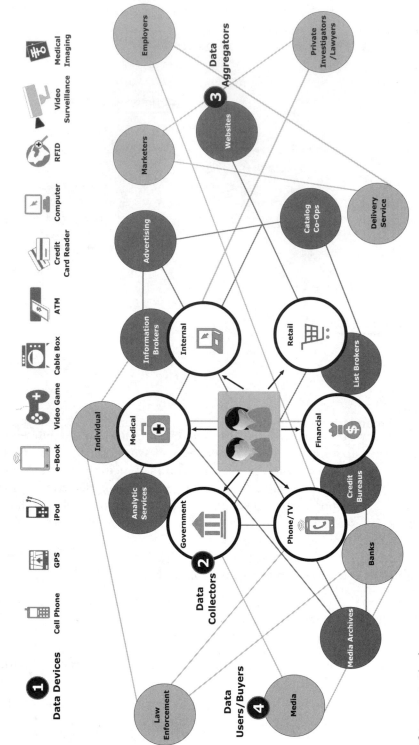

**Figure 1-3:** Big data ecosystem

Traditional IT infrastructure and data processing tools and methodologies are inadequate to handle the volume, variety, dynamism, and complexity of big data. Analyzing big data in real time requires new techniques, architectures, and tools that provide high performance, massively parallel processing (MPP) data platforms, and advanced analytics on the data sets.

Data science is an emerging discipline, which enables organizations to derive business value from big data. Data science represents the synthesis of several existing disciplines, such as statistics, math, data visualization, and computer science to enable data scientists to develop advanced algorithms for the purpose of analyzing vast amounts of information to drive new value and make more data-driven decisions.

Several industries and markets currently looking to employ data science techniques include medical and scientific research, health care, public administration, fraud detection, social media, banks, insurance companies, and other digital information-based entities that benefit from the analytics of big data.

### 1.1.4 Information

Data, whether structured or unstructured, does not fulfill any purpose for individuals or businesses unless it is presented in a meaningful form. *Information* is the intelligence and knowledge derived from data.

Businesses analyze raw data to identify meaningful trends. On the basis of these trends, a company can plan or modify its strategy. For example, a retailer identifies customers' preferred products and brand names by analyzing their purchase patterns and maintaining an inventory of those products. Effective data analysis not only extends its benefits to existing businesses, but also creates the potential for new business opportunities by using the information in creative ways.

### 1.1.5 Storage

Data created by individuals or businesses must be stored so that it is easily accessible for further processing. In a computing environment, devices designed for storing data are termed *storage devices* or simply *storage*. The type of storage used varies based on the type of data and the rate at which it is created and used. Devices, such as a media card in a cell phone or digital camera, DVDs, CD-ROMs, and disk drives in personal computers are examples of storage devices.

Businesses have several options available for storing data, including internal hard disks, external disk arrays, and tapes.

## 1.2 Evolution of Storage Architecture

Historically, organizations had centralized computers (mainframes) and information storage devices (tape reels and disk packs) in their data center. The evolution of open systems, their affordability, and ease of deployment made it possible for business units/departments to have their own servers and storage. In earlier implementations of open systems, the storage was typically internal to the server. These storage devices could not be shared with any other servers. This approach is referred to as *server-centric storage architecture* (see Figure 1-4 [a]). In this architecture, each server has a limited number of storage devices, and any administrative tasks, such as maintenance of the server or increasing storage capacity, might result in unavailability of information. The proliferation of departmental servers in an enterprise resulted in unprotected, unmanaged, fragmented islands of information and increased capital and operating expenses..

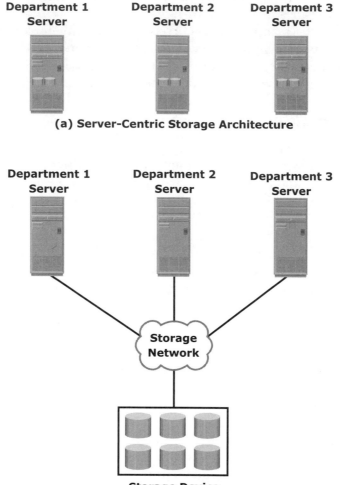

**(a) Server-Centric Storage Architecture**

**Storage Device**

**(b) Information-Centric Storage Architecture**

**Figure 1-4:** Evolution of storage architecture

To overcome these challenges, storage evolved from server-centric to *informa-tion-centric architecture* (see Figure 1-4 [b]). In this architecture, storage devices are managed centrally and independent of servers. These centrally-managed storage devices are shared with multiple servers. When a new server is deployed in the environment, storage is assigned from the same shared storage devices to that server. The capacity of shared storage can be increased dynamically by adding more storage devices without impacting information availability. In this architecture, information management is easier and cost-effective.

Storage technology and architecture continue to evolve, which enables organizations to consolidate, protect, optimize, and leverage their data to achieve the highest return on information assets.

# 1.3 Data Center Infrastructure

Organizations maintain data centers to provide centralized data-processing capabilities across the enterprise. Data centers house and manage large amounts of data. The data center infrastructure includes hardware components, such as computers, storage systems, network devices, and power backups; and software components, such as applications, operating systems, and management software. It also includes environmental controls, such as air conditioning, fire suppression, and ventilation.

Large organizations often maintain more than one data center to distribute data processing workloads and provide backup if a disaster occurs.

## 1.3.1 Core Elements of a Data Center

Five core elements are essential for the functionality of a data center:

- **Application:** A computer program that provides the logic for computing operations

- **Database management system (DBMS):** Provides a structured way to store data in logically organized tables that are interrelated

- **Host or compute:** A computing platform (hardware, firmware, and software) that runs applications and databases

- **Network:** A data path that facilitates communication among various networked devices

- **Storage:** A device that stores data persistently for subsequent use

These core elements are typically viewed and managed as separate entities, but all the elements must work together to address data-processing requirements.

**In this book, host, compute, and server are used interchangeably to represent the element that runs applications.**

Figure 1-5 shows an example of an online order transaction system that involves the five core elements of a data center and illustrates their functionality in a business process.

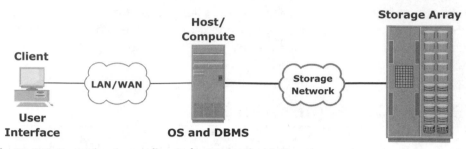

**Figure 1-5:** Example of an online order transaction system

A customer places an order through a client machine connected over a LAN/WAN to a host running an order-processing application. The client accesses the DBMS on the host through the application to provide order-related information, such as the customer name, address, payment method, products ordered, and quantity ordered.

The DBMS uses the host operating system to write this data to the physical disks in the storage array. The storage networks provide the communication link between the host and the storage array and transports the request to read or write data between them. The storage array, after receiving the read or write request from the host, performs the necessary operations to store the data on physical disks.

## 1.3.2 Key Characteristics of a Data Center

Uninterrupted operation of data centers is critical to the survival and success of a business. Organizations must have a reliable infrastructure that ensures that data is accessible at all times. Although the characteristics shown in Figure 1-6 are applicable to all elements of the data center infrastructure, the focus here is on storage systems. This book covers the various technologies and solutions to meet these requirements.

- **Availability:** A data center should ensure the availability of information when required. Unavailability of information could cost millions of dollars per hour to businesses, such as financial services, telecommunications, and e-commerce.

- **Security:** Data centers must establish policies, procedures, and core element integration to prevent unauthorized access to information.

- **Scalability:** Business growth often requires deploying more servers, new applications, and additional databases. Data center resources should scale based on requirements, without interrupting business operations.

- **Performance:** All the elements of the data center should provide optimal performance based on the required service levels.

- **Data integrity:** Data integrity refers to mechanisms, such as error correction codes or parity bits, which ensure that data is stored and retrieved exactly as it was received.

- **Capacity:** Data center operations require adequate resources to store and process large amounts of data, efficiently. When capacity requirements increase, the data center must provide additional capacity without interrupting availability or with minimal disruption. Capacity may be managed by reallocating the existing resources or by adding new resources.

- **Manageability:** A data center should provide easy and integrated management of all its elements. Manageability can be achieved through automation and reduction of human (manual) intervention in common tasks.

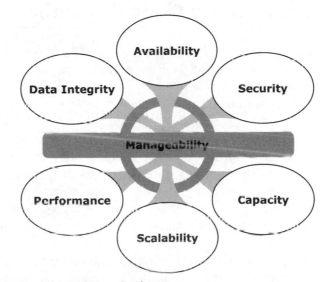

**Figure 1-6:** Key characteristics of a data center

## 1.3.3 Managing a Data Center

Managing a data center involves many tasks. The key management activities include the following:

- **Monitoring:** It is a continuous process of gathering information on various elements and services running in a data center. The aspects of a data center that are monitored include security, performance, availability, and capacity.

- **Reporting:** It is done periodically on resource performance, capacity, and utilization. Reporting tasks help to establish business justifications and chargeback of costs associated with data center operations.

- **Provisioning:** It is a process of providing the hardware, software, and other resources required to run a data center. Provisioning activities primarily include resources management to meet capacity, availability, performance, and security requirements.

Virtualization and cloud computing have dramatically changed the way data center infrastructure resources are provisioned and managed. Organizations are rapidly deploying virtualization on various elements of data centers to optimize their utilization. Further, continuous cost pressure on IT and on-demand data processing requirements have resulted in the adoption of cloud computing.

# 1.4 Virtualization and Cloud Computing

Virtualization is a technique of abstracting physical resources, such as compute, storage, and network, and making them appear as logical resources. Virtualization has existed in the IT industry for several years and in different forms. Common examples of virtualization are virtual memory used on compute systems and partitioning of raw disks.

Virtualization enables pooling of physical resources and providing an aggregated view of the physical resource capabilities. For example, storage virtualization enables multiple pooled storage devices to appear as a single large storage entity. Similarly, by using compute virtualization, the CPU capacity of the pooled physical servers can be viewed as the aggregation of the power of all CPUs (in megahertz). Virtualization also enables centralized management of pooled resources.

Virtual resources can be created and provisioned from the pooled physical resources. For example, a virtual disk of a given capacity can be created from a storage pool or a virtual server with specific CPU power and memory can be configured from a compute pool. These virtual resources share pooled physical resources, which improves the utilization of physical IT resources. Based on business requirements, capacity can be added to or removed from the virtual resources without any disruption to applications or users. With improved utilization of IT assets, organizations save the costs associated with procurement and management of new physical resources. Moreover, fewer physical resources means less space and energy, which leads to better economics and green computing.

In today's fast-paced and competitive environment, organizations must be agile and flexible to meet changing market requirements. This leads to rapid expansion and upgrade of resources while meeting shrinking or stagnant IT budgets. *Cloud computing*, addresses these challenges efficiently. Cloud computing enables individuals or businesses to use IT resources as a service over the network. It provides highly scalable and flexible computing that enables provisioning of resources on demand. Users can scale up or scale down the demand of computing resources, including storage capacity, with minimal management effort or service provider interaction. Cloud computing empowers self-service requesting through a fully automated request-fulfillment process. Cloud computing enables consumption-based metering; therefore, consumers pay only for the resources they use, such as CPU hours used, amount of data transferred, and gigabytes of data stored.

Cloud infrastructure is usually built upon virtualized data centers, which provide resource pooling and rapid provisioning of resources. Information storage in virtualized and cloud environments is detailed later in the book.

## Summary

This chapter described the importance of data, information, and storage infrastructure. Meeting today's storage needs begins with understanding the type of data, its value, and key attributes of a data center.

The evolution of storage architecture and the core elements of a data center covered in this chapter provided the foundation for information storage and management. The emergence of virtualization has provided the opportunity to transform classic data centers into virtualized data centers. Cloud computing is further changing the way IT resources are provisioned and consumed.

The subsequent chapters in the book provide comprehensive details on various aspects of information storage and management in both classic and virtualized environments. It begins with describing the core elements of a data center with a focus on storage systems and RAID (covered in Chapters 2, 3, and 4). Chapters 5 through 8 of this book detail various storage networking technologies, such as storage area network (SAN), network attached storage (NAS), and object-based and unified storage. Chapters 9 through 12 cover various business continuity solutions, such as backup and replication, along with archival technologies. Chapter 13 introduces cloud infrastructure and services. Chapters 14 and 15 describe securing and managing storage in traditional and virtualized environments.

**EXERCISES**

1. What is structured and unstructured data? Research the challenges of storing and managing unstructured data.

2. Discuss the benefits of information-centric storage architecture over server-centric storage architecture.

3. What are the attributes of big data? Research and prepare a presentation on big data analytics.

4. Research how businesses use their information assets to derive competitive advantage and new business opportunities.

5. Research and prepare a presentation on personal data management.

# Chapter 2
# Data Center Environment

Today, data centers are essential and integral parts of any business, whether small, medium, or large in size. The core elements of a data center are host, storage, connectivity (or network), applications, and DBMS that are managed centrally. These elements work together to process and store data. With the evolution of virtualization, data centers have also evolved from a classic data center to a virtualized data center (VDC). In a VDC, physical resources from a classic data center are pooled together and provided as virtual resources. This abstraction hides the complexity and limitation of physical resources from the user. By consolidating IT resources using virtualization, organizations can optimize their infrastructure utilization and reduce the total cost of owning an infrastructure. Moreover, in a VDC, virtual resources are created using software that enables faster deployment, compared to deploying physical

resources in classic data centers. This chapter covers all the key components of a data center, including virtualization at compute, memory, desktop, and application. Storage and network virtualization is discussed later in the book.

With the increase in the criticality of information assets to businesses, storage — one of the core elements of a data center — is recognized as a distinct resource. Storage needs special focus and attention for its implementation and management. This chapter also focuses on storage subsystems and provides details on components, geometry, and performance parameters of a disk drive. The connectivity between the host and storage facilitated by various technologies is also explained.

## 2.1 Application

An *application* is a computer program that provides the logic for computing operations. The application sends requests to the underlying operating system to perform read/write (R/W) operations on the storage devices. Applications can be layered on the database, which in turn uses the OS services to perform R/W operations on the storage devices. Applications deployed in a data center environment are commonly categorized as business applications, infrastructure management applications, data protection applications, and security applications. Some examples of these applications are e-mail, enterprise resource planning (ERP), decision support system (DSS), resource management, backup, authentication and antivirus applications, and so on.

The characteristics of I/Os (Input/Output) generated by the application influence the overall performance of storage system and storage solution designs. For more information on application I/O characteristics, refer to Appendix A.

**APPLICATION VIRTUALIZATION**

*Application virtualization* **breaks the dependency between the application and the underlying platform (OS and hardware). Application virtualization encapsulates the application and the required OS resources within a virtualized container. This technology provides the ability to deploy applications without making any change to the underlying OS, file system, or registry of the computing platform on which they are deployed. Because virtualized applications run in an isolated environment, the underlying OS and other applications are protected from potential corruptions. There are many scenarios in which conflicts might arise if multiple applications or multiple versions of the same application are installed on the same computing platform. Application virtualization eliminates this conflict by isolating different versions of an application and the associated O/S resources.**

## 2.2 Database Management System (DBMS)

A database is a structured way to store data in logically organized tables that are interrelated. A database helps to optimize the storage and retrieval of data. A DBMS controls the creation, maintenance, and use of a database. The DBMS processes an application's request for data and instructs the operating system to transfer the appropriate data from the storage.

## 2.3 Host (Compute)

Users store and retrieve data through applications. The computers on which these applications run are referred to as *hosts* or *compute systems*. Hosts can be physical or virtual machines. A compute virtualization software enables creating virtual machines on top of a physical compute infrastructure. Compute virtualization and virtual machines are discussed later in this chapter. Examples of physical hosts include desktop computers, servers or a cluster of servers, laptops, and mobile devices. A host consists of CPU, memory, I/O devices, and a collection of software to perform computing operations. This software includes the operating system, file system, logical volume manager, device drivers, and so on. This software can be installed as separate entities or as part of the operating system.

The CPU consists of four components: Arithmetic Logic Unit (ALU), control unit, registers, and L1 cache. There are two types of memory on a host, Random Access Memory (RAM) and Read-Only Memory (ROM). I/O devices enable communication with a host. Examples of I/O devices are keyboard, mouse, monitor, etc.

Software runs on a host and enables processing of input and output (I/O) data. The following section details various software components that are essential parts of a host system.

### 2.3.1 Operating System

In a traditional computing environment, an *operating system* controls all aspects of computing. It works between the application and the physical components of a compute system. One of the services it provides to the application is data access. The operating system also monitors and responds to user actions and the environment. It organizes and controls hardware components and manages the allocation of hardware resources. It provides basic security for the access and usage of all managed resources. An operating system also performs basic storage management tasks while managing other underlying components, such as the file system, volume manager, and device drivers.

In a virtualized compute environment, the virtualization layer works between the operating system and the hardware resources. Here the OS might work differently based on the type of compute virtualization implemented. In a typical implementation, the OS works as a guest and performs only the activities related to application interaction. In this case, hardware management functions are handled by the virtualization layer.

### Memory Virtualization

Memory has been, and continues to be, an expensive component of a host. It determines both the size and number of applications that can run on a host. *Memory virtualization* enables multiple applications and processes, whose aggregate memory requirement is greater than the available physical memory, to run on a host without impacting each other.

Memory virtualization is an operating system feature that virtualizes the physical memory (RAM) of a host. It creates virtual memory with an address space larger than the physical memory space present in the compute system. The virtual memory encompasses the address space of the physical memory and part of the disk storage. The operating system utility that manages the virtual memory is known as the *virtual memory manager* (VMM). The VMM manages the virtual-to-physical memory mapping and fetches data from the disk storage when a process references a virtual address that points to data at the disk storage. The space used by the VMM on the disk is known as a swap space. A *swap space* (also known as *page file* or *swap file*) is a portion of the disk drive that appears to be physical memory to the operating system.

In a virtual memory implementation, the memory of a system is divided into contiguous blocks of fixed-size pages. A process known as *paging* moves inactive physical memory pages onto the swap file and brings them back to the physical memory when required. This enables efficient use of the available physical memory among different applications. The operating system typically moves the least used pages into the swap file so that enough RAM is available for processes that are more active. Access to swap file pages is slower than access to physical memory pages because swap file pages are allocated on the disk drive, which is slower than physical memory.

## 2.3.2 Device Driver

A *device driver* is special software that permits the operating system to interact with a specific device, such as a printer, a mouse, or a disk drive. A device driver enables the operating system to recognize the device and to access and control devices. Device drivers are hardware-dependent and operating-system-specific.

## 2.3.3 Volume Manager

In the early days, disk drives appeared to the operating system as a number of continuous disk blocks. The entire disk drive would be allocated to the file system or other data entity used by the operating system or application. The disadvantage was lack of flexibility. When a disk drive ran out of space, there was no easy way to extend the file system's size. Also, as the storage capacity of the disk drive increased, allocating the entire disk drive for the file system often resulted in underutilization of storage capacity.

The evolution of *Logical Volume Managers* (LVMs) enabled dynamic extension of file system capacity and efficient storage management. The LVM is software that runs on the compute system and manages logical and physical storage. LVM is an intermediate layer between the file system and the physical disk. It can partition a larger-capacity disk into virtual, smaller-capacity volumes (the process is called *partitioning*) or aggregate several smaller disks to form a larger virtual volume. (The process is called *concatenation*.) These volumes are then presented to applications.

*Disk partitioning* was introduced to improve the flexibility and utilization of disk drives. In partitioning, a disk drive is divided into logical containers called *logical volumes* (LVs) (see Figure 2-1). For example, a large physical drive can be partitioned into multiple LVs to maintain data according to the file system and application requirements. The partitions are created from groups of contiguous cylinders when the hard disk is initially set up on the host. The host's file system accesses the logical volumes without any knowledge of partitioning and physical structure of the disk.

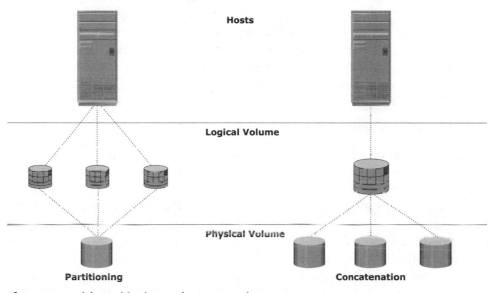

**Figure 2-1:** Disk partitioning and concatenation

*Concatenation* is the process of grouping several physical drives and presenting them to the host as one big logical volume (see Figure 2-1).

The LVM provides optimized storage access and simplifies storage resource management. It hides details about the physical disk and the location of data on the disk. It enables administrators to change the storage allocation even when the application is running.

The basic LVM components are physical volumes, volume groups, and logical volumes. In LVM terminology, each physical disk connected to the host system is a *physical volume* (PV). The LVM converts the physical storage provided by the physical volumes to a logical view of storage, which is then used by the operating system and applications. A *volume group* is created by grouping together one or more physical volumes. A unique *physical volume identifier* (PVID) is assigned to each physical volume when it is initialized for use by the LVM. Physical volumes can be added or removed from a volume group dynamically. They cannot be shared between different volume groups, which means that the entire physical volume becomes part of a volume group. Each physical volume is partitioned into equal-sized data blocks called *physical extents* when the volume group is created.

*Logical volumes* are created within a given volume group. A logical volume can be thought of as a disk partition, whereas the volume group itself can be thought of as a disk. A volume group can have a number of logical volumes. The size of a logical volume is based on a multiple of the physical extents.

The logical volume appears as a physical device to the operating system. A logical volume is made up of noncontiguous physical extents and may span multiple physical volumes. A file system is created on a logical volume. These logical volumes are then assigned to the application. A logical volume can also be mirrored to provide enhanced data availability.

## 2.3.4 File System

A *file* is a collection of related records or data stored as a unit with a name. A *file system* is a hierarchical structure of files. A file system enables easy access to data files residing within a disk drive, a disk partition, or a logical volume. A file system consists of logical structures and software routines that control access to files. It provides users with the functionality to create, modify, delete, and access files. Access to files on the disks is controlled by the permissions assigned to the file by the owner, which are also maintained by the file system.

A file system organizes data in a structured hierarchical manner via the use of directories, which are containers for storing pointers to multiple files. All file systems maintain a pointer map to the directories, subdirectories, and files that are part of the file system. Examples of common file systems are:

- FAT 32 (File Allocation Table) for Microsoft Windows
- NT File System (NTFS) for Microsoft Windows
- UNIX File System (UFS) for UNIX
- Extended File System (EXT2/3) for Linux

Apart from the files and directories, the file system also includes a number of other related records, which are collectively called the *metadata*. For example, the metadata in a UNIX environment consists of the *superblock*, the *inodes*, and the list of data blocks free and in use. The metadata of a file system must be consistent for the file system to be considered healthy.

A superblock contains important information about the file system, such as the file system type, creation and modification dates, size, and layout. It also contains the count of available resources (such as the number of free blocks, inodes, and so on) and a flag indicating the mount status of the file system. An inode is associated with every file and directory and contains information such as the file length, ownership, access privileges, time of last access/modification, number of links, and the address of the data.

A file system *block* is the smallest "unit" allocated for storing data. Each file system block is a contiguous area on the physical disk. The block size of a file system is fixed at the time of its creation. The file system size depends on the block size and the total number of file system blocks. A file can span multiple file system blocks because most files are larger than the predefined block size of the file system. File system blocks cease to be contiguous and become fragmented when new blocks are added or deleted. Over time, as files grow larger, the file system becomes increasingly fragmented.

The following list shows the process of mapping user files to the disk storage subsystem with an LVM (see Figure 2-2):

1. Files are created and managed by users and applications.
2. These files reside in the file systems.
3. The file systems are mapped to file system blocks.
4. The file system blocks are mapped to logical extents of a logical volume.
5. These logical extents in turn are mapped to the disk physical extents either by the operating system or by the LVM.
6. These physical extents are mapped to the disk sectors in a storage subsystem.

If there is no LVM, then there are no logical extents. Without LVM, file system blocks are directly mapped to disk sectors.

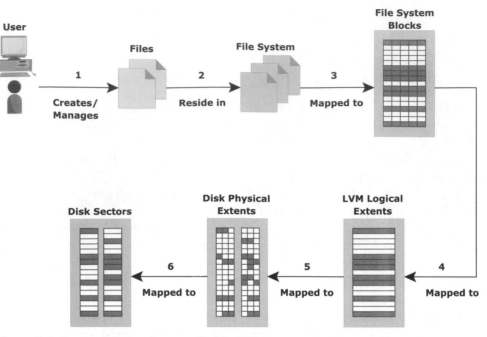

**Figure 2-2:** Process of mapping user files to disk storage

The *file system tree* starts with the *root directory*. The root directory has a number of subdirectories. A file system should be mounted before it can be used.

 The system utility `fsck` is run to check file system consistency in UNIX and Linux hosts. An example of the file system in an inconsistent state is when the file system has outstanding changes and the computer system crashes before the changes are committed to disk. At the time of booting, the `fsck` command first checks for consistency of file systems for a successful boot. If the file systems are found to be consistent, the command checks the consistency of all other file systems. If any file system is found to be inconsistent, it is not mounted. The inconsistent file system might be repaired automatically by the `fsck` command or might require user interaction for confirmation of corrective actions. `CHKDSK` is the command used on DOS, OS/2, and Microsoft Windows operating systems.

A file system can be either a journaling file system or a nonjournaling file system. *Nonjournaling file systems* cause a potential loss of files because they use separate writes to update their data and metadata. If the system crashes during the write process, the metadata or data might be lost or corrupted. When the system reboots, the file system attempts to update the metadata structures by examining and repairing them. This operation takes a long time on large file systems. If there is insufficient information to re-create the wanted or original structure, the files might be misplaced or lost, resulting in corrupted file systems.

A *journaling file system* uses a separate area called a *log* or *journal*. This journal might contain all the data to be written (*physical journal*) or just the metadata to be updated (*logical journal*). Before changes are made to the file system, they are written to this separate area. After the journal has been updated, the operation on the file system can be performed. If the system crashes during the operation, there is enough information in the log to "replay" the log record and complete the operation. Journaling results in a quick file system check because it looks only at the active, most recently accessed parts of a large file system. In addition, because information about the pending operation is saved, the risk of files being lost is reduced.

A disadvantage of journaling file systems is that they are slower than other file systems. This slowdown is the result of the extra operations that have to be performed on the journal each time the file system is changed. However, the much shortened time for file system checks and the file system integrity provided by journaling far outweighs its disadvantage. Nearly all file system implementations today use journaling.

Dedicated file servers may be installed to manage and share a large number of files over a network. These file servers support multiple file systems and use file-sharing protocols specific to the operating system — for example, NFS and CIFS. These protocols are detailed in Chapter 7.

## 2.3.5 Compute Virtualization

Compute virtualization is a technique for masking or abstracting the physical hardware from the operating system. It enables multiple operating systems to run concurrently on single or clustered physical machines. This technique enables creating portable virtual compute systems called *virtual machines* (VMs). Each VM runs an operating system and application instance in an isolated manner. Compute virtualization is achieved by a virtualization layer that resides between the hardware and virtual machines. This layer is also called the *hypervisor*. The hypervisor provides hardware resources, such as CPU, memory, and network to all the virtual machines. Within a physical server, a large number of virtual machines can be created depending on the hardware capabilities of the physical server.

A virtual machine is a logical entity but appears like a physical host to the operating system, with its own CPU, memory, network controller, and disks. However, all VMs share the same underlying physical hardware in an isolated manner. From a hypervisor perspective, virtual machines are discrete sets of files that include VM configuration file, data files, and so on.

Typically, a physical server often faces resource-conflict issues when two or more applications running on the server have conflicting requirements. For example, applications might need different values in the same registry entry, different versions of the same DLL, and so on. These issues are further compounded with an application's high-availability requirements. As a result, the servers are limited to serve only one application at a time, as shown in Figure 2-3 (a). This causes organizations to purchase new physical machines for every application they deploy, resulting in expensive and inflexible infrastructure. On the other hand, many applications do not take full advantage of the hardware capabilities available to them. Consequently, resources such as processors, memory, and storage remain underutilized. Compute virtualization enables users to overcome these challenges (see Figure 2-3 [b]) by allowing multiple operating systems and applications to run on a single physical machine. This technique significantly improves server utilization and provides server consolidation.

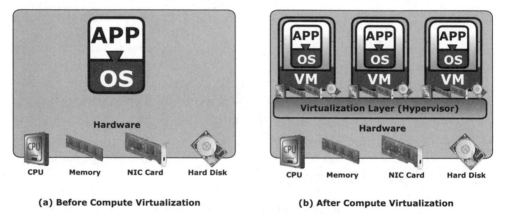

(a) Before Compute Virtualization          (b) After Compute Virtualization

**Figure 2-3:** Server virtualization

Server consolidation enables organizations to run their data center with fewer servers. This, in turn, cuts down the cost of new server acquisition, reduces operational cost, and saves data center floor and rack space. Creation of VMs takes less time compared to a physical server setup; organizations can provision servers faster and with ease. Individual VMs can be restarted, upgraded, or even crashed, without affecting the other VMs on the same physical machine. Moreover, VMs can be copied or moved from one physical machine to another without causing application downtime. Nondisruptive migration of VMs is required for load balancing among physical machines, hardware maintenance, and availability purposes.

**DESKTOP VIRTUALIZATION**

With the traditional desktop, the OS, applications, and user profiles are all tied to a specific piece of hardware. With legacy desktops, business productivity is impacted greatly when a client device is broken or lost. *Desktop virtualization* breaks the dependency between the hardware and its OS, applications, user profiles, and settings. This enables the IT staff to change, update, and deploy these elements independently. Desktops hosted at the data center run on virtual machines; users remotely access these desktops from a variety of client devices, such as laptops, desktops, and mobile devices (also called Thin devices). Application execution and data storage are performed centrally at the data center instead of at the client devices. Because desktops run as virtual machines within an organization's data center, it mitigates the risk of data leakage and theft. It also helps to perform centralized backup and simplifies compliance procedures. Virtual desktops are easy to maintain because it is simple to apply patches, deploy new applications and OS, and provision or remove users centrally.

# 2.4 Connectivity

Connectivity refers to the interconnection between hosts or between a host and peripheral devices, such as printers or storage devices. The discussion here focuses only on the connectivity between the host and the storage device. Connectivity and communication between host and storage are enabled using physical components and interface protocols.

## 2.4.1 Physical Components of Connectivity

The *physical components* of connectivity are the hardware elements that connect the host to storage. Three physical components of connectivity between the host and storage are the host interface device, port, and cable (Figure 2-4).

A *host interface device* or *host adapter* connects a host to other hosts and storage devices. Examples of host interface devices are host bus adapter (HBA) and network interface card (NIC). *Host bus adaptor* is an *application-specific integrated circuit* (ASIC) board that performs I/O interface functions between the host and storage, relieving the CPU from additional I/O processing workload. A host typically contains multiple HBAs.

A *port* is a specialized outlet that enables connectivity between the host and external devices. An HBA may contain one or more ports to connect the host to the storage device. *Cables* connect hosts to internal or external devices using copper or fiber optic media.

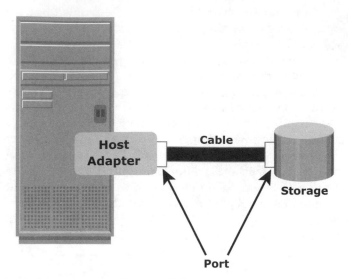

**Figure 2-4:** Physical components of connectivity

## 2.4.2 Interface Protocols

A *protocol* enables communication between the host and storage. Protocols are implemented using interface devices (or controllers) at both source and destination. The popular interface protocols used for host to storage communications are *Integrated Device Electronics/Advanced Technology Attachment* (IDE/ATA), *Small Computer System Interface* (SCSI), *Fibre Channel* (FC) and *Internet Protocol* (IP).

### IDE/ATA and Serial ATA

IDE/ATA is a popular interface protocol standard used for connecting storage devices, such as disk drives and CD-ROM drives. This protocol supports parallel transmission and therefore is also known as Parallel ATA (PATA) or simply ATA. IDE/ATA has a variety of standards and names. The Ultra DMA/133 version of ATA supports a throughput of 133 MB per second. In a master-slave configuration, an ATA interface supports two storage devices per connector. However, if the performance of the drive is important, sharing a port between two devices is not recommended.

The serial version of this protocol supports single bit serial transmission and is known as Serial ATA (SATA). High performance and low cost SATA has largely replaced PATA in newer systems. SATA revision 3.0 provides a data transfer rate up to 6 Gb/s.

### SCSI and Serial SCSI

SCSI has emerged as a preferred connectivity protocol in high-end computers. This protocol supports parallel transmission and offers improved performance, scalability, and compatibility compared to ATA. However, the high cost associated with SCSI limits its popularity among home or personal desktop users. Over the years, SCSI has been enhanced and now includes a wide variety of related technologies and standards. SCSI supports up to 16 devices on a single bus and provides data transfer rates up to 640 MB/s (for the Ultra-640 version).

Serial attached SCSI (SAS) is a point-to-point serial protocol that provides an alternative to parallel SCSI. A newer version of serial SCSI (SAS 2.0) supports a data transfer rate up to 6 Gb/s. This book's Appendix B provides more details on the SCSI architecture and interface.

### Fibre Channel

Fibre Channel is a widely used protocol for high-speed communication to the storage device. The Fibre Channel interface provides gigabit network speed. It provides a serial data transmission that operates over copper wire and optical fiber. The latest version of the FC interface (16FC) allows transmission of data up to 16 Gb/s. The FC protocol and its features are covered in more detail in Chapter 5.

### Internet Protocol (IP)

IP is a network protocol that has been traditionally used for host-to-host traffic. With the emergence of new technologies, an IP network has become a viable option for host-to-storage communication. IP offers several advantages in terms of cost and maturity and enables organizations to leverage their existing IP-based network. iSCSI and FCIP protocols are common examples that leverage IP for host-to-storage communication. These protocols are detailed in Chapter 6.

## 2.5 Storage

Storage is a core component in a data center. A storage device uses magnetic, optic, or solid state media. Disks, tapes, and diskettes use magnetic media, whereas CD/DVD uses optical media for storage. Removable Flash memory or Flash drives are examples of solid state media.

In the past, *tapes* were the most popular storage option for backups because of their low cost. However, tapes have various limitations in terms of performance and management, as listed here:

- Data is stored on the tape linearly along the length of the tape. Search and retrieval of data are done sequentially, and it invariably takes several seconds to access the data. As a result, random data access is slow and time-consuming. This limits tapes as a viable option for applications that require real-time, rapid access to data.

■ In a shared computing environment, data stored on tape cannot be accessed by multiple applications simultaneously, restricting its use to one application at a time.

■ On a tape drive, the read/write head touches the tape surface, so the tape degrades or wears out after repeated use.

■ The storage and retrieval requirements of data from the tape and the overhead associated with managing the tape media are significant.

Due to these limitations and availability of low-cost disk drives, tapes are no longer a preferred choice as a backup destination for enterprise-class data centers.

*Optical disc storage* is popular in small, single-user computing environments. It is frequently used by individuals to store photos or as a backup medium on personal or laptop computers. It is also used as a distribution medium for small applications, such as games, or as a means to transfer small amounts of data from one computer system to another. Optical discs have limited capacity and speed, which limit the use of optical media as a business data storage solution.

The capability to *write once and read many* (WORM) is one advantage of optical disc storage. A CD-ROM is an example of a WORM device. Optical discs, to some degree, guarantee that the content has not been altered. Therefore, it can be used as a low-cost alternative for long-term storage of relatively small amounts of fixed content that do not change after it is created. Collections of optical discs in an array, called a *jukebox*, are still used as a fixed-content storage solution. Other forms of optical discs include CD-RW, Blu-ray disc, and other variations of DVD.

*Disk drives* are the most popular storage medium used in modern computers for storing and accessing data for performance-intensive, online applications. Disks support rapid access to random data locations. This means that data can be written or retrieved quickly for a large number of simultaneous users or applications. In addition, disks have a large capacity. Disk storage arrays are configured with multiple disks to provide increased capacity and enhanced performance.

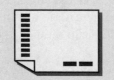 **Disk drives are accessed through predefined protocols, such as ATA, Serial ATA (SATA), SAS (Serial Attached SCSI), and FC. These protocols are implemented on the disk interface controllers. Earlier, disk interface controllers were implemented as separate cards, which were connected to the motherboard to provide communication with storage devices. Modern disk interface controllers are integrated with the disk drives; therefore, disk drives are known by the protocol interface they support, for example SATA disk, FC disk, and so on.**

## 2.6 Disk Drive Components

The key components of a hard disk drive are platter, spindle, read-write head, actuator arm assembly, and controller board (see Figure 2-5).

I/O operations in a HDD are performed by rapidly moving the arm across the rotating flat platters coated with magnetic particles. Data is transferred between the disk controller and magnetic platters through the read-write (R/W) head which is attached to the arm. Data can be recorded and erased on magnetic platters any number of times. Following sections detail the different components of the disk drive, the mechanism for organizing and storing data on disks, and the factors that affect disk performance.

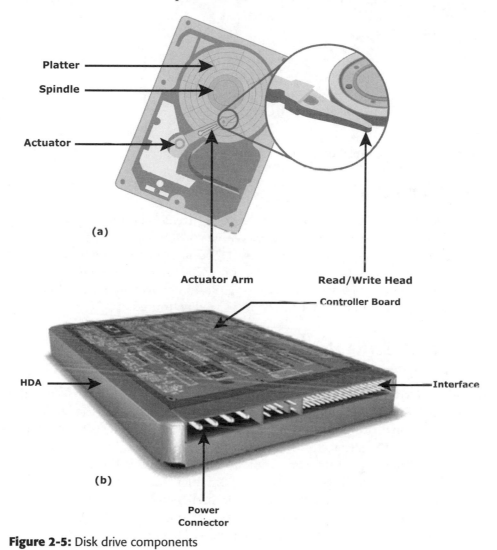

**Figure 2-5:** Disk drive components

### 2.6.1 Platter

A typical HDD consists of one or more flat circular disks called *platters* (Figure 2-6). The data is recorded on these platters in binary codes (0s and 1s). The set of rotating platters is sealed in a case, called the *Head Disk Assembly* (HDA). A platter is a rigid, round disk coated with magnetic material on both surfaces (top and bottom). The data is encoded by polarizing the magnetic area, or domains, of the disk surface. Data can be written to or read from both surfaces of the platter. The number of platters and the storage capacity of each platter determine the total capacity of the drive.

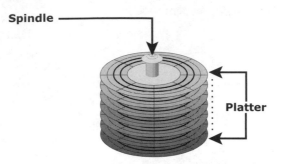

**Figure 2-6:** Spindle and platter

## 2.6.2 Spindle

A spindle connects all the platters (refer to Figure 2-6) and is connected to a motor. The motor of the spindle rotates with a constant speed.

The disk platter spins at a speed of several thousands of revolutions per minute (rpm). Common spindle speeds are 5,400 rpm, 7,200 rpm, 10,000 rpm, and 15,000 rpm. The speed of the platter is increasing with improvements in technology, although the extent to which it can be improved is limited.

## 2.6.3 Read/Write Head

*Read/Write (R/W) heads,* as shown in Figure 2-7, read and write data from or to platters. Drives have two R/W heads per platter, one for each surface of the platter. The R/W head changes the magnetic polarization on the surface of the platter when writing data. While reading data, the head detects the magnetic polarization on the surface of the platter. During reads and writes, the R/W head senses the magnetic polarization and never touches the surface of the platter. When the spindle is rotating, there is a microscopic air gap maintained between the R/W heads and the platters, known as the *head flying height*. This air gap is removed when the spindle stops rotating and the R/W head rests on a special area on the platter near the spindle. This area is called the *landing zone*. The landing zone is coated with a lubricant to reduce friction between the head and the platter.

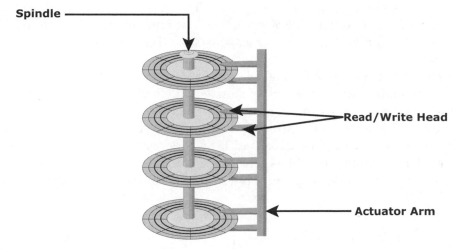

**Figure 2-7:** Actuator arm assembly

The logic on the disk drive ensures that heads are moved to the landing zone before they touch the surface. If the drive malfunctions and the R/W head accidentally touches the surface of the platter outside the landing zone, a *head crash* occurs. In a head crash, the magnetic coating on the platter is scratched and may cause damage to the R/W head. A head crash generally results in data loss.

## 2.6.4 Actuator Arm Assembly

R/W heads are mounted on the *actuator arm assembly*, which positions the R/W head at the location on the platter where the data needs to be written or read (refer to Figure 2-7). The R/W heads for all platters on a drive are attached to one actuator arm assembly and move across the platters simultaneously.

## 2.6.5 Drive Controller Board

The controller (refer to Figure 2-5 [b]) is a printed circuit board, mounted at the bottom of a disk drive. It consists of a microprocessor, internal memory, circuitry, and firmware. The firmware controls the power to the spindle motor and the speed of the motor. It also manages the communication between the drive and the host. In addition, it controls the R/W operations by moving the actuator arm and switching between different R/W heads, and performs the optimization of data access.

## 2.6.6 Physical Disk Structure

Data on the disk is recorded on *tracks*, which are concentric rings on the platter around the spindle, as shown in Figure 2-8. The tracks are numbered, starting from zero, from the outer edge of the platter. The number of *tracks per inch* (TPI) on the platter (or the *track density*) measures how tightly the tracks are packed on a platter.

Each track is divided into smaller units called *sectors*. A sector is the smallest, individually addressable unit of storage. The track and sector structure is written on the platter by the drive manufacturer using a low-level formatting operation. The number of sectors per track varies according to the drive type. The first personal computer disks had 17 sectors per track. Recent disks have a much larger number of sectors on a single track. There can be thousands of tracks on a platter, depending on the physical dimensions and recording density of the platter.

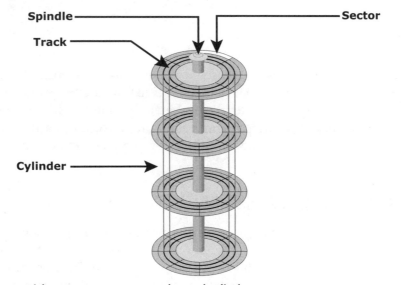

**Figure 2-8:** Disk structure: sectors, tracks, and cylinders

Typically, a sector holds 512 bytes of user data, although some disks can be formatted with larger sector sizes. In addition to user data, a sector also stores other information, such as the sector number, head number or platter number, and track number. This information helps the controller to locate the data on the drive.

A cylinder is a set of identical tracks on both surfaces of each drive platter. The location of R/W heads is referred to by the cylinder number, not by the track number.

## DISK ADVERTISED CAPACITY VERSUS AVAILABLE CAPACITY

A difference exists between the advertised capacity of a disk and the actual space available for data storage. For example, a disk advertised as 500 GB has only 465.7 GB of user-data capacity. The reason for this difference is that drive manufacturers use a base of 10 for the disk capacity, which means 1 kilobyte is equal to 1,000 bytes instead of 1,024 bytes; therefore, the actual available capacity of a disk is always less than the advertised capacity.

## 2.6.7 Zoned Bit Recording

Platters are made of concentric tracks; the outer tracks can hold more data than the inner tracks because the outer tracks are physically longer than the inner tracks. On older disk drives, the outer tracks had the same number of sectors as the inner tracks, so data density was low on the outer tracks. This was an inefficient use of the available space, as shown in Figure 2-9 (a).

*Zoned bit recording* uses the disk efficiently. As shown in Figure 2-9 (b), this mechanism groups tracks into zones based on their distance from the center of the disk. The zones are numbered, with the outermost zone being zone 0. An appropriate number of sectors per track are assigned to each zone, so a zone near the center of the platter has fewer sectors per track than a zone on the outer edge. However, tracks within a particular zone have the same number of sectors.

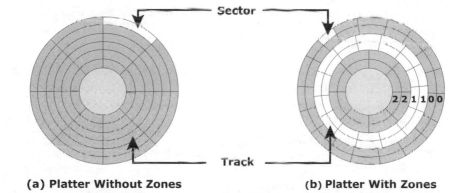

(a) Platter Without Zones          (b) Platter With Zones

**Figure 2-9:** Zoned bit recording

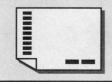

The data transfer rate drops while accessing data from zones closer to the center of the platter. Applications that demand high performance should have their data on the outer zones of the platter.

### 2.6.8 Logical Block Addressing

Earlier drives used physical addresses consisting of the *cylinder, head,* and *sector* (CHS) number to refer to specific locations on the disk, as shown in Figure 2-10 (a), and the host operating system had to be aware of the geometry of each disk used. *Logical block addressing* (LBA), as shown in Figure 2-10 (b), simplifies addressing by using a linear address to access physical blocks of data. The disk controller translates LBA to a CHS address, and the host needs to know only the size of the disk drive in terms of the number of blocks. The logical blocks are mapped to physical sectors on a 1:1 basis.

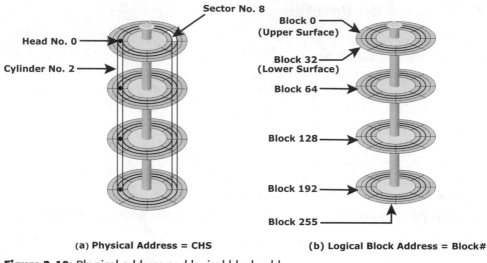

**(a) Physical Address = CHS**          **(b) Logical Block Address = Block#**

**Figure 2-10:** Physical address and logical block address

In Figure 2-10 (b), the drive shows eight sectors per track, eight heads, and four cylinders. This means a total of 8 × 8 × 4 = 256 blocks, so the block number ranges from 0 to 255. Each block has its own unique address. Assuming that the sector holds 512 bytes, a 500 GB drive with a formatted capacity of 465.7 GB has in excess of 976,000,000 blocks.

## 2.7 Disk Drive Performance

A disk drive is an electromechanical device that governs the overall performance of the storage system environment. The various factors that affect the performance of disk drives are discussed in this section.

## 2.7.1 Disk Service Time

*Disk service time* is the time taken by a disk to complete an I/O request. Components that contribute to the service time on a disk drive are *seek time, rotational latency,* and *data transfer rate.*

### Seek Time

The *seek time* (also called *access time*) describes the time taken to position the R/W heads across the platter with a radial movement (moving along the radius of the platter). In other words, it is the time taken to position and settle the arm and the head over the correct track. Therefore, the lower the seek time, the faster the I/O operation. Disk vendors publish the following seek time specifications:

- **Full Stroke:** The time taken by the R/W head to move across the entire width of the disk, from the innermost track to the outermost track.

- **Average:** The average time taken by the R/W head to move from one random track to another, normally listed as the time for one-third of a full stroke.

- **Track-to-Track:** The time taken by the R/W head to move between adjacent tracks.

Each of these specifications is measured in milliseconds. The seek time of a disk is typically specified by the drive manufacturer. The average seek time on a modern disk is typically in the range of 3 to 15 milliseconds. Seek time has more impact on the read operation of random tracks rather than adjacent tracks. To minimize the seek time, data can be written to only a subset of the available cylinders. This results in lower usable capacity than the actual capacity of the drive. For example, a 500 GB disk drive is set up to use only the first 40 percent of the cylinders and is effectively treated as a 200 GB drive. This is known as *short-stroking* the drive.

### Rotational Latency

To access data, the actuator arm moves the R/W head over the platter to a particular track while the platter spins to position the requested sector under the R/W head. The time taken by the platter to rotate and position the data under the R/W head is called *rotational latency.* This latency depends on the rotation speed of the spindle and is measured in milliseconds. The average rotational latency is one-half of the time taken for a full rotation. Similar to the seek time, rotational latency has more impact on the reading/writing of random sectors on the disk than on the same operations on adjacent sectors.

Average rotational latency is approximately 5.5 ms for a 5,400-rpm drive, and around 2.0 ms for a 15,000-rpm (or 250-rps revolution per second) drive as shown here:

> Average rotational latency for a 15,000 rpm (or 250 rps)
> drive = 0.5/250 = 2 milliseconds.

## Data Transfer Rate

The *data transfer rate* (also called *transfer rate*) refers to the average amount of data per unit time that the drive can deliver to the HBA. It is important to first understand the process of read/write operations to calculate data transfer rates. In a *read operation*, the data first moves from disk platters to R/W heads; then it moves to the drive's internal *buffer*. Finally, data moves from the buffer through the interface to the host HBA. In a *write operation*, the data moves from the HBA to the internal buffer of the disk drive through the drive's interface. The data then moves from the buffer to the R/W heads. Finally, it moves from the R/W heads to the platters.

The data transfer rates during the R/W operations are measured in terms of internal and external transfer rates, as shown in Figure 2-11.

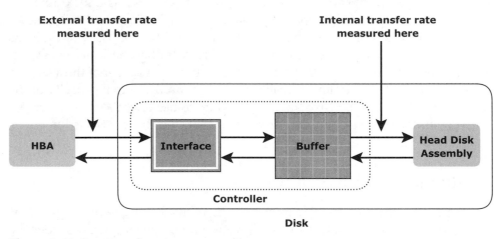

**Figure 2-11:** Data transfer rate

*Internal transfer rate* is the speed at which data moves from a platter's surface to the internal buffer (cache) of the disk. The internal transfer rate takes into account factors such as the seek time and rotational latency. *External transfer rate* is the rate at which data can move through the interface to the HBA. The external transfer rate is generally the advertised speed of the interface, such as 133 MB/s for ATA. The sustained external transfer rate is lower than the interface speed.

## 2.7.2 Disk I/O Controller Utilization

Utilization of a disk I/O controller has a significant impact on the I/O response time. To understand this impact, consider that a disk can be viewed as a black box consisting of two elements:

- **Queue:** The location where an I/O request waits before it is processed by the I/O controller
- **Disk I/O Controller:** Processes I/Os waiting in the queue one by one

The I/O requests arrive at the controller at the rate generated by the application. This rate is also called the *arrival rate*. These requests are held in the I/O queue, and the I/O controller processes them one by one, as shown in Figure 2-12. The I/O arrival rate, the queue length, and the time taken by the I/O controller to process each request determines the I/O response time. If the controller is busy or heavily utilized, the queue size will be large and the response time will be high.

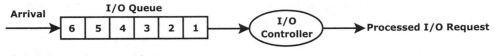

**Figure 2-12:** I/O processing

Based on the fundamental laws of disk drive performance, the relationship between controller utilization and average response time is given as

Average response time $(T_R)$ = Service time $(T_S)$ / (1 − Utilization)

where $T_S$ is the time taken by the controller to serve an I/O.

As the utilization reaches 100 percent — that is, as the I/O controller saturates — the response time is closer to infinity. In essence, the saturated component, or the bottleneck, forces the serialization of I/O requests, meaning that each I/O request must wait for the completion of the I/O requests that preceded it. Figure 2-13 shows a graph plotted between utilization and response time.

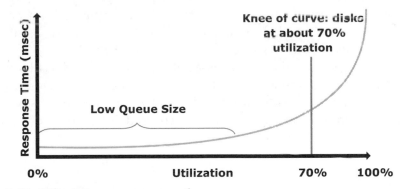

**Figure 2-13:** Utilization versus response time

The graph indicates that the response time changes are nonlinear as the utilization increases. When the average queue sizes are low, the response time remains low. The response time increases slowly with added load on the queue and increases exponentially when the utilization exceeds 70 percent. Therefore, for performance-sensitive applications, it is common to utilize disks below their 70 percent of I/O serving capability.

## 2.8 Host Access to Data

Data is accessed and stored by applications using the underlying infrastructure. The key components of this infrastructure are the operating system (or file system), connectivity, and storage. The storage device can be internal and (or) external to the host. In either case, the host controller card accesses the storage devices using predefined protocols, such as IDE/ATA, SCSI, or Fibre Channel (FC). IDE/ATA and SCSI are popularly used in small and personal computing environments for accessing internal storage. FC and iSCSI protocols are used for accessing data from an external storage device (or subsystems). External storage devices can be connected to the host directly or through the storage network. When the storage is connected directly to the host, it is referred as *direct-attached storage* (DAS), which is detailed later in this chapter.

Understanding access to data over a network is important because it lays the foundation for storage networking technologies. Data can be accessed over a network in one of the following ways: block level, file level, or object level.

In general, the application requests data from the file system (or operating system) by specifying the filename and location. The file system maps the file attributes to the logical block address of the data and sends the request to the storage device. The storage device converts the logical block address (LBA) to a cylinder-head-sector (CHS) address and fetches the data.

In a block-level access, the file system is created on a host, and data is accessed on a network at the block level, as shown in Figure 2-14 (a). In this case, raw disks or logical volumes are assigned to the host for creating the file system.

In a file-level access, the file system is created on a separate file server or at the storage side, and the file-level request is sent over a network, as shown in Figure 2-14 (b). Because data is accessed at the file level, this method has higher overhead, as compared to the data accessed at the block level. Object-level access is an intelligent evolution, whereby data is accessed over a network in terms of self-contained objects with a unique object identifier. Details of storage networking technologies and deployments are covered in Section II of this book, "Storage Networking Technologies."

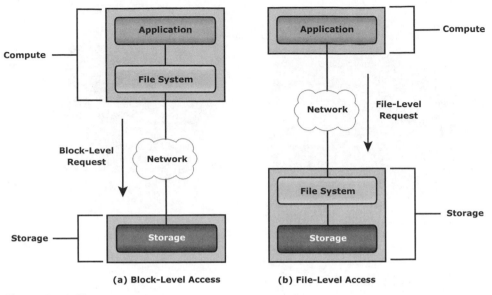

(a) Block-Level Access   (b) File-Level Access

**Figure 2-14:** Host access to storage

## 2.9 Direct-Attached Storage

DAS is an architecture in which storage is connected directly to the hosts. The internal disk drive of a host and the directly-connected external storage array are some examples of DAS. Although the implementation of storage networking technologies is gaining popularity, DAS has remained suitable for localized data access in a small environment, such as personal computing and workgroups. DAS is classified as internal or external, based on the location of the storage device with respect to the host.

In *internal DAS* architectures, the storage device is internally connected to the host by a serial or parallel bus (see Figure 2-15 [a]). The physical bus has distance limitations and can be sustained only over a shorter distance for high-speed connectivity. In addition, most internal buses can support only a limited number of devices, and they occupy a large amount of space inside the host, making maintenance of other components difficult.

On the other hand, in *external DAS* architectures, the host connects directly to the external storage device, and data is accessed at the block level (see Figure 2-15 [b]). In most cases, communication between the host and the storage device takes place over a SCSI or FC protocol. Compared to internal DAS, an external DAS overcomes the distance and device count limitations and provides centralized management of storage devices.

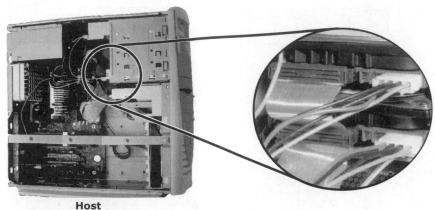

**Host**

**(a) Internal DAS**

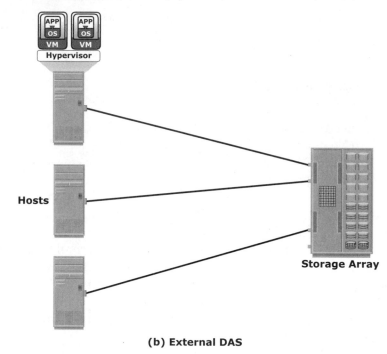

**(b) External DAS**

**Figure 2-15:** Internal and external DAS architecture

## 2.9.1 DAS Benefits and Limitations

DAS requires a relatively lower initial investment than storage networking architectures. The DAS configuration is simple and can be deployed easily and rapidly. The setup is managed using host-based tools, such as the host OS, which makes storage management tasks easy for small environments. Because

DAS has a simple architecture, it requires fewer management tasks and less hardware and software elements to set up and operate.

However, DAS does not scale well. A storage array has a limited number of ports, which restricts the number of hosts that can directly connect to the storage. When capacities are reached, the service availability may be compromised. DAS does not make optimal use of resources due to its limited capability to share front-end ports. In DAS environments, unused resources cannot be easily re-allocated, resulting in islands of over-utilized and under-utilized storage pools.

## 2.10 Storage Design Based on Application Requirements and Disk Performance

Determining storage requirements for an application begins with determining the required storage capacity. This is easily estimated by the size and number of file systems and database components used by applications. The I/O size, I/O characteristics, and the number of I/Os generated by the application at peak workload are other factors that affect disk performance, I/O response time, and design of storage systems. The I/O block size depends on the file system and the database on which the application is built. Block size in a database environment is controlled by the underlying database engine and the environment variables.

The disk service time ($T_S$) for an I/O is a key measure of disk performance; $T_S$, along with disk utilization rate (U), determines the I/O response time for an application. As discussed earlier in this chapter, the total disk service time ($T_S$) is the sum of the seek time (T), rotational latency (L), and internal transfer time (X):

$$T_S = T + L + X$$

Consider an example with the following specifications provided for a disk:

- The average seek time is 5 ms in a random I/O environment; therefore, $T = 5$ ms.

- Disk rotation speed of 15,000 revolutions per minute or 250 revolutions per second — from which rotational latency (L) can be determined, which is one-half of the time taken for a full rotation or L = (0.5/250 rps expressed in ms).

- 40 MB/s internal data transfer rate, from which the internal transfer time (X) is derived based on the block size of the I/O — for example, an I/O with a block size of 32 KB; therefore X = 32 KB/40 MB.

Consequently, the time taken by the I/O controller to serve an I/O of block size 32 KB is ($T_S$) = 5 ms + (0.5/250) + 32 KB/40 MB = 7.8 ms.

Therefore, the maximum number of I/Os serviced per second or IOPS is $(1/T_S) = 1/(7.8 \times 10^{-3}) = 128$ IOPS.

Table 2-1 lists the maximum IOPS that can be serviced for different block sizes using the previous disk specifications.

**Table 2-1:** IOPS Performed by Disk Drive

| BLOCK SIZE | $T_S = T + L + X$ | IOPS = $1/T_S$ |
|---|---|---|
| 4 KB | 5 ms + (0.5/250 rps) + 4 K/40 MB = 5 + 2 + 0.1 = 7.1 | 140 |
| 8 KB | 5 ms + (0.5/250 rps) + 8 K/40 MB = 5 + 2 + 0.2 = 7.2 | 139 |
| 16 KB | 5 ms + (0.5/250 rps) + 16 K/40 MB = 5 + 2 + 0.4 = 7.4 | 135 |
| 32 KB | 5 ms + (0.5/250 rps) + 32 K/40 MB = 5 + 2 + 0.8 = 7.8 | 128 |
| 64 KB | 5 ms + (0.5/250 rps) + 64 K/40 MB = 5 + 2 + 1.6 = 8.6 | 116 |

The IOPS ranging from 116 to 140 for different block sizes represents the IOPS that can be achieved at potentially high levels of utilization (close to 100 percent). As discussed in Section 2.7.2, the application response time, R, increases with an increase in disk controller utilization. For the same preceding example, the response time (R) for an I/O with a block size of 32 KB at 96 percent disk controller utilization is

$$R = T_S/(1 - U) = 7.8/(1 - 0.96) = 195 \text{ ms}$$

If the application demands a faster response time, then the utilization for the disks should be maintained below 70 percent. For the same 32-KB block size, at 70-percent disk utilization, the response time reduces drastically to 26 ms. However, at lower disk utilization, the number of IOPS a disk can perform is also reduced. In the case of a 32-KB block size, a disk can perform 128 IOPS at almost 100 percent utilization, whereas the number of IOPS it can perform at 70-percent utilization is 89 (128 x 0.7). This indicates that the number of I/Os a disk can perform is an important factor that needs to be considered while designing the storage requirement for an application.

Therefore, the storage requirement for an application is determined in terms of both the capacity and IOPS. If an application needs 200 GB of disk space, then this capacity can be provided simply with a single disk. However, if the application IOPS requirement is high, then it results in performance degradation because just a single disk might not provide the required response time for I/O operations.

Based on this discussion, the total number of disks required ($D_R$) for an application is computed as follows:

$$D_R = \text{Max} (D_C, D_I)$$

Where $D_C$ is the number of disks required to meet the capacity, and $D_I$ is the number of disks required to meet the application IOPS requirement. Let's understand this with the help of an example.

Consider an example in which the capacity requirement for an application is 1.46 TB. The number of IOPS generated by the application at peak workload is estimated at 9,000 IOPS. The vendor specifies that a 146-GB, 15,000-rpm drive is capable of doing a maximum 180 IOPS.

In this example, the number of disks required to meet the capacity requirements will be 1.46 TB/146 GB = 10 disks.

To meet the application IOPS requirements, the number of disks required is 9,000/180 = 50. However, if the application is response-time sensitive, the number of IOPS a disk drive can perform should be calculated based on 70-percent disk utilization. Considering this, the number of IOPS a disk can perform at 70 percent utilization is $180 \times 0.7 = 126$ IOPS. Therefore, the number of disks required to meet the application IOPS requirement will be 9,000/126 = 72.

As a result, the number of disks required to meet the application requirements will be Max (10, 72) = 72 disks.

The preceding example indicates that from a capacity-perspective, 10 disks are sufficient; however, the number of disks required to meet application performance is 72. To optimize disk requirements from a performance perspective, various solutions are deployed in a real-time environment. Examples of these solutions are disk native command queuing, use of flash drives, RAID, and the use of cache memory. RAID and cache are detailed in Chapters 3 and 4 respectively.

## 2.11 Disk Native Command Queuing

Command queuing is a technique implemented on modern disk drives that determines the execution order of received I/Os and reduces unnecessary drive-head movements to improve disk performance. When an I/O is received for execution at the disk controller, the command queuing algorithms assign a tag that defines a sequence in which the commands should be executed. With command queuing, commands are executed based on the organization of data on the disk, regardless of the order in which the commands are received.

The commonly used algorithm for command queuing is *seek time optimization*. Commands are executed based on optimizing read/write head movements, which might result in the reordering of commands. Without seek time optimization, the commands are executed in the order they are received. For example, as shown in Figure 2-16 (a), the commands are executed in the order A, B, C, and D. The radial movement required by the head to execute C immediately after A is less than what would be required to execute B. With seek time optimization, the command execution sequence would be A, C, B, and D, as shown in Figure 2-16 (b).

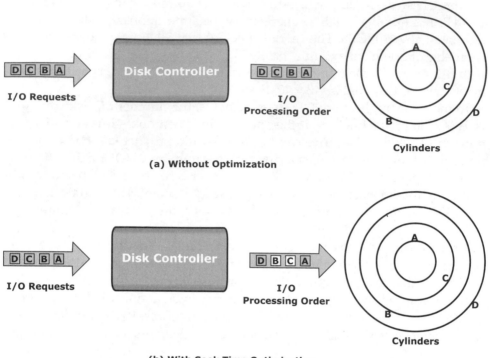

(a) Without Optimization

(b) With Seek Time Optimization

**Figure 2-16:** Disk command queuing

*Access Time Optimization* is another command queuing algorithm. With this algorithm, commands are executed based on the combination of seek time optimization and an analysis of rotational latency for optimal performance.

Command queuing is also implemented on modern storage array controllers, which might further supplement the command queuing implemented on the disk drive.

## 2.12 Introduction to Flash Drives

With the growth of information, storage users continue to demand ever-increasing performance requirements for their business applications. Traditionally, high I/O requirements were met by simply using more disks. Availability of enterprise class flash drives (EFD) has changed the scenario.

Flash drives, also referred as solid state drives (SSDs), are new generation drives that deliver ultra-high performance required by performance-sensitive applications. Flash drives use semiconductor-based solid state memory (flash memory) to store and retrieve data. Unlike conventional mechanical disk drives, flash drives contain no moving parts; therefore, they do not have seek and rotational latencies. Flash drives deliver a high number of IOPS with very low response times. Also, being a semiconductor-based device, flash drives consume less power, compared to mechanical drives. Flash drives are especially suited for applications with small block size and random-read workloads that require consistently low (less than 1 millisecond) response times. Applications that need to process massive amounts of information quickly, such as currency exchange, electronic trading systems, and real-time data feed processing benefit from flash drives.

Compared to conventional mechanical disk drives, EFD provides up to 30 times the throughput and up to one-tenth the response time (<1 ms compared with 6-10 ms). In addition, flash drives can store data using up to 38 percent less energy per TB than traditional disk drives, which translates into approximately 98 percent less power consumption per I/O.

Overall, flash drives provide better total cost of ownership (TCO) even though they cost more on $/GB basis. By implementing flash drives, businesses can meet application performance requirements with far fewer drives (approximately 20 to 30 times less number of drives compared to conventional mechanical drives). This reduction not only provides savings in terms of drive cost, but also translates to savings for power, cooling, and space consumption. Fewer numbers of drives in the environment also means less cost for managing the storage.

## 2.12.1 Components and Architecture of Flash Drives

Flash drives use similar physical form factor and connectors as mechanical disk drives to maintain compatibility. This enables easy replacement of a mechanical disk drive with a flash drive in a storage array enclosure. The key components of a flash drive are the controller, I/O interface, mass storage (collection of memory chips), and cache. The controller manages the functioning of the drive, and the I/O interface provides power and data access. Mass storage is an array of nonvolatile NAND (negated AND) memory chips used for storing data. Cache serves as a temporary space or buffer for data transaction and operations.

A flash drive uses multiple parallel I/O channels (from its drive controller to the flash memory chips) for data access. Generally, the larger the number of flash memory chips and channels, the higher the drive's internal bandwidth, and ultimately the higher the drive's performance. Flash drives typically have eight to 24 channels.

Memory chips in flash drives are logically organized in blocks and pages. A *page* is the smallest object that can be read or written on a flash drive. Pages are grouped together into *blocks*. (These blocks should not be confused with the 512-byte blocks in mechanical disk drive sectors.) A block may have 32, 64, or 128 pages. Pages do not have a standard size; typical page sizes are 4 KB, 8 KB, and 16 KB. Because flash drives emulate mechanical drives that use logical block addresses (LBAs), a page spans across a consecutive series of data blocks. For example, a 4-KB page would span across eight 512-byte data blocks with consecutive addresses. In flash drives, a read operation can happen at the page level, whereas a write or an erase operation happens only at the block level.

## 2.12.2 Features of Enterprise Flash Drives

The key features of enterprise class flash drives are as follows:

- **NAND flash memory technology:** NAND memory technology is well suited for accessing random data. A NAND device uses bad block tracking and error-correcting code (ECC) to maintain data integrity and provide the fastest write speeds.

- **Single-Level Cell (SLC)-based flash:** NAND technology is available in two different cell designs. A multi-level cell (MLC) stores more than one bit per cell by virtue of its capability to register multiple states, versus a single-level cell that can store only 1 bit. SLC is the preferred technology for enterprise data applications due to its performance and longevity. SLC read speeds are typically rated at twice those of MLC devices, and write speeds are up to four times higher. SLC devices typically have 10 times higher write erase cycles, compared to MLC designs. In addition, the SLC flash memory has higher reliability because it stores only 1 bit per cell. Hence, the likelihood for error is reduced.

- **Write leveling technique:** An important element of maximizing a flash drive's useful life is ensuring that the individual memory cells experience uniform use. This means that data that is frequently updated is written to different locations to avoid rewriting the same cells. In EFDs, the device is designed to ensure that with any new write operation, the youngest block is used.

## 2.13 Concept in Practice: VMware ESXi

VMware is the leading provider for a server virtualization solution. VMware ESXi provides a platform called hypervisor. The hypervisor abstracts CPU, memory, and storage resources to run multiple virtual machines concurrently on the same physical server.

VMware ESXi is a hypervisor that installs on x86 hardware to enable server virtualization. It enables creating multiple virtual machines (VMs) that can run simultaneously on the same physical machine. A VM is a discrete set of files that can be moved, copied, and used as a template. All the files that make up a VM are typically stored in a single directory on a cluster file system called Virtual Machine File System (VMFS). The physical machine that houses ESXi is called the ESXi host. ESXi hosts provide physical resources used to run virtual machines. ESXi has two key components: VMkernel and Virtual Machine Monitor.

VMkernel provides functionality similar to that found in other operating systems, such as process creation, file system management, and process scheduling. It is designed to specifically support running multiple VMs and provide core functionality such as resource scheduling, I/O stacks, and so on.

The virtual machine monitor is responsible for executing commands on the CPUs and performing Binary Translation (BT). A virtual machine monitor performs hardware abstraction to appear as a physical machine with its own CPU, memory, and I/O devices. Each VM is assigned a virtual machine monitor that has a share of the CPU, memory, and I/O devices to successfully run the VM.

## Summary

This chapter detailed the key elements of a data center environment — application, DBMS, host, connectivity, and storage. The data flows from an application to storage through these elements. Physical and logical components of these entities affect the overall performance of the application. Virtualization at different components of the data center provides better utilization and management of these components.

Storage is a core component in the data center environment. The disk drive is the most popular storage device that uses magnetic media for accessing and storing data. Flash-based solid-state drives (SSDs) are a recent innovation, and in many ways, superior to mechanical disk drives.

Modern disk storage systems use hundreds of disks to meet application performance requirements. Managing the capacity, performance, and reliability of these large numbers of disks poses significant challenges. RAID (redundant array of independent disk), as detailed in the next chapter, is an enabling technology to manage capacity, performance, and reliability of disk drives.

## EXERCISES

1. What are the advantages of a virtualized data center over a classic data center?

2. An application specifies a requirement of 200 GB to host a database and other files. It also specifies that the storage environment should support 5,000 IOPS during its peak workloads. The disks available for configuration provide 66 GB of usable capacity, and the manufacturer specifies that they can support a maximum of 140 IOPS. The application is response time-sensitive, and disk utilization beyond 60 percent does not meet the response time requirements. Compute and explain the theoretical basis for the minimum number of disks that should be configured to meet the requirements of the application.

3. Which components constitute the disk service time? Which component contributes the largest percentage of the disk service time in a random I/O operation?

4. The average I/O size of an application is 64 KB. The following specifications are available from the disk manufacturer: average seek time = 5 ms, 7,200 RPM, and transfer rate = 40 MB/s. Determine the maximum IOPS that could be performed with this disk for the application. Using this case as an example, explain the relationship between disk utilization and IOPS.

5. Refer to Question 4. Based on the calculated disk service time, plot a graph showing the response time versus utilization, considering the utilization of the I/O controller at 20 percent, 40 percent, 60 percent, 80 percent, and 100 percent. Describe the conclusion that could be derived from the graph.

6. Research other elements of a data center besides the core elements discussed in this chapter, including environmental control parameters such as HVAC (heat, ventilation, and air-condition), power supplies, and security.

# Chapter 3
# Data Protection: RAID

In the late 1980s, rapid adoption of computers for business processes stimulated the growth of new applications and databases, significantly increasing the demand for storage capacity and performance. At that time, data was stored on a single large, expensive disk drive called *Single Large Expensive Drive* (SLED). Use of single disks could not meet the required performance levels because they were capable of serving only a limited number of I/Os.

Today's data centers house hundreds of disk drives in their storage infrastructure. Disk drives are inherently susceptible to failures due to mechanical wear and tear and other environmental factors, which could result in data loss. The greater the number of disk drives in a storage array, the greater the probability of a disk failure in the array. For example, consider a storage array of 100 disk drives, each with an average life expectancy of 750,000 hours. The average life expectancy of this collection in the array, therefore, is 750,000/100 or 7,500 hours. This means that a disk drive in this array is likely to fail at least once in 7,500 hours.

RAID is an enabling technology that leverages multiple drives as part of a set that provides data protection against drive failures. In general, RAID implementations also improve the storage system performance by serving I/Os from multiple disks simultaneously. Modern arrays with flash drives also benefit in terms of protection and performance by using RAID.

In 1987, Patterson, Gibson, and Katz at the University of California, Berkeley, published a paper titled "A Case for Redundant Arrays of Inexpensive Disks

(RAID)." This paper described the use of small-capacity, inexpensive disk drives as an alternative to large-capacity drives common on mainframe computers. The term *RAID* has been redefined to refer to *independent* disks to reflect advances in the storage technology. RAID technology has now grown from an academic concept to an industry standard and is common implementation in today's storage arrays.

This chapter details RAID technology, RAID levels, and different types of RAID implementations and their benefits.

# 3.1 RAID Implementation Methods

The two methods of RAID implementation are hardware and software. Both have their advantages and disadvantages, and are discussed in this section.

## 3.1.1 Software RAID

*Software RAID* uses host-based software to provide RAID functions. It is implemented at the operating-system level and does not use a dedicated hardware controller to manage the RAID array.

Software RAID implementations offer cost and simplicity benefits when compared with hardware RAID. However, they have the following limitations:

- **Performance:** Software RAID affects overall system performance. This is due to additional CPU cycles required to perform RAID calculations.

- **Supported features:** Software RAID does not support all RAID levels.

- **Operating system compatibility:** Software RAID is tied to the host operating system; hence, upgrades to software RAID or to the operating system should be validated for compatibility. This leads to inflexibility in the data-processing environment.

## 3.1.2 Hardware RAID

In *hardware RAID* implementations, a specialized hardware controller is implemented either on the host or on the array.

*Controller card RAID* is a host-based hardware RAID implementation in which a specialized RAID controller is installed in the host, and disk drives are connected to it. Manufacturers also integrate RAID controllers on motherboards. A host-based RAID controller is not an efficient solution in a data center environment with a large number of hosts.

The external RAID controller is an array-based hardware RAID. It acts as an interface between the host and disks. It presents storage volumes to the host, and the host manages these volumes as physical drives. The key functions of the RAID controllers are as follows:

- Management and control of disk aggregations
- Translation of I/O requests between logical disks and physical disks
- Data regeneration in the event of disk failures

## 3.2 RAID Array Components

A *RAID array* is an enclosure that contains a number of disk drives and supporting hardware to implement RAID. A subset of disks within a RAID array can be grouped to form logical associations called logical arrays, also known as a *RAID set* or a *RAID group* (see Figure 3-1).

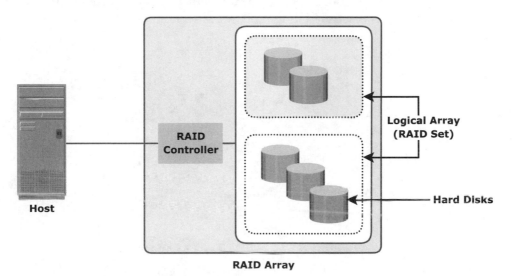

**Figure 3-1:** Components of a RAID array

## 3.3 RAID Techniques

RAID techniques — striping, mirroring, and parity — form the basis for defining various RAID levels. These techniques determine the data availability and performance characteristics of a RAID set.

### 3.3.1 Striping

*Striping* is a technique to spread data across multiple drives (more than one) to use the drives in parallel. All the read-write heads work simultaneously, allowing more data to be processed in a shorter time and increasing performance, compared to reading and writing from a single disk.

Within each disk in a RAID set, a predefined number of contiguously addressable disk blocks are defined as a *strip*. The set of aligned strips that spans across all the disks within the RAID set is called a *stripe*. Figure 3-2 shows physical and logical representations of a striped RAID set.

*Strip size* (also called *stripe depth*) describes the number of blocks in a strip and is the maximum amount of data that can be written to or read from a single disk in the set, assuming that the accessed data starts at the beginning of the strip. All strips in a stripe have the same number of blocks. Having a smaller strip size means that data is broken into smaller pieces while spread across the disks.

Stripe size is a multiple of strip size by the number of *data* disks in the RAID set. For example, in a five disk striped RAID set with a strip size of 64 KB, the stripe size is 320 KB(64KB × 5). *Stripe width* refers to the number of data strips in a stripe. Striped RAID does not provide any data protection unless parity or mirroring is used, as discussed in the following sections.

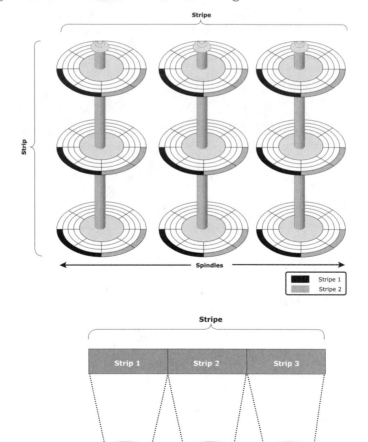

**Figure 3-2:** Striped RAID set

### 3.3.2 Mirroring

*Mirroring* is a technique whereby the same data is stored on two different disk drives, yielding two copies of the data. If one disk drive failure occurs, the data is intact on the surviving disk drive (see Figure 3-3) and the controller continues to service the host's data requests from the surviving disk of a mirrored pair.

When the failed disk is replaced with a new disk, the controller copies the data from the surviving disk of the mirrored pair. This activity is transparent to the host.

In addition to providing complete data redundancy, mirroring enables fast recovery from disk failure. However, disk mirroring provides only data protection and is not a substitute for data backup. Mirroring constantly captures changes in the data, whereas a backup captures point-in-time images of the data.

Mirroring involves duplication of data — the amount of storage capacity needed is twice the amount of data being stored. Therefore, mirroring is considered expensive and is preferred for mission-critical applications that cannot afford the risk of any data loss. Mirroring improves read performance because read requests can be serviced by both disks. However, write performance is slightly lower than that in a single disk because each write request manifests as two writes on the disk drives. Mirroring does not deliver the same levels of write performance as a striped RAID.

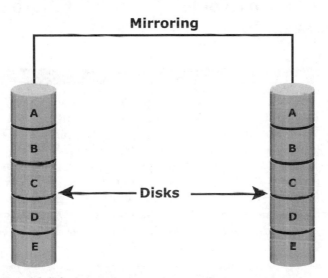

**Figure 3-3:** Mirrored disks in an array

### 3.3.3 Parity

*Parity* is a method to protect striped data from disk drive failure without the cost of mirroring. An additional disk drive is added to hold parity, a mathematical construct that allows re-creation of the missing data. Parity is a redundancy technique that ensures protection of data without maintaining a full set of duplicate data. Calculation of parity is a function of the RAID controller.

Parity information can be stored on separate, dedicated disk drives or distributed across all the drives in a RAID set. Figure 3-4 shows a parity RAID set. The first four disks, labeled "Data Disks," contain the data. The fifth disk, labeled "Parity Disk," stores the parity information, which, in this case, is the sum of the elements in each row. Now, if one of the data disks fails, the missing value can be calculated by subtracting the sum of the rest of the elements from the parity value. Here, for simplicity, the computation of parity is represented as an arithmetic sum of the data. However, parity calculation is a *bitwise XOR* operation.

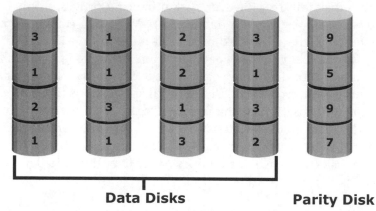

**Data Disks**      **Parity Disk**

**Figure 3-4:** Parity RAID

---

### XOR OPERATION

A bit-by-bit Exclusive -OR (XOR) operation takes two bit patterns of equal length and performs the logical XOR operation on each pair of corresponding bits. The result in each position is 1 if the two bits are different, and 0 if they are the same. The truth table of the XOR operation is shown next. (A and B denote the inputs and C, the output after performing the XOR operation.) If any of the data from A, B, or C is lost, it can be reproduced by performing an XOR operation on the remaining available data. For example, if a disk containing all the data from A fails, the data can be regenerated by performing an XOR between B and C.

| A | B | C |
|---|---|---|
| 0 | 0 | 0 |
| 0 | 1 | 1 |
| 1 | 0 | 1 |
| 1 | 1 | 0 |

Compared to mirroring, parity implementation considerably reduces the cost associated with data protection. Consider an example of a parity RAID configuration with five disks where four disks hold data, and the fifth holds the parity information. In this example, parity requires only 25 percent extra disk space compared to mirroring, which requires 100 percent extra disk space. However, there are some disadvantages of using parity. Parity information is generated from data on the data disk. Therefore, parity is recalculated every time there is a change in data. This recalculation is time-consuming and affects the performance of the RAID array.

For parity RAID, the stripe size calculation does not include the parity strip. For example in a five (4 + 1) disk parity RAID set with a strip size of 64 KB, the stripe size will be 256 KB (64 KB × 4).

## 3.4 RAID Levels

Application performance, data availability requirements, and cost determine the RAID level selection. These RAID levels are defined on the basis of striping, mirroring, and parity techniques. Some RAID levels use a single technique, whereas others use a combination of techniques. Table 3-1 shows the commonly used RAID levels.

**Table 3-1:** Raid Levels

| LEVELS | BRIEF DESCRIPTION |
| --- | --- |
| RAID 0 | Striped set with no fault tolerance |
| RAID 1 | Disk mirroring |
| Nested | Combinations of RAID levels. Example: RAID 1 + RAID 0 |
| RAID 3 | Striped set with parallel access and a dedicated parity disk |
| RAID 4 | Striped set with independent disk access and a dedicated parity disk |
| RAID 5 | Striped set with independent disk access and distributed parity |
| RAID 6 | Striped set with independent disk access and dual distributed parity |

### 3.4.1 RAID 0

RAID 0 configuration uses data striping techniques, where data is striped across all the disks within a RAID set. Therefore it utilizes the full storage capacity of a RAID set. To read data, all the strips are put back together by the controller. Figure 3-5 shows RAID 0 in an array in which data is striped across five disks. When the number of drives in the RAID set increases, performance improves because more data can be read or written simultaneously. RAID 0 is a good option for applications that need high I/O throughput. However, if these applications require high availability during drive failures, RAID 0 does not provide data protection and availability.

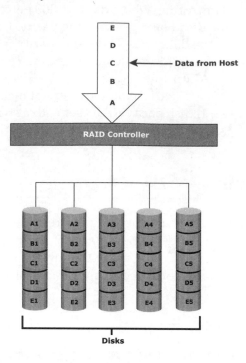

**Figure 3-5:** RAID 0

## 3.4.2 RAID 1

RAID 1 is based on the mirroring technique. In this RAID configuration, data is mirrored to provide fault tolerance (see Figure 3-6). A RAID 1 set consists of two disk drives and every write is written to both disks. The mirroring is transparent to the host. During disk failure, the impact on data recovery in RAID 1 is the least among all RAID implementations. This is because the RAID controller uses the mirror drive for data recovery. RAID 1 is suitable for applications that require high availability and cost is no constraint.

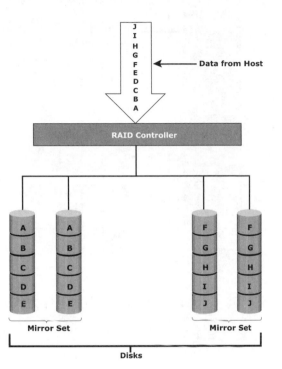

**Figure 3-6:** RAID 1

## 3.4.3 Nested RAID

Most data centers require data redundancy and performance from their RAID arrays. RAID 1+0 and RAID 0+1combine the performance benefits of RAID 0 with the redundancy benefits of RAID 1. They use striping and mirroring techniques and combine their benefits. These types of RAID require an even number of disks, the minimum being four (see Figure 3-7).

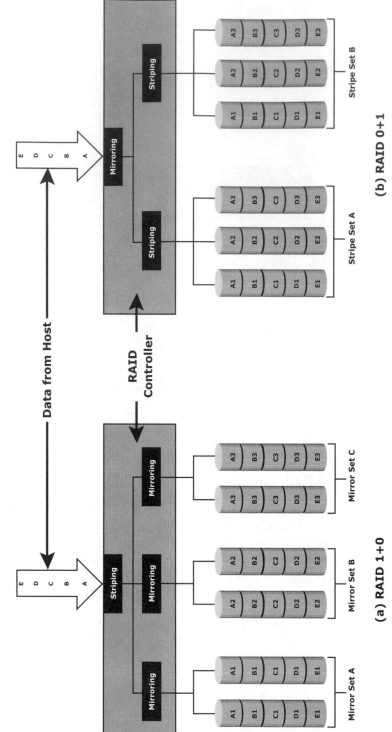

**Figure 3-7:** Nested RAID

RAID 1+0 is also known as RAID 10 (Ten) or RAID 1/0. Similarly, RAID 0+1 is also known as RAID 01 or RAID 0/1. RAID 1+0 performs well for workloads with small, random, write-intensive I/Os. Some applications that benefit from RAID 1+0 include the following:

- High transaction rate Online Transaction Processing (OLTP)
- Large messaging installations
- Database applications with write intensive random access workloads

A common misconception is that RAID 1+0 and RAID 0+1 are the same. Under normal conditions, RAID levels 1+0 and 0+1 offer identical benefits. However, rebuild operations in the case of disk failure differ between the two.

RAID 1+0 is also called striped mirror. The basic element of RAID 1+0 is a mirrored pair, which means that data is first mirrored and then both copies of the data are striped across multiple disk drive pairs in a RAID set. When replacing a failed drive, only the mirror is rebuilt. In other words, the disk array controller uses the surviving drive in the mirrored pair for data recovery and continuous operation. Data from the surviving disk is copied to the replacement disk.

To understand the working of RAID 1+0, consider an example of six disks forming a RAID 1+0 (RAID 1 first and then RAID 0) set. These six disks are paired into three sets of two disks, where each set acts as a RAID 1 set (mirrored pair of disks). Data is then striped across all the three mirrored sets to form RAID 0. Following are the steps performed in RAID 1+0 (see Figure 3-7 [a]):

Drives 1+2 = RAID 1 (Mirror Set A)
Drives 3+4 = RAID 1 (Mirror Set B)
Drives 5+6 = RAID 1 (Mirror Set C)

Now, RAID 0 striping is performed across sets A through C. In this configuration, if drive 5 fails, then the mirror set C alone is affected. It still has drive 6 and continues to function and the entire RAID 1+0 array also keeps functioning. Now, suppose drive 3 fails while drive 5 was being replaced. In this case the array still continues to function because drive 3 is in a different mirror set. So, in this configuration, up to three drives can fail without affecting the array, as long as they are all in different mirror sets.

RAID 0+1 is also called a mirrored stripe. The basic element of RAID 0+1 is a stripe. This means that the process of striping data across disk drives is performed initially, and then the entire stripe is mirrored. In this configuration if one drive fails, then the entire stripe is faulted. Consider the same example of six disks to understand the working of RAID 0+1 (that is, RAID 0 first and then RAID 1). Here, six disks are paired into two sets of three disks each. Each of these sets, in turn, act as a RAID 0 set that contains three disks and then these two sets are mirrored to form RAID 1. Following are the steps performed in RAID 0+1 (see Figure 3-7 [b]):

$$\text{Drives } 1 + 2 + 3 = \text{RAID } 0 \text{ (Stripe Set A)}$$
$$\text{Drives } 4 + 5 + 6 = \text{RAID } 0 \text{ (Stripe Set B)}$$

Now, these two stripe sets are mirrored. If one of the drives, say drive 3, fails, the entire stripe set A fails. A rebuild operation copies the entire stripe, copying the data from each disk in the healthy stripe to an equivalent disk in the failed stripe. This causes increased and unnecessary I/O load on the surviving disks and makes the RAID set more vulnerable to a second disk failure.

## 3.4.4 RAID 3

RAID 3 stripes data for performance and uses parity for fault tolerance. Parity information is stored on a dedicated drive so that the data can be reconstructed if a drive fails in a RAID set. For example, in a set of five disks, four are used for data and one for parity. Therefore, the total disk space required is 1.25 times the size of the data disks. RAID 3 always reads and writes complete stripes of data across all disks because the drives operate in parallel. There are no partial writes that update one out of many strips in a stripe. Figure 3-8 illustrates the RAID 3 implementation.

RAID 3 provides good performance for applications that involve large sequential data access, such as data backup or video streaming.

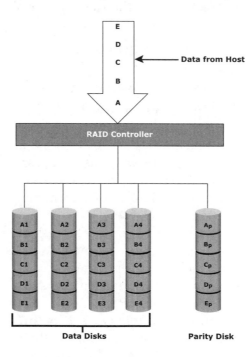

**Figure 3-8:** RAID 3

## 3.4.5 RAID 4

Similar to RAID 3, RAID 4 stripes data for high performance and uses parity for improved fault tolerance. Data is striped across all disks except the parity disk in the array. Parity information is stored on a dedicated disk so that the data can be rebuilt if a drive fails.

Unlike RAID 3, data disks in RAID 4 can be accessed independently so that specific data elements can be read or written on a single disk without reading or writing an entire stripe. RAID 4 provides good read throughput and reasonable write throughput.

## 3.4.6 RAID 5

RAID 5 is a versatile RAID implementation. It is similar to RAID 4 because it uses striping. The drives (strips) are also independently accessible. The difference between RAID 4 and RAID 5 is the parity location. In RAID 4, parity is written to a dedicated drive, creating a write bottleneck for the parity disk. In RAID 5, parity is distributed across all disks to overcome the write bottleneck of a dedicated parity disk. Figure 3-9 illustrates the RAID 5 implementation.

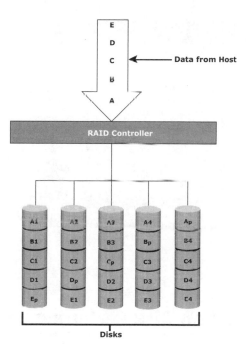

**Figure 3-9:** RAID 5

RAID 5 is good for random, read-intensive I/O applications and preferred for messaging, data mining, medium-performance media serving, and relational database management system (RDBMS) implementations, in which database administrators (DBAs) optimize data access.

### 3.4.7 RAID 6

RAID 6 works the same way as RAID 5, except that RAID 6 includes a second parity element to enable survival if two disk failures occur in a RAID set (see Figure 3-10). Therefore, a RAID 6 implementation requires at least four disks. RAID 6 distributes the parity across all the disks. The write penalty (explained later in this chapter) in RAID 6 is more than that in RAID 5; therefore, RAID 5 writes perform better than RAID 6. The rebuild operation in RAID 6 may take longer than that in RAID 5 due to the presence of two parity sets.

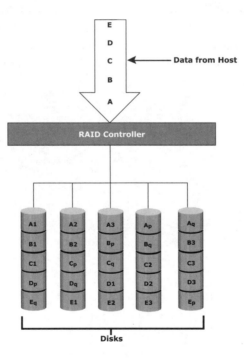

**Figure 3-10:** RAID 6

# 3.5 RAID Impact on Disk Performance

When choosing a RAID type, it is imperative to consider its impact on disk performance and application IOPS.

In both mirrored and parity RAID configurations, every write operation translates into more I/O overhead for the disks, which is referred to as a *write penalty*. In a RAID 1 implementation, every write operation must be performed on two disks configured as a mirrored pair, whereas in a RAID 5 implementation, a write operation may manifest as four I/O operations. When performing I/Os to a disk configured with RAID 5, the controller has to read, recalculate, and write a parity segment for every data write operation.

Figure 3-11 illustrates a single write operation on RAID 5 that contains a group of five disks.

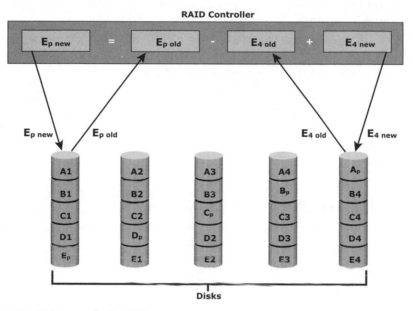

**Figure 3-11:** Write penalty in RAID 5

The parity (P) at the controller is calculated as follows:

$$E_p = E_1 + E_2 + E_3 + E_4 \text{ (XOR operations)}$$

Whenever the controller performs a write I/O, parity must be computed by reading the old parity ($E_p$ old) and the old data ($E_{4\,old}$) from the disk, which means two read I/Os. Then, the new parity ($E_p$ new) is computed as follows:

$$E_{p\,new} = E_{p\,old} - E_{4\,old} + E_{4\,new} \text{ (XOR operations)}$$

After computing the new parity, the controller completes the write I/O by writing the new data and the new parity onto the disks, amounting to two write I/Os. Therefore, the controller performs two disk reads and two disk writes for every write operation, and the write penalty is 4.

In RAID 6, which maintains dual parity, a disk write requires three read operations: two parity and one data. After calculating both new parities, the controller performs three write operations: two parity and an I/O. Therefore, in a RAID 6 implementation, the controller performs six I/O operations for each write I/O, and the write penalty is 6.

## 3.5.1 Application IOPS and RAID Configurations

When deciding the number of disks required for an application, it is important to consider the impact of RAID based on IOPS generated by the application. The total disk load should be computed by considering the type of RAID configuration and the ratio of read compared to write from the host.

The following example illustrates the method to compute the disk load in different types of RAID.

Consider an application that generates 5,200 IOPS, with 60 percent of them being reads.

The disk load in RAID 5 is calculated as follows:

RAID 5 disk load (reads + writes) = $0.6 \times 5{,}200 + \mathbf{4} \times (0.4 \times 5{,}200)$ [because the write penalty for RAID 5 is 4]

= $3{,}120 + 4 \times 2{,}080$

= $3{,}120 + 8{,}320$

= 11,440 IOPS

The disk load in RAID 1 is calculated as follows:

RAID 1 disk load = $0.6 \times 5{,}200 + \mathbf{2} \times (0.4 \times 5{,}200)$ [because every write manifests as two writes to the disks]

= $3{,}120 + 2 \times 2{,}080$

= $3{,}120 + 4{,}160$

= 7,280 IOPS

The computed disk load determines the number of disks required for the application. If in this example a disk drive with a specification of a maximum 180 IOPS needs to be used, the number of disks required to meet the workload for the RAID configuration would be as follows:

RAID 5: 11,440/180 = 64 disks

RAID 1: 7,280/180 = 42 disks (approximated to the nearest even number)

## 3.6 RAID Comparison

Table 3-2 compares the common types of RAID levels.

**Table 3-2:** Comparison of Common RAID Types

| RAID | MIN. DISKS | STORAGE EFFICIENCY % | COST | READ PERFORMANCE | WRITE PERFORMANCE | WRITE PENALTY | PROTECTION |
|---|---|---|---|---|---|---|---|
| 0 | 2 | 100 | Low | Good for both random and sequential reads | Good | No | No protection |
| 1 | 2 | 50 | High | Better than single disk | Slower than single disk because every write must be committed to all disks | Moderate | Mirror protection |
| 3 | 3 | $[(n-1)/n] \times 100$ where n= number of disks | Moderate | Fair for random reads and good for sequential reads | Poor to fair for small random writes and fair for large, sequential writes | High | Parity protection for single disk failure |
| 4 | 3 | $[(n-1)/n] \times 100$ where n= number of disks | Moderate | Good for random and sequential reads | Fair for random and sequential writes | High | Parity protection for single disk failure |
| 5 | 3 | $[(n-1)/n] \times 100$ where n= number of disks | Moderate | Good for random and sequential reads | Fair for random and sequential writes | High | Parity protection for single disk failure |
| 6 | 4 | $[(n-2)/n] \times 100$ where n= number of disks | Moderate but more than RAID 5. | Good for random and sequential reads | Poor to fair for random writes and fair for sequential writes | Very High | Parity protection for two disk failures |
| 1+0 and 0+1 | 4 | 50 | High | Good | Good | Moderate | Mirror protection |

# 3.7 Hot Spares

A *hot spare* refers to a spare drive in a RAID array that temporarily replaces a failed disk drive by taking the identity of the failed disk drive. With the hot spare, one of the following methods of data recovery is performed depending on the RAID implementation:

- If parity RAID is used, the data is rebuilt onto the hot spare from the parity and the data on the surviving disk drives in the RAID set.
- If mirroring is used, the data from the surviving mirror is used to copy the data onto the hot spare.

When a new disk drive is added to the system, data from the hot spare is copied to it. The hot spare returns to its idle state, ready to replace the next failed drive. Alternatively, the hot spare replaces the failed disk drive permanently. This means that it is no longer a hot spare, and a new hot spare must be configured on the array.

A hot spare should be large enough to accommodate data from a failed drive. Some systems implement multiple hot spares to improve data availability.

A hot spare can be configured as automatic or user initiated, which specifies how it will be used in the event of disk failure. In an automatic configuration, when the recoverable error rates for a disk exceed a predetermined threshold, the disk subsystem tries to copy data from the failing disk to the hot spare automatically. If this task is completed before the damaged disk fails, the subsystem switches to the hot spare and marks the failing disk as unusable. Otherwise, it uses parity or the mirrored disk to recover the data. In the case of a user-initiated configuration, the administrator has control of the rebuild process. For example, the rebuild could occur overnight to prevent any degradation of system performance. However, the system is at risk of data loss if another disk failure occurs.

# Summary

Individual disks are prone to failures and pose the threat of data unavailability. RAID addresses data availability requirements by using mirroring and parity techniques. RAID implementations with striping enhance I/O performance by spreading data across multiple disk drives, in addition to redundancy benefits.

This chapter explained the fundamental constructs of striping, mirroring, and parity, which form the basis for various RAID levels. Selection of a RAID level depends on the performance, cost, and data protection requirements of an application.

RAID is the cornerstone technology for several advancements in storage. The intelligent storage systems discussed in the next chapter implement RAID along with a specialized operating environment that offers high performance and availability.

**EXERCISES**

1. Why is RAID 1 not a substitute for a backup?

2. Research  RAID 6 and its second parity computation.

3. Explain the process of data recovery in case of a drive failure in RAID 5.

4. What are the benefits of using RAID 3 in a backup application?

5. Discuss the impact of random and sequential I/Os in different RAID configurations.

6. An application has 1,000 heavy users at a peak of 2 IOPS each and 2,000 typical users at a peak of 1 IOPS each. It is estimated that the application also experiences an overhead of 20 percent for other workloads. The read/write ratio for the application is 2:1. Calculate RAID corrected IOPS for RAID 1/0, RAID 5, and RAID 6.

7. For Question 6, compute the number of drives required to support the application in different RAID environments if 10 K RPM drives with a rating of 130 IOPS per drive were used.

8. What is the stripe size of a five-disk RAID 5 set with a strip size of 32 KB? Compare it with the stripe size of a five-disk RAID 0 array with the same strip size.

# Chapter 4
# Intelligent Storage Systems

B usiness-critical applications require high levels of performance, availability, security, and scalability. A disk drive is a core element of storage that governs the performance of any storage system. Some of the older disk-array technologies could not overcome performance constraints due to the limitations of disk drives and their mechanical components. RAID technology made an important contribution to enhancing storage performance and reliability, but disk drives, even with a RAID implementation, could not meet the performance requirements of today's applications.

With advancements in technology, a new breed of storage solutions, known as *intelligent storage systems*, has evolved. These intelligent storage systems are feature-rich RAID arrays that provide highly optimized I/O processing capabilities. These storage systems are configured with a large amount of memory (called *cache*) and multiple I/O paths and use sophisticated algorithms to meet the requirements of performance-sensitive applications. These arrays have an operating environment that intelligently and optimally handles the management, allocation, and utilization of storage resources. Support for flash drives and other modern-day technologies, such as virtual storage provisioning and automated storage tiering, has added a new dimension to storage system performance, scalability, and availability.

This chapter covers components of intelligent storage systems along with storage provisioning to applications.

# 4.1 Components of an Intelligent Storage System

An intelligent storage system consists of four key components: *front end*, *cache*, *back end*, and *physical disks*. Figure 4-1 illustrates these components and their interconnections. An I/O request received from the host at the front-end port is processed through cache and back end, to enable storage and retrieval of data from the physical disk. A read request can be serviced directly from cache if the requested data is found in the cache. In modern intelligent storage systems, front end, cache, and back end are typically integrated on a single board (referred to as a *storage processor* or *storage controller*).

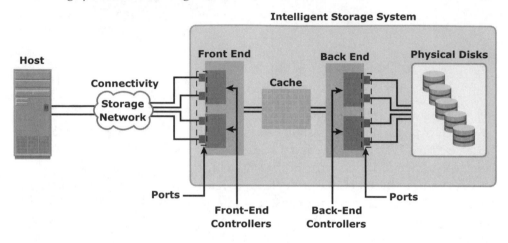

**Figure 4-1:** Components of an intelligent storage system

## 4.1.1 Front End

The front end provides the interface between the storage system and the host. It consists of two components: front-end ports and front-end controllers. Typically, a front end has redundant controllers for high availability, and each controller contains multiple ports that enable large numbers of hosts to connect to the intelligent storage system. Each front-end controller has processing logic that executes the appropriate transport protocol, such as Fibre Channel, iSCSI, FICON, or FCoE for storage connections.

*Front-end controllers* route data to and from cache via the internal data bus. When the cache receives the write data, the controller sends an acknowledgment message back to the host.

## 4.1.2 Cache

*Cache* is semiconductor memory where data is placed temporarily to reduce the time required to service I/O requests from the host.

Cache improves storage system performance by isolating hosts from the mechanical delays associated with rotating disks or hard disk drives (HDD). Rotating disks are the slowest component of an intelligent storage system. Data access on rotating disks usually takes several millisecond because of seek time and rotational latency. Accessing data from cache is fast and typically takes less than a millisecond. On intelligent arrays, write data is first placed in cache and then written to disk.

### Structure of Cache

Cache is organized into pages, which is the smallest unit of cache allocation. The size of a cache page is configured according to the application I/O size. Cache consists of the *data store* and *tag RAM*. The data store holds the data whereas the tag RAM tracks the location of the data in the data store (see Figure 4-2) and in the disk.

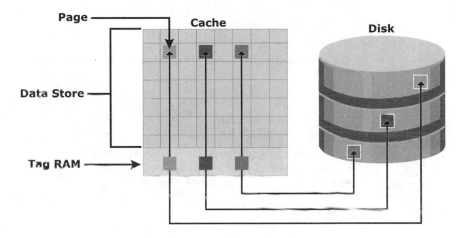

**Figure 4-2:** Structure of cache

Entries in tag RAM indicate where data is found in cache and where the data belongs on the disk. Tag RAM includes a *dirty bit* flag, which indicates whether the data in cache has been committed to the disk. It also contains time-based information, such as the time of last access, which is used to identify cached information that has not been accessed for a long period and may be freed up.

### Read Operation with Cache

When a host issues a read request, the storage controller reads the tag RAM to determine whether the required data is available in cache. If the requested data is found in the cache, it is called a *read cache hit* or *read hit* and data is sent directly to the host, without any disk operation (see Figure 4-3 [a]). This provides a fast response time to the host (about a millisecond). If the requested data is not found in cache, it is called a *cache miss* and the data must be read from the disk (see Figure 4-3 [b]). The back end accesses the appropriate disk and retrieves the requested data. Data is then placed in cache and finally sent to the host through the front end. Cache misses increase the I/O response time.

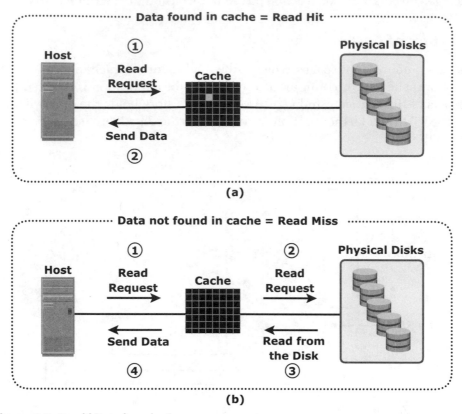

**Figure 4-3:** Read hit and read miss

A *prefetch* or *read-ahead* algorithm is used when read requests are sequential. In a sequential read request, a contiguous set of associated blocks is retrieved. Several other blocks that have not yet been requested by the host can be read from the disk and placed into cache in advance. When the host subsequently requests these blocks, the read operations will be read hits. This process significantly improves the response time experienced by the host. The intelligent storage system offers fixed and variable prefetch sizes. In *fixed prefetch*, the intelligent storage system prefetches a fixed amount of data. It is most suitable when host I/O sizes are uniform. In *variable prefetch*, the storage system prefetches an amount of data in multiples of the size of the host request. *Maximum prefetch* limits the number of data blocks that can be prefetched to prevent the disks from being rendered busy with prefetch at the expense of other I/Os.

Read performance is measured in terms of the *read hit ratio*, or the *hit rate*, usually expressed as a percentage. This ratio is the number of read hits with respect to the total number of read requests. A higher read hit ratio improves the read performance.

## Write Operation with Cache

Write operations with cache provide performance advantages over writing directly to disks. When an I/O is written to cache and acknowledged, it is completed in far less time (from the host's perspective) than it would take to write directly to disk. Sequential writes also offer opportunities for optimization because many smaller writes can be coalesced for larger transfers to disk drives with the use of cache.

A write operation with cache is implemented in the following ways:

- **Write-back cache:** Data is placed in cache and an acknowledgment is sent to the host immediately. Later, data from several writes are committed (de-staged) to the disk. Write response times are much faster because the write operations are isolated from the mechanical delays of the disk. However, uncommitted data is at risk of loss if cache failures occur.

- **Write-through cache:** Data is placed in the cache and immediately written to the disk, and an acknowledgment is sent to the host. Because data is committed to disk as it arrives, the risks of data loss are low, but the write-response time is longer because of the disk operations.

Cache can be bypassed under certain conditions, such as large size write I/O. In this implementation, if the size of an I/O request exceeds the predefined size, called *write aside size*, writes are sent to the disk directly to reduce the impact of large writes consuming a large cache space. This is particularly useful in an environment where cache resources are constrained and cache is required for small random I/Os.

## Cache Implementation

Cache can be implemented as either dedicated cache or global cache. With dedicated cache, separate sets of memory locations are reserved for reads and writes. In global cache, both reads and writes can use any of the available memory addresses. Cache management is more efficient in a global cache implementation because only one global set of addresses has to be managed.

Global cache allows users to specify the percentages of cache available for reads and writes for cache management. Typically, the read cache is small, but it should be increased if the application being used is read-intensive. In other global cache implementations, the ratio of cache available for reads versus writes is dynamically adjusted based on the workloads.

## Cache Management

Cache is a finite and expensive resource that needs proper management. Even though modern intelligent storage systems come with a large amount of cache, when all cache pages are filled, some pages have to be freed up to accommodate new data and avoid performance degradation. Various cache management algorithms are implemented in intelligent storage systems to proactively maintain a set of free pages and a list of pages that can be potentially freed up whenever required. The most commonly used algorithms are discussed in the following list:

- **Least Recently Used (LRU):** An algorithm that continuously monitors data access in cache and identifies the cache pages that have not been accessed for a long time. LRU either frees up these pages or marks them for reuse. This algorithm is based on the assumption that data that has not been accessed for a while will not be requested by the host. However, if a page contains write data that has not yet been committed to disk, the data is first written to disk before the page is reused.

- **Most Recently Used (MRU):** This algorithm is the opposite of LRU, where the pages that have been accessed most recently are freed up or marked for reuse. This algorithm is based on the assumption that recently accessed data may not be required for a while.

As cache fills, the storage system must take action to flush dirty pages (data written into the cache but not yet written to the disk) to manage space availability. *Flushing* is the process that commits data from cache to the disk. On the basis of the I/O access rate and pattern, high and low levels called *watermarks* are set in cache to manage the flushing process. *High watermark* (*HWM*) is the cache utilization level at which the storage system starts high-speed flushing of cache data. *Low watermark* (*LWM*) is the point at which the storage system stops flushing data to the disks. The cache utilization level, as shown in Figure 4-4, drives the mode of flushing to be used:

- **Idle flushing:** Occurs continuously, at a modest rate, when the cache utilization level is between the high and low watermark.

- **High watermark flushing:** Activated when cache utilization hits the high watermark. The storage system dedicates some additional resources for flushing. This type of flushing has some  impact on I/O processing.

- **Forced flushing:** Occurs in the event of a large I/O burst when cache reaches 100 percent of its capacity, which significantly affects the I/O response time. In forced flushing, system flushes the cache on priority by allocating more resources.

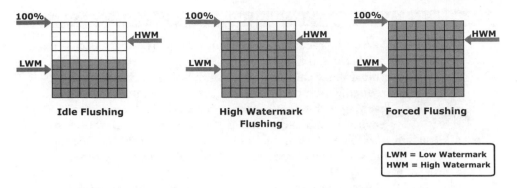

**Figure 4-4:** Types of flushing

## Cache Data Protection

Cache is volatile memory, so a power failure or any kind of cache failure will cause loss of the data that is not yet committed to the disk. This risk of losing uncommitted data held in cache can be mitigated using *cache mirroring* and *cache vaulting*:

- **Cache mirroring:** Each write to cache is held in two different memory locations on two independent memory cards. If a cache failure occurs, the write data will still be safe in the mirrored location and can be committed to the disk. Reads are staged from the disk to the cache; therefore, if a cache failure occurs, the data can still be accessed from the disk. Because only writes are mirrored, this method results in better utilization of the available cache.

  In cache mirroring approaches, the problem of maintaining *cache coherency* is introduced. Cache coherency means that data in two different cache locations must be identical at all times. It is the responsibility of the array operating environment to ensure coherency.

- **Cache vaulting:** The risk of data loss due to power failure can be addressed in various ways: powering the memory with a battery until the AC power is restored or using battery power to write the cache content to the disk. If an extended power failure occurs, using batteries is not a viable option. This is because in intelligent storage systems, large amounts of data might need to be committed to numerous disks, and batteries might not provide power for sufficient time to write each piece of data to its intended disk. Therefore, storage vendors use a set of physical disks to dump the contents of cache during power failure. This is called *cache vaulting* and the disks are called *vault drives*. When power is restored, data from these disks is written back to write cache and then written to the intended disks.

**SERVER FLASH-CACHING TECHNOLOGY**

Server flash-caching technology uses intelligent caching software and a PCI Express (PCIe) flash card on the host. This dramatically improves application performance by reducing latency, and accelerates throughput. Server flash-caching technology works in both physical and virtual environments and provides performance acceleration for read-intensive workloads. This technology uses minimal CPU and memory resources from the server by offloading flash management onto the PCIe card.

It intelligently determines which data would benefit by sitting in the server on PCIe flash and closer to the application. This avoids the latencies associated with I/O access over the network to the storage array. With this, the processing power required for an application's most frequently referenced data is offloaded from the back-end storage to the PCIe card. Therefore, the storage array can allocate greater processing power to other applications.

## 4.1.3 Back End

The *back end* provides an interface between cache and the physical disks. It consists of two components: back-end ports and back-end controllers. The back-end controls data transfers between cache and the physical disks. From cache, data is sent to the back end and then routed to the destination disk. Physical disks are connected to ports on the back end. The back-end controller communicates with the disks when performing reads and writes and also provides additional, but limited, temporary data storage. The algorithms implemented on back-end controllers provide error detection and correction, along with RAID functionality.

For high data protection and high availability, storage systems are configured with dual controllers with multiple ports. Such configurations provide an alternative path to physical disks if a controller or port failure occurs. This reliability is further enhanced if the disks are also dual-ported. In that case, each disk port can connect to a separate controller. Multiple controllers also facilitate load balancing.

## 4.1.4 Physical Disk

Physical disks are connected to the back-end storage controller and provide persistent data storage. Modern intelligent storage systems provide support to a variety of disk drives with different speeds and types, such as FC, SATA, SAS, and flash drives. They also support the use of a mix of flash, FC, or SATA within the same array.

# 4.2 Storage Provisioning

*Storage provisioning* is the process of assigning storage resources to hosts based on capacity, availability, and performance requirements of applications running on the hosts. Storage provisioning can be performed in two ways: traditional and virtual. *Virtual provisioning* leverages virtualization technology for provisioning storage for applications. This section details both traditional and virtual storage provisioning.

## 4.2.1 Traditional Storage Provisioning

In traditional storage provisioning, physical disks are logically grouped together and a required RAID level is applied to form a set, called a RAID set. The number of drives in the RAID set and the RAID level determine the availability, capacity, and performance of the RAID set. It is highly recommend that the RAID set be created from drives of the same type, speed, and capacity to ensure maximum usable capacity, reliability, and consistency in performance. For example, if drives of different capacities are mixed in a RAID set, the capacity of the smallest drive is used from each disk in the set to make up the RAID set's overall capacity. The remaining capacity of the larger drives remains unused. Likewise, mixing higher revolutions per minute (RPM) drives with lower RPM drives lowers the overall performance of the RAID set.

RAID sets usually have a large capacity because they combine the total capacity of individual drives in the set. *Logical units* are created from the RAID sets by partitioning (seen as slices of the RAID set) the available capacity into smaller units. These units are then assigned to the host based on their storage requirements.

Logical units are spread across all the physical disks that belong to that set. Each logical unit created from the RAID set is assigned a unique ID, called a *logical unit number* (LUN). LUNs hide the organization and composition of the RAID set from the hosts. LUNs created by traditional storage provisioning methods are also referred to as *thick LUNs* to distinguish them from the LUNs created by virtual provisioning methods.

Figure 4-5 shows a RAID set consisting of five disks that have been sliced, or partitioned, into two LUNs: LUN 0 and LUN 1. These LUNs are then assigned to Host1 and Host 2 for their storage requirements.

When a LUN is configured and assigned to a non-virtualized host, a bus scan is required to identify the LUN. This LUN appears as a raw disk to the operating system. To make this disk usable, it is formatted with a file system and then the file system is mounted.

In a virtualized host environment, the LUN is assigned to the hypervisor, which recognizes it as a raw disk. This disk is configured with the hypervisor file system, and then virtual disks are created on it. *Virtual disks* are files on the hypervisor file system. The virtual disks are then assigned to virtual machines and appear as raw disks to them. To make the virtual disk usable to the virtual machine, similar steps are followed as in a non-virtualized environment. Here, the LUN space may be shared and accessed simultaneously by multiple virtual machines.

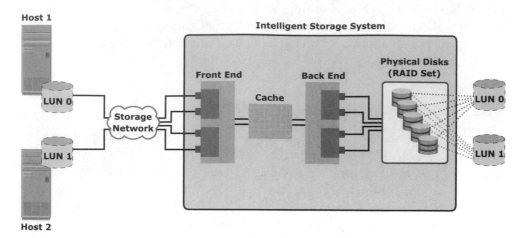

**Figure 4-5:** RAID set and LUNs

Virtual machines can also access a LUN directly on the storage system. In this method the entire LUN is allocated to a single virtual machine. Storing data in this way is recommended when the applications running on the virtual machine are response-time sensitive, and sharing storage with other virtual machines may impact their response time. The direct access method is also used when a virtual machine is clustered with a physical machine. In this case, the virtual machine is required to access the LUN that is being accessed by the physical machine.

### LUN Expansion: MetaLUN

*MetaLUN* is a method to expand LUNs that require additional capacity or performance. A metaLUN can be created by combining two or more LUNs. A metaLUN consists of a base LUN and one or more component LUNs. MetaLUNs can be either *concatenated* or *striped*.

Concatenated expansion simply adds additional capacity to the base LUN. In this expansion, the component LUNs are not required to be of the same capacity as the base LUN. All LUNs in a concatenated metaLUN must be either protected (parity or mirrored) or unprotected (RAID 0). RAID types within a metaLUN can be mixed. For example, a RAID 1/0 LUN can be concatenated with a RAID 5 LUN. However, a RAID 0 LUN can be concatenated only with another RAID 0 LUN.

Concatenated expansion is quick but does not provide any performance benefit. (See Figure 4-6.)

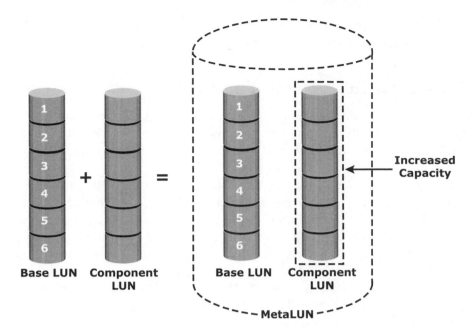

**Figure 4-6:** Concatenated metaLUN

Striped expansion restripes the base LUN's data across the base LUN and component LUNs. In striped expansion, all LUNs must be of the same capacity and RAID level. Striped expansion provides improved performance due to the increased number of drives being striped (see Figure 4-7).

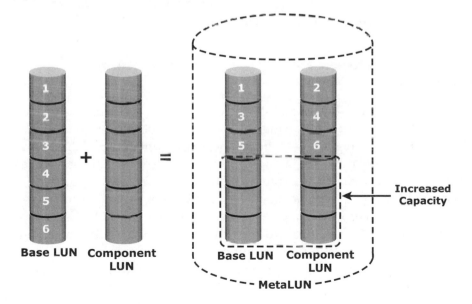

**Figure 4-7:** Striped metaLUN

All LUNs in both concatenated and striped expansion must reside on the same disk-drive type: either all Fibre Channel or all ATA.

## 4.2.2 Virtual Storage Provisioning

*Virtual provisioning* enables creating and presenting a LUN with more capacity than is physically allocated to it on the storage array. The LUN created using virtual provisioning is called a *thin LUN* to distinguish it from the traditional LUN.

Thin LUNs do not require physical storage to be completely allocated to them at the time they are created and presented to a host. Physical storage is allocated to the host "on-demand" from a shared pool of physical capacity. A *shared pool* consists of physical disks. A shared pool in virtual provisioning is analogous to a RAID group, which is a collection of drives on which LUNs are created. Similar to a RAID group, a shared pool supports a single RAID protection level. However, unlike a RAID group, a shared pool might contain large numbers of drives. Shared pools can be homogeneous (containing a single drive type) or heterogeneous (containing mixed drive types, such as flash, FC, SAS, and SATA drives).

Virtual provisioning enables more efficient allocation of storage to hosts. Virtual provisioning also enables oversubscription, where more capacity is presented to the hosts than is actually available on the storage array. Both shared pool and thin LUN can be expanded nondisruptively as the storage requirements of the hosts grow. Multiple shared pools can be created within a storage array, and a shared pool may be shared by multiple thin LUNs. Figure 4-8 illustrates the provisioning of thin LUNs.

### *Comparison between Virtual and Traditional Storage Provisioning*

Administrators typically allocate storage capacity based on anticipated storage requirements. This generally results in the over provisioning of storage capacity, which then leads to higher costs and lower capacity utilization. Administrators often over-provision storage to an application for various reasons, such as, to avoid frequent provisioning of storage if the LUN capacity is exhausted, and to reduce disruption to application availability. Over provisioning of storage often leads to additional storage acquisition and operational costs.

Virtual provisioning addresses these challenges. Virtual provisioning improves storage capacity utilization and simplifies storage management. Figure 4-9 shows an example, comparing virtual provisioning with traditional storage provisioning.

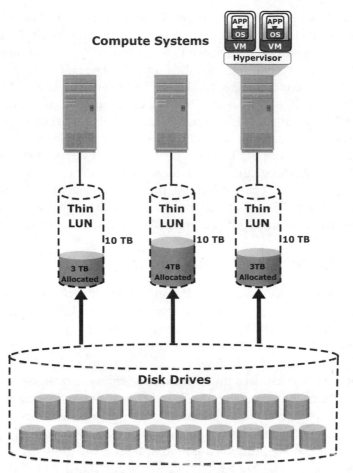

**Figure 4-8:** Virtual provisioning

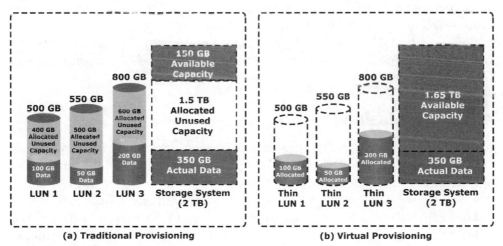

**Figure 4-9:** Traditional versus virtual provisioning

With traditional provisioning, three LUNs are created and presented to one or more hosts (see Figure 4-9 [a]). The total storage capacity of the storage system is 2 TB. The allocated capacity of LUN 1 is 500 GB, of which only 100 GB is consumed, and the remaining 400 GB is unused. The size of LUN 2 is 550 GB, of which 50 GB is consumed, and 500 GB is unused. The size of LUN 3 is 800 GB, of which 200 GB is consumed, and 600 GB is unused. In total, the storage system has 350 GB of data, 1.5 TB of allocated but unused capacity, and only 150 GB of remaining capacity available for other applications.

Now consider the same 2 TB storage system with virtual provisioning (see Figure 4-9 [b]). Here, three thin LUNs of the same sizes are created. However, there is no allocated unused capacity. In total, the storage system with virtual provisioning has the same 350 GB of data, but 1.65 TB of capacity is available for other applications, whereas only 150 GB is available in traditional storage provisioning.

### Use Cases for Thin and Traditional LUNs

Virtual provisioning and thin LUN offer many benefits, although in some cases traditional LUN is better suited for an application. Thin LUNs are appropriate for applications that can tolerate performance variations. In some cases, performance improvement is perceived when using a thin LUN, due to striping across a large number of drives in the pool. However, when multiple thin LUNs contend for shared storage resources in a given pool, and when utilization reaches higher levels, the performance can degrade. Thin LUNs provide the best storage space efficiency and are suitable for applications where space consumption is difficult to forecast. Using thin LUNs benefits organizations in reducing power and acquisition costs and in simplifying their storage management.

Traditional LUNs are suited for applications that require predictable performance. Traditional LUNs provide full control for precise data placement and allow an administrator to create LUNs on different RAID groups if there is any workload contention. Organizations that are not highly concerned about storage space efficiency may still use traditional LUNs.

Both traditional and thin LUNs can coexist in the same storage array. Based on the requirement, an administrator may migrate data between thin and traditional LUNs.

## 4.2.3 LUN Masking

*LUN masking* is a process that provides data access control by defining which LUNs a host can access. The LUN masking function is implemented on the storage array. This ensures that volume access by hosts is controlled appropriately, preventing unauthorized or accidental use in a shared environment.

For example, consider a storage array with two LUNs that store data of the sales and finance departments. Without LUN masking, both departments can easily see and modify each other's data, posing a high risk to data integrity and security. With LUN masking, LUNs are accessible only to the designated hosts.

# 4.3 Types of Intelligent Storage Systems

Intelligent storage systems generally fall into one of the following two categories:

- High-end storage systems
- Midrange storage systems

Traditionally, high-end storage systems have been implemented with *active-active configuration*, whereas midrange storage systems have been implemented with *active-passive configuration*. The distinctions between these two implementations are becoming increasingly insignificant.

## 4.3.1 High-End Storage Systems

High-end storage systems, referred to as *active-active arrays*, are generally aimed at large enterprise applications. These systems are designed with a large number of controllers and cache memory. An active-active array implies that the host can perform I/Os to its LUNs through any of the available controllers (see Figure 4-10).

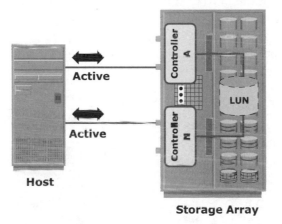

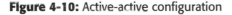

**Figure 4-10:** Active-active configuration

To address enterprise storage needs, these arrays provide the following capabilities:

- Large storage capacity
- Large amounts of cache to service host I/Os optimally

- Fault tolerance architecture to improve data availability
- Connectivity to mainframe computers and open systems hosts
- Availability of multiple front-end ports and interface protocols to serve a large number of hosts
- Availability of multiple back-end controllers to manage disk processing
- Scalability to support increased connectivity, performance, and storage capacity requirements
- Ability to handle large amounts of concurrent I/Os from a number of hosts and applications
- Support for array-based local and remote data replication

In addition to these features, high-end systems possess some unique features that are required for mission-critical applications.

## 4.3.2 Midrange Storage Systems

Midrange storage systems are also referred to as *active-passive arrays* and are best suited for small- and medium-sized enterprise applications. They also provide optimal storage solutions at a lower cost. In an active-passive array, a host can perform I/Os to a LUN only through the controller that owns the LUN. As shown in Figure 4-11, the host can perform reads or writes to the LUN only through the path to controller A because controller A is the owner of that LUN. The path to controller B remains passive and no I/O activity is performed through this path.

Midrange storage systems are typically designed with two controllers, each of which contains host interfaces, cache, RAID controllers, and interface to disk drives.

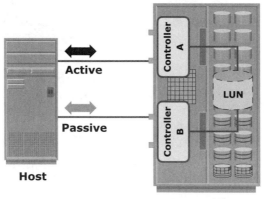

**Figure 4-11:** Active-passive configuration

Midrange arrays are designed to meet the requirements of small and medium enterprise applications; therefore, they host less storage capacity and cache than high-end storage arrays. There are also fewer front-end ports for connection to hosts. However, they ensure high redundancy and high performance for applications with predictable workloads. They also support array-based local and remote replication.

# 4.4 Concepts in Practice: EMC Symmetrix and VNX

To illustrate the concepts discussed in this chapter, this section covers the EMC implementation of intelligent storage arrays.

The EMC Symmetrix storage array is an active-active array implementation. Symmetrix is a solution for customers who require an uncompromising level of service, performance, and the most advanced business continuity solution to support large and unpredictable application workloads. Symmetrix also provides built-in, advanced-level security features and offers the most efficient use of power and cooling to support enterprise-level data storage requirements.

The EMC VNX storage array is an active-passive array implementation. It is EMC's midrange storage offering that delivers enterprise-quality features and functionalities. EMC VNX is a unified storage platform that offers storage for block, file, and object-based data within the same array. It is ideally suited for applications with predictable workloads that require moderate-to-high throughput. Details of unified storage and EMC VNX are covered in Chapter 8.

For the latest information on Symmetrix and VNX, visit www.emc.com.

## 4.4.1 EMC Symmetrix Storage Array

EMC Symmetrix establishes the highest standards for performance and capacity for an enterprise information storage solution and is recognized as the industry's most trusted storage platform. Symmetrix offers the highest level of scalability and performance to meet even unpredictable I/O workload requirements. The EMC Symmetrix offering includes the Symmetrix Virtual Matrix (VMAX) series.

The EMC Symmetrix VMAX series is an innovative platform built around a scalable Virtual Matrix architecture to support the future storage growth demands of virtual IT environments. Figure 4-12 shows the Symmetrix VMAX storage array. The key features supported by Symmetrix VMAX follows:

- Incrementally scalable to 2,400 disks
- Supports up to 8 VMAX engines (Each VMAX engine contains a pair of directors.)
- Supports flash drives, fully automated storage tiering (FAST), virtual provisioning, and Cloud computing

- Supports up to 1 TB of global cache memory

- Supports FC, iSCSI, GigE, and FICON for host connectivity

- Supports RAID levels 1, 1+0, 5, and 6

- Supports storage-based replication through EMC TimeFinder and EMC SRDF

- Highly fault-tolerant design that allows nondisruptive upgrades and full component-level redundancy with hot-swappable replacements

**Figure 4-12:** EMC Symmetrix VMAX

## 4.4.2 EMC Symmetrix VMAX Component

EMC Symmetrix VMAX contains one system bay and up to ten storage bays. A storage bay supports up to 16 drive array enclosures (DAEs), and each drive enclosure can house up to 15 drives. The system bay houses the system components, which include VMAX Engines, Matrix Interface Board Enclosure (MIBE), standby power supply (SPS) modules, and service processor:

- **VMAX Engine:** Consists of a pair of directors that contains four quad-core Intel processors, up to 128 GB of memory, and up to16 front-end ports for host access or SRDF channels.

- **Matrix Interface Board Enclosure (MIBE):** Contains two independent matrix switches that provide point-to point communication between directors. Each director has two connections to the V-Max Matrix Interface Board Enclosure. Because every director has two separate physical paths to every other director via the Virtual Matrix, this is a highly available interconnect with no single point of failure. This design eliminates the need for separate interconnects for data, control, messaging, and environmental and system tests. A single highly available interconnect suffices for all communications between the directors, which reduces complexity.

- **Service Processor:** Used for system configuration and the management console. It also provides notification and support capabilities to allow access to the system locally or remotely. The Service Processor automatically notifies the vendor's Customer Support Center whenever a component failure or environmental violation is detected.

- **Symmetrix Enginuity:** The operating environment for EMC Symmetrix. Enginuity manages and ensures the optimal flow and integrity of information through the various hardware components of the Symmetrix system. It manages all Symmetrix operations and system resources to optimize performance intelligently. Enginuity ensures system availability through advanced fault monitoring, detection, and correction capabilities and provides concurrent maintenance and serviceability features. It also offers a foundation for specific software features for disaster recovery, business continuance, and storage management.

## 4.4.3 Symmetrix VMAX Architecture

Each VMAX engine contains a portion of global memory and two directors capable of managing front-end, back-end, and remote connections simultaneously. The VMAX engine is connected to Virtual Matrix and allows all system resources, including CPU, memory, drives, and host ports, to be dynamically accessed and shared by any host. Additional VMAX engines can be added nondisruptively to efficiently scale system resources. The Virtual Matrix supports up to eight VMAX engines in a system, as shown in Figure 4-13.

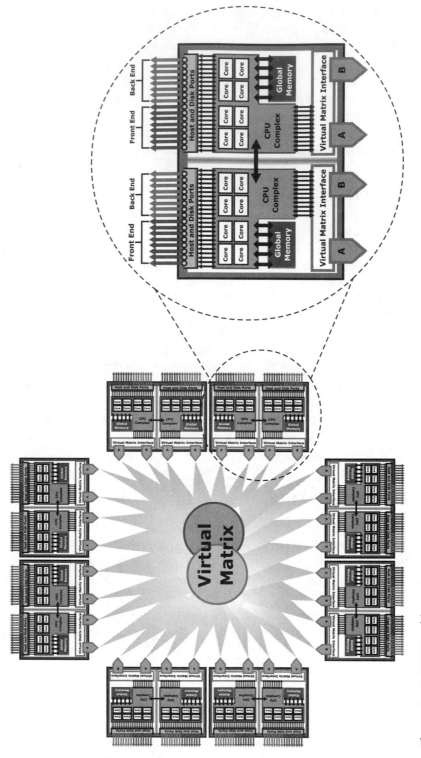

**Figure 4-13:** VMAX architecture

# Summary

This chapter detailed the features and key components of modern intelligent storage systems. The different types of storage systems, high-end and midrange, and their characteristics were also explained. An intelligent storage system provides the following benefits to an organization:

- Increased storage capacity
- Improved I/O performance
- Easier storage management
- Improved data availability
- Improved scalability and flexibility
- Improved business continuity
- Improved security and access control

An intelligent storage system is an integral part of every data center. The large capacity and high performance supported by the intelligent storage system makes it necessary to share it among multiple hosts. Intelligent storage systems enable enterprises to share data easily and securely.

Storage networking is a flexible information-centric strategy that extends the reach of intelligent storage systems throughout an enterprise. It provides a common way to manage, share, and protect enterprise-information assets. Storage networking is detailed in the next part of this book.

## EXERCISES

1. Research Cache Coherency mechanisms, and explain how they address the environment with multiple shared caches.

2. Which type of application benefits the most by bypassing write cache? Justify your answer.

3. Research various cache parameters: cache page size, read versus write cache allocation, cache prefetch size, and write aside size.

4. An Oracle database uses a block size of 4 KB for its I/O operation. The application that uses this database primarily performs a sequential read operation. Suggest and explain the appropriate values for the following cache parameters: cache page size, cache allocation (read versus write), prefetch type, and write aside size.

5. Research and prepare a presentation on EMC VMAX architecture.

# Section

# II

# Storage Networking Technologies

## In This Section

# Chapter 5
# Fibre Channel Storage Area Networks

Organizations are experiencing an explosive growth in information. This information needs to be stored, protected, optimized, and managed efficiently. Data center managers are burdened with the challenging task of providing low-cost, high-performance information management solutions. An effective information management solution must provide the following:

| KEY CONCEPTS |
| --- |
| Fibre Channel (FC) Architecture |
| Fibre Channel Protocol Stack |
| Ports in Fibre Channel SAN |
| Fibre Channel Addressing |
| World Wide Names |
| Zoning |
| Fibre Channel SAN Topologies |
| Block-level Storage Virtualization |
| Virtual SAN |

- **Just-in-time information to business users:** Information must be available to business users when they need it. 24 x 7 data availability is becoming one of the key requirements of today's storage infrastructure. The explosive growth in storage, proliferation of new servers and applications, and the spread of mission-critical data throughout enterprises are some of the challenges that need to be addressed to provide information availability in real time.

- **Integration of information infrastructure with business processes:** The storage infrastructure should be integrated with various business processes without compromising its security and integrity.

- **Flexible and resilient storage infrastructure:** The storage infrastructure must provide flexibility and resilience that aligns with changing business requirements. Storage should scale without compromising the performance requirements of applications and, at the same time, the total cost of managing information must be low.

*Direct-attached storage* (DAS) is often referred to as a stovepiped storage environment. Hosts "own" the storage, and it is difficult to manage and share resources on these isolated storage devices. Efforts to organize this dispersed data led to the emergence of the *storage area network* (SAN). SAN is a high-speed, dedicated network of servers and shared storage devices. A SAN provides storage consolidation and facilitates centralized data management. It meets the storage demands efficiently with better economies of scale and also provides effective maintenance and protection of data. Virtualized SAN and block storage virtualization provide enhanced utilization and collaboration among dispersed storage resources. The implementation of virtualization in SAN provides improved productivity, resource utilization, and manageability.

Common SAN deployments are Fibre Channel (FC) SAN and IP SAN. Fibre Channel SAN uses Fibre Channel protocol for the transport of data, commands, and status information between servers (or hosts) and storage devices. IP SAN uses IP-based protocols for communication.

This chapter provides detailed insight into the FC technology on which an FC SAN is deployed. It also covers FC SAN components, topologies, and block storage virtualization.

# 5.1 Fibre Channel: Overview

The FC architecture forms the fundamental construct of the FC SAN infrastructure. *Fibre Channel* is a high-speed network technology that runs on high-speed optical fiber cables and serial copper cables. The FC technology was developed to meet the demand for increased speeds of data transfer between servers and mass storage systems. Although FC networking was introduced in 1988, the FC standardization process began when the American National Standards Institute (ANSI) chartered the Fibre Channel Working Group (FCWG). By 1994, the new high-speed computer interconnection standard was developed and the Fibre Channel Association (FCA) was founded with 70 charter member companies. Technical Committee T11, which is the committee within International Committee for Information Technology Standards (INCITS), is responsible for Fibre Channel interface standards.

High data transmission speed is an important feature of the FC networking technology. The initial implementation offered a throughput of 200 MB/s (equivalent to a raw bit rate of 1Gb/s), which was greater than the speeds of Ultra SCSI (20 MB/s), commonly used in DAS environments. In comparison with Ultra SCSI, FC is a significant leap in storage networking technology. The latest FC implementations of 16 GFC (Fibre Channel) offer a throughput of 3200 MB/s (raw bit rates of 16 Gb/s), whereas Ultra640 SCSI is available with a throughput of 640 MB/s. The FC architecture is highly scalable, and theoretically, a single FC network can accommodate approximately 15 million devices.

## 5.2 The SAN and Its Evolution

A SAN carries data between servers (or *hosts*) and storage devices through Fibre Channel network (see Figure 5-1). A SAN enables storage consolidation and enables storage to be shared across multiple servers. This improves the utilization of storage resources compared to direct-attached storage architecture and reduces the total amount of storage an organization needs to purchase and manage. With consolidation, storage management becomes centralized and less complex, which further reduces the cost of managing information. SAN also enables organizations to connect geographically dispersed servers and storage.

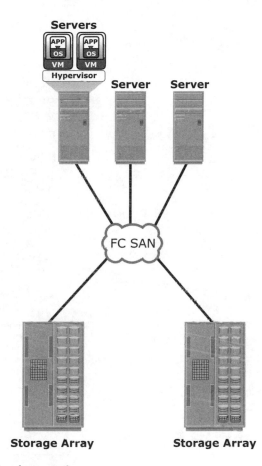

**Figure 5-1:** FC SAN implementation

In its earliest implementation, the FC SAN was a simple grouping of hosts and storage devices connected to a network using an FC hub as a connectivity device. This configuration of an FC SAN is known as a *Fibre Channel Arbitrated*

*Loop* (FC-AL). Use of hubs resulted in isolated FC-AL SAN islands because hubs provide limited connectivity and bandwidth.

The inherent limitations associated with hubs gave way to high-performance FC *switches*. Use of switches in SAN improved connectivity and performance and enabled FC SANs to be highly scalable. This enhanced data accessibility to applications across the enterprise. Now, FC-AL has been almost abandoned for FC SANs due to its limitations but still survives as a back-end connectivity option to disk drives. Figure 5-2 illustrates the FC SAN evolution from FC-AL to enterprise SANs.

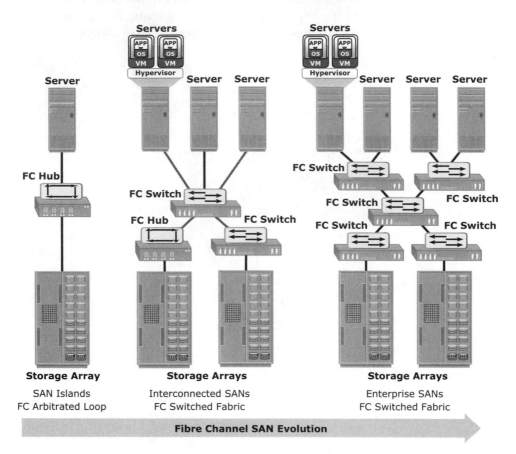

**Figure 5-2:** FC SAN evolution

## 5.3 Components of FC SAN

FC SAN is a network of servers and shared storage devices. Servers and storage are the end points or devices in the SAN (called *nodes*). FC SAN infrastructure consists of node ports, cables, connectors, and interconnecting devices (such as FC switches or hubs), along with SAN management software.

### 5.3.1 Node Ports

In a Fibre Channel network, the end devices, such as hosts, storage arrays, and tape libraries, are all referred to as *nodes*. Each node is a source or destination of information. Each node requires one or more ports to provide a physical interface for communicating with other nodes. These ports are integral components of host adapters, such as HBA, and storage front-end controllers or adapters. In an FC environment a port operates in full-duplex data transmission mode with a *transmit* (Tx) link and a *receive* (Rx) link (see Figure 5-3).

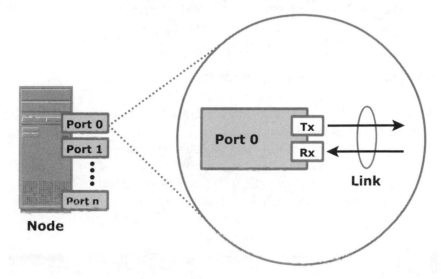

**Figure 5-3:** Nodes, ports, and links

### 5.3.2 Cables and Connectors

SAN implementations use optical fiber cabling. Copper can be used for shorter distances for back-end connectivity because it provides an acceptable signal-to-noise ratio for distances up to 30 meters. Optical fiber cables carry data in the form of light. There are two types of optical cables: multimode and single-mode. *Multimode fiber* (MMF) cable carries multiple beams of light projected at different angles simultaneously onto the core of the cable (see Figure 5-4 [a]). Based on the bandwidth, multimode fibers are classified as OM1 (62.5µm core), OM2 (50µm core), and laser-optimized OM3 (50µm core). In an MMF transmission, multiple light beams traveling inside the cable tend to disperse and collide. This collision weakens the signal strength after it travels a certain distance — a process known as *modal dispersion*. An MMF cable is typically used for short distances because of signal degradation (attenuation) due to modal dispersion.

*Single-mode fiber* (SMF) carries a single ray of light projected at the center of the core (see Figure 5-4 [b]). These cables are available in core diameters of 7 to 11 microns;

the most common size is 9 microns. In an SMF transmission, a single light beam travels in a straight line through the core of the fiber. The small core and the single light wave help to limit modal dispersion. Among all types of fiber cables, single-mode provides minimum signal attenuation over maximum distance (up to 10 km). A single-mode cable is used for long-distance cable runs, and distance usually depends on the power of the laser at the transmitter and sensitivity of the receiver.

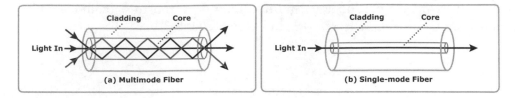

**Figure 5-4:** Multimode fiber and single-mode fiber

MMFs are generally used within data centers for shorter distance runs, whereas SMFs are used for longer distances.

A connector is attached at the end of a cable to enable swift connection and disconnection of the cable to and from a port. A *Standard connector* (SC) (see Figure 5-5 [a]) and a *Lucent connector* (LC) (see Figure 5-5 [b]) are two commonly used connectors for fiber optic cables. *Straight Tip* (ST) is another fiber-optic connector, which is often used with fiber patch panels (see Figure 5.5 [c]).

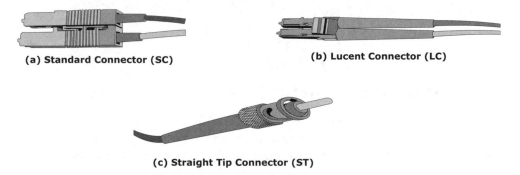

**(a) Standard Connector (SC)**    **(b) Lucent Connector (LC)**

**(c) Straight Tip Connector (ST)**

**Figure 5-5:** SC, LC, and ST connectors

## 5.3.3 Interconnect Devices

FC hubs, switches, and directors are the interconnect devices commonly used in FC SAN.

*Hubs* are used as communication devices in FC-AL implementations. Hubs physically connect nodes in a logical loop or a physical star topology. All the nodes must share the loop because data travels through all the connection points. Because of the availability of low-cost and high-performance switches, hubs are no longer used in FC SANs.

*Switches* are more intelligent than hubs and directly route data from one physical port to another. Therefore, nodes do not share the bandwidth. Instead, each node has a dedicated communication path.

*Directors* are high-end switches with a higher port count and better fault-tolerance capabilities.

Switches are available with a fixed port count or with modular design. In a modular switch, the port count is increased by installing additional port cards to open slots. The architecture of a director is always modular, and its port count is increased by inserting additional line cards or blades to the director's chassis. High-end switches and directors contain redundant components to provide high availability. Both switches and directors have management ports (Ethernet or serial) for connectivity to SAN management servers.

A port card or blade has multiple ports for connecting nodes and other FC switches. Typically, a Fibre Channel transceiver is installed at each port slot that houses the transmit (Tx) and receive (Rx) link. In a transceiver, the Tx and Rx links share common circuitry. Transceivers inside a port card are connected to an application specific integrated circuit, also called port ASIC. Blades in a director usually have more than one ASIC for higher throughput.

## 5.3.4 SAN Management Software

SAN management software manages the interfaces between hosts, interconnect devices, and storage arrays. The software provides a view of the SAN environment and enables management of various resources from one central console.

It provides key management functions, including mapping of storage devices, switches, and servers, monitoring and generating alerts for discovered devices, and *zoning* (discussed in section 5.9 "Zoning" later in this chapter).

**FC SWITCH VERSUS FC HUB**

Scalability and performance are the primary differences between switches and hubs. Addressing in a switched fabric supports more than 15 million nodes within the fabric, whereas the FC-AL implemented in hubs supports only a maximum of 126 nodes.

Fabric switches provide full bandwidth between multiple pairs of ports in a fabric, resulting in a scalable architecture that supports multiple simultaneous communications.

Hubs support only one communication at a time. They provide a low-cost connectivity expansion solution. Switches, conversely, can be used to build dynamic, high-performance fabrics through which multiple communications can take place simultaneously. Switches are more expensive than hubs.

# 5.4 FC Connectivity

The FC architecture supports three basic interconnectivity options: point-to-point, arbitrated loop, and Fibre Channel switched fabric.

## 5.4.1 Point-to-Point

*Point-to-point* is the simplest FC configuration — two devices are connected directly to each other, as shown in Figure 5-6. This configuration provides a dedicated connection for data transmission between nodes. However, the point-to-point configuration offers limited connectivity, because only two devices can communicate with each other at a given time. Moreover, it cannot be scaled to accommodate a large number of nodes. Standard DAS uses point-to-point connectivity.

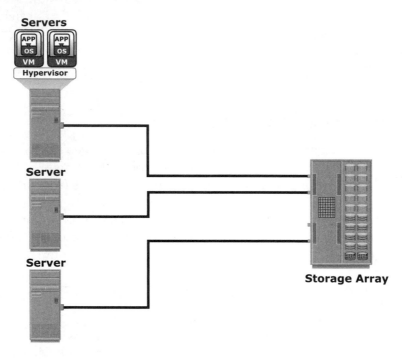

**Figure 5-6:** Point-to-point connectivity

## 5.4.2 Fibre Channel Arbitrated Loop

In the FC-AL configuration, devices are attached to a shared loop. FC-AL has the characteristics of a token ring topology and a physical star topology. In FC-AL, each device contends with other devices to perform I/O operations. Devices on the loop must "arbitrate" to gain control of the loop. At any given time, only one device can perform I/O operations on the loop (see Figure 5-7).

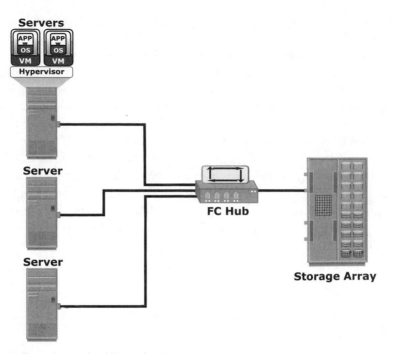

**Figure 5-7:** Fibre Channel Arbitrated Loop

As a loop configuration, FC-AL can be implemented without any interconnecting devices by directly connecting one device to another two devices in a ring through cables.

However, FC-AL implementations may also use hubs whereby the arbitrated loop is physically connected in a star topology.

The FC-AL configuration has the following limitations in terms of scalability:

- FC-AL shares the loop and only one device can perform I/O operations at a time. Because each device in a loop must wait for its turn to process an I/O request, the overall performance in FC-AL environments is low.

- FC-AL uses only 8-bits of 24-bit Fibre Channel addressing (the remaining 16-bits are masked) and enables the assignment of 127 valid addresses to the ports. Hence, it can support up to 127 devices on a loop. One address is reserved for optionally connecting the loop to an FC switch port. Therefore, up to 126 nodes can be connected to the loop.

- Adding or removing a device results in loop re-initialization, which can cause a momentary pause in loop traffic.

## 5.4.3 Fibre Channel Switched Fabric

Unlike a loop configuration, a Fibre Channel switched fabric (FC-SW) network provides dedicated data path and scalability. The addition or removal of a device in a switched fabric is minimally disruptive; it does not affect the ongoing traffic between other devices.

FC-SW is also referred to as *fabric connect*. A fabric is a logical space in which all nodes communicate with one another in a network. This virtual space can be created with a switch or a network of switches. Each switch in a fabric contains a unique domain identifier, which is part of the fabric's addressing scheme. In FC-SW, nodes do not share a loop; instead, data is transferred through a dedicated path between the nodes. Each port in a fabric has a unique 24-bit Fibre Channel address for communication. Figure 5-8 shows an example of the FC-SW fabric.

In a switched fabric, the link between any two switches is called an *Interswitch link* (ISL). ISLs enable switches to be connected together to form a single, larger fabric. ISLs are used to transfer host-to-storage data and fabric management traffic from one switch to another. By using ISLs, a switched fabric can be expanded to connect a large number of nodes.

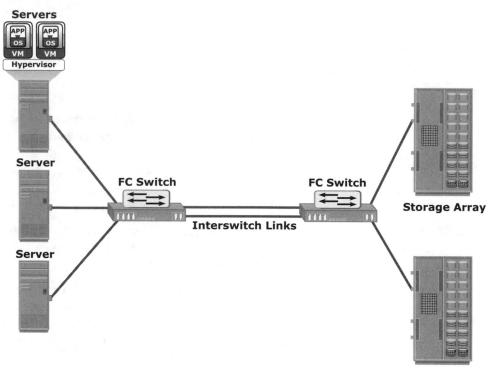

**Figure 5-8:** Fibre Channel switched fabric

A fabric can be described by the number of tiers it contains. The number of tiers in a fabric is based on the number of switches traversed between two points that are farthest from each other. This number is based on the infrastructure constructed by the fabric instead of how the storage and server are connected across the switches.

When the number of tiers in a fabric increases, the distance that the fabric management traffic must travel to reach each switch also increases. This increase in the distance also increases the time taken to propagate and complete a fabric reconfiguration event, such as the addition of a new switch or a zone set propagation event. Figure 5-9 illustrates two-tier and three-tier fabric architecture.

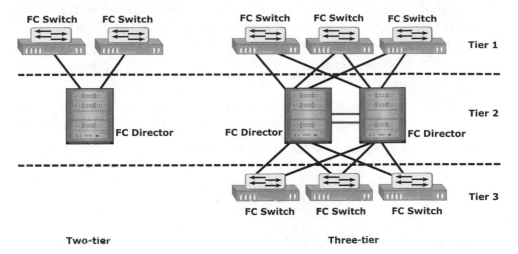

**Figure 5-9:** Tiered structure of Fibre Channel switched fabric

### FC-SW Transmission

FC-SW uses switches that can switch data traffic between nodes directly through switch ports. Frames are routed between source and destination by the fabric.

As shown in Figure 5-10, if node B wants to communicate with node D, the nodes should individually login first and then transmit data via the FC-SW. This link is considered a dedicated connection between the initiator and the target.

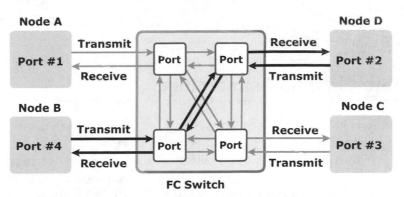

**Figure 5-10:** Data transmission in Fibre Channel switched fabric

## 5.5 Switched Fabric Ports

Ports in a switched fabric can be one of the following types:

- **N_Port:** An end point in the fabric. This port is also known as the *node port*. Typically, it is a host port (HBA) or a storage array port connected to a switch in a switched fabric.

- **E_Port:** A port that forms the connection between two FC switches. This port is also known as the *expansion port*. The E_Port on an FC switch connects to the E_Port of another FC switch in the fabric through ISLs.

- **F_Port:** A port on a switch that connects an N_Port. It is also known as a *fabric port*.

- **G_Port:** A generic port on a switch that can operate as an E_Port or an F_Port and determines its functionality automatically during initialization.

Figure 5-11 shows various FC ports located in a switched fabric.

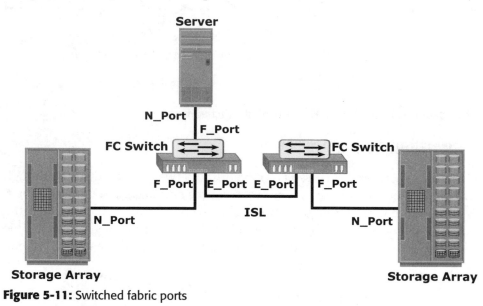

**Figure 5-11:** Switched fabric ports

## 5.6 Fibre Channel Architecture

Traditionally, host computer operating systems have communicated with peripheral devices over channel connections, such as ESCON and SCSI. Channel technologies provide high levels of performance with low protocol overheads. Such performance is achievable due to the static nature of channels and the high level of hardware and software integration provided by the channel technologies.

However, these technologies suffer from inherent limitations in terms of the number of devices that can be connected and the distance between these devices.

In contrast to channel technology, network technologies are more flexible and provide greater distance capabilities. Network connectivity provides greater scalability and uses shared bandwidth for communication. This flexibility results in greater protocol overhead and reduced performance.

The FC architecture represents true channel/network integration and captures some of the benefits of both channel and network technology. FC SAN uses the *Fibre Channel Protocol* (FCP) that provides both channel speed for data transfer with low protocol overhead and scalability of network technology.

FCP forms the fundamental construct of the FC SAN infrastructure. Fibre Channel provides a serial data transfer interface that operates over copper wire and optical fiber. FCP is the implementation of serial SCSI over an FC network. In FCP architecture, all external and remote storage devices attached to the SAN appear as local devices to the host operating system. The key advantages of FCP are as follows:

- Sustained transmission bandwidth over long distances.
- Support for a larger number of addressable devices over a network. Theoretically, FC can support more than 15 million device addresses on a network.
- Support speeds up to 16 Gbps (16 GFC).

## 5.6.1 Fibre Channel Protocol Stack

It is easier to understand a communication protocol by viewing it as a structure of independent layers. FCP defines the communication protocol in five layers: FC-0 through FC-4 (except FC-3 layer, which is not implemented). In a layered communication model, the peer layers on each node talk to each other through defined protocols. Figure 5-12 illustrates the Fibre Channel protocol stack.

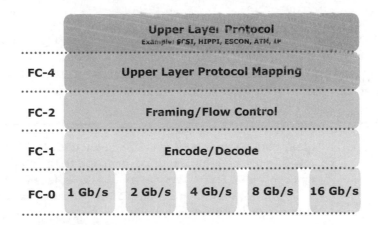

**Figure 5-12:** Fibre Channel protocol stack

### FC-4 Layer

FC-4 is the uppermost layer in the FCP stack. This layer defines the application interfaces and the way *Upper Layer Protocols* (ULPs) are mapped to the lower FC layers. The FC standard defines several protocols that can operate on the FC-4 layer (see Figure 5-12). Some of the protocols include SCSI, High Performance Parallel Interface (HIPPI) Framing Protocol, Enterprise Storage Connectivity (ESCON), Asynchronous Transfer Mode (ATM), and IP.

### FC-2 Layer

The FC-2 layer provides Fibre Channel addressing, structure, and organization of data (frames, sequences, and exchanges). It also defines fabric services, classes of service, flow control, and routing.

### FC-1 Layer

The FC-1 layer defines how data is encoded prior to transmission and decoded upon receipt. At the transmitter node, an 8-bit character is encoded into a 10-bit transmissions character. This character is then transmitted to the receiver node. At the receiver node, the 10-bit character is passed to the FC-1 layer, which decodes the 10-bit character into the original 8-bit character. FC links with speeds of 10 Gbps and above use 64-bit to 66-bit encoding algorithms. The FC-1 layer also defines the transmission words, such as FC frame delimiters, which identify the start and end of a frame and primitive signals that indicate events at a transmitting port. In addition to these, the FC-1 layer performs link initialization and error recovery.

### FC-0 Layer

FC-0 is the lowest layer in the FCP stack. This layer defines the physical interface, media, and transmission of bits. The FC-0 specification includes cables, connectors, and optical and electrical parameters for a variety of data rates. The FC transmission can use both electrical and optical media.

 Mainframe SANs use *Fibre Connectivity* (FICON) for a low-latency, high-bandwidth connection to the storage controller. FICON was designed as a replacement for *Enterprise System Connection* (ESCON) to support mainframe-attached storage systems.

## 5.6.2 Fibre Channel Addressing

An FC address is dynamically assigned when a node port logs on to the fabric. The FC address has a distinct format, as shown in Figure 5-13. The addressing mechanism provided here corresponds to the fabric with the switch as an interconnecting device.

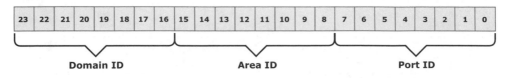

| 23 | 22 | 21 | 20 | 19 | 18 | 17 | 16 | 15 | 14 | 13 | 12 | 11 | 10 | 9 | 8 | 7 | 6 | 5 | 4 | 3 | 2 | 1 | 0 |

Domain ID                    Area ID                    Port ID

**Figure 5-13:** 24-bit FC address of N_Port

The first field of the FC address contains the domain ID of the switch. A *domain ID* is a unique number provided to each switch in the fabric. Although this is an 8-bit field, there are only 239 available addresses for domain ID because some addresses are deemed special and reserved for fabric management services. For example, FFFFFC is reserved for the name server, and FFFFFE is reserved for the fabric login service. The *area ID* is used to identify a group of switch ports used for connecting nodes. An example of a group of ports with a common area ID is a port card on the switch. The last field, the *port ID*, identifies the port within the group.

Therefore, the maximum possible number of node ports in a switched fabric is calculated as:

239 domains × 256 areas × 256 ports = 15,663,104

---

**N_PORT ID VIRTUALIZATION (NPIV)**

*NPIV* is a Fibre Channel configuration that enables multiple N_Port IDs to share a single physical N_Port. A typical use of NPIV would be for SAN storage provisioning to virtual machines in a virtualized server environment. With NPIV, several virtual machines on a host may share a common physical N_Port in the host, with each virtual machine using its own N_Port_ID for that physical node port. For this to work, the FC switch must be NPIV-enabled.

---

## 5.6.3 World Wide Names

Each device in the FC environment is assigned a 64-bit unique identifier called the *World Wide Name* (WWN). The Fibre Channel environment uses two types of WWNs: *World Wide Node Name* (WWNN) and *World Wide Port Name* (WWPN). Unlike an FC address, which is assigned dynamically, a WWN is a static name for each node on an FC network. WWNs are similar to the Media Access Control (MAC) addresses used in IP networking. WWNs are *burned* into the hardware or assigned through software. Several configuration definitions in a SAN use WWN for identifying storage devices and HBAs. The name server in an FC environment keeps the association of WWNs to the dynamically created FC addresses for nodes. Figure 5-14 illustrates the WWN structure examples for an array and an HBA.

| World Wide Name - Array | | | | | | | | | | | | | | | |
|---|---|---|---|---|---|---|---|---|---|---|---|---|---|---|---|
| 5 | 0 | 0 | 6 | 0 | 1 | 6 | 0 | 0 | 0 | 6 | 0 | 0 | 1 | B | 2 |
| 0101 | 0000 | 0000 | 0110 | 0000 | 0001 | 0110 | 0000 | 0000 | 0000 | 0110 | 0000 | 0000 | 0001 | 1011 | 0010 |
| Format Type | Company ID 24 bits | | | | | | Port | Model Seed 32 bits | | | | | | | |

| World Wide Name - HBA | | | | | | | | | | | | | | | |
|---|---|---|---|---|---|---|---|---|---|---|---|---|---|---|---|
| 1 | 0 | 0 | 0 | 0 | 0 | 0 | 0 | c | 9 | 2 | 0 | d | c | 4 | 0 |
| Format Type | Reserved 12 bits | | | Company ID 24 bits | | | | | | Company Specific 24 bits | | | | | |

**Figure 5-14:** World Wide Names

## 5.6.4 FC Frame

An FC frame (Figure 5-15) consists of five parts: *start of frame* (SOF), *frame header, data field, cyclic redundancy check* (CRC), and *end of frame* (EOF).

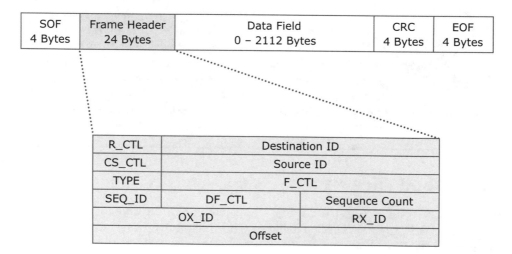

**Figure 5-15:** FC frame

The SOF and EOF act as delimiters. In addition to this role, the SOF also indicates whether the frame is the first frame in a sequence of frames.

The frame header is 24 bytes long and contains addressing information for the frame. It includes the following information: Source ID (S_ID), Destination ID (D_ID), Sequence ID (SEQ_ID), Sequence Count (SEQ_CNT), Originating Exchange ID (OX_ID), and Responder Exchange ID (RX_ID), in addition to some control fields.

The S_ID and D_ID are FC addresses for the source port and the destination port, respectively. The SEQ_ID and OX_ID identify the frame as a component of a specific sequence and exchange, respectively.

The frame header also defines the following fields:

■ **Routing Control (R_CTL):** This field denotes whether the frame is a link control frame or a data frame. Link control frames are frames that do not carry any user data. These frames are used for setup and messaging. In contrast, data frames carry the user data.

■ **Class Specific Control (CS_CTL):** This field specifies link speeds for class 1 and class 4 data transmission. (Class of service is discussed in section 5.6.7 "Classes of Service" later in the chapter.)

■ **TYPE:** This field describes the upper layer protocol (ULP) to be carried on the frame if it is a data frame. However, if it is a link control frame, this field is used to signal an event such as "fabric busy." For example, if the TYPE is 08, and the frame is a data frame, it means that the SCSI will be carried on an FC.

■ **Data Field Control (DF_CTL):** A 1-byte field that indicates the existence of any optional headers at the beginning of the data payload. It is a mechanism to extend header information into the payload.

■ **Frame Control (F_CTL):** A 3-byte field that contains control information related to frame content. For example, one of the bits in this field indicates whether this is the first sequence of the exchange.

The data field in an FC frame contains the data payload, up to 2,112 bytes of actual data with 36 bytes of fixed overhead.

The CRC checksum facilitates error detection for the content of the frame. This checksum verifies data integrity by checking whether the content of the frames are received correctly. The CRC checksum is calculated by the sender before encoding at the FC-1 layer. Similarly, it is calculated by the receiver after decoding at the FC-1 layer.

## 5.6.5. Structure and Organization of FC Data

In an FC network, data transport is analogous to a conversation between two people, whereby a frame represents a word, a sequence represents a sentence, and an exchange represents a conversation.

- **Exchange:** An exchange operation enables two node ports to identify and manage a set of information units. Each upper layer protocol has its protocol-specific information that must be sent to another port to perform certain operations. This protocol-specific information is called an information unit. The structure of these information units is defined in the FC-4 layer. This unit maps to a sequence. An exchange is composed of one or more sequences.

- **Sequence:** A sequence refers to a contiguous set of frames that are sent from one port to another. A sequence corresponds to an information unit, as defined by the ULP.

- **Frame:** A frame is the fundamental unit of data transfer at Layer 2. Each frame can contain up to 2,112 bytes of payload.

## 5.6.6 Flow Control

Flow control defines the pace of the flow of data frames during data transmission. FC technology uses two flow-control mechanisms: buffer-to-buffer credit (BB_Credit) and end-to-end credit (EE_Credit).

### BB_Credit

FC uses the *BB_Credit* mechanism for flow control. BB_Credit controls the maximum number of frames that can be present over the link at any given point in time. In a switched fabric, BB_Credit management may take place between any two FC ports. The transmitting port maintains a count of free receiver buffers and continues to send frames if the count is greater than 0. The BB_Credit mechanism uses *Receiver Ready* (R_RDY) primitive that indicates a buffer has been freed on the port that transmitted the R_RDY.

### EE_Credit

The function of end-to-end credit, known as *EE_Credit*, is similar to that of BB_Credit. When an initiator and a target establish themselves as nodes communicating with each other, they exchange the EE_Credit parameters (part of Port login). The EE_Credit mechanism provides the flow control for class 1 and class 2 traffic only.

## 5.6.7 Classes of Service

The FC standards define different classes of service to meet the requirements of a wide range of applications. Table 5-1 shows three classes of services and their features.

**Table 5-1:** FC Class of Services

|  | CLASS 1 | CLASS 2 | CLASS 3 |
|---|---|---|---|
| Communication type | Dedicated connection | Nondedicated connection | Nondedicated connection |
| Flow control | End-to-end credit | End-to-end credit B-to-B credit | B-to-B credit |
| Frame delivery | In order delivery | Order not guaranteed | Order not guaranteed |
| Frame acknowledgment | Acknowledged | Acknowledged | Not acknowledged |
| Multiplexing | No | Yes | Yes |
| Bandwidth utilization | Poor | Moderate | High |

Another class of service is *class F*, which is used for fabric management. Class F is similar to Class 2 and provides notification of nondelivery of frames.

# 5.7 Fabric Services

All FC switches, regardless of the manufacturer, provide a common set of services as defined in the Fibre Channel standards. These services are available at certain predefined addresses. Some of these services are Fabric Login Server, Fabric Controller, Name Server, and Management Server (see Figure 5-16).

The *Fabric Login Server* is located at the predefined address of FFFFFE and is used during the initial part of the node's fabric login process.

The *Name Server* (formally known as *Distributed Name Server*) is located at the predefined address FFFFFC and is responsible for name registration and management of node ports. Each switch exchanges its Name Server information with other switches in the fabric to maintain a synchronized, distributed name service.

Each switch has a *Fabric Controller* located at the predefined address FFFFFD. The Fabric Controller provides services to both node ports and other switches. The Fabric Controller is responsible for managing and distributing Registered State Change Notifications (RSCNs) to the node ports registered with the

Fabric Controller. If there is a change in the fabric, RSCNs are sent out by a switch to the attached node ports. The Fabric Controller also generates Switch Registered State Change Notifications (SW-RSCNs) to every other domain (switch) in the fabric. These RSCNs keep the name server up-to-date on all switches in the fabric.

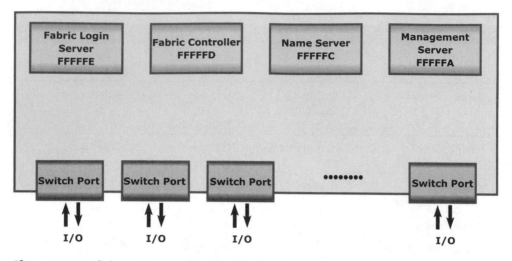

**Figure 5-16:** Fabric services provided by FC switches

FFFFFA is the Fibre Channel address for the *Management Server*. The Management Server is distributed to every switch within the fabric. The Management Server enables the FC SAN management software to retrieve information and administer the fabric.

## 5.8 Switched Fabric Login Types

Fabric services define three login types:

- *Fabric login* (**FLOGI**): Performed between an N_Port and an F_Port. To log on to the fabric, a node sends a FLOGI frame with the WWNN and WWPN parameters to the login service at the predefined FC address FFFFFE (Fabric Login Server). In turn, the switch accepts the login and returns an Accept (ACC) frame with the assigned FC address for the node. Immediately after the FLOGI, the N_Port registers itself with the local Name Server on the switch, indicating its WWNN, WWPN, port type, class of service, assigned FC address and so on. After the N_Port has logged in, it can query the name server database for information about all other logged in ports.

- *Port login* **(PLOGI):** Performed between two N_Ports to establish a session. The initiator N_Port sends a PLOGI request frame to the target N_Port, which accepts it. The target N_Port returns an ACC to the initiator N_Port. Next, the N_Ports exchange service parameters relevant to the session.

- *Process login* **(PRLI):** Also performed between two N_Ports. This login relates to the FC-4 ULPs, such as SCSI. If the ULP is SCSI, N_Ports exchange SCSI-related service parameters.

## 5.9 Zoning

*Zoning* is an FC switch function that enables node ports within the fabric to be logically segmented into groups and to communicate with each other within the group (see Figure 5-17).

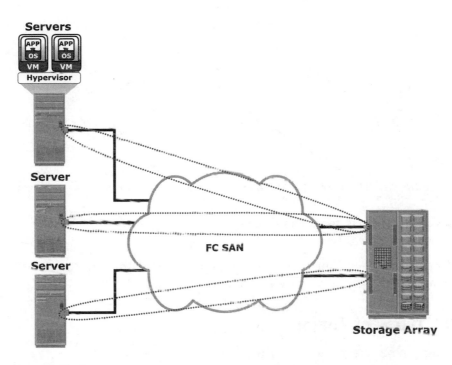

**Figure 5-17:** Zoning

Whenever a change takes place in the name server database, the fabric controller sends a Registered State Change Notification (RSCN) to all the nodes impacted by the change. If zoning is not configured, the fabric controller sends an RSCN to all the nodes in the fabric. Involving the nodes that are not impacted by the change results in increased fabric-management traffic. For a large fabric, the amount of FC traffic generated due to this process can be significant and might impact the host-to-storage data traffic. Zoning helps to limit the number of RSCNs in a fabric. In the presence of zoning, a fabric sends the RSCN to only those nodes in a zone where the change has occurred.

Zone members, zones, and zone sets form the hierarchy defined in the zoning process (see Figure 5-18). A *zone set* is composed of a group of zones that can be activated or deactivated as a single entity in a fabric. Multiple zone sets may be defined in a fabric, but only one zone set can be active at a time. *Members* are nodes within the SAN that can be included in a zone. Switch ports, HBA ports, and storage device ports can be members of a zone. A port or node can be a member of multiple zones. Nodes distributed across multiple switches in a switched fabric may also be grouped into the same zone. Zone sets are also referred to as *zone configurations*.

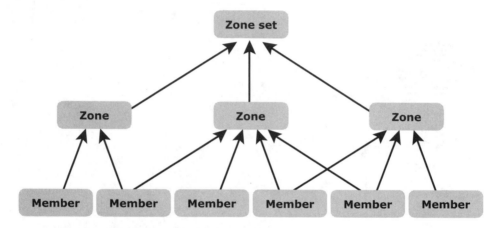

**Figure 5-18:** Members, zones, and zone sets

Zoning provides control by allowing only the members in the same zone to establish communication with each other.

## 5.9.1 Types of Zoning

Zoning can be categorized into three types:

- **Port zoning:** Uses the physical address of switch ports to define zones. In port zoning, access to node is determined by the physical switch port to which a node is connected. The zone members are the port identifier (switch domain ID and port number) to which HBA and its targets (storage devices) are connected. If a node is moved to another switch port in the fabric, then zoning must be modified to allow the node, in its new port, to participate in its original zone. However, if an HBA or storage device port fails, an administrator just has to replace the failed device without changing the zoning configuration.

- **WWN zoning:** Uses World Wide Names to define zones. The zone members are the unique WWN addresses of the HBA and its targets (storage devices). A major advantage of WWN zoning is its flexibility. WWN zoning allows nodes to be moved to another switch port in the fabric and maintain connectivity to its zone partners without having to modify the zone configuration. This is possible because the WWN is static to the node port.

- **Mixed zoning:** Combines the qualities of both WWN zoning and port zoning. Using mixed zoning enables a specific node port to be tied to the WWN of another node.

Figure 5-19 shows the three types of zoning on an FC network.

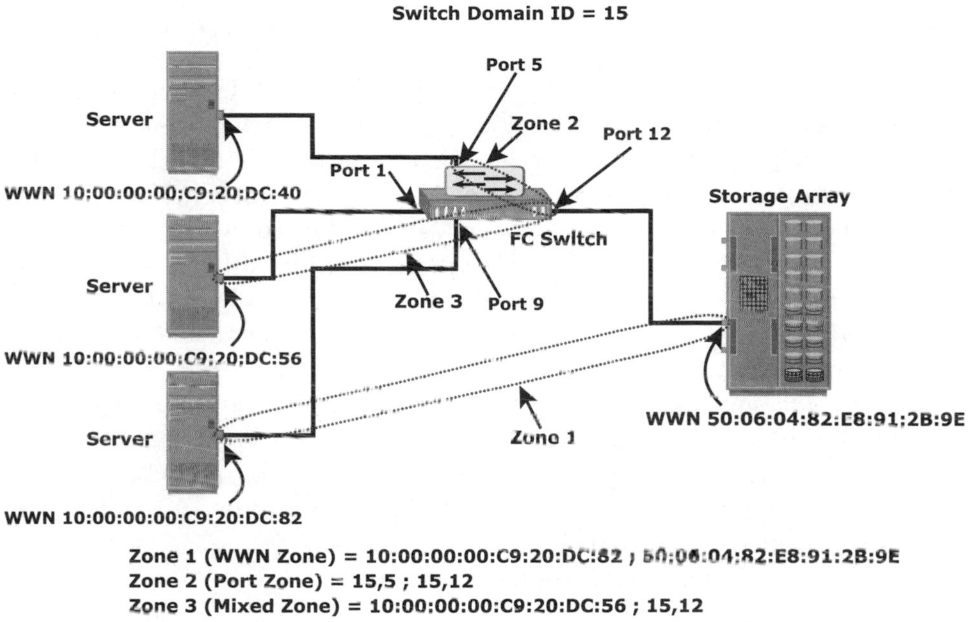

**Switch Domain ID = 15**

Server
WWN 10:00:00:00:C9:20:DC:40

Server
WWN 10:00:00:00:C9:20:DC:56

Server
WWN 10:00:00:00:C9:20:DC:82

Port 5
Zone 2    Port 12
Port 1
FC Switch
Zone 3    Port 9
Zone 1

Storage Array
WWN 50:06:04:82:E8:91:2B:9E

Zone 1 (WWN Zone) = 10:00:00:00:C9:20:DC:82 ; 50:06:04:82:E8:91:2B:9E
Zone 2 (Port Zone) = 15,5 ; 15,12
Zone 3 (Mixed Zone) = 10:00:00:00:C9:20:DC:56 ; 15,12

**Figure 5-19:** Types of zoning

Zoning is used with LUN masking to control server access to storage. However, these are two different activities. Zoning takes place at the fabric level and LUN masking is performed at the array level.

**SINGLE HBA ZONING**

Single HBA zoning is considered as an industry best practice to configure a zone set. A single HBA zone consists of one HBA port and one or more storage device ports. Single HBA zoning eliminates unnecessary host-to-host interaction and minimizes RSCNs. Single HBA zoning in a large fabric leads to configuring a large number of zones and more administrative actions. However, this practice improves the FC SAN performance and reduces the time to troubleshoot FC SAN-related problems.

# 5.10 FC SAN Topologies

Fabric design follows standard topologies to connect devices. Core-edge fabric is one of the popular topologies for fabric designs. Variations of core-edge fabric and mesh topologies are most commonly deployed in FC SAN implementations.

## 5.10.1 Mesh Topology

A mesh topology may be one of the two types: full mesh or partial mesh. In a *full mesh*, every switch is connected to every other switch in the topology. A full mesh topology may be appropriate when the number of switches involved is small. A typical deployment would involve up to four switches or directors, with each of them servicing highly localized host-to-storage traffic. In a full mesh topology, a maximum of one ISL or hop is required for host-to-storage traffic. However, with the increase in the number of switches, the number of switch ports used for ISL also increases. This reduces the available switch ports for node connectivity.

In a *partial mesh topology*, several hops or ISLs may be required for the traffic to reach its destination. Partial mesh offers more scalability than full mesh topology. However, without proper placement of host and storage devices, traffic management in a partial mesh fabric might be complicated and ISLs could become overloaded due to excessive traffic aggregation. Figure 5-20 depicts both partial mesh and full mesh topologies.

**A SINGLE-SWITCH TOPOLOGY**

A single-switch fabric consists of only a single switch or single director. This topology is becoming popular, especially in large data centers, due to their inherent simplicity. Larger port count and modular and scalable architecture of switches and directors allow SAN design to start small and grow as needed by adding port cards/blades in the switch rather than adding new switches.

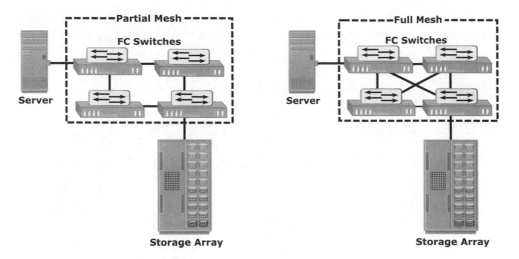

**Figure 5-20:** Partial mesh and full mesh topologies

## 5.10.2 Core-Edge Fabric

The *core-edge fabric* topology has two types of switch tiers. The *edge tier* is usually composed of switches and offers an inexpensive approach to adding more hosts in a fabric. Each switch at the edge tier is attached to a switch at the core tier through ISLs.

The *core tier* is usually composed of enterprise directors that ensure high fabric availability. In addition, typically all traffic must either traverse this tier or terminate at this tier. In this configuration, all storage devices are connected to the core tier, enabling host-to-storage traffic to traverse only one ISL. Hosts that require high performance may be connected directly to the core tier and consequently avoid ISL delays.

In *core-edge topology*, the edge-tier switches are not connected to each other. The core-edge fabric topology increases connectivity within the SAN while conserving the overall port utilization. If fabric expansion is required, additional edge switches are connected to the core. The core of the fabric is also extended by adding more switches or directors at the core tier. Based on the number of core-tier switches, this topology has different variations, such as, *single-core topology* (see Figure 5-21) and *dual-core topology* (see Figure 5-22). To transform a single-core topology to dual-core, new ISLs are created to connect each edge switch to the new core switch in the fabric.

### Benefits and Limitations of Core-Edge Fabric

The core-edge fabric provides maximum one-hop storage access to all storage devices in the system. Because traffic travels in a deterministic pattern (from the edge to the core and vice versa), a core-edge provides easier calculation of the ISL load and traffic patterns. In this topology, because each tier's switch port is used for either storage or hosts, it's easy to identify which network resources are approaching their capacity, making it easier to develop a set of rules for scaling and apportioning.

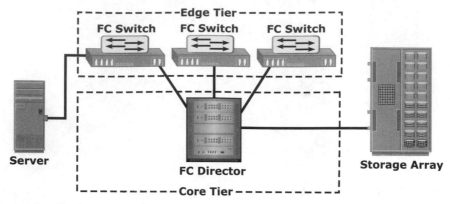

**Figure 5-21:** Single-core topology

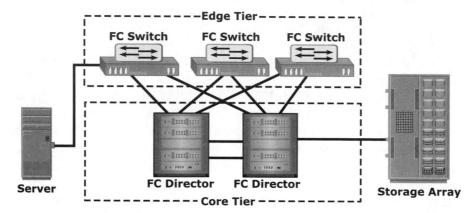

**Figure 5-22:** Dual-core topology

Core-edge fabrics are scaled to larger environments by adding more core switches and linking them, or adding more edge switches. This method enables extending the existing simple core-edge model or expanding the fabric into a compound or complex core-edge model.

However, the core-edge fabric might lead to some performance-related problems because scaling a core-edge topology involves increasing the number of hop counts in the fabric. *Hop count* represents the total number of ISLs traversed by a packet between its source and destination. A common best practice is to keep the number of host-to-storage hops unchanged, at one hop, in a core-edge. Generally, a large hop count means a high data transmission delay between the source and destination.

As the number of cores increases, it is prohibitive to continue to maintain ISLs from each core to each edge switch. When this happens, the fabric design is changed to a compound or complex core-edge design (see Figure 5-23).

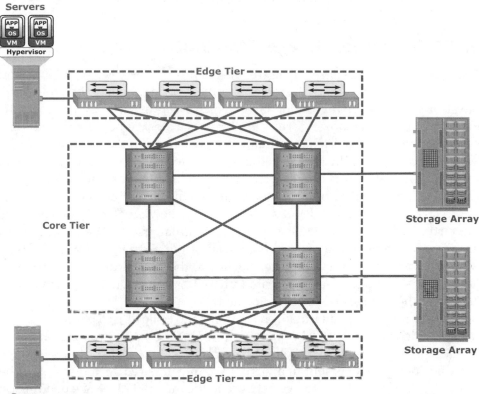

**Figure 5-23:** Compound core-edge topology

---

**FAN-OUT AND FAN-IN**

*Fan-out* enables multiple server ports to communicate to a single storage port. A four-server connection to a single-storage port results in a fan-out ratio of 4. The fan-out ratio of a storage port is dependent on the capabilities of the storage system. The key parameter that governs the fan-out ratio of a storage port is the front-end processing capability of the storage system. Typically, the product vendor specifies the fan-out ratio of a storage system.

*Fan-in* refers to the number of storage ports that a single server port uses. Similar to fan-out, the restriction on fan-in is based on the capability of the host-bus adapter.

# 5.11 Virtualization in SAN

This section details two network-based virtualization techniques in a SAN environment: block-level storage virtualization and virtual SAN (VSAN).

## 5.11.1 Block-level Storage Virtualization

*Block-level storage virtualization* aggregates block storage devices (LUNs) and enables provisioning of virtual storage volumes, independent of the underlying physical storage. A virtualization layer, which exists at the SAN, abstracts the identity of physical storage devices and creates a storage pool from heterogeneous storage devices. Virtual volumes are created from the storage pool and assigned to the hosts. Instead of being directed to the LUNs on the individual storage arrays, the hosts are directed to the virtual volumes provided by the virtualization layer. For hosts and storage arrays, the virtualization layer appears as the target and initiator devices, respectively. The virtualization layer maps the virtual volumes to the LUNs on the individual arrays. The hosts remain unaware of the mapping operation and access the virtual volumes as if they were accessing the physical storage attached to them. Typically, the virtualization layer is managed via a dedicated virtualization appliance to which the hosts and the storage arrays are connected.

Figure 5-24 illustrates a virtualized environment. It shows two physical servers, each of which has one virtual volume assigned. These virtual volumes are used by the servers. These virtual volumes are mapped to the LUNs in the storage arrays. When an I/O is sent to a virtual volume, it is redirected through the virtualization layer at the storage network to the mapped LUNs. Depending on the capabilities of the virtualization appliance, the architecture may allow for more complex mapping between array LUNs and virtual volumes.

Block-level storage virtualization enables extending the storage volumes online to meet application growth requirements. It consolidates heterogeneous storage arrays and enables transparent volume access.

Block-level storage virtualization also provides the advantage of nondisruptive data migration. In a traditional SAN environment, LUN migration from one array to another is an offline event because the hosts needed to be updated to reflect the new array configuration. In other instances, host CPU cycles were required to migrate data from one array to the other, especially in a multivendor environment. With a block-level virtualization solution in place, the virtualization layer handles the back-end migration of data, which enables LUNs to remain online and accessible while data is migrating. No physical changes are required because the host still points to the same virtual targets on the virtualization layer. However, the mappings information on the virtualization layer should be changed. These changes can be executed dynamically and are transparent to the end user.

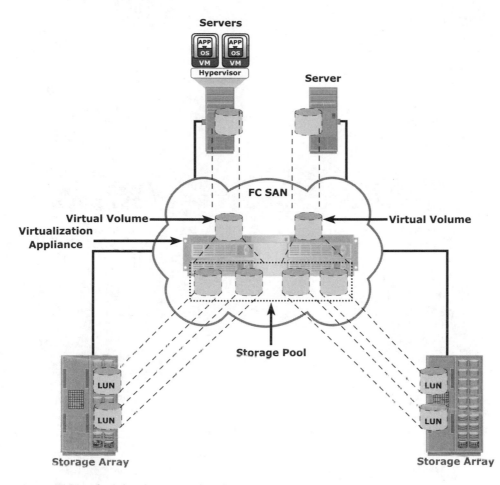

**Figure 5-24:** Block-level storage virtualization

Previously, block-level storage virtualization provided nondisruptive data migration only within a data center. The new generation of block-level storage virtualization enables nondisruptive data migration both within and between data centers. It provides the capability to connect the virtualization layers at multiple data centers. The connected virtualization layers are managed centrally and work as a single virtualization layer stretched across data centers (see Figure 5-25). This enables the federation of block-storage resources both within and across data centers. The virtual volumes are created from the federated storage resources.

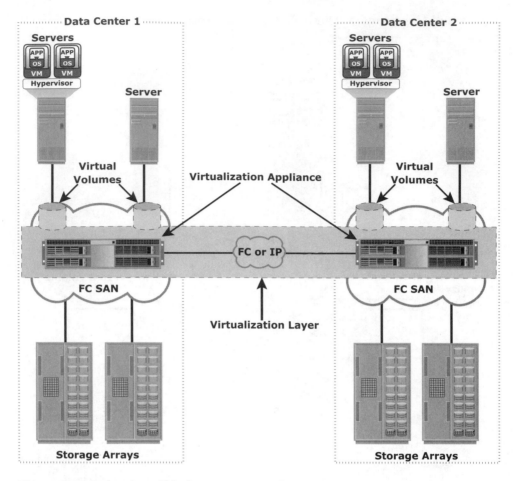

**Figure 5-25:** Federation of block storage across data centers

## 5.11.2 Virtual SAN (VSAN)

*Virtual SAN* (also called *virtual fabric*) is a logical fabric on an FC SAN, which enables communication among a group of nodes regardless of their physical location in the fabric. In a VSAN, a group of hosts or storage ports communicate with each other using a virtual topology defined on the physical SAN. Multiple VSANs may be created on a single physical SAN. Each VSAN acts as an independent fabric with its own set of fabric services, such as name server, and zoning. Fabric-related configurations in one VSAN do not affect the traffic in another.

VSANs improve SAN security, scalability, availability, and manageability. VSANs provide enhanced security by isolating the sensitive data in a VSAN and by restricting access to the resources located within that VSAN. The same Fibre Channel address can be assigned to nodes in different VSANs, thus increasing the fabric scalability. Events causing traffic disruptions in one VSAN are contained within that VSAN and are not propagated to other VSANs. VSANs facilitate an easy, flexible, and less expensive way to manage networks. Configuring VSANs is easier and quicker compared to building separate physical FC SANs for various node groups. To regroup nodes, an administrator simply changes the VSAN configurations without moving nodes and recabling. VSAN is further discussed in Chapter 14.

## 5.12 Concepts in Practice: EMC Connectrix and EMC VPLEX

The EMC Connectrix family represents the industry's most extensive selection of networked storage connectivity products. Connectrix integrates high-speed Fibre Channel connectivity, highly resilient switching technology, options for intelligent IP storage networking, and I/O consolidation with products that support Fibre Channel over Ethernet.

EMC VPLEX is the next-generation solution for block-level virtualization and data mobility within, across, and between data centers. EMC VPLEX provides storage federation by aggregating storage arrays that can be located either in a single data center or multiple data centers. VPLEX is also used as the data mobility solution for environments like cloud computing.

For the latest information on Connectrix connectivity products and VPLEX, visit www.emc.com.

### 5.12.1 EMC Connectrix

EMC offers the following connectivity products under the Connectrix brand (see Figure 5-26):

- Enterprise directors
- Departmental switches
- Multi-purpose switches

Enterprise directors are ideal for large enterprise connectivity. They offer high port density and high component redundancy. Enterprise directors are deployed in high-availability or large-scale environments. Connectrix directors offer several hundred ports per domain. Departmental switches are best suited for workgroup, mid-tier environments. Multi-purpose switches support various protocols such as iSCSI, FCIP, FCoE, FICON, in addition to FC protocol. In addition to FC ports, Connectrix switches and directors have Ethernet ports and serial ports for communication and switch management functions. The Connectrix management software enables configuration, monitoring, and management of Connectrix switches.

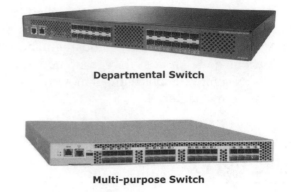

**Departmental Switch**

**Enterprise Director**

**Multi-purpose Switch**

**Figure 5-26:** EMC Connectrix

### Connectrix Switches

B-series and MDS-series make up the Connectrix family of switches offered by EMC. These switches are designed to meet workgroup, department-level, and enterprise-level requirements. They are designed with a nonblocking architecture and can operate in heterogeneous environments. Nonblocking architecture refers to the capability of a switch to handle independent packets simultaneously because the switch has sufficient internal resources to handle maximum transfer rates from all ports. The features of these switches that ensure their high availability are their nondisruptive software and port upgrade, and redundant and hot-swappable components. These switches can be managed through CLI, HTTP, and standalone GUI applications.

### Connectrix Directors

EMC offers the high-end Connectrix family of directors. Their modular architectural design offers high scalability by providing over 500 ports. They are suitable for server and storage consolidation across enterprises. These directors have redundant components for high availability and provide multiprotocol connectivity for both mainframe and open system environments. Connectrix directors offer high speeds (up to 16 Gb/s) and support ISL aggregation. Similar to switches, directors can also be managed through CLI or with other GUI tools.

### Connectrix Multi-purpose Switches

Multi-purpose switches provide support for multiple protocols, such as FC, FCIP, iSCSI, FCoE, and FICON. They perform protocol translation and route frames between two dissimilar networks, such as FC and IP. These multiprotocol capabilities offer many benefits, including long-distance SAN extension, greater resource sharing, and simplified management. Connectrix multi-purpose switches include FCoE switches, FCIP routers, iSCSI gateways, and so on.

### Connectrix Management Tools

There are several ways to monitor and manage FC switches in a fabric. Individual switch management is accomplished through the CLI or browser-based tools.

Command-line utilities such as Telnet and Secure Shell (SSH) are used to log on to the switch over IP and issue CLI commands. The primary purpose of the CLI is to automate the management of a large number of switches or directors with the use of scripts. The browser-based tools provide GUIs. These tools also display the topology map.

Fabric-wide management and monitoring is accomplished by using vendor-specific tools and Simple Network Management Protocol (SNMP)-based, third-party software.

EMC ControlCenter SAN Manager provides a single interface for managing a Storage Area Network. With SAN Manager, an administrator can discover, monitor, manage, and configure complex heterogeneous SAN environments. It streamlines and centralizes SAN management operations across multivendor storage networks and storage devices. It enables storage administrators to manage SAN zones and LUN masking consistently across multivendor SAN arrays and switches. EMC ControlCenter SAN Manager also supports virtual environments, including VMware, and virtual SANs.

EMC ProSphere is a newly launched tool with additional features specifically for the cloud computing environment. A future release of EMC ProSphere will include all the functionalities of EMC ControlCenter.

## 5.12.2 EMC VPLEX

EMC VPLEX provides a virtual storage infrastructure that enables federation of heterogeneous storage resources both within and across datacenters. The VPLEX appliance resides between the servers and heterogeneous storage devices. It forms a pool of distributed block storage resources and enables creating virtual storage volumes from the pool. These virtual volumes are then allocated to the servers. The virtual-to-physical-storage mapping remains hidden to the servers.

VPLEX provides nondisruptive data mobility among physical storage devices to balance the application workload and to enable both local and remote data access. The mapping of virtual volumes to physical volumes can be changed dynamically by the administrator. This allows for a virtual volume to be moved across storage arrays while still in production.

VPLEX uses a unique clustering architecture and distributed cache coherency that enable multiple hosts located across two locations to access a single copy of data. This eliminates the operational overhead and time required to copy and distribute data across locations VPLEX also provides the capability to mirror data of a virtual volume both within and across locations. This enables hosts at different data centers to access cache-coherent copies of the same virtual volume. Practical applications of this capability include mobility, load-balancing, and high availability across data centers.

To avoid application downtime due to outage at a data center, the workload can be moved quickly to another data center. Applications continue accessing the same virtual volume and remain uninterrupted by the data mobility.

### VPLEX Family of Products

The VPLEX family consists of three products: VPLEX Local, VPLEX Metro, and VPLEX Geo.

EMC VPLEX Local delivers local federation, which provides simplified management and nondisruptive data mobility across heterogeneous arrays within a data center. EMC VPLEX Metro delivers distributed federation, which provides data access and mobility between two VPEX clusters within synchronous distances that support round-trip latency up to 5 ms. EMC VPLEX Geo delivers data access and mobility between two VPLEX clusters within asynchronous distances (that support round-trip latency up to 50 ms).

## Summary

The FC SAN has enabled the consolidation of storage and benefited organizations by lowering the cost of storage infrastructure. FC SAN reduces overall operational cost and downtime. Virtualization of storage and storage networks further minimizes resource management complexity and cost. The adoption of FC SANs has increased with the decline of hardware prices and has enhanced to the maturity of storage network standards.

This chapter detailed the components of an FC SAN, its topologies, and the FC technology that forms its backbone. FC meets today's demands for reliable, and high-performance applications. The chapter also covered virtualization in a SAN environment.

The interoperability between FC switches from different vendors has enhanced significantly compared to early SAN deployments. The standards published by a dedicated study group within T11 on FC SAN routing, and the new product offerings from vendors, are now revolutionizing the way FC SANs are deployed and operated.

Although FC SANs have eliminated islands of storage, their implementation requires additional equipment and infrastructure in an enterprise. The emergence of the iSCSI and FCIP technologies, detailed in Chapter 6, has pushed the convergence of FC SAN with IP technology, providing a cost-effective method to leverage existing IP based infrastructure for storage networking.

## EXERCISES

1. **What is zoning? Discuss a scenario:**
   a. **Where WWN zoning is preferred over port zoning.**
   b. **Where port zoning is preferred over WWN zoning.**

2. **Describe the process of assigning an FC address to a node when logging on to the network for the first time.**

3. **Seventeen switches, with 16 ports each, are connected in a full mesh topology. How many ports are available for host and storage connectivity?**

4. **Discuss the roles of the name server and fabric controller in an FC-switched fabric.**

5. **How does flow control work in an FC network?**

6. **Explain storage migration using block-level storage virtualization. Compare this migration with traditional migration methods.**

7. **How do VSANs improve the manageability of an FC SAN?**

# Chapter 6
# IP SAN and FCoE

Traditional SAN enables the transfer of block I/O over Fibre Channel and provides high performance and scalability. These advantages of FC SAN come with the additional cost of buying FC components, such as FC HBA and switches. Organizations typically have an existing Internet Protocol (IP)-based infrastructure, which could be leveraged for storage networking. Advancements in technology have enabled IP to be used for transporting block I/O over the IP network. This technology of transporting block I/Os over an IP is referred to as IP SAN. IP is a mature technology, and using IP as a storage networking option provides several advantages. When block I/O is run over IP, the existing network infrastructure can be leveraged, which is more economical than investing in a new SAN infrastructure. In addition, many robust and mature security options are now available for IP networks. Many long-distance, disaster recovery (DR) solutions are already leveraging IP-based networks. With IP SAN, organizations can extend the geographical reach of their storage infrastructure.

Two primary protocols that leverage IP as the transport mechanism are *Internet SCSI* (iSCSI) and *Fibre Channel over IP* (FCIP). iSCSI is encapsulation of SCSI I/O over IP. FCIP is a protocol in which an FCIP entity such as an FCIP gateway is used to tunnel FC fabrics through an IP network. In FCIP, FC frames are encapsulated onto the IP payload. An FCIP implementation is capable of merging interconnected fabrics into a single fabric. Frequently, only a small subset of nodes at either end require connectivity across fabrics. Thus, the majority of FCIP implementations today use switch-specific features such as IVR (Inter-VSAN Routing) or FCRS

(Fibre Channel Routing Services) to create a tunnel. In this manner, traffic may be routed between specific nodes without actually merging the fabrics.

This chapter describes both iSCSI and FCIP protocols, components, and topologies in detail. This chapter also covers an emerging protocol, *Fibre Channel over Ethernet* (FCoE). FCoE converges Ethernet and FC traffic over a single physical link. Therefore, it eliminates the complexity of managing two separate networks in the data center.

# 6.1 iSCSI

iSCSI is an IP based protocol that establishes and manages connections between host and storage over IP, as shown in Figure 6-1. iSCSI encapsulates SCSI commands and data into an IP packet and transports them using TCP/IP. iSCSI is widely adopted for connecting servers to storage because it is relatively inexpensive and easy to implement, especially in environments in which an FC SAN does not exist.

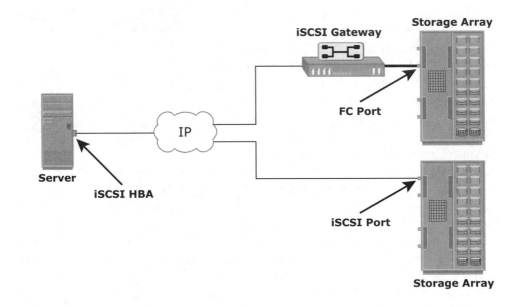

**Figure 6-1:** iSCSI implementation

## 6.1.1 Components of iSCSI

An initiator (host), target (storage or iSCSI gateway), and an IP-based network are the key iSCSI components. If an iSCSI-capable storage array is deployed, then a host with the iSCSI initiator can directly communicate with the storage array over an IP network. However, in an implementation that uses an existing FC array for iSCSI communication, an iSCSI gateway is used. These devices perform the translation of IP packets to FC frames and vice versa, thereby bridging the connectivity between the IP and FC environments.

## 6.1.2 iSCSI Host Connectivity

A standard NIC with software iSCSI initiator, a TCP offload engine (TOE) NIC with software iSCSI initiator, and an iSCSI HBA are the three iSCSI host connectivity options. The function of the iSCSI initiator is to route the SCSI commands over an IP network.

A standard NIC with a software iSCSI initiator is the simplest and least expensive connectivity option. It is easy to implement because most servers come with at least one, and in many cases two, embedded NICs. It requires only a software initiator for iSCSI functionality. Because NICs provide standard IP function, encapsulation of SCSI into IP packets and decapsulation are carried out by the host CPU. This places additional overhead on the host CPU. If a standard NIC is used in heavy I/O load situations, the host CPU might become a bottleneck. TOE NIC helps alleviate this burden. A TOE NIC offloads TCP management functions from the host and leaves only the iSCSI functionality to the host processor. The host passes the iSCSI information to the TOE card, and the TOE card sends the information to the destination using TCP/IP. Although this solution improves performance, the iSCSI functionality is still handled by a software initiator that requires host CPU cycles.

An iSCSI HBA is capable of providing performance benefits because it offloads the entire iSCSI and TCP/IP processing from the host processor. The use of an iSCSI HBA is also the simplest way to boot hosts from a SAN environment via iSCSI. If there is no iSCSI HBA, modifications must be made to the basic operating system to boot a host from the storage devices because the NIC needs to obtain an IP address before the operating system loads. The functionality of an iSCSI HBA is similar to the functionality of an FC HBA.

## 6.1.3 iSCSI Topologies

Two topologies of iSCSI implementations are native and bridged. *Native topology* does not have FC components. The initiators may be either directly attached to targets or connected through the IP network. *Bridged topology* enables the coexistence of FC with IP by providing iSCSI-to-FC bridging functionality. For example, the initiators can exist in an IP environment while the storage remains in an FC environment.

### Native iSCSI Connectivity

FC components are not required for iSCSI connectivity if an iSCSI-enabled array is deployed. In Figure 6-2 (a), the array has one or more iSCSI ports configured with an IP address and is connected to a standard Ethernet switch.

After an initiator is logged on to the network, it can access the available LUNs on the storage array. A single array port can service multiple hosts or initiators as long as the array port can handle the amount of storage traffic that the hosts generate.

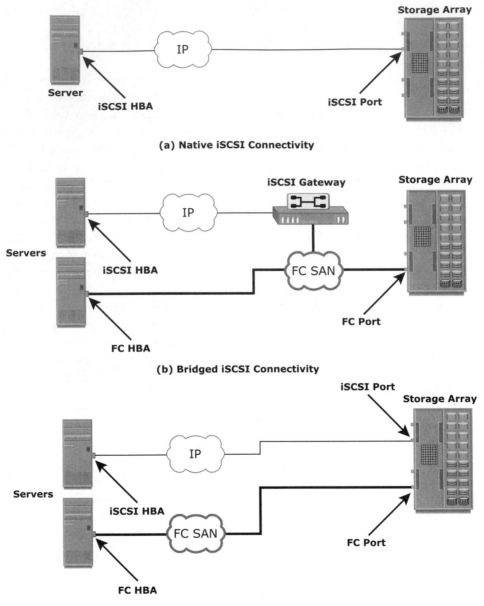

**(a) Native iSCSI Connectivity**

**(b) Bridged iSCSI Connectivity**

**(c) Combining FC and Native iSCSI Connectivity**

**Figure 6-2:** iSCSI Topologies

### Bridged iSCSI Connectivity

A bridged iSCSI implementation includes FC components in its configuration. Figure 6-2 (b) illustrates iSCSI host connectivity to an FC storage array.

In this case, the array does not have any iSCSI ports. Therefore, an external device, called a gateway or a multiprotocol router, must be used to facilitate the communication between the iSCSI host and FC storage. The gateway converts IP packets to FC frames and vice versa. The bridge devices contain both FC and Ethernet ports to facilitate the communication between the FC and IP environments.

In a bridged iSCSI implementation, the iSCSI initiator is configured with the gateway's IP address as its target destination. On the other side, the gateway is configured as an FC initiator to the storage array.

### Combining FC and Native iSCSI Connectivity

The most common topology is a combination of FC and native iSCSI. Typically, a storage array comes with both FC and iSCSI ports that enable iSCSI and FC connectivity in the same environment, as shown in Figure 6-2 (c).

## 6.1.4 iSCSI Protocol Stack

Figure 6-3 displays a model of the iSCSI protocol layers and depicts the encapsulation order of the SCSI commands for their delivery through a physical carrier.

SCSI is the command protocol that works at the application layer of the Open System Interconnection (OSI) model. The initiators and targets use SCSI commands and responses to talk to each other. The SCSI command descriptor blocks, data, and status messages are encapsulated into TCP/IP and transmitted across the network between the initiators and targets.

iSCSI is the session-layer protocol that initiates a reliable session between devices that recognize SCSI commands and TCP/IP. The iSCSI session-layer interface is responsible for handling login, authentication, target discovery, and session management. TCP is used with iSCSI at the transport layer to provide reliable transmission.

TCP controls message flow, windowing, error recovery, and retransmission. It relies upon the network layer of the OSI model to provide global addressing and connectivity. The Layer 2 protocols at the data link layer of this model enable node-to-node communication through a physical network.

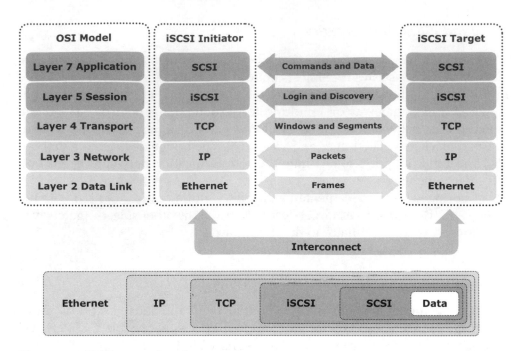

**Figure 6-3:** iSCSI protocol stack

## 6.1.5 iSCSI PDU

A *protocol data unit* (PDU) is the basic "information unit" in the iSCSI environment. The iSCSI initiators and targets communicate with each other using iSCSI
PDUs. This communication includes establishing iSCSI connections and iSCSI
sessions, performing iSCSI discovery, sending SCSI commands and data, and
receiving SCSI status. All iSCSI PDUs contain one or more header segments
followed by zero or more data segments. The PDU is then encapsulated into an
IP packet to facilitate the transport.

A PDU includes the components shown in Figure 6-4. The IP header provides
packet-routing information to move the packet across a network. The TCP
header contains the information required to guarantee the packet delivery to
the target. The iSCSI header (basic header segment) describes how to extract
SCSI commands and data for the target. iSCSI adds an optional CRC, known
as the *digest*, to ensure datagram integrity. This is in addition to TCP checksum
and Ethernet CRC. The header and the data digests are optionally used in the
PDU to validate integrity and data placement.

As shown in Figure 6-5, each iSCSI PDU does not correspond in a 1:1 relationship with an IP packet. Depending on its size, an iSCSI PDU can span an
IP packet or even coexist with another PDU in the same packet.

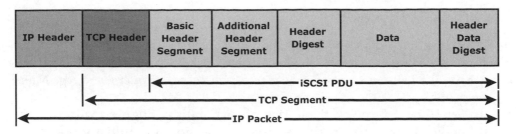

| IP Header | TCP Header | Basic Header Segment | Additional Header Segment | Header Digest | Data | Header Data Digest |
|---|---|---|---|---|---|---|

**Figure 6-4:** iSCSI PDU encapsulated in an IP packet

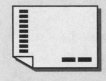 A message transmitted on a network is divided into a number of packets. If necessary, each packet can be sent by a different route across the network. Packets can arrive in a different order than the order in which they were sent. IP only delivers them; it is up to TCP to organize them in the right sequence. The target extracts the SCSI commands and data on the basis of the information in the iSCSI header.

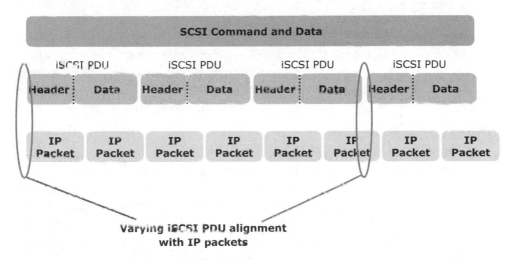

**Figure 6-5:** Alignment of iSCSI PDUs with IP packets

To achieve the 1:1 relationship between the IP packet and the iSCSI PDU, the maximum transmission unit (MTU) size of the IP packet is modified. This eliminates fragmentation of the IP packet, which improves the transmission efficiency.

## 6.1.6 iSCSI Discovery

An initiator must discover the location of its targets on the network and the names of the targets available to it before it can establish a session. This discovery can take place in two ways: *SendTargets discovery* or *internet Storage Name Service* (iSNS).

In *SendTargets discovery*, the initiator is manually configured with the target's network portal to establish a discovery session. The initiator issues the SendTargets command, and the target network portal responds with the names and addresses of the targets available to the host.

iSNS (see Figure 6-6) enables automatic discovery of iSCSI devices on an IP network. The initiators and targets can be configured to automatically register themselves with the iSNS server. Whenever an initiator wants to know the targets that it can access, it can query the iSNS server for a list of available targets.

The discovery can also take place by using service location protocol (SLP). However, this is less commonly used than SendTargets discovery and iSNS.

## 6.1.7 iSCSI Names

A unique worldwide iSCSI identifier, known as an *iSCSI name*, is used to identify the initiators and targets within an iSCSI network to facilitate communication. The unique identifier can be a combination of the names of the department, application, or manufacturer, serial number, asset number, or any tag that can be used to recognize and manage the devices. Following are two types of iSCSI names commonly used:

- **iSCSI Qualified Name (IQN):** An organization must own a registered domain name to generate iSCSI Qualified Names. This domain name does not need to be active or resolve to an address. It just needs to be reserved to prevent other organizations from using the same domain name to generate iSCSI names. A date is included in the name to avoid potential conflicts caused by the transfer of domain names. An example of an IQN is iqn.2008-02.com.example:*optional_string*.

  The *optional_string* provides a serial number, an asset number, or any other device identifiers. An iSCSI Qualified Name enables storage administrators to assign meaningful names to iSCSI devices, and therefore, manage those devices more easily.

■ **Extended Unique Identifier (EUI):** An EUI is a globally unique identifier based on the IEEE EUI-64 naming standard. An EUI is composed
of the eui prefix followed by a 16-character hexadecimal name, such as
`eui.0300732A32598D26`.

In either format, the allowed special characters are dots, dashes, and
blank spaces.

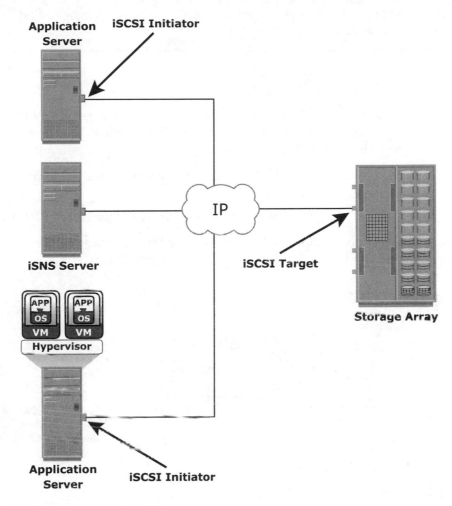

**Figure 6-6:** Discovery using iSNS

**NETWORK ADDRESS AUTHORITY**

*Network Address Authority* (NAA) is an additional iSCSI node name type to enable a worldwide naming format as defined by the InterNational Committee for Information Technology Standards (INCITS) T11. This format enables the SCSI storage devices that contain both iSCSI ports and SAS ports to use the same NAA-based SCSI device name. This format is defined by RFC 3980, "T11 Network Address Authority (NAA) Naming Format for iSCSI Node Names."

## 6.1.8 iSCSI Session

An iSCSI session is established between an initiator and a target, as shown in Figure 6-7. A session is identified by a session ID (SSID), which includes part of an initiator ID and a target ID. The session can be intended for one of the following:

- The discovery of the available targets by the initiators and the location of a specific target on a network

- The normal operation of iSCSI (transferring data between initiators and targets)

There might be one or more TCP connections within each session. Each TCP connection within the session has a unique connection ID (CID).

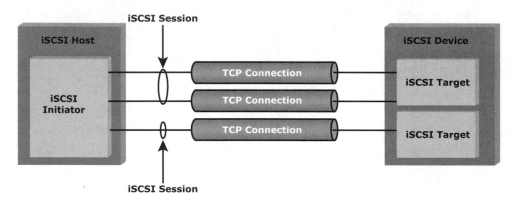

**Figure 6-7:** iSCSI session

An iSCSI session is established via the iSCSI login process. The login process is started when the initiator establishes a TCP connection with the required target either via the well-known port 3260 or a specified target port. During the login phase, the initiator and the target authenticate each other and negotiate on various parameters.

After the login phase is successfully completed, the iSCSI session enters the full-feature phase for normal SCSI transactions. In this phase, the initiator may send SCSI commands and data to the various LUNs on the target by encapsulating them in iSCSI PDUs that travel over the established TCP connection.

The final phase of the iSCSI session is the connection termination phase, which is referred to as the logout procedure. The initiator is responsible for commencing the logout procedure; however, the target may also prompt termination by sending an iSCSI message, indicating the occurrence of an internal error condition. After the logout request is sent from the initiator and accepted by the target, no further request and response can be sent on that connection.

## 6.1.9 iSCSI Command Sequencing

The iSCSI communication between the initiators and targets is based on the request-response command sequences. A command sequence may generate multiple PDUs. A *command sequence number* (CmdSN) within an iSCSI session is used for numbering all initiator-to-target command PDUs belonging to the session. This number ensures that every command is delivered in the same order in which it is transmitted, regardless of the TCP connection that carries the command in the session.

Command sequencing begins with the first login command, and the CmdSN is incremented by one for each subsequent command. The iSCSI target layer is responsible for delivering the commands to the SCSI layer in the order of their CmdSN. This ensures the correct order of data and commands at a target even when there are multiple TCP connections between an initiator and the target that use portal groups.

Similar to command numbering, a *status sequence number* (StatSN) is used to sequentially number status responses, as shown in Figure 6-8. These unique numbers are established at the level of the TCP connection.

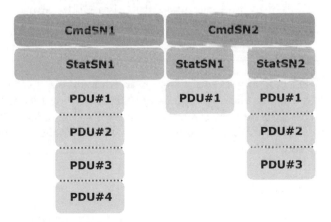

**Figure 6-8:** Command and status sequence number

A target sends *request-to-transfer* (R2T) PDUs to the initiator when it is ready to accept data. A *data sequence number* (DataSN) is used to ensure in-order delivery of data within the same command. The DataSN and R2TSN are used to sequence data PDUs and R2Ts, respectively. Each of these sequence numbers is stored locally as an unsigned 32-bit integer counter defined by iSCSI. These numbers are communicated between the initiator and target in the appropriate iSCSI PDU fields during command, status, and data exchanges.

For read operations, the DataSN begins at zero and is incremented by one for each subsequent data PDU in that command sequence. For a write operation, the first unsolicited data PDU or the first data PDU in response to an R2T begins with a DataSN of zero and increments by one for each subsequent data PDU. R2TSN is set to zero at the initiation of the command and incremented by one for each subsequent R2T sent by the target for that command.

# 6.2 FCIP

FC SAN provides a high-performance infrastructure for localized data movement. Organizations are now looking for ways to transport data over a long distance between their disparate SANs at multiple geographic locations. One of the best ways to achieve this goal is to interconnect geographically dispersed SANs through reliable, high-speed links. This approach involves transporting the FC block data over the IP infrastructure. FCIP is a tunneling protocol that enables distributed FC SAN islands to be interconnected over the existing IP-based networks.

The FCIP standard has rapidly gained acceptance as a manageable, cost-effective way to blend the best of the two worlds: FC SAN and the proven, widely deployed IP infrastructure. As a result, organizations now have a better way to store, protect and move their data by leveraging investments in their existing IP infrastructure. FCIP is extensively used in disaster recovery implementations in which data is duplicated to the storage located at a remote site.

> **FCIP might require high network bandwidth when replicating or backing up data. FCIP does not handle data traffic throttling or flow control; these are controlled by the communicating FC switches and devices within the fabric.**

## 6.2.1 FCIP Protocol Stack

The FCIP protocol stack is shown in Figure: 6-9. Applications generate SCSI commands and data, which are processed by various layers of the protocol stack.

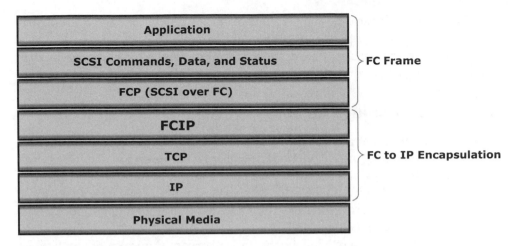

**Figure 6-9:** FCIP protocol stack

The upper layer protocol SCSI includes the SCSI driver program that executes the read-and-write commands. Below the SCSI layer is the Fibre Channel Protocol (FCP) layer, which is simply a Fibre Channel frame whose payload is SCSI. The FCP layer rides on top of the Fibre Channel transport layer. This enables the FC frames to run natively within a SAN fabric environment. In addition, the FC frames can be encapsulated into the IP packet and sent to a remote SAN over the IP. The FCIP layer encapsulates the Fibre Channel frames onto the IP payload and passes them to the TCP layer (see Figure 6-10). TCP and IP are used for transporting the encapsulated information across Ethernet, wireless, or other media that support the TCP/IP traffic.

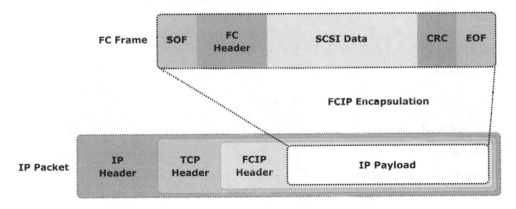

**Figure 6-10:** FCIP encapsulation

Encapsulation of FC frame into an IP packet could cause the IP packet to be fragmented when the data link cannot support the maximum transmission unit

(MTU) size of an IP packet. When an IP packet is fragmented, the required parts of the header must be copied by all fragments. When a TCP packet is segmented, normal TCP operations are responsible for receiving and re-sequencing the data prior to passing it on to the FC processing portion of the device.

## 6.2.2 FCIP Topology

In an FCIP environment, an FCIP gateway is connected to each fabric via a standard FC connection (see Figure 6-11). The FCIP gateway at one end of the IP network encapsulates the FC frames into IP packets. The gateway at the other end removes the IP wrapper and sends the FC data to the layer 2 fabric. The fabric treats these gateways as layer 2 fabric switches. An IP address is assigned to the port on the gateway, which is connected to an IP network. After the IP connectivity is established, the nodes in the two independent fabrics can communicate with each other.

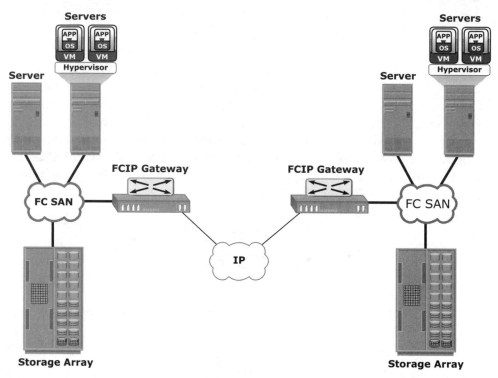

**Figure 6-11:** FCIP topology

## 6.2.3 FCIP Performance and Security

Performance, reliability, and security should always be taken into consideration when implementing storage solutions. The implementation of FCIP is also subject to the same considerations.

From the perspective of performance, configuring multiple paths between FCIP gateways eliminates single points of failure and provides increased bandwidth. In a scenario of extended distance, the IP network might be a bottleneck if sufficient bandwidth is not available. In addition, because FCIP creates a unified fabric, disruption in the underlying IP network can cause instabilities in the SAN environment. These instabilities include a segmented fabric, excessive RSCNs, and host timeouts.

The vendors of FC switches have recognized some of the drawbacks related to FCIP and have implemented features to enhance stability, such as the capability to segregate the FCIP traffic into a separate virtual fabric.

Security is also a consideration in an FCIP solution because the data is transmitted over public IP channels. Various security options are available to protect the data based on the router's support. IPSec is one such security measure that can be implemented in the FCIP environment.

## 6.3 FCoE

Data centers typically have multiple networks to handle various types of I/O traffic — for example, an Ethernet network for TCP/IP communication and an FC network for FC communication. TCP/IP is typically used for client-server communication, data backup, infrastructure management communication, and so on. FC is typically used for moving block-level data between storage and servers. To support multiple networks, servers in a data center are equipped with multiple redundant physical network interfaces — for example, multiple Ethernet and FC cards/adapters. In addition, to enable the communication, different types of networking switches and physical cabling infrastructure are implemented in data centers. The need for two different kinds of physical network infrastructure increases the overall cost and complexity of data center operation.

Fibre Channel over Ethernet (FCoE) protocol provides consolidation of LAN and SAN traffic over a single physical interface infrastructure. FCoE helps organizations address the challenges of having multiple discrete network infrastructures. FCoE uses the Converged Enhanced Ethernet (CEE) link (10 Gigabit Ethernet) to send FC frames over Ethernet.

### 6.3.1 I/O Consolidation Using FCoE

The key benefit of FCoE is I/O consolidation. Figure 6-12 represents the infrastructure before FCoE deployment. Here, the storage resources are accessed using HBAs, and the IP network resources are accessed using NICs by the servers. Typically, in a data center, a server is configured with 2 to 4 NIC cards and redundant HBA cards. If the data center has hundreds of servers, it would require a large number of adapters, cables, and switches. This leads to a complex environment, which is difficult to manage and scale. The cost of power, cooling, and floor space further adds to the challenge.

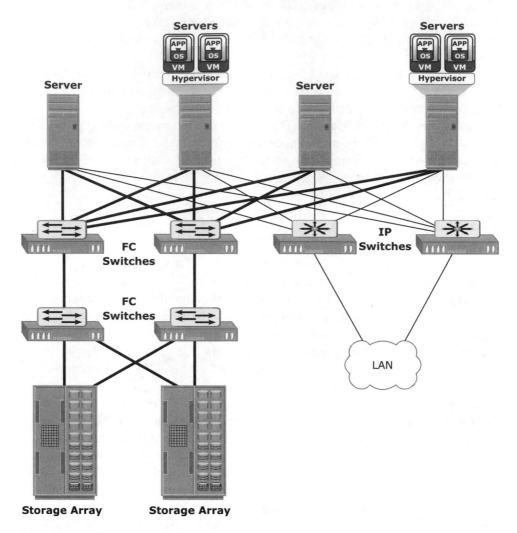

**Figure 6-12:** Infrastructure before using FCoE

Figure 6-13 shows the I/O consolidation with FCoE using FCoE switches and Converged Network Adapters (CNAs). A CNA (discussed in the section "Converged Network Adapter") replaces both HBAs and NICs in the server and consolidates both the IP and FC traffic. This reduces the requirement of multiple network adapters at the server to connect to different networks. Overall, this reduces the requirement of adapters, cables, and switches. This also considerably reduces the cost and management overhead.

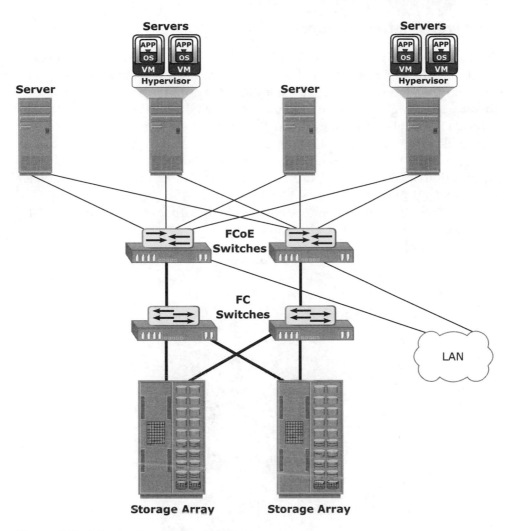

**Figure 6-13:** Infrastructure after using FCoE

## 6.3.2 Components of an FCoE Network

This section describes the key physical components required to implement FCoE in a data center. The key FCoE components are:

- Converged Network Adapter (CNA)
- Cables
- FCoE switches

### Converged Network Adapter

A CNA provides the functionality of both a standard NIC and an FC HBA in a single adapter and consolidates both types of traffic. CNA eliminates the need to deploy separate adapters and cables for FC and Ethernet communications, thereby reducing the required number of server slots and switch ports. CNA offloads the FCoE protocol processing task from the server, thereby freeing the server CPU resources for application processing. As shown in Figure 6-14, a CNA contains separate modules for 10 Gigabit Ethernet, Fibre Channel, and FCoE Application Specific Integrated Circuits (ASICs). The FCoE ASIC encapsulates FC frames into Ethernet frames. One end of this ASIC is connected to 10GbE and FC ASICs for server connectivity, while the other end provides a 10GbE interface to connect to an FCoE switch.

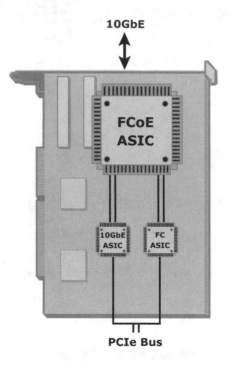

**Figure 6-14:** Converged Network Adapter

### Cables

Currently two options are available for FCoE cabling: Copper based Twinax and standard fiber optical cables. A Twinax cable is composed of two pairs of copper cables covered with a shielded casing. The Twinax cable can transmit data at the speed of 10 Gbps over shorter distances up to 10 meters. Twinax cables require less power and are less expensive than fiber optic cables. The Small Form Factor Pluggable Plus (SFP+) connector is the primary connector used for FCoE links and can be used with both optical and copper cables.

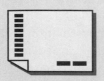 A typical strategy for FCoE deployment is the *top of rack* implementation. Here, a pair of redundant FCoE switches is installed at the top of each rack of servers. Both FC and IP connectivity to each server is accomplished using inexpensive Twinax cabling from the server to the top of rack FCoE switches. This short distance is well supported with Twinax. Connectivity from the top of rack switches to existing backbone LAN and SAN infrastructures, that is connections across racks, is typically done with optical links, which can support the longer cable runs that may be required.

## FCoE Switches

An FCoE switch has both Ethernet switch and Fibre Channel switch functionalities. The FCoE switch has a Fibre Channel Forwarder (FCF), Ethernet Bridge, and set of Ethernet ports and optional FC ports, as shown in Figure 6-15. The function of the FCF is to encapsulate the FC frames, received from the FC port, into the FCoE frames and also to de-encapsulate the FCoE frames, received from the Ethernet Bridge, to the FC frames.

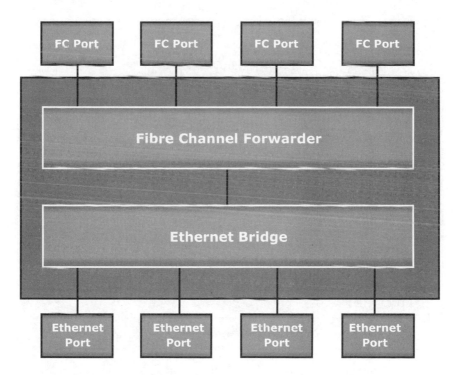

**Figure 6-15:** FCoE switch generic architecture

Upon receiving the incoming traffic, the FCoE switch inspects the Ethertype (used to indicate which protocol is encapsulated in the payload of an Ethernet frame) of the incoming frames and uses that to determine the destination. If the Ethertype of the frame is FCoE, the switch recognizes that the frame contains an FC payload and forwards it to the FCF. From there, the FC is extracted from the FCoE frame and transmitted to FC SAN over the FC ports. If the Ethertype is not FCoE, the switch handles the traffic as usual Ethernet traffic and forwards it over the Ethernet ports.

### 6.3.3 FCoE Frame Structure

An FCoE frame is an Ethernet frame that contains an FCoE Protocol Data Unit. Figure 6-16 shows the FCoE frame structure. The first 48-bits in the frame are used to specify the destination MAC address, and the next 48-bits specify the source MAC address. The 32-bit IEEE 802.1Q tag supports the creation of multiple virtual networks (VLANs) across a single physical infrastructure. FCoE has its own Ethertype, as designated by the next 16 bits, followed by the 4-bit version field. The next 100-bits are reserved and are followed by the 8-bit Start of Frame and then the actual FC frame. The 8-bit End of Frame delimiter is followed by 24 reserved bits. The frame ends with the final 32-bits dedicated to the Frame Check Sequence (FCS) function that provides error detection for the Ethernet frame.

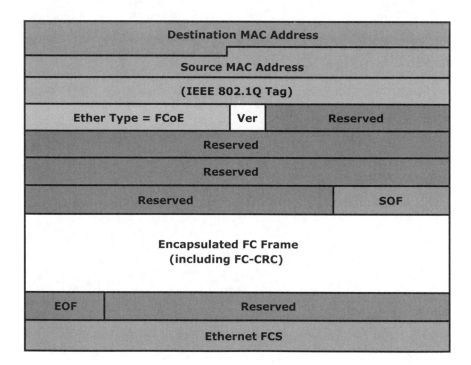

**Figure 6-16:** FCoE frame structure

The encapsulated Fibre Channel frame consists of the original 24-byte FC header and the data being transported (including the Fibre Channel CRC). The FC frame structure is maintained such that when a traditional FC SAN is connected to an FCoE capable switch, the FC frame is de-encapsulated from the FCoE frame and transported to FC SAN seamlessly. This capability enables FCoE to integrate with the existing FC SANs without the need for a gateway.

Frame size is also an important factor in FCoE. A typical Fibre Channel data frame has a 2,112-byte payload, a 24-byte header, and an FCS. A standard Ethernet frame has a default payload capacity of 1,500 bytes. To maintain good performance, FCoE must use jumbo frames to prevent a Fibre Channel frame from being split into two Ethernet frames. The next chapter discusses jumbo frames in detail. FCoE requires Converged Enhanced Ethernet, which provides lossless Ethernet and jumbo frame support.

### FCoE Frame Mapping

The encapsulation of the Fibre Channel frame occurs through the mapping of the FC frames onto Ethernet, as shown in Figure 6-17. Fibre Channel and traditional networks have stacks of layers where each layer in the stack represents a set of functionalities. The FC stack consists of five layers: FC-0 through FC-4. Ethernet is typically considered as a set of protocols that operates at the physical and data link layers in the seven layer OSI stack. The FCoE protocol specification replaces the FC-0 and FC-1 layers of the FC stack with Ethernet. This provides the capability to carry the FC-2 to the FC-4 layer over the Ethernet layer.

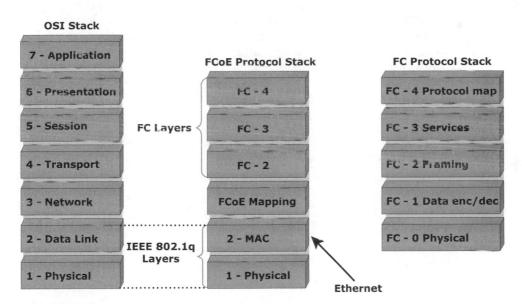

**Figure 6-17:** FCoE frame mapping

**FCoE PORTS**

To transport FC frames, the FCoE ports need to emulate the behavior of FC ports and become virtual FC ports. FCoE uses similar terminology as FC to define various ports in the network. FCoE has the following ports (See the figure following this list):

- **VN_Port (Virtual N_Port):** Port in an Enhanced Ethernet node (or Enode). Enodes are end points, such as a server, with CNA.

- **VF_Port (Virtual F_Port):** Virtual Fabric Port in an FCoE Switch

- **VE_Port (Virtual E_Port):** Virtual Extension Port in an FCoE Switch for ISLs

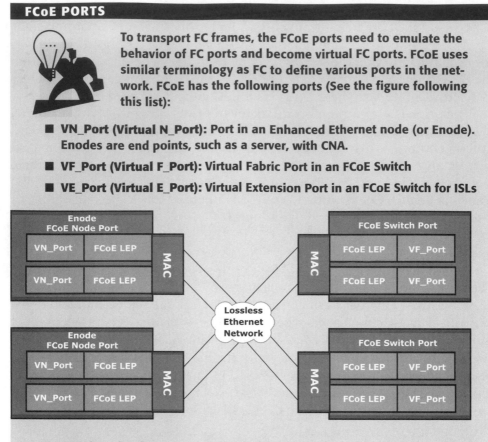

FCoE Link End Points (LEP) are located between the MAC and the virtual ports. LEPs are responsible for FC frame encapsulation/de-capsulation and for transmitting and receiving the encapsulated frames through a virtual port.

## 6.3.4 FCoE Enabling Technologies

Conventional Ethernet is lossy in nature, which means that frames might be dropped or lost during transmission. *Converged Enhanced Ethernet* (CEE), or lossless Ethernet, provides a new specification to the existing Ethernet standard that eliminates the lossy nature of Ethernet. This makes 10 Gb Ethernet a viable storage networking option, similar to FC. Lossless Ethernet requires certain functionalities. These functionalities are defined and maintained by the data center bridging (DCB) task group, which is a part of the IEEE 802.1 working group, and they are:

- Priority-based flow control
- Enhanced transmission selection

- Congestion Notification
- Data center bridging exchange protocol

### Priority-Based Flow Control (PFC)

Traditional FC manages congestion through the use of a link-level, credit-based flow control that guarantees no loss of frames. Typical Ethernet, coupled with TCP/IP, uses a packet drop flow control mechanism. The packet drop flow control is not lossless. This challenge is eliminated by using an IEEE 802.3x Ethernet PAUSE control frame to create a lossless Ethernet. A receiver can send a PAUSE request to a sender when the receiver's buffer is filling up. Upon receiving a PAUSE frame, the sender stops transmitting frames, which guarantees no loss of frames. The downside of using the Ethernet PAUSE frame is that it operates on the entire link, which might be carrying multiple traffic flows.

PFC provides a link level flow control mechanism. PFC creates eight separate virtual links on a single physical link and allows any of these links to be paused and restarted independently. PFC enables the pause mechanism based on user priorities or classes of service. Enabling the pause based on priority allows creating lossless links for traffic, such as FCoE traffic. This PAUSE mechanism is typically implemented for FCoE while regular TCP/IP traffic continues to drop frames. Figure 6-18 illustrates how a physical Ethernet link is divided into eight virtual links and allows a PAUSE for a single virtual link without affecting the traffic for the others.

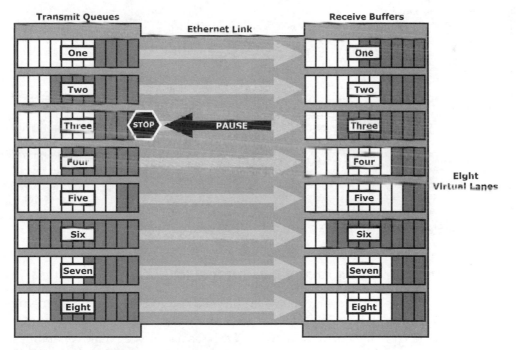

**Figure 6-18:** Priority-based flow control

### Enhanced Transmission Selection (ETS)

Enhanced transmission selection provides a common management framework for the assignment of bandwidth to different traffic classes, such as LAN, SAN, and Inter Process Communication (IPC). When a particular class of traffic does not use its allocated bandwidth, ETS enables other traffic classes to use the available bandwidth.

### Congestion Notification (CN)

Congestion notification provides end-to-end congestion management for protocols, such as FCoE, that do not have built-in congestion control mechanisms. Link level congestion notification provides a mechanism for detecting congestion and notifying the source to move the traffic flow away from the congested links. Link level congestion notification enables a switch to send a signal to other ports that need to stop or slow down their transmissions. The process of congestion notification and its management is shown in Figure 6-19, which represents the communication between the nodes A (sender) and B (receiver). If congestion at the receiving end occurs, the algorithm running on the switch generates a congestion notification message to the sending node (Node A). In response to the CN message, the sending end limits the rate of data transfer.

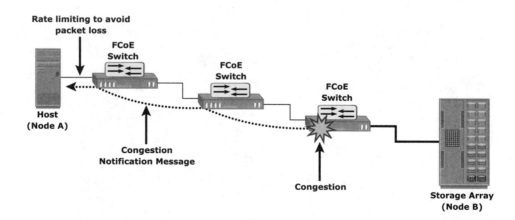

**Figure 6-19:** Congestion Notification

### Data Center Bridging Exchange Protocol (DCBX)

DCBX protocol is a discovery and capability exchange protocol, which helps Converged Enhanced Ethernet devices to convey and configure their features with the other CEE devices in the network. DCBX is used to negotiate capabilities between the switches and the adapters, and it allows the switch to distribute the configuration values to all the attached adapters. This helps to ensure consistent configuration across the entire network.

## Summary

IP SAN has enabled IT organizations to adopt storage networking infrastructure at reasonable costs. Storage networks can now be geographically distributed with the help of the IP SAN technology, which enhances storage utilization across enterprises. FCIP has emerged as a solution for implementing viable business continuity across data centers.

Because IP SANs are based on standard IP protocols, the concepts, security mechanisms, and management tools are familiar to network administrators. This has enabled the rapid adoption of IP SAN in organizations. This chapter detailed the two IP SAN technologies: iSCSI and FCIP. This chapter also detailed the emerging FCoE technology that enables transportation of both the LAN and SAN traffic on a single physical network infrastructure.

SAN offers a high-performance storage networking solution; however, SAN does not enable sharing of data among multiple hosts. Organizations might require sharing of data or files among multiple heterogeneous clients for collaboration purposes.

The next chapter details network-attached storage (NAS), a solution that provides a file-sharing environment to heterogeneous clients. Because NAS is dedicated for file sharing, it provides better performance than traditional file servers.

## EXERCISES

1. How does iSCSI handle the process of authentication? Research the available options.

2. Compared to a standard IP packet, what percentage of reduction can be realized in protocol overhead in an iSCSI, configured to use jumbo frames with an MTU value of 9,000 bytes?

3. Why should an MTU value of at least 2,500 bytes be configured in a bridged iSCSI environment?

4. Why does the lossy nature of standard Ethernet make it unsuitable for a layered FCoE implementation? How does Converged Enhanced Ethernet (CEE) address this problem?

5. Compare various data center protocols that use Ethernet as the physical medium for transporting storage traffic.

# Chapter 7
# Network-Attached Storage

File sharing, as the name implies, enables users to share files with other users. Traditional methods of file sharing involve copying files to portable media such as floppy diskette, CD, DVD, or USB drives and delivering them to other users with whom it is being shared. However, this approach is not suitable in an enterprise environment in which a large number of users at different locations need access to common files.

Network-based file sharing provides the flexibility to share files over long distances among a large number of users. File servers use client-server technology to enable file sharing over a network. To address the tremendous growth of file data in enterprise environments, organizations have been deploying large numbers of file servers. These servers are either connected to direct-attached storage (DAS) or storage area network (SAN)-attached storage. This has resulted in the proliferation of islands of over-utilized and under-utilized file servers and storage. In

## KEY CONCEPTS

NAS Devices

Network File Sharing

Unified, Gateway, and Scale-Out NAS

NAS Connectivity and Protocols

NAS Performance

MTU and Jumbo Frames

TCP Window and Link Aggregation

File-Level Virtualization

addition, such environments have poor scalability, higher management cost, and greater complexity. *Network-attached storage* (NAS) emerged as a solution to these challenges.

NAS is a dedicated, high-performance file sharing and storage device. NAS enables its clients to share files over an IP network. NAS provides the advantages of server consolidation by eliminating the need for multiple file servers. It also consolidates the storage used by the clients onto a single system, making it easier to manage the storage. NAS uses network and file-sharing protocols to provide access to the file data. These protocols include TCP/IP for data transfer, and Common Internet File System (CIFS) and Network File System (NFS) for network file service. NAS enables both UNIX and Microsoft Windows users to share the same data seamlessly.

A NAS device uses its own operating system and integrated hardware and software components to meet specific file-service needs. Its operating system is optimized for file I/O and, therefore, performs file I/O better than a general-purpose server. As a result, a NAS device can serve more clients than general-purpose servers and provide the benefit of server consolidation.

A network-based file sharing environment is composed of multiple file servers or NAS devices. It might be required to move the files from one device to another due to reasons such as cost or performance. File-level virtualization, implemented in the file sharing environment, provides a simple, nondisruptive file-mobility solution. It enables the movement of files across NAS devices, even if the files are being accessed.

This chapter describes the components of NAS, different types of NAS implementations, and the file-sharing protocols used in NAS implementations. The chapter also explains factors that affect NAS performance, and file-level virtualization.

# 7.1 General-Purpose Servers versus NAS Devices

A NAS device is optimized for file-serving functions such as storing, retrieving, and accessing files for applications and clients. As shown in Figure 7-1, a general-purpose server can be used to host any application because it runs a general-purpose operating system. Unlike a general-purpose server, a NAS device is dedicated to file-serving. It has specialized operating system dedicated to file serving by using industry-standard protocols. Some NAS vendors support features, such as native clustering for high availability.

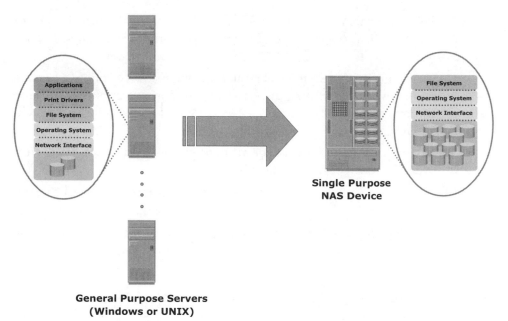

**Figure 7-1:** General purpose server versus NAS device

## 7.2 Benefits of NAS

NAS offers the following benefits:

- **Comprehensive access to information:** Enables efficient file sharing and supports many-to-one and one-to-many configurations. The many-to-one configuration enables a NAS device to serve many clients simultaneously. The one-to-many configuration enables one client to connect with many NAS devices simultaneously.

- **Improved efficiency:** NAS delivers better performance compared to a general-purpose file server because NAS uses an operating system specialized for file serving.

- **Improved flexibility:** Compatible with clients on both UNIX and Windows platforms using industry-standard protocols. NAS is flexible and can serve requests from different types of clients from the same source.

- **Centralized storage:** Centralizes data storage to minimize data duplication on client workstations, and ensure greater data protection

- **Simplified management:** Provides a centralized console that makes it possible to manage file systems efficiently

- **Scalability:** Scales well with different utilization profiles and types of business applications because of the high-performance and low-latency design

- **High availability:** Offers efficient replication and recovery options, enabling high data availability. NAS uses redundant components that provide maximum connectivity options. A NAS device supports clustering technology for failover.

- **Security:** Ensures security, user authentication, and file locking with industry-standard security schemas

- **Low cost:** NAS uses commonly available and inexpensive Ethernet components.

- **Ease of deployment:** Configuration at the client is minimal, because the clients have required NAS connection software built in.

# 7.3 File Systems and Network File Sharing

A *file system* is a structured way to store and organize data files. Many file systems maintain a file access table to simplify the process of searching and accessing files.

## 7.3.1 Accessing a File System

A file system must be mounted before it can be used. In most cases, the operating system mounts a local file system during the boot process. The mount process creates a link between the file system on the NAS and the operating system on the client. When mounting a file system, the operating system organizes files and directories in a tree-like structure and grants the privilege to the user to access this structure. The tree is rooted at a mount point. The mount point is named using operating system conventions. Users and applications can traverse the entire tree from the root to the leaf nodes as file system permissions allow. Files are located at leaf nodes, and directories and subdirectories are located at intermediate roots. The access to the file system terminates when the file system is unmounted. Figure 7-2 shows an example of a UNIX directory structure.

## 7.3.2 Network File Sharing

Network file sharing refers to storing and accessing files over a network. In a file-sharing environment, the user who creates a file (the creator or owner of a file) determines the type of access (such as read, write, execute, append, and delete) to be given to other users and controls changes to the file. When multiple users try to access a shared file at the same time, a locking scheme is required to maintain data integrity and, at the same time, make this sharing possible.

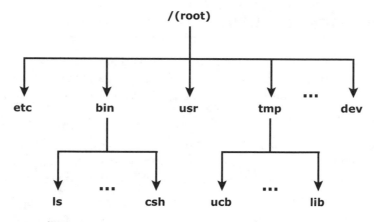

**Figure 7-2:** UNIX directory structure

Some examples of file-sharing methods are file transfer protocol (FTP), Distributed File System (DFS), client-server models that use file-sharing protocols such as NFS and CIFS, and the peer-to-peer (P2P) model

*FTP* is a client-server protocol that enables data transfer over a network. An FTP server and an FTP client communicate with each other using TCP as the transport protocol. FTP, as defined by the standard, is not a secure method of data transfer because it uses unencrypted data transfer over a network. FTP over Secure Shell (SSH) adds security to the original FTP specification. When FTP is used over SSH, it is referred to as Secure FTP (SFTP).

A *distributed file system* (DFS) is a file system that is distributed across several hosts. A DFS can provide hosts with direct access to the entire file system, while ensuring efficient management and data security. Standard client-server file-sharing protocols, such as NFS and CIFS, enable the owner of a file to set the required type of access, such as read-only or read-write, for a particular user or group of users. Using this protocol, the clients mount remote file systems that are available on dedicated file servers.

A *name service*, such as Domain Name System (DNS), and directory services such as Microsoft Active Directory, and Network Information Services (NIS), helps users identify and access a unique resource over the network. A *name service protocol* such as the Lightweight Directory Access Protocol (LDAP) creates a namespace, which holds the unique name of every network resource and helps recognize resources on the network.

A *peer-to-peer* (P2P) file sharing model uses a peer-to-peer network. P2P enables client machines to directly share files with each other over a network. Clients use a file sharing software that searches for other peer clients. This differs from the client-server model that uses file servers to store files for sharing.

# 7.4 Components of NAS

A NAS device has two key components: NAS head and storage (see Figure 7-3). In some NAS implementations, the storage could be external to the NAS device and shared with other hosts. The NAS head includes the following components:

- CPU and memory
- One or more network interface cards (NICs), which provide connectivity to the client network. Examples of network protocols supported by NIC include Gigabit Ethernet, Fast Ethernet, ATM, and Fiber Distributed Data Interface (FDDI).
- An optimized operating system for managing the NAS functionality. It translates file-level requests into block-storage requests and further converts the data supplied at the block level to file data.
- NFS, CIFS, and other protocols for file sharing
- Industry-standard storage protocols and ports to connect and manage physical disk resources

The NAS environment includes clients accessing a NAS device over an IP network using file-sharing protocols.

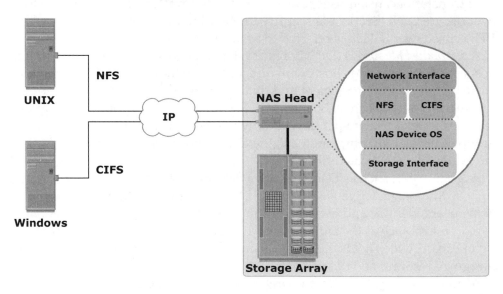

**Figure 7-3:** Components of NAS

## 7.5 NAS I/O Operation

NAS provides file-level data access to its clients. File I/O is a high-level request that specifies the file to be accessed. For example, a client may request a file by specifying its name, location, or other attributes. The NAS operating system keeps track of the location of files on the disk volume and converts client file I/O into block-level I/O to retrieve data. The process of handling I/Os in a NAS environment is as follows:

1. The requestor (client) packages an I/O request into TCP/IP and forwards it through the network stack. The NAS device receives this request from the network.

2. The NAS device converts the I/O request into an appropriate physical storage request, which is a block-level I/O, and then performs the operation on the physical storage.

3. When the NAS device receives data from the storage, it processes and repackages the data into an appropriate file protocol response.

4. The NAS device packages this response into TCP/IP again and forwards it to the client through the network.

Figure 7-4 illustrates this process.

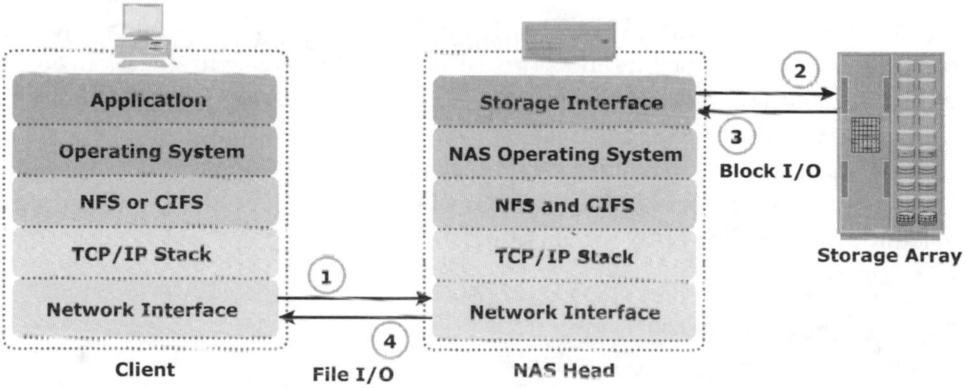

**Figure 7-4:** NAS I/O operation

## 7.6 NAS Implementations

Three common NAS implementations are unified, gateway, and scale-out. The *unified* NAS consolidates NAS-based and SAN-based data access within a unified storage platform and provides a unified management interface for managing both the environments.

In a *gateway* implementation, the NAS device uses external storage to store and retrieve data, and unlike unified storage, there are separate administrative tasks for the NAS device and storage.

The *scale-out* NAS implementation pools multiple nodes together in a cluster. A node may consist of either the NAS head or storage or both. The cluster performs the NAS operation as a single entity.

### 7.6.1 Unified NAS

Unified NAS performs file serving and storing of file data, along with providing access to block-level data. It supports both CIFS and NFS protocols for file access and iSCSI and FC protocols for block level access. Due to consolidation of NAS-based and SAN-based access on a single storage platform, unified NAS reduces an organization's infrastructure and management costs.

A unified NAS contains one or more NAS heads and storage in a single system. NAS heads are connected to the storage controllers (SCs), which provide access to the storage. These storage controllers also provide connectivity to iSCSI and FC hosts. The storage may consist of different drive types, such as SAS, ATA, FC, and flash drives, to meet different workload requirements.

### 7.6.2 Unified NAS Connectivity

Each NAS head in a unified NAS has front-end Ethernet ports, which connect to the IP network. The front-end ports provide connectivity to the clients and service the file I/O requests. Each NAS head has back-end ports, to provide connectivity to the storage controllers.

iSCSI and FC ports on a storage controller enable hosts to access the storage directly or through a storage network at the block level. Figure 7-5 illustrates an example of unified NAS connectivity.

### 7.6.3 Gateway NAS

A gateway NAS device consists of one or more NAS heads and uses external and independently managed storage. Similar to unified NAS, the storage is shared with other applications that use block-level I/O. Management functions in this type of solution are more complex than those in a unified NAS environment because there are separate administrative tasks for the NAS head and the storage. A gateway solution can use the FC infrastructure, such as switches and directors for accessing SAN-attached storage arrays or direct-attached storage arrays.

The gateway NAS is more scalable compared to unified NAS because NAS heads and storage arrays can be independently scaled up when required.

For example, NAS heads can be added to scale up the NAS device performance. When the storage limit is reached, it can scale up, adding capacity on the SAN, independent of NAS heads. Similar to a unified NAS, a gateway NAS also enables high utilization of storage capacity by sharing it with the SAN environment.

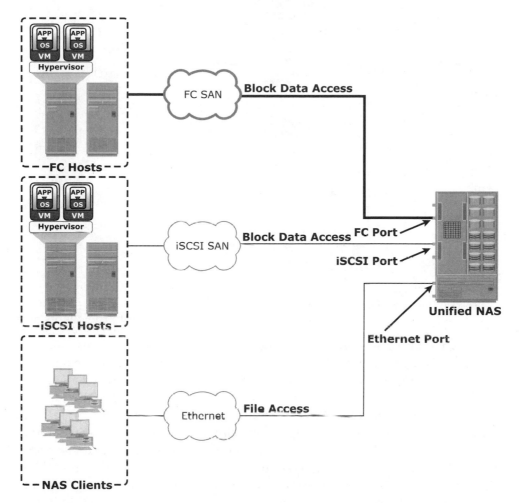

**Figure 7-5:** Unified NAS connectivity

## 7.6.4 Gateway NAS Connectivity

In a gateway solution, the front-end connectivity is similar to that in a unified storage solution. Communication between the NAS gateway and the storage system in a gateway solution is achieved through a traditional FC SAN. To deploy a gateway NAS solution, factors, such as multiple paths for data, redundant fabrics, and load distribution, must be considered. Figure 7-6 illustrates an example of gateway NAS connectivity.

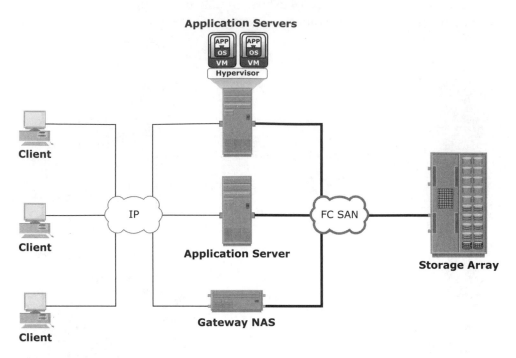

**Figure 7-6:** Gateway NAS connectivity

Implementation of both unified and gateway solutions requires analysis of the SAN environment. This analysis is required to determine the feasibility of combining the NAS workload with the SAN workload. Analyze the SAN to determine whether the workload is primarily read or write, and if it is random or sequential. Also determine the predominant I/O size in use. Typically, NAS workloads are random with small I/O sizes. Introducing sequential workload with random workloads can be disruptive to the sequential workload. Therefore, it is recommended to separate the NAS and SAN disks. Also, determine whether the NAS workload performs adequately with the configured cache in the storage system.

## 7.6.5 Scale-Out NAS

Both unified and gateway NAS implementations provide the capability to scale-up their resources based on data growth and rise in performance requirements. Scaling up these NAS devices involves adding CPUs, memory, and storage to the NAS device. Scalability is limited by the capacity of the NAS device to house and use additional NAS heads and storage.

Scale-out NAS enables grouping multiple nodes together to construct a clustered NAS system. A scale-out NAS provides the capability to scale its resources by simply adding nodes to a clustered NAS architecture. The cluster works as a single NAS device and is managed centrally. Nodes can be added to the cluster, when more performance or more capacity is needed, without causing any downtime. Scale-out NAS provides the flexibility to use many nodes of moderate performance and availability characteristics to produce a total system that has better aggregate performance and availability. It also provides ease of use, low cost, and theoretically unlimited scalability.

Scale-out NAS creates a single file system that runs on all nodes in the cluster. All information is shared among nodes, so the entire file system is accessible by clients connecting to any node in the cluster. Scale-out NAS stripes data across all nodes in a cluster along with mirror or parity protection. As data is sent from clients to the cluster, the data is divided and allocated to different nodes in parallel. When a client sends a request to read a file, the scale-out NAS retrieves the appropriate blocks from multiple nodes, recombines the blocks into a file, and presents the file to the client. As nodes are added, the file system grows dynamically and data is evenly distributed to every node. Each node added to the cluster increases the aggregate storage, memory, CPU, and network capacity. Hence, cluster performance also increases.

Scale-out NAS is suitable to solve the "Big Data" challenges that enterprises and customers face today. It provides the capability to manage and store large, high-growth data in a single place with the flexibility to meet a broad range of performance requirements.

## 7.6.6 Scale-Out NAS Connectivity

Scale-out NAS clusters use separate internal and external networks for back-end and front-end connectivity, respectively. An internal network provides connections for intracluster communication, and an external network connection enables clients to access and share file data. Each node in the cluster connects to the internal network. The internal network offers high throughput and low latency and uses high-speed networking technology, such as InfiniBand or Gigabit Ethernet. To enable clients to access a node, the node must be connected to the external Ethernet network. Redundant internal or external networks may be used for high availability. Figure 7-7 illustrates an example of scale-out NAS connectivity.

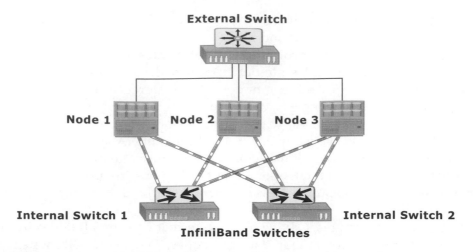

**Figure 7-7:** Scale-out NAS with dual internal and single external networks

**INFINIBAND**

InfiniBand is a networking technology that provides a low-latency, high-bandwidth communication link between hosts and peripherals. It provides serial connection and is often used for inter-server communications in high-performance computing environments. InfiniBand enables remote direct memory access (RDMA) that enables a device (host or peripheral) to access data directly from the memory of a remote device. InfiniBand also enables a single physical link to carry multiple channels of data simultaneously using a multiplexing technique. The InfiniBand networking infrastructure consists of host channel adapters (HCAs), target channel adapters (TCAs), and InfiniBand switches. HCAs are located within hosts. HCAs provide the mechanism to connect CPUs and memory of the hosts to the InfiniBand network. Similarly, TCAs enable storage and other peripheral devices to connect to the InfiniBand network. InfiniBand switches provide connectivity among HCAs and TCAs.

## 7.7 NAS File-Sharing Protocols

Most NAS devices support multiple file-service protocols to handle file I/O requests to a remote file system. As discussed earlier, NFS and CIFS are the common protocols for file sharing. NAS devices enable users to share file data across different operating environments and provide a means for users to migrate transparently from one operating system to another.

## 7.7.1 NFS

*NFS* is a client-server protocol for file sharing that is commonly used on UNIX systems. NFS was originally based on the connectionless *User Datagram Protocol* (UDP). It uses a machine-independent model to represent user data. It also uses Remote Procedure Call (RPC) as a method of inter-process communication between two computers. The NFS protocol provides a set of RPCs to access a remote file system for the following operations:

- Searching files and directories
- Opening, reading, writing to, and closing a file
- Changing file attributes
- Modifying file links and directories

NFS creates a connection between the client and the remote system to transfer data. NFS (NFSv3 and earlier) is a *stateless protocol*, which means that it does not maintain any kind of table to store information about open files and associated pointers. Therefore, each call provides a full set of arguments to access files on the server. These arguments include a file handle reference to the file, a particular position to read or write, and the versions of NFS.

Currently, three versions of NFS are in use:

- **NFS version 2 (NFSv2):** Uses UDP to provide a stateless network connection between a client and a server. Features, such as locking, are handled outside the protocol.

- **NFS version 3 (NFSv3):** The most commonly used version, which uses UDP or TCP, and is based on the stateless protocol design. It includes some new features, such as a 64-bit file size, asynchronous writes, and additional file attributes to reduce refetching.

- **NFS version 4 (NFSv4):** Uses TCP and is based on a stateful protocol design. It offers enhanced security. The latest NFS version 4.1 is the enhancement of NFSv4 and includes some new features, such as session model, parallel NFS (pNFS), and data retention.

---

**PNFS AND MPFS**

pNFS, as part of NFSv4.1, separates the file system protocol processing into two parts: metadata processing and data processing. The metadata includes information about a file system object, such as its name, location within the namespace, owner, access control list (ACL), and other attributes. The pNFS server, also called a metadata server,

*(Continued)*

**PNFS AND MPFS** *(continued)*

does the metadata processing and is kept out of the data path. pNFS clients send the metadata information to the pNFS server. The pNFS clients access storage devices directly using multiple parallel data paths. The pNFS client uses a storage network protocol, such as iSCSI or FC, to perform I/O to storage devices. The pNFS clients get information about the storage devices from the metadata server. Because the pNFS server is relieved of data processing and pNFS clients can access the storage devices directly using parallel paths, the pNFS mechanism significantly improves the pNFS client performance.

The EMC-patented Multi-Path File System (MPFS) protocol works similar to pNFS. The MPFS driver software, installed at the NAS clients, sends the file's metadata to the NAS device (MPFS server) via the IP network. The MPFS driver obtains information about the location of the data from the NAS device over the IP network. After knowing the data location, the MPFS driver communicates directly to the storage devices and enables the NAS clients to access the data over SAN. The following Figure shows the MPFS architecture that provides different paths for transferring a file's metadata and data.

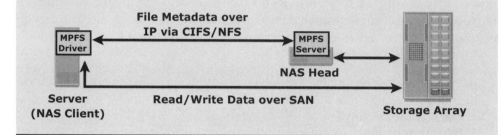

## 7.7.2 CIFS

CIFS is a client-server application protocol that enables client programs to make requests for files and services on remote computers over TCP/IP. It is a public, or open, variation of Server Message Block (SMB) protocol.

The CIFS protocol enables remote clients to gain access to files on a server. CIFS enables file sharing with other clients by using special locks. Filenames in CIFS are encoded using unicode characters. CIFS provides the following features to ensure data integrity:

- It uses file and record locking to prevent users from overwriting the work of another user on a file or a record.

- It supports fault tolerance and can automatically restore connections and reopen files that were open prior to an interruption. The fault tolerance features of CIFS depend on whether an application is written to take advantage of these features. Moreover, CIFS is a stateful protocol because the CIFS server maintains connection information regarding every connected client. If a network failure or CIFS server failure occurs, the client receives a disconnection notification. User disruption is minimized if the application has the embedded intelligence to restore the connection. However, if the embedded intelligence is missing, the user must take steps to reestablish the CIFS connection.

Users refer to remote file systems with an easy-to-use file-naming scheme:

`\\server\share` or `\\servername.domain.suffix\share`.

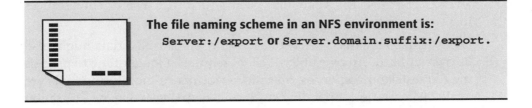

**The file naming scheme in an NFS environment is:**
`Server:/export` or `Server.domain.suffix:/export.`

## 7.8 Factors Affecting NAS Performance

NAS uses IP network; therefore, bandwidth and latency issues associated with IP affect NAS performance. Network congestion is one of the most significant sources of latency (Figure 7-8) in a NAS environment. Other factors that affect NAS performance at different levels follow:

1. **Number of hops:** A large number of hops can increase latency because IP processing is required at each hop, adding to the delay caused at the router.

2. **Authentication with a directory service such as Active Directory or NIS:** The authentication service must be available on the network with enough resources to accommodate the authentication load. Otherwise, a large number of authentication requests can increase latency.

3. **Retransmission:** Link errors and buffer overflows can result in retransmission. This causes packets that have not reached the specified destination to be re-sent. Care must be taken to match both speed and duplex settings on the network devices and the NAS heads. Improper configuration might result in errors and retransmission, adding to latency.

4. **Overutilized routers and switches:** The amount of time that an overutilized device in a network takes to respond is always more than the response time of an optimally utilized or underutilized device. Network administrators can view utilization statistics to determine the optimum utilization of switches and routers in a network. Additional devices should be added if the current devices are overutilized.

5. **File system lookup and metadata requests:** NAS clients access files on NAS devices. The processing required to reach the appropriate file or directory can cause delays. Sometimes a delay is caused by deep directory structures and can be resolved by flattening the directory structure. Poor file system layout and an overutilized disk system can also degrade performance.

6. **Over utilized NAS devices:** Clients accessing multiple files can cause high utilization levels on a NAS device, which can be determined by viewing utilization statistics. High memory, CPU, or disk subsystem utilization levels can be caused by a poor file system structure or insufficient resources in a storage subsystem.

7. **Over utilized clients:** The client accessing CIFS or NFS data might also be over utilized. An overutilized client requires a longer time to process the requests and responses. Specific performance-monitoring tools are available for various operating systems to help determine the utilization of client resources.

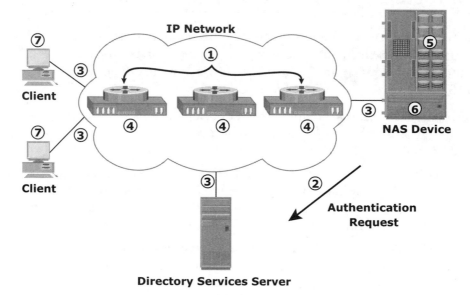

**Figure 7-8:** Causes of latency

Configuring *virtual LANs* (VLANs), setting proper Maximum Transmission Unit (MTU) and TCP window sizes, and link aggregation can improve NAS performance. Link aggregation and redundant network configurations also ensure high availability.

A VLAN is a logical segment of a switched network or logical grouping of end devices connected to different physical networks. An end device could be a client or a NAS device. The segmentation or grouping can be done based on business functions, project teams, or applications. VLAN is a Layer 2 (data link layer) construct and works similar to a physical LAN. A network switch can be logically divided among multiple VLANs, enabling better utilization of the switch and reducing the overall cost of deploying a network infrastructure.

The broadcast traffic on one VLAN is not transmitted outside that VLAN, which substantially reduces the broadcast overhead, makes bandwidth available for applications, and reduces the network's vulnerability to broadcast storms.

VLANs also provide enhanced security by restricting user access, flagging network intrusions, and controlling the size and composition of the broadcast domain. The *MTU* setting determines the size of the largest packet that can be transmitted without data fragmentation. *Path maximum transmission unit discovery* is the process of discovering the maximum size of a packet that can be sent across a network without fragmentation. The default MTU setting for an Ethernet interface card is 1,500 bytes. A feature called *jumbo frames* sends, receives, or transports Ethernet frames with an MTU of more than 1,500 bytes. The most common deployments of jumbo frames have an MTU of 9,000 bytes. However not all vendors use the same MTU size for jumbo frames. Servers send and receive larger frames more efficiently than smaller ones in heavy network traffic conditions. Jumbo frames ensure increased efficiency because it takes fewer, larger frames to transfer the same amount of data. Larger packets also reduce the amount of raw network bandwidth being consumed for the same amount of payload. Larger frames also help to smooth sudden I/O bursts.

The *TCP window size* is the maximum amount of data that can be sent at any time for a connection. For example, if a pair of hosts is talking over a TCP connection that has a TCP window size of 64 KB, the sender can send only 64 KB of data and must then wait for an acknowledgment from the receiver. If the receiver acknowledges that all the data has been received, then the sender is free to send another 64 KB of data. If the sender receives an acknowledgment from the receiver that only the first 32 KB of data has been received, which can happen only if another 32 KB of data is in transit or was lost, the sender can send only another 32 KB of data because the transmission cannot have more than 64 KB of unacknowledged data outstanding.

In theory, the TCP window size should be set to the product of the available bandwidth of the network and the round-trip time of data sent over the network.

For example, if a network has a bandwidth of 100 Mbps and the round-trip time is 5 milliseconds, the TCP window should be as follows:

100 Mb/s × .005 seconds = 524,288 bits or 65,536 bytes

The size of the TCP window field that controls the flow of data is between 2 bytes and 65,535 bytes.

*Link aggregation* is the process of combining two or more network interfaces into a logical network interface, enabling higher throughput, load sharing or load balancing, transparent path failover, and scalability. Due to link aggregation, multiple active Ethernet connections to the same switch appear as one link. If a connection or a port in the aggregation is lost, then all the network traffic on that link is redistributed across the remaining active connections.

## 7.9 File-Level Virtualization

*File-level virtualization* eliminates the dependencies between the data accessed at the file level and the location where the files are physically stored. Implementation of file-level virtualization is common in NAS or file-server environments. It provides non-disruptive file mobility to optimize storage utilization.

Before virtualization, each host knows exactly where its file resources are located. This environment leads to underutilized storage resources and capacity problems because files are bound to a specific NAS device or file server. It may be required to move the files from one server to another because of performance reasons or when the file server fills up. Moving files across the environment is not easy and may make files inaccessible during file movement. Moreover, hosts and applications need to be reconfigured to access the file at the new location. This makes it difficult for storage administrators to improve storage efficiency while maintaining the required service level.

File-level virtualization simplifies file mobility. It provides user or application independence from the location where the files are stored. File-level virtualization creates a logical pool of storage, enabling users to use a logical path, rather than a physical path, to access files. File-level virtualization facilitates the movement of files across the online file servers or NAS devices. This means that while the files are being moved, clients can access their files nondisruptively. Clients can also read their files from the old location and write them back to the new location without realizing that the physical location has changed. A global namespace is used to map the logical path of a file to the physical path names.

Figure 7-9 illustrates a file-serving environment before and after the implementation of file-level virtualization.

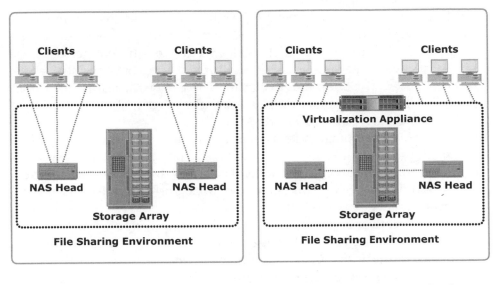

**(a) Before File-Level Virtualization**          **(b) After File-Level Virtualization**

**Figure 7-9:** File-serving environment before and after file-level virtualization

# 7.10 Concepts in Practice: EMC Isilon and EMC VNX Gateway

EMC Isilon is the scale-out NAS solution. Isilon offers high scalability of both performance and storage capacity. It provides the capability to address big-data challenges.

The VNX Gateway, a member of the EMC VNX family, provides a gateway NAS solution. It provides multiprotocol file access, dynamic expansion of file systems, high availability, and high performance.

For more information on EMC Isilon and VNX Gateway, visit www.emc.com.

## 7.10.1 EMC Isilon

Isilon has a specialized operating system called OneFS that enables the scale-out NAS architecture. OneFS combines the three layers of traditional storage architectures — file system, volume manager, and RAID — into one unified software layer, creating a single file system that spans across all nodes in an Isilon cluster. OneFS enables data protection and automated data balancing. It provides the ability to seamlessly add storage and other resources without system downtime. With OneFS, throughput scales linearly with the number of nodes in a cluster.

OneFS enables different node types to be mixed in a single cluster through the addition of the SmartPools application software. SmartPools enables deploying a single file system to span multiple nodes that have different performance characteristics and capacities. Isilon offers different types of nodes, such as the X-Series, S-Series, NL-Series, and Accelerator. These nodes have different prices, performance levels, and storage capabilities. Each type of node is optimized for handling a specific type of workload.

OneFS enables the storage system administrator to specify the access pattern (random, concurrent, or sequential) on a per-file or per-directory basis. This unique capability enables OneFS to tailor data layout decisions, cache-retention policies, and data prefetch policies to maximize performance of individual workflows.

OneFS constantly monitors the health of all files and disks within a cluster, and if components are at risk, the file system automatically flags the problem components for replacement and transparently relocates those files to healthy components. OneFS also ensures data integrity if the file system has an unexpected failure during a write operation.

When a new storage node is added, the Autobalance feature of OneFS automatically moves data onto this new node via the Infiniband based internal network. This automatic rebalancing ensures that the new node does not become a hot spot for new data. The Autobalance feature is transparent to the clients and can be adjusted to minimize the impact on high-performance workloads.

OneFS includes a core technology, called FlexProtect, to provide data protection. FlexProtect provides protection for up to four simultaneous failures of either nodes or individual drives per stripe. FlexProtect ensures minimal data reconstruction time if a failure occurs. FlexProtect provides file-specific protection capabilities. Different protection levels can be assigned to individual files, directories, or to portions of a file system. These protection levels are aligned based on the importance of data and workflow.

## 7.10.2 EMC VNX Gateway

The VNX Series Gateway contains one or more NAS heads, called X-Blades, that access external storage arrays, such as Symmetrix, block-based VNX, or CLARiiON storage array, via SAN. X-Blades run the VNX operating environment that is optimized for high-performance and multiprotocol network file system access. Each X-Blade consists of processors, redundant data paths, power supplies, Gigabit Ethernet, and 10-Gigabit Ethernet optical ports. All the X-Blades in a VNX gateway system are managed by Control Station, which provides a single point for configuring VNX Gateway. The VNX Gateway supports both pNFS and EMC patented Multi-Path File System (MPFS) protocols, which further improves the VNX Gateway performance.

VNX Series Gateway offers two models: VG2 and VG8. VG8 supports up to eight X-Blades, whereas VG2 supports up to two. X-Blades may be configured as either primary or standby. A primary X-Blade is the operating NAS head, whereas a standby X-Blade becomes operational if the primary X-Blade fails. The Control Station handles an X-Blade failover. The Control Station also provides other high-availability features, such as fault monitoring, fault reporting, call home, and remote diagnostics.

## Summary

Decisions for choosing an appropriate storage infrastructure are based on maintaining the balance between cost and performance. Organizations look for the performance and scalability of SAN combined with the ease of use and lower total cost of ownership of NAS solutions. Both SAN and NAS have enjoyed unique advantages in enterprises, and advances in IP technology have scaled NAS solutions to meet the demands of performance-sensitive applications. With the advancement of storage networking technology, both SAN-based and NAS-based accesses have converged to a single platform.

Although NAS invariably imposes higher protocol overhead, it tends to be the most efficient for file-sharing tasks. NAS performance has significantly improved with the emergence of MPFS and pNFS protocols. These protocols use SAN speed to provide access to file data. They also offload the file-data processing load from the NAS device. NAS can also provide file-level access control to its clients. Organizations can also deploy NAS solutions for their database applications. Scale-out NAS fulfills the need for big-data performance and big-data capacity. Applications generating big data are optimized and more easily managed by using a single-expandable file system. File-level virtualization provides the flexibility to move files across NAS devices without disrupting the access to the files.

NAS devices impose additional latency to the client traffic while converting file I/O to block I/Os and vice versa. Also, nested directory structure and management of permission for individual files and directories add overhead to NAS. The overhead increases as the NAS file system grows. Hence, NAS clients are limited by the performance of the NAS device. Although the use of pNFS and MPFS protocols has considerably improved the NAS performance, these protocols might pose some security challenges. Object-based storage, detailed in the following chapter, addresses the performance and security challenges in the file-serving environment. Unified storage, also detailed in the following chapter, provides a single-storage platform for accessing files, blocks, and objects simultaneously. Unified storage brings ease of management and eliminates the additional cost of deploying separate storage systems for storing file-, block-, and object-based data.

**EXERCISES**

1. SAN is configured for a backup–to-disk environment, and the storage configuration has additional capacity available. Can you have a NAS gateway configuration use this SAN-attached storage? Discuss the implications of sharing the backup-to-disk SAN environment with NAS.

2. Explain how the performance of NAS can be affected if the TCP window size at the sender and receiver are not synchronized.

3. How does the use of jumbo frames affect the NAS performance?

4. Research the file access and sharing features of pNFS.

5. A NAS implementation configured jumbo frames on the NAS head with 9,000 as its MTU. However, the implementers did not see any performance improvement and actually experienced performance degradation. What could be the cause? Research the end-to-end jumbo frame support requirements in a network.

6. How does file-level virtualization ensure nondisruptive file mobility?

# Chapter 8
# Object-Based and
# Unified Storage

R ecent studies have shown that more than 90 percent of data generated is unstructured. This growth of unstructured data has posed new challenges to IT administrators and storage managers. With this growth, traditional NAS, which is a dominant solution for storing unstructured data, has become inefficient. Data growth adds high

**KEY CONCEPTS**

Object-Based Storage

Content Addressed Storage

Unified Storage

overhead to the network-attached storage (NAS) in terms of managing a large number of permissions and nested directories. In an enterprise environment, NAS also manages large amounts of metadata generated by hosts, storage systems, and individual applications. Typically this metadata is stored as part of the file and distributed throughout the environment. This adds to the complexity and latency in searching and retrieving files. These challenges demand a smarter approach to manage unstructured data based on its content rather than metadata about its name, location, and so on. *Object-based storage* is a way to store file data in the form of objects based on its content and other attributes rather than the name and location.

Due to varied application requirements, organizations have been deploying storage area networks (SANs), NAS, and object-based storage devices (OSDs) in their data centers. Deploying these disparate storage solutions adds management complexity, cost and environmental overhead. An ideal solution would be to have an integrated storage solution that supports block, file, and object access. Unified storage has emerged as a solution that consolidates block, file, and object-based access within one unified platform. It supports multiple protocols for data access and can be managed using a single management interface.

This chapter details object-based storage, its components, and operation. It also details *content addressed storage* (CAS), a special type of OSD. Further, this chapter covers the components and data access method in unified storage.

# 8.1 Object-Based Storage Devices

An OSD is a device that organizes and stores unstructured data, such as movies, office documents, and graphics, as objects. Object-based storage provides a scalable, self-managed, protected, and shared storage option. OSD stores data in the form of *objects*. OSD uses flat address space to store data. Therefore, there is no hierarchy of directories and files; as a result, a large number of objects can be stored in an OSD system (see Figure 8-1).

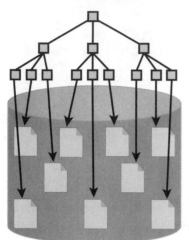
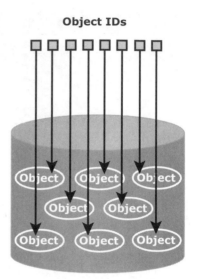

**(a) Hierarchical File System**    **(b) Flat Address Space**

**Figure 8-1:** Hierarchical file system versus flat address space

An object might contain user data, related metadata (size, date, ownership, and so on), and other attributes of data (retention, access pattern, and so on); see Figure 8-2. Each object stored in the system is identified by a unique ID called the *object ID*. The object ID is generated using specialized algorithms such as hash function on the data and guarantees that every object is uniquely identified.

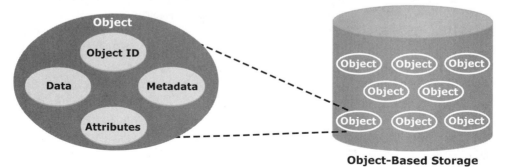

**Object-Based Storage**

**Figure 8-2:** Object structure

## 8.1.1 Object-Based Storage Architecture

An I/O in the traditional block access method passes through various layers in the I/O path. The I/O generated by an application passes through the file system, the channel, or network and reaches the disk drive. When the file system receives the I/O from an application, the file system maps the incoming I/O to the disk blocks. The block interface is used for sending the I/O over the channel or network to the storage device. The I/O is then written to the block allocated on the disk drive. Figure 8-3 (a) illustrates the block-level access.

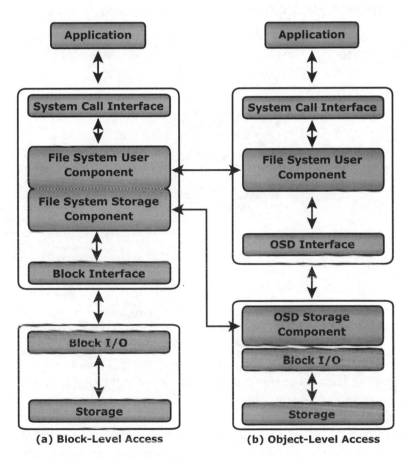

**Figure 8-3:** Block-level access versus object-level access

The file system has two components: user component and storage component. The user component of the file system performs functions such as hierarchy management, naming, and user access control. The storage component maps the files to the physical location on the disk drive.

When an application accesses data stored in OSD, the request is sent to the file system user component. The file system user component communicates to the OSD interface, which in turn sends the request to the storage device. The storage device has the OSD storage component responsible for managing the access to the object on a storage device. Figure 8-3 (b) illustrates the object-level access. After the object is stored, the OSD sends an acknowledgment to the application server. The OSD storage component manages all the required low-level storage and space management functions. It also manages security and access control functions for the objects.

## 8.1.2 Components of OSD

The OSD system is typically composed of three key components: nodes, private network, and storage. Figure 8-4 illustrates the components of OSD.

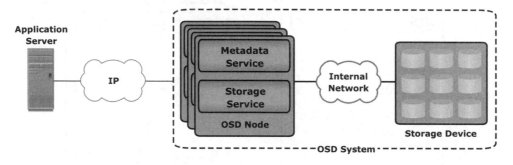

**Figure 8-4:** OSD components

The OSD system is composed of one or more *nodes*. A node is a server that runs the OSD operating environment and provides services to store, retrieve, and manage data in the system. The OSD node has two key services: metadata service and storage service. The metadata service is responsible for generating the object ID from the contents (and can also include other attributes of data) of a file. It also maintains the mapping of the object IDs and the file system namespace. The storage service manages a set of disks on which the user data is stored. The OSD nodes connect to the storage via an internal network. The internal network provides node-to-node connectivity and node-to-storage connectivity. The application server accesses the node to store and retrieve data over an external network. In some implementations, such as CAS, the metadata service might reside on the application server or on a separate server.

OSD typically uses low-cost and high-density disk drives to store the objects. As more capacity is required, more disk drives can be added to the system.

## 8.1.3 Object Storage and Retrieval in OSD

The process of storing objects in OSD is illustrated in Figure 8-5. The data storage process in an OSD system is as follows:

1. The application server presents the file to be stored to the OSD node.

2. The OSD node divides the file into two parts: user data and metadata.

3. The OSD node generates the object ID using a specialized algorithm. The algorithm is executed against the contents of the user data to derive an ID unique to this data.

4. For future access, the OSD node stores the metadata and object ID using the metadata service.

5. The OSD node stores the user data (objects) in the storage device using the storage service.

6. An acknowledgment is sent to the application server stating that the object is stored.

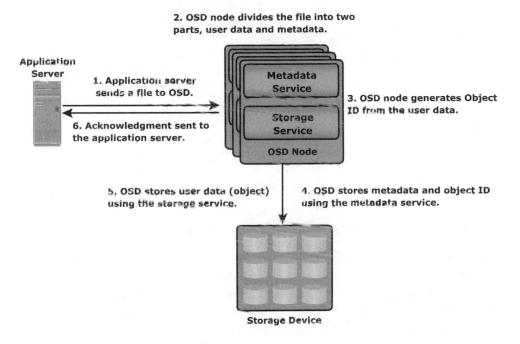

**Figure 8-5:** Storing objects on OSD

After an object is stored successfully, it is available for retrieval. A user accesses the data stored on OSD by the same filename. The application server retrieves the stored content using the object ID. This process is transparent to the user.

The process of retrieving objects in OSD is illustrated in Figures 8-6. The process of data retrieval from OSD is as follows:

1. The application server sends a read request to the OSD system.
2. The metadata service retrieves the object ID for the requested file.
3. The metadata service sends the object ID to the application server.
4. The application server sends the object ID to the OSD storage service for object retrieval.
5. The OSD storage service retrieves the object from the storage device.
6. The OSD storage service sends the file to the application server.

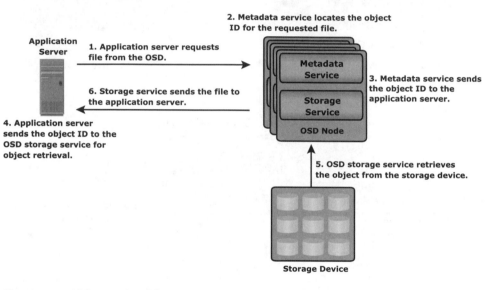

**Figure 8-6:** Object retrieval from an OSD system

## 8.1.4 Benefits of Object-Based Storage

For unstructured data, object-based storage devices provide numerous benefits over traditional storage solutions. An ideal storage architecture should provide performance, scalability, security, and data sharing across multiple platforms. Traditional storage solutions, such as SAN and NAS, do not offer all these benefits as a single solution. Object-based storage combines benefits of both the worlds. It provides platform and location independence, and at the same time, provides scalability, security, and data-sharing capabilities. The key benefits of object-based storage are as follows:

▪ **Security and reliability:** Data integrity and content authenticity are the key features of object-based storage devices. OSD uses specialized algorithms to create objects that provide strong data encryption capability. In OSD, request authentication is performed at the storage device rather than with an external authentication mechanism.

▪ **Platform independence:** Objects are abstract containers of data, including metadata and attributes. This feature allows objects to be shared across heterogeneous platforms locally or remotely. This platform-independence capability makes object-based storage the best candidate for cloud computing environments.

▪ **Scalability:** Due to the use of flat address space, object-based storage can handle large amounts of data without impacting performance. Both storage and OSD nodes can be scaled independently in terms of performance and capacity.

▪ **Manageability:** Object-based storage has an inherent intelligence to manage and protect objects. It uses self-healing capability to protect and replicate objects. Policy-based management capability helps OSD to handle routine jobs automatically.

## 8.1.5 Common Use Cases for Object-Based Storage

A data archival solution is a promising use case for OSD. Data integrity and protection is the primary requirement for any data archiving solution. Traditional archival solutions — CD and DVD-ROM — do not provide scalability and performance. OSD stores data in the form of objects, associates them with a unique object ID, and ensures high data integrity. Along with integrity, it provides scalability and data protection. These capabilities make OSD a viable option for long term data archiving for fixed content. Content addressed storage (CAS) is a special type of object-based storage device purposely built for storing fixed content. CAS is covered in the following section.

Another use case for OSD is cloud-based storage. OSD uses a web interface to access storage resources. OSD provides inherent security, scalability, and automated data management. It also enables data sharing across heterogeneous platforms or tenants while ensuring integrity of data. These capabilities make OSD a strong option for cloud-based storage. Cloud service providers can leverage OSD to offer storage-as-a-service.

OSD supports web service access via *representational state transfer* (REST) and *simple object access protocol* (SOAP). REST and SOAP APIs can be easily integrated with business applications that access OSD over the web.

## REST AND SOAP

 REST is an architectural style developed for modern web applications. REST provides lightweight web services to access resources (for example, documents, blogs, and so on) on which a few basic operations can be performed, such as retrieving, modifying, creating, and deleting resources. REST-style web services are resource-oriented services. Resources can be uniquely located and identified by a Universal Resource Identifier (URI), and operations can be performed on those resources using an HTTP specification. For example, if a user accesses a blog using REST via a unique identifier, the request returns the representation of the blog in a particular format (XML or HTML).

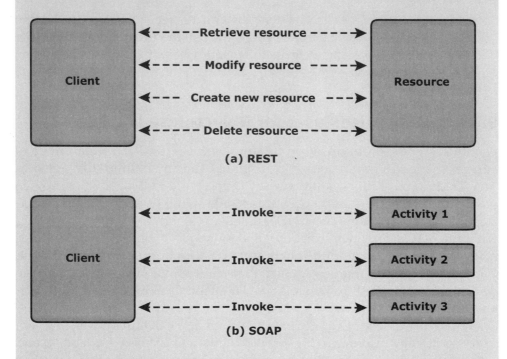

SOAP is an XML-based protocol that enables communication between the web applications running on different OSes and based on different programming languages. SOAP provides processes to encode HTTP headers and XML files to enable and pass information between different computers.

# 8.2 Content-Addressed Storage

CAS is an object-based storage device designed for secure online storage and retrieval of fixed content. CAS stores user data and its attributes as an object. The stored object is assigned a globally unique address, known as a *content address* (CA). This address is derived from the object's binary representation. CAS provides an optimized and centrally managed storage solution. Data access in CAS differs from other OSD devices. In CAS, the application server access the CAS device only via the CAS API running on the application server. However, the way CAS stores data is similar to the other OSD systems.

CAS provides all the features required for storing fixed content. The key features of CAS are as follows:

- **Content authenticity:** It assures the genuineness of stored content. This is achieved by generating a unique content address for each object and validating the content address for stored objects at regular intervals. Content authenticity is assured because the address assigned to each object is as unique as a fingerprint. Every time an object is read, CAS uses a hashing algorithm to recalculate the object's content address as a validation step and compares the result to its original content address. If the object fails validation, CAS rebuilds the object using a mirror or parity protection scheme.

- **Content integrity:** It provides assurance that the stored content has not been altered. CAS uses a hashing algorithm for content authenticity and integrity. If the fixed content is altered, CAS generates a new address for the altered content, rather than overwrite the original fixed content.

- **Location independence:** CAS uses a unique content address, rather than directory path names or URLs, to retrieve data. This makes the physical location of the stored data irrelevant to the application that requests the data.

- **Single-instance storage (SIS):** CAS uses a unique content address to guarantee the storage of only a single instance of an object. When a new object is written, the CAS system is polled to see whether an object is already available with the same content address. If the object is available in the system, it is not stored; instead, only a pointer to that object is created.

- **Retention enforcement:** Protecting and retaining objects is a core requirement of an archive storage system. After an object is stored in the CAS system and the retention policy is defined, CAS does not make the object available for deletion until the policy expires.

- **Data protection:** CAS ensures that the content stored on the CAS system is available even if a disk or a node fails. CAS provides both local and remote protection to the data objects stored on it. In the local protection option, data objects are either mirrored or parity protected. In mirror protection, two copies of the data object are stored on two different nodes in the same cluster. This decreases the total available capacity by 50 percent. In parity protection, the data object is split in multiple parts and parity is generated from them. Each part of the data and its parity are stored on a different node. This method consumes less capacity to protect the stored data, but takes slightly longer to regenerate the data if corruption of data occurs.

In the remote replication option, data objects are copied to a secondary CAS at the remote location. In this case, the objects remain accessible from the secondary CAS if the primary CAS system fails.

- **Fast record retrieval:** CAS stores all objects on disks, which provides faster access to the objects compared to tapes and optical discs.
- **Load balancing:** CAS distributes objects across multiple nodes to provide maximum throughput and availability.
- **Scalability:** CAS allows the addition of more nodes to the cluster without any interruption to data access and with minimum administrative overhead.
- **Event notification:** CAS continuously monitors the state of the system and raises an alert for any event that requires the administrator's attention. The event notification is communicated to the administrator through SNMP, SMTP, or e-mail.
- **Self diagnosis and repair:** CAS automatically detects and repairs corrupted objects and alerts the administrator about the potential problem. CAS systems can be configured to alert remote support teams who can diagnose and repair the system remotely.
- **Audit trails:** CAS keeps track of management activities and any access or disposition of data. Audit trails are mandated by compliance requirements.

## 8.3 CAS Use Cases

Organizations have deployed CAS solutions to solve several business challenges. Two solutions are described in detail in the following sections.

### 8.3.1 Healthcare Solution: Storing Patient Studies

Large healthcare centers examine hundreds of patients every day and generate large volumes of medical records. Each record might be composed of one or more images that range in size from approximately 15 MB for a standard digital X-ray to more than 1 GB for oncology studies. The patient records are stored online for a specific period of time for immediate use by the attending physicians. Even if a patient's record is no longer needed, compliance requirements might stipulate that the records be kept in the original format for several years.

Medical image solution providers offer hospitals the capability to view medical records, such as X-ray images, with acceptable response times and resolution to enable rapid assessments of patients. Figure 8-7 illustrates the use of CAS in this scenario. Patients' records are retained on the primary storage for 60 days after which they are moved to the CAS system. CAS facilitates long-term storage and at the same time, provides immediate access to data, when needed.

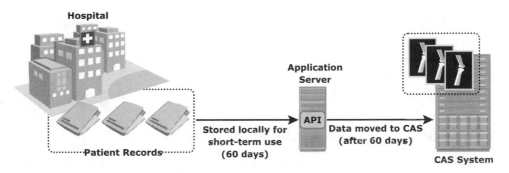

**Figure 8-7:** Storing patient studies on a CAS system

## 8.3.2 Finance Solution: Storing Financial Records

In a typical banking scenario, images of checks, each approximately 25 KB in size, are created and sent to archive services over an IP network. A check imaging service provider might process approximately 90 million check images per month. Typically, check images are actively processed in transactional systems for about 5 days.

For the next 60 days, check images may be requested by banks or individual consumers for verification purposes; beyond 60 days, access requirements drop drastically. Figure 8-8 illustrates the use of CAS in this scenario. The check images are moved from the primary storage to the CAS system after 60 days, and can be held there for long term based on retention policy. Check imaging is one example of a financial service application that is best serviced with CAS. Customer transactions initiated by e-mail, contracts, and security transaction records might need to be kept online for 30 years; CAS is the preferred storage solution in such cases.

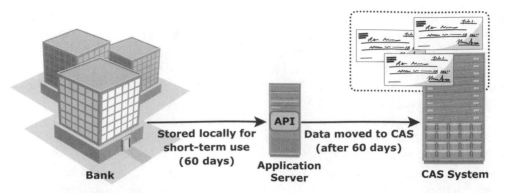

**Figure 8-8:** Storing financial records on a CAS system

# 8.4 Unified Storage

Unified storage consolidates block, file, and object access into one storage solution. It supports multiple protocols, such as CIFS, NFS, iSCSI, FC, FCoE, REST (representational state transfer), and SOAP (simple object access protocol).

## 8.4.1 Components of Unified Storage

A unified storage system consists of the following key components: storage controller, NAS head, OSD node, and storage. Figure 8-9 illustrates the block diagram of a unified storage platform.

The *storage controller* provides block-level access to application servers through iSCSI, FC, or FCoE protocols. It contains iSCSI, FC, and FCoE front-end ports for direct block access. The storage controller is also responsible for managing the back-end storage pool in the storage system. The controller configures LUNs and presents them to application servers, NAS heads, and OSD nodes. The LUNs presented to the application server appear as local physical disks. A file system is configured on these LUNs and is made available to applications for storing data.

A *NAS head* is a dedicated file server that provides file access to NAS clients. The NAS head is connected to the storage via the storage controller typically using a FC or FCoE connection. The system typically has two or more NAS heads for redundancy. The LUNs presented to the NAS head appear as physical disks. The NAS head configures the file systems on these disks, creates a NFS, CIFS, or mixed share, and exports the share to the NAS clients.

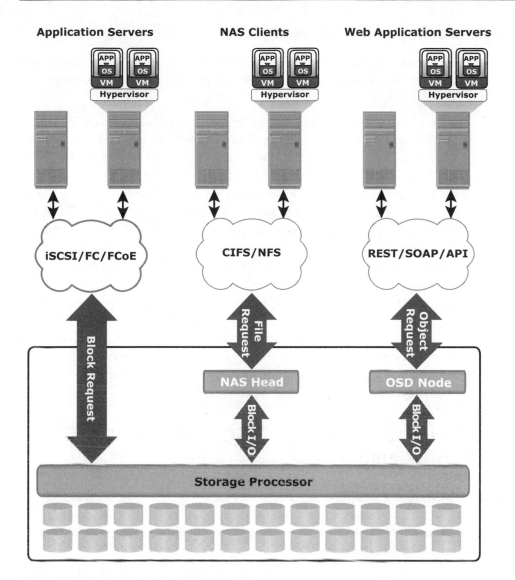

**Figure 8-9:** Unified storage platform

The *OSD node* accesses the storage through the storage controller using a FC or FCoE connection. The LUNs assigned to the OSD node appear as physical disks. These disks are configured by the OSD nodes, enabling them to store the data from the web application servers.

### Data Access from Unified Storage

In a unified storage system, block, file, and object requests to the storage travel through different I/O paths. Figure 8-9 illustrates the different I/O paths for block, file, and object access.

- **Block I/O request:** The application servers are connected to an FC, iSCSI, or FCoE port on the storage controller. The server sends a block request over an FC, iSCSI, or FCoE connection. The storage processor (SP) processes the I/O and responds to the application server.

- **File I/O request:** The NAS clients (where the NAS share is mounted or mapped) send a file request to the NAS head using the NFS or CIFS protocol. The NAS head receives the request, converts it into a block request, and forwards it to the storage controller. Upon receiving the block data from the storage controller, the NAS head again converts the block request back to the file request and sends it to the clients.

- **Object I/O request:** The web application servers send an object request, typically using REST or SOAP protocols, to the OSD node. The OSD node receives the request, converts it into a block request, and sends it to the disk through the storage controller. The controller in turn processes the block request and responds back to the OSD node, which in turn provides the requested object to the web application server.

## 8.5 Concepts in Practice: EMC Atmos, EMC VNX, and EMC Centera

EMC Atmos supports object-based storage for unstructured data, such as pictures and videos. Atmos combines massive scalability with specialized intelligence to address the cost, distribution, and management challenges associated with vast amounts of unstructured data.

EMC VNX is a unified storage platform that consolidates block, file, and object access in one solution. It implements a modular architecture that integrates hardware components for block, file, and object access. EMC VNX delivers file access (NAS) functionality via X-Blades (Data Movers) and block access functionality via storage processors. Optionally, it offers object access to the storage using EMC Atmos Virtual Edition (Atmos VE).

EMC Centera is a simple, affordable, and secure repository for information archiving. EMC Centera is designed and optimized specifically to deal with the storage and retrieval of fixed content by meeting performance, compliance, and regulatory requirements. Compared to traditional archive storage, EMC Centera provides faster record retrieval, Single instance storage (SIS), guaranteed content authenticity, self-healing, and support for numerous industry and regulatory standards.

For the latest information on EMC Atmos, EMC VNX, and EMC Centera, visit www.emc.com.

## 8.5.1 EMC Atmos

Atmos can be deployed in two ways: as a purpose-built hardware appliance or as software in VMware environments, where AtmosVE can leverage the existing servers and storage.

Figure 8-10 illustrates the EMC Atmos hardware appliance. The hardware appliance is comprised of servers (nodes) connected to standard disk enclosures. The rack includes a 24-port Gigabit Ethernet switch to provide internode communication. The Atmos software is installed on each node.

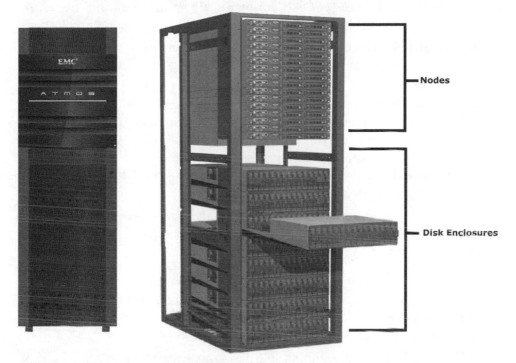

**Figure 8-10:** EMC Atmos storage system

Atmos VE enables users to exploit the power of Atmos in a virtualized environment. It can be deployed on a virtual machine in VMware ESXi hosts and configured with the VMware certified back-end storage.

Following are the key features offered by EMC Atmos:

- **Policy-based management:** EMC Atmos improves operational efficiency by automatically distributing content based on business policy. The administrator-defined policies dictate how, when, and where the information resides.

- **Protection:** Atmos offers two options to protect the objects, replication and Geo Parity:

  - *Replication* ensures that the content is available and accessible by creating redundant copies of an object at redundant designated locations.

  - *Geo Parity* ensures that the content is available and accessible by dividing objects into multiple segments plus parity segments and distributing them to one or more designated locations.

- **Data services:** EMC Atmos includes the data services, such as compression and deduplication. These features are native to Atmos and can be managed and accessed via a policy.

- **Web services and legacy protocols:** EMC Atmos provides flexible web services access (REST/SOAP) for web-scale applications and file access (CIFS/NFS/Installable File System/Centera API) for traditional applications.

- **Automated system management:** EMC Atmos provides auto-configuring, auto-managing, and auto-healing capabilities to reduce administration and downtime.

- **Multitenancy:** EMC Atmos enables multiple applications to be served from the same infrastructure. Each application is securely partitioned and cannot access the other application's data. Multitenancy is ideal for service providers or large enterprises that want to provide cloud computing services to multiple customers or departments allowing logical and secure separation within a single infrastructure.

- **Flexible administration:** EMC Atmos can be managed via a graphical user interface (GUI) or command-line interface (CLI).

## 8.5.2 EMC VNX

VNX is EMC's unified storage product offering. Figure 8-11 illustrates the EMC VNX storage array.

VNX storage systems include the following components:

- *Storage processors* (SPs) support block I/O access to storage with FC, iSCSI, and FCoE protocols.

- *X-Blades* access data from the back end and provide host access with NFS, CIFS, MPFS, pNFS, and FTP protocols. The X-Blades in each array are scalable and provide redundancy to ensure no single point of failure.

- *Control Stations* provide management functions to the X-Blades. The Control Station is also responsible for X-Blade failover. The Control Station may optionally be configured with a matching secondary Control Station to ensure management redundancy on the VNX array.

- *Standby power supplies* provide enough power to each storage processor and first DAE to ensure that any data in flight is stored in the vault area if a power failure occurs. This ensures that no writes are lost.

- *Disk-array enclosures* (DAEs) house the drives used in the array. Different sized DAEs are available that can each hold a maximum of 15, 25, or 60 drives. More DAEs can be added to meet growing storage demands.

**Figure 8-11:** EMC VNX storage system

## 8.5.3 EMC Centera

EMC Centera is offered in three different models to meet different types of user requirements — EMC Centera Basic, EMC Centera Governance Edition, and EMC Centera Compliance Edition Plus (CE+):

- **EMC Centera Basic:** Provides all functionalities without the enforcement of retention periods.

■ **EMC Centera Governance Edition:** Provides the retention capabilities required by organizations to manage digital records in addition to the features provided by EMC Centera Basic.

■ **EMC Centera Compliance Edition Plus:** Provides extensive compliance capabilities. CE+ is designed to meet the requirements of the most stringent regulated business environments for electronic storage media, as established by regulations from the Securities and Exchange Commission (SEC), or other national and international regulatory groups.

### EMC Centera Architecture

The Centera architecture is shown in Figure 8-12. A client accesses the Centera over a LAN. The client can access Centera only through the server that runs the Centera API (application programming interface). The Centera API is responsible for performing functions that enable an application to store and retrieve the data.

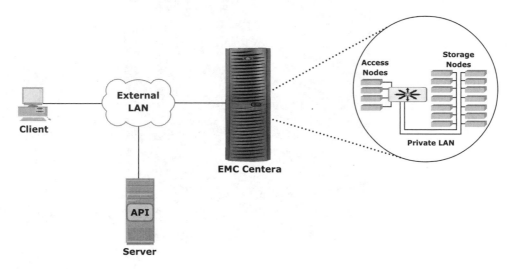

**Figure 8-12:** Centera architecture

Centera architecture is a *Redundant Array of Independent Nodes* (RAIN). It contains storage nodes and access nodes that are networked as a cluster by using a private LAN. The internal LAN reconfigures automatically when it detects configuration changes, such as the addition of storage or access nodes. The application server accesses the Centera via an external LAN.

The nodes are configured with low-cost, high-capacity SATA disk drives. These nodes run CentraStar, the operating environment for Centera, which provides the features and functionalities required in a Centera system.

When nodes are installed, they are configured with a "role" that defines the functionality provided to the node. A node can be configured as a storage node, an access node, or a dual-role node.

*Storage nodes* store and protect data objects. They are sometimes referred to as *back-end nodes*.

*Access nodes* provide connectivity to application servers through an external LAN. They establish connectivity with the storage nodes in the cluster through a private LAN. The number of access nodes is determined by the amount of throughput required from the cluster. If a node is configured solely as an "access node," its disk space cannot be used to store data objects. Storage and retrieval requests are sent to the access node via the external LAN.

*Dual-role nodes* provide both storage and access-node capabilities. This configuration is more common than a pure access-node configuration.

## Summary

Object-based storage systems are a potential solution for storing ever-growing unstructured data. They also provide a solution for long-term retention of data to meet compliance regulations. An object's attributes enable automated policy-based management of data. The features of OSD also make it an attractive solution for cloud deployments. This chapter covered the OSD architecture, its components, operation, and content-addressed storage.

This chapter also covered unified storage that allows block, file, and object access to data through a single solution. This solution offers low cost of ownership while providing storage access to different applications. This chapter covered the components of unified storage and the processes of accessing the data from the system.

Modern storage systems are equipped with capabilities that can ensure performance, capacity, and protection of the system. These systems have built-in redundancy to avoid any disruption due to a single component failure. However, resources and data are still vulnerable to natural disasters and other planned and unplanned outages, which can affect data availability. The next chapter covers business continuity and describes disaster recovery solutions that ensure high availability and uninterrupted business operations.

**EXERCISES**

1. Discuss the object storage and retrieval process in an OSD system.

2. Explain the storage and retrieval process for block, file, and object access in a unified storage system.

3. Research and prepare a presentation to demonstrate a scenario in which object-based storage is a better choice over SAN and NAS.

4. Research REST and SOAP and their implementations.

5. When is unified storage a suitable option for a data center? Justify your answer by comparing the unified storage offering with traditional storage solutions.

**Section**

**III**

# Backup, Archive, and Replication

## In This Section

# Chapter 9
# Introduction to Business Continuity

In today's world, continuous access to information is a must for the smooth functioning of business operations. The cost of unavailability of information is greater than ever, and outages in key industries cost millions of dollars per hour. There are many threats to information availability, such as natural disasters, unplanned occurrences, and planned occurrences, that could result in the inaccessibility of information. Therefore it is critical for businesses to define an appropriate strategy that can help them overcome these crises. Business continuity is an important process to define and implement these strategies.

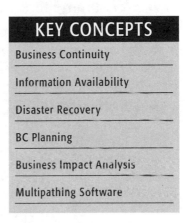

**KEY CONCEPTS**

Business Continuity

Information Availability

Disaster Recovery

BC Planning

Business Impact Analysis

Multipathing Software

*Business continuity* (BC) is an integrated and enterprise-wide process that includes all activities (internal and external to IT) that a business must perform to mitigate the impact of planned and unplanned downtime. BC entails preparing for, responding to, and recovering from a system outage that adversely affects business operations. It involves proactive measures, such as business impact analysis, risk assessments, BC technology solutions deployment (backup and replication), and reactive measures, such as disaster recovery and restart, to be invoked in the event of a failure. The goal of a BC solution is to ensure the "information availability" required to conduct vital business operations.

In a virtualized environment, BC technology solutions need to protect both physical and virtualized resources. Virtualization considerably simplifies the implementation of BC strategy and solutions.

This chapter describes the factors that affect information availability and the consequences of information unavailability. It also explains the key parameters that govern any BC strategy and the roadmap to develop an effective BC plan.

# 9.1 Information Availability

*Information availability* (IA) refers to the ability of an IT infrastructure to function according to business expectations during its specified time of operation. IA ensures that people (employees, customers, suppliers, and partners) can access information whenever they need it. IA can be defined in terms of accessibility, reliability, and timeliness of information.

- **Accessibility:** Information should be accessible at the right place, to the right user.

- **Reliability:** Information should be reliable and correct in all aspects. It is "the same" as what was stored, and there is no alteration or corruption to the information.

- **Timeliness:** Defines the exact moment or the time window (a particular time of the day, week, month, and year as specified) during which information must be accessible. For example, if online access to an application is required between 8:00 a.m. and 10:00 p.m. each day, any disruptions to data availability outside of this time slot are not considered to affect timeliness.

## 9.1.1 Causes of Information Unavailability

Various planned and unplanned incidents result in information unavailability. *Planned outages* include installation/integration/maintenance of new hardware, software upgrades or patches, taking backups, application and data restores, facility operations (renovation and construction), and refresh/migration of the testing to the production environment. *Unplanned outages* include failure caused by human errors, database corruption, and failure of physical and virtual components.

Another type of incident that may cause data unavailability is natural or man-made disasters, such as flood, fire, earthquake, and contamination. As illustrated in Figure 9-1, the majority of outages are planned. Planned outages are expected and scheduled but still cause data to be unavailable. Statistically, the cause of information unavailability due to unforeseen disasters is less than 1 percent.

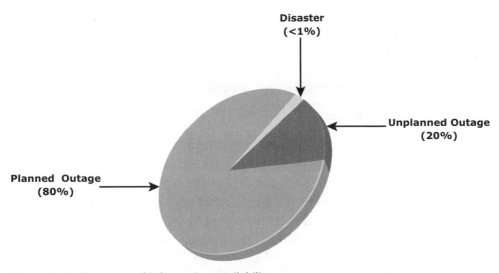

**Figure 9-1:** Disruptors of information availability

## 9.1.2 Consequences of Downtime

Information unavailability or downtime results in loss of productivity, loss of revenue, poor financial performance, and damage to reputation. Loss of productivity includes reduced output per unit of labor, equipment, and capital. Loss of revenue includes direct loss, compensatory payments, future revenue loss, billing loss, and investment loss. Poor financial performance affects revenue recognition, cash flow, discounts, payment guarantees, credit rating, and stock price. Damages to reputations may result in a loss of confidence or credibility with customers, suppliers, financial markets, banks, and business partners. Other possible consequences of downtime include the cost of additional equipment rental, overtime, and extra shipping

The business impact of downtime is the sum of all losses sustained as a result of a given disruption. An important metric, *average cost of downtime per hour*, provides a key estimate in determining the appropriate BC solutions. It is calculated as follows:

Average cost of downtime per hour = average productivity loss
per hour + average revenue loss per hour

Where:

Productivity loss per hour = (total salaries and benefits of all employees
per week)/(average number of working hours per week)

Average revenue loss per hour = (total revenue of an organization
per week)/(average number of hours per week that
an organization is open for business)

The average downtime cost per hour may also include estimates of projected revenue loss due to other consequences, such as damaged reputations, and the additional cost of repairing the system.

### 9.1.3 Measuring Information Availability

IA relies on the availability of both physical and virtual components of a data center. Failure of these components might disrupt IA. A failure is the termination of a component's capability to perform a required function. The component's capability can be restored by performing an external corrective action, such as a manual reboot, repair, or replacement of the failed component(s). Repair involves restoring a component to a condition that enables it to perform a required function. Proactive risk analysis, performed as part of the BC planning process, considers the component failure rate and average repair time, which are measured by mean time between failure (MTBF) and mean time to repair (MTTR):

- **Mean Time Between Failure (MTBF):** It is the average time available for a system or component to perform its normal operations between failures. It is the measure of system or component reliability and is usually expressed in hours.

- **Mean Time To Repair (MTTR):** It is the average time required to repair a failed component. While calculating MTTR, it is assumed that the fault responsible for the failure is correctly identified and the required spares and personnel are available. A fault is a physical defect at the component level, which may result in information unavailability. MTTR includes the total time required to do the following activities: Detect the fault, mobilize the maintenance team, diagnose the fault, obtain the spare parts, repair, test, and restore the data. Figure 9-2 illustrates the various information availability metrics that represent system uptime and downtime.

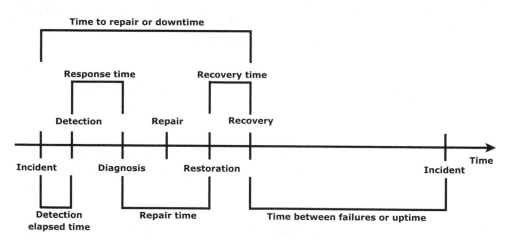

**Figure 9-2:** Information availability metrics

IA is the time period during which a system is in a condition to perform its intended function upon demand. It can be expressed in terms of system uptime and downtime and measured as the amount or percentage of system uptime:

IA = system uptime/(system uptime + system downtime)

Where *system uptime* is the period of time during which the system is in an accessible state; when it is not accessible, it is termed as *system downtime*. In terms of MTBF and MTTR, IA could also be expressed as

IA = MTBF/(MTBF + MTTR)

Uptime per year is based on the exact timeliness requirements of the service. This calculation leads to the number of "9s" representation for availability metrics. Table 9-1 lists the approximate amount of downtime allowed for a service to achieve certain levels of 9s availability.

For example, a service that is said to be "five 9s available" is available for 99.999 percent of the scheduled time in a year (24 × 365).

**Table 9-1:** Availability Percentage and Allowable Downtime

| UPTIME (%) | DOWNTIME (%) | DOWNTIME PER YEAR | DOWNTIME PER WEEK |
|---|---|---|---|
| 98 | 2 | 7.3 days | 3 hr, 22 minutes |
| 99 | 1 | 3.65 days | 1 hr, 41 minutes |
| 99.8 | 0.2 | 17 hr, 31 minutes | 20 minutes, 10 secs |
| 99.9 | 0.1 | 8 hr, 45 minutes | 10 minutes, 5 secs |
| 99.99 | 0.01 | 52.5 minutes | 1 minute |
| 99.999 | 0.001 | 5.25 minutes | 6 secs |
| 99.9999 | 0.0001 | 31.5 secs | 0.6 secs |

# 9.2 BC Terminology

This section introduces and defines common terms related to BC operations, which are used in the next few chapters to explain advanced concepts:

- **Disaster recovery:** This is the coordinated process of restoring systems, data, and the infrastructure required to support ongoing business operations after a disaster occurs. It is the process of restoring a previous copy of the data and applying logs or other necessary processes to that copy to bring it to a known point of consistency. After all recovery efforts are completed, the data is validated to ensure that it is correct.

- **Disaster restart:** This is the process of restarting business operations with mirrored consistent copies of data and applications.

- **Recovery-Point Objective (RPO):** This is the point in time to which systems and data must be recovered after an outage. It defines the amount of data loss that a business can endure. A large RPO signifies high tolerance to information loss in a business. Based on the RPO, organizations plan for the frequency with which a backup or replica must be made. For example, if the RPO is 6 hours, backups or replicas must be made at least once in 6 hours. Figure 9-3 (a) shows various RPOs and their corresponding ideal recovery strategies. An organization can plan for an appropriate BC technology solution on the basis of the RPO it sets. For example:

  - **RPO of 24 hours:** Backups are created at an offsite tape library every midnight. The corresponding recovery strategy is to restore data from the set of last backup tapes.

  - **RPO of 1 hour:** Shipping database logs to the remote site every hour. The corresponding recovery strategy is to recover the database to the point of the last log shipment.

  - **RPO in the order of minutes:** Mirroring data asynchronously to a remote site

  - **Near zero RPO:** Mirroring data synchronously to a remote site

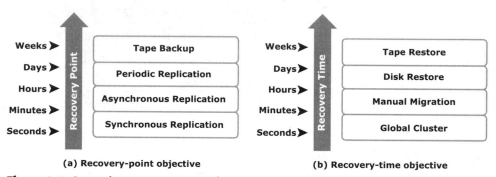

**(a) Recovery-point objective**　　　　　**(b) Recovery-time objective**

**Figure 9-3:** Strategies to meet RPO and RTO targets

- **Recovery-Time Objective (RTO):** The time within which systems and applications must be recovered after an outage. It defines the amount of downtime that a business can endure and survive. Businesses can optimize disaster recovery plans after defining the RTO for a given system. For example, if the RTO is 2 hours, it requires disk-based backup because it enables a faster restore than a tape backup. However, for an RTO of 1 week, tape backup will likely meet the requirements. Some examples of RTOs and the recovery strategies to ensure data availability are listed here (refer to Figure 9-3 [b]):

- **RTO of 72 hours:** Restore from tapes available at a cold site.

- **RTO of 12 hours:** Restore from tapes available at a hot site.

- **RTO of few hours:** Use of data vault at a hot site

- **RTO of a few seconds:** Cluster production servers with bidirectional mirroring, enabling the applications to run at both sites simultaneously.

- **Data vault:** A repository at a remote site where data can be periodically or continuously copied (either to tape drives or disks) so that there is always a copy at another site

- **Hot site:** A site where an enterprise's operations can be moved in the event of disaster. It is a site with the required hardware, operating system, application, and network support to perform business operations, where the equipment is available and running at all times.

- **Cold site:** A site where an enterprise's operations can be moved in the event of disaster, with minimum IT infrastructure and environmental facilities in place, but not activated

- **Server Clustering:** A group of servers and other necessary resources coupled to operate as a single system. Clusters can ensure high availability and load balancing. Typically, in failover clusters, one server runs an application and updates the data, and another server is kept as standby to take over completely, as required. In more sophisticated clusters, multiple servers may access data, and typically one server is kept as standby. Server clustering provides load balancing by distributing the application load evenly among multiple servers within the cluster.

## 9.3 BC Planning Life Cycle

BC planning must follow a disciplined approach like any other planning process. Organizations today dedicate specialized resources to develop and maintain BC plans. From the conceptualization to the realization of the BC plan, a life cycle of activities can be defined for the BC process. The BC planning life cycle includes five stages (see Figure 9-4):

1. Establishing objectives

2. Analyzing

3. Designing and developing

4. Implementing

5. Training, testing, assessing, and maintaining

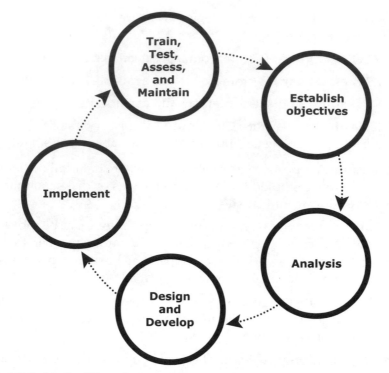

**Figure 9-4:** BC planning life cycle

Several activities are performed at each stage of the BC planning life cycle, including the following key activities:

1. Establish objectives:

   ▪ Determine BC requirements.

   ▪ Estimate the scope and budget to achieve requirements.

   ▪ Select a BC team that includes subject matter experts from all areas of the business, whether internal or external.

   ▪ Create BC policies.

2. Analysis:

   ▪ Collect information on data profiles, business processes, infrastructure support, dependencies, and frequency of using business infrastructure.

   ▪ Conduct a Business Impact Analysis (BIA).

   ▪ Identify critical business processes and assign recovery priorities.

   ▪ Perform risk analysis for critical functions and create mitigation strategies.

- Perform cost benefit analysis for available solutions based on the mitigation strategy.
- Evaluate options.

3. Design and develop:
   - Define the team structure and assign individual roles and responsibilities. For example, different teams are formed for activities, such as emergency response, damage assessment, and infrastructure and application recovery.
   - Design data protection strategies and develop infrastructure.
   - Develop contingency solutions.
   - Develop emergency response procedures.
   - Detail recovery and restart procedures.

4. Implement:
   - Implement risk management and mitigation procedures that include backup, replication, and management of resources.
   - Prepare the disaster recovery sites that can be utilized if a disaster affects the primary data center.
   - Implement redundancy for every resource in a data center to avoid single points of failure.

5. Train, test, assess, and maintain:
   - Train the employees who are responsible for backup and replication of business-critical data on a regular basis or whenever there is a modification in the BC plan.
   - Train employees on emergency response procedures when disasters are declared.
   - Train the recovery team on recovery procedures based on contingency scenarios.
   - Perform damage-assessment processes and review recovery plans.
   - Test the BC plan regularly to evaluate its performance and identify its limitations.
   - Assess the performance reports and identify limitations.
   - Update the BC plans and recovery/restart procedures to reflect regular changes within the data center.

# 9.4 Failure Analysis

Failure analysis involves analyzing both the physical and virtual infrastructure components to identify systems that are susceptible to a single point of failure and implementing fault-tolerance mechanisms.

## 9.4.1 Single Point of Failure

A *single point of failure* refers to the failure of a component that can terminate the availability of the entire system or IT service. Figure 9-5 depicts a system setup in which an application, running on a VM, provides an interface to the client and performs I/O operations. The client is connected to the server through an IP network, and the server is connected to the storage array through an FC connection.

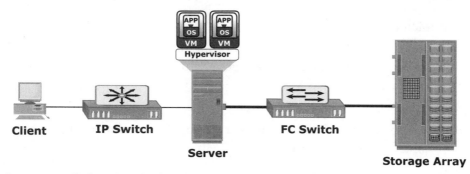

**Figure 9-5:** Single point of failure

In a setup in which each component must function as required to ensure data availability, the failure of a single physical or virtual component causes the unavailability of an application. This failure results in disruption of business operations. For example, failure of a hypervisor can affect all the running VMs and the virtual network, which are hosted on it. In the setup shown in Figure 9-5, several single points of failure can be identified. A VM, a hypervisor, an HBA/NIC on the server, the physical server, the IP network, the FC switch, the storage array ports, or even the storage array could be a potential single point of failure.

## 9.4.2 Resolving Single Points of Failure

To mitigate single points of failure, systems are designed with redundancy, such that the system fails only if all the components in the redundancy group fail. This ensures that the failure of a single component does not affect data availability. Data centers follow stringent guidelines to implement fault tolerance for uninterrupted information availability. Careful analysis is performed to eliminate every single point of failure. The example shown in Figure 9-6 represents all enhancements in the infrastructure to mitigate single points of failure:

- Configuration of redundant HBAs at a server to mitigate single HBA failure

- Configuration of NIC teaming at a server allows protection against single physical NIC failure. It allows grouping of two or more physical NICs and treating them as a single logical device. With NIC teaming, if one of the underlying physical NICs fails or its cable is unplugged, the traffic is redirected to another physical NIC in the team. Thus, NIC teaming eliminates the single point of failure associated with a single physical NIC.

- Configuration of redundant switches to account for a switch failure

- Configuration of multiple storage array ports to mitigate a port failure

- RAID and hot spare configuration to ensure continuous operation in the event of disk failure

- Implementation of a redundant storage array at a remote site to mitigate local site failure

- Implementing server (or compute) clustering, a fault-tolerance mechanism whereby two or more servers in a cluster access the same set of data volumes. Clustered servers exchange a *heartbeat* to inform each other about their health. If one of the servers or hypervisors fails, the other server or hypervisor can take up the workload.

- Implementing a VM Fault Tolerance mechanism ensures BC in the event of a server failure. This technique creates duplicate copies of each VM on another server so that when a VM failure is detected, the duplicate VM can be used for failover. The two VMs are kept in synchronization with each other in order to perform successful failover.

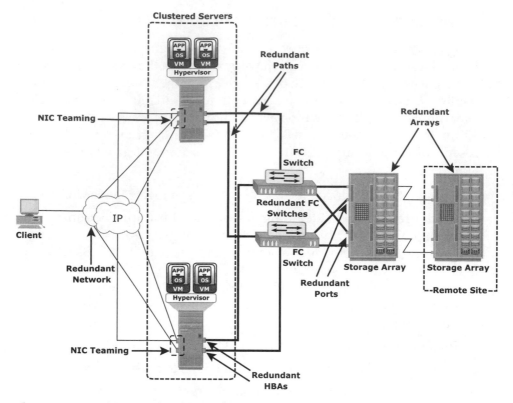

**Figure 9-6:** Resolving single points of failure

## 9.4.3 Multipathing Software

Configuration of multiple paths increases the data availability through path failover. If servers are configured with one I/O path to the data, there will be no access to the data if that path fails. Redundant paths to the data eliminate the possibility of the path becoming a single point of failure. Multiple paths to data also improve I/O performance through load balancing among the paths and maximize server, storage, and data path utilization.

In practice, merely configuring multiple paths does not serve the purpose. Even with multiple paths, if one path fails, I/O does not reroute unless the system recognizes that it has an alternative path. Multipathing software provides the functionality to recognize and utilize alternative I/O paths to data. Multipathing software also manages the load balancing by distributing I/Os to all available, active paths.

Multipathing software intelligently manages the paths to a device by sending I/O down the optimal path based on the load balancing and failover policy setting for the device. It also takes into account path usage and availability before deciding the path through which to send the I/O. If a path to the device fails, it automatically reroutes the I/O to an alternative path.

In a virtual environment, multipathing is enabled either by using the hypervisor's built-in capability or by running a third-party software module, added to the hypervisor.

## 9.5 Business Impact Analysis

A *business impact analysis* (BIA) identifies which business units, operations, and processes are essential to the survival of the business. It evaluates the financial, operational, and service impacts of a disruption to essential business processes. Selected functional areas are evaluated to determine resilience of the infrastructure to support information availability. The BIA process leads to a report detailing the incidents and their impact over business functions. The impact may be specified in terms of money or in terms of time. Based on the potential impacts associated with downtime, businesses can prioritize and implement countermeasures to mitigate the likelihood of such disruptions. These are detailed in the BC plan. A BIA includes the following set of tasks:

- Determine the business areas.
- For each business area, identify the key business processes critical to its operation.
- Determine the attributes of the business process in terms of applications, databases, and hardware and software requirements.
- Estimate the costs of failure for each business process.
- Calculate the maximum tolerable outage and define RTO and RPO for each business process.
- Establish the minimum resources required for the operation of business processes.
- Determine recovery strategies and the cost for implementing them.
- Optimize the backup and business recovery strategy based on business priorities.
- Analyze the current state of BC readiness and optimize future BC planning.

## 9.6 BC Technology Solutions

After analyzing the business impact of an outage, designing the appropriate solutions to recover from a failure is the next important activity. One or more copies of the data are maintained using any of the following strategies so that data can be recovered or business operations can be restarted using an alternative copy:

- **Backup:** Data backup is a predominant method of ensuring data availability. The frequency of backup is determined based on RPO, RTO, and the frequency of data changes.

- **Local replication:** Data can be replicated to a separate location within the same storage array. The replica is used independently for other business operations. Replicas can also be used for restoring operations if data corruption occurs.

- **Remote replication:** Data in a storage array can be replicated to another storage array located at a remote site. If the storage array is lost due to a disaster, business operations can be started from the remote storage array.

# 9.7 Concept in Practice: EMC PowerPath

EMC PowerPath is host-based multipathing software that provides path failover and load-balancing functionality for SAN environments. PowerPath resides between the operating system and device drivers. EMC PowerPath/VE software allows optimizing virtual environments with PowerPath multipathing features.

Refer to www.emc.com for the latest information.

## 9.7.1 PowerPath Features

PowerPath provides the following features:

- **Dynamic path configuration and management:** PowerPath provides the flexibility to define some paths to a device as "active" and some as "standby." The standby paths are used when all active paths to a logical device have failed. Paths can be dynamically added and removed by setting them in standby or active mode.

- **Dynamic load balancing across multiple paths:** PowerPath intelligently distributes I/O requests across all available paths to the logical storage device. This reduces path bottlenecks and improves application performance.

- **Automatic path failover:** In the event of a path failure, PowerPath fails over seamlessly to an alternative path without disrupting application operations. PowerPath redistributes I/O to the best available path to achieve optimal host performance.

- **Proactive path testing and automatic path recovery:** PowerPath uses the autoprobe and autorestore functions to proactively test the dead and restored paths, respectively. The PowerPath *autoprobe* function periodically probes all the paths to check failed paths before sending the application I/O. This process enables PowerPath to proactively close paths before an application experiences a timeout when sending I/O over failed paths. The PowerPath *autorestore* function runs every 5 minutes and tests every failed or closed path to determine whether it has been restored.

- **Cluster support:** The deployment of PowerPath in a server cluster eliminates invoking cluster failover due to a path failure.

## 9.7.2 Dynamic Load Balancing

PowerPath provides significant performance improvement in environments where the I/O workload is not balanced. For every I/O, the PowerPath filter driver selects the path based on the load-balancing policy and failover setting for the logical storage device. The driver identifies all available paths to a device and builds a routing table, called a volume path set, for the devices. PowerPath supports certain user-specified load-balancing policies such as the following:

- **Round-Robin policy:** I/O requests are assigned to each available path in rotation.
- **Least I/Os policy:** I/O requests are routed to the path with the fewest queued I/O requests, regardless of the total number of I/O blocks.
- **Least Blocks policy:** I/O requests are routed to the path with the fewest queued I/O blocks, regardless of the number of requests involved.
- **Priority-Based policy:** I/O requests are balanced across multiple paths based on the composition of reads, writes, user-assigned devices, or application priorities.

### *I/O Operation without PowerPath*

Figure 9-7 illustrates I/O operations in a storage system in the absence of PowerPath. The applications running on a host have four paths to the storage array. This example illustrates how I/O throughput is unbalanced without PowerPath. Two paths get high I/O traffic and are highly loaded, whereas the other two paths are less loaded. As a result, applications cannot achieve optimal performance.

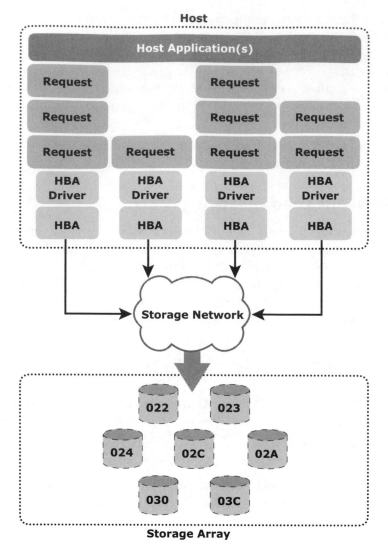

**Figure 9-7:** I/O without PowerPath

## I/O Operation with PowerPath

Figure 9-8 shows I/O operations in a storage system environment that has PowerPath. PowerPath ensures that I/O requests are balanced across all the paths to storage, based on the load-balancing algorithm chosen. As a result, the applications can effectively utilize all the paths, thereby improving their performance.

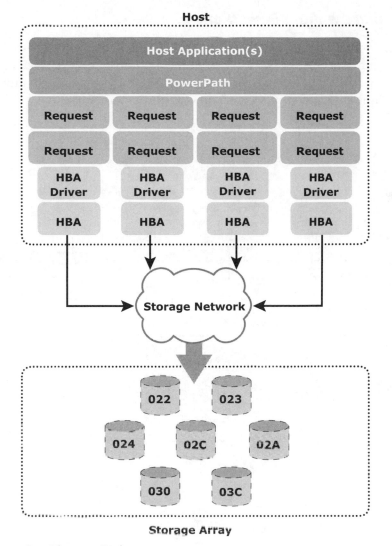

**Figure 9-8:** I/O with PowerPath

## 9.7.3 Automatic Path Failover

The next two examples demonstrate how PowerPath performs path failover operations if a path failure occurs for active-active and active-passive array configurations.

## Path Failure without PowerPath

Figure 9-9 shows a scenario without PowerPath. The loss of a path (the path failure is marked by a cross "X") due to single points of failure, such as the loss of an HBA, storage array front-end connectivity, switch port, or a failed cable, can result in an outage for one or more applications that use that path.

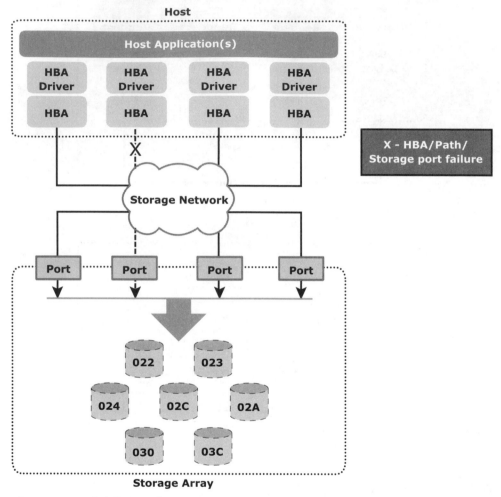

**Figure 9-9:** Path failure without PowerPath

## Path Failover with PowerPath: Active-Active Array

Figure 9-10 shows a storage system environment in which an application uses PowerPath with an active-active array configuration to perform I/O operations. In an active-active storage array, if multiple paths to a logical device exist, they all are active and provide access to the device. If a path to the device fails, PowerPath redirects the application I/Os through an alternative active path therefore preventing any application outage.

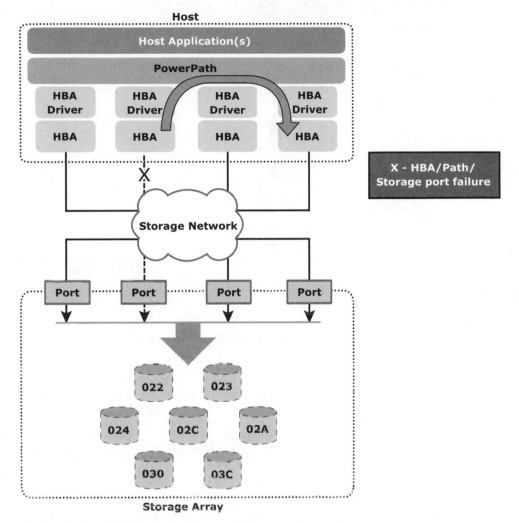

**Figure 9-10:** Path failover with PowerPath for an active-active array

## Path Failover with PowerPath: Active-Passive Array

Figure 9-11 shows a scenario in which a logical device is assigned to a storage processor B (SP B) and therefore, all I/Os are directed down the path through SP B to the device. The logical device can also be accessed through SP A but only after SP B is unavailable and the device is re-assigned to SP A.

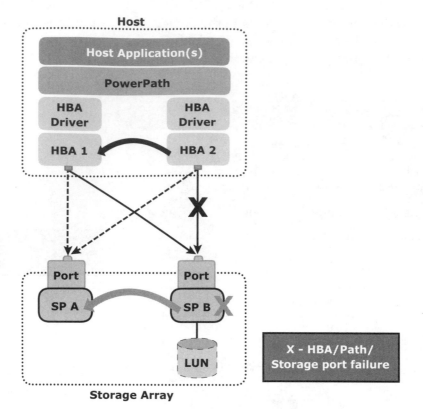

**Figure 9-11:** Path failover with PowerPath for an active-passive array

Path failure can occur due to a failure of the link, HBA, or storage processor (SP). If a path failure occurs, PowerPath with an active-passive configuration performs the path failover operation in the following way:

- If an I/O path to SP B either through HBA 2 or through HBA 1 fails, PowerPath uses the remaining available path to SP B to send all the I/Os.

- If SP B fails, PowerPath stops all I/O to SP B and *trespasses* the device over to SP A. All I/O is sent down the paths to SP A (paths which were previously standby but are now active for the given LUN). This process is referred as *LUN trespassing*. When SP B is brought back online, PowerPath recognizes that it is available and resumes sending I/O down to SP B after the LUN has been trespassed back to SP B.

# Summary

Technology innovations have led to a rich set of options in terms of storage devices and solutions to meet business continuity (BC) needs. The goal of any business continuity plan is to identify and implement the most appropriate risk management and risk mitigation procedures to protect against possible failures. The process of analyzing the hardware and software configuration to identify any single points of failure and their impact on business operations is critical. A business impact analysis (BIA) helps an organization to develop an appropriate BC plan. This plan ensures that the storage infrastructure and services are designed to meet business requirements. BC provides the framework for organizations to implement effective and cost-efficient disaster recovery and restart procedures in both physical and virtual environments. In a constantly changing business environment, BC can become a demanding endeavor.

The next three chapters discuss specific BC technology solutions, backup, local replication, and remote replication.

**EXERCISES**

1. A system has three components and requires all three to be operational 24 hours, Monday through Friday. Failure of component 1 occurs as follows:

   - ▪ Monday = No failure
   - ▪ Tuesday = 5 a.m. to 7 a.m.
   - ▪ Wednesday = No failure
   - ▪ Thursday = 4 p.m. to 8 p.m.
   - ▪ Friday = 8 a.m. to 11 a.m.

   Calculate the MTBF and MTTR of component 1.

2. A system has three components and requires all three to be operational during 8 a.m. to 5 p.m. business hours, Monday through Friday. Failure of component 2 occurs as follows:

   - ▪ Monday = 8 a.m. to 11 a.m.
   - ▪ Tuesday = No failure
   - ▪ Wednesday = 4 p.m. to 7 p.m.
   - ▪ Thursday = 5 p.m. to 8 p.m.
   - ▪ Friday = 1 p.m. to 2 p.m.

   Calculate the availability of component 2.

3. The IT department of a bank provide customers access to the currency conversion rate table between 9:00 a.m. and 4:00 p.m. from Monday through Friday. It updates the table every day at 8:00 a.m. with a feed from the mainframe system. The update process takes 35 minutes to complete. On Thursday, due to a database corruption, the rate table could not be updated. At 9:05 a.m., it was identified that the table had errors. A rerun of the update was done, and the table was re-created at 9:45 a.m. Verification was run for 15 minutes, and the rate table became available to the bank branches. What was the availability of the rate table for the week in which this incident took place, assuming there were no other issues?

4. Research various planned and unplanned occurances of information unavailability in the context of data center operations.

5. Research server clustering technology used in a data center.

6. Refer to the storage configuration shown in the following figure:

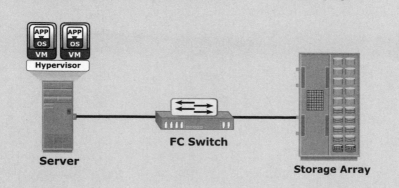

Perform the single point of failure analysis for this configuration and provide an alternative configuration that eliminates all single points of failure.

# Chapter 10
# Backup and Archive

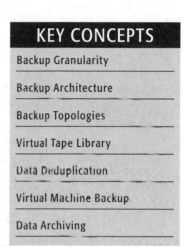

**KEY CONCEPTS**

Backup Granularity

Backup Architecture

Backup Topologies

Virtual Tape Library

Data Deduplication

Virtual Machine Backup

Data Archiving

A *backup* is an additional copy of production data, created and retained for the sole purpose of recovering lost or corrupted data. With growing business and regulatory demands for data storage, retention, and availability, organizations are faced with the task of backing up an ever-increasing amount of data. This task becomes more challenging with the growth of information, stagnant IT budgets, and less time for taking backups. Moreover, organizations need a quick restore of backed up data to meet business service-level agreements (SLAs).

Evaluating the various backup methods along with their recovery considerations and retention requirements is an essential step to implement a successful backup and recovery solution.

Organizations generate and maintain large volumes of data, and most of the data is fixed content. This fixed content is rarely accessed after a period of time. Still, this data needs to be retained for several years to meet regulatory compliance. Accumulation of this data on the primary storage increases the overall storage cost to the organization. Further, this increases the amount of data to be backed up, which in turn increases the time required to perform the backup.

*Data archiving* is the process of moving data that is no longer actively used, from primary storage to a low-cost secondary storage. The data is retained in the secondary storage for a long term to meet regulatory requirements. Moving the data from primary storage reduces the amount of data to be backed up. This reduces the time required to back up the data.

This chapter includes details about the purposes of the backup, backup and recovery considerations, backup methods, architecture, topologies, and backup targets. Backup optimization using data deduplication and backup in a virtualized environment are also covered in the chapter. Further, this chapter covers types of data archives and archiving solution architecture.

# 10.1 Backup Purpose

Backups are performed to serve three purposes: disaster recovery, operational recovery, and archival. These are covered in the following sections.

## 10.1.1 Disaster Recovery

One purpose of backups is to address disaster recovery needs. The backup copies are used for restoring data at an alternate site when the primary site is incapacitated due to a disaster. Based on recovery-point objective (RPO) and recovery-time objective (RTO) requirements, organizations use different data protection strategies for disaster recovery. When tape-based backup is used as a disaster recovery option, the backup tape media is shipped and stored at an offsite location. Later, these tapes can be recalled for restoration at the disaster recovery site. Organizations with stringent RPO and RTO requirements use remote replication technology to replicate data to a disaster recovery site. This allows organizations to bring production systems online in a relatively short period of time if a disaster occurs. Remote replication is covered in detail in Chapter 12.

## 10.1.2 Operational Recovery

Data in the production environment changes with every business transaction and operation. Backups are used to restore data if data loss or logical corruption occurs during routine processing. The majority of restore requests in most organizations fall in this category. For example, it is common for a user to accidentally delete an important e-mail or for a file to become corrupted, which can be restored using backup data.

## 10.1.3 Archival

Backups are also performed to address archival requirements. Although content addressed storage (CAS) has emerged as the primary solution for archives (CAS is discussed in Chapter 8), traditional backups are still used by small and medium enterprises for long-term preservation of transaction records, e-mail messages, and other business records required for regulatory compliance.

**BACKUP WINDOW**

The period during which a source is available to perform a data backup is called a *backup window*. Performing a backup from the source sometimes requires the production operation to be suspended because the data being backed up is exclusively locked for the use of the backup process.

## 10.2 Backup Considerations

The amount of data loss and downtime that a business can endure in terms of RPO and RTO are the primary considerations in selecting and implementing a specific backup strategy. RPO refers to the point in time to which data must be recovered, and the point in time from which to restart business operations. This specifies the time interval between two backups. In other words, the RPO determines backup frequency. For example, if an application requires an RPO of 1 day, it would need the data to be backed up at least once every day. Another consideration is the retention period, which defines the duration for which a business needs to retain the backup copies. Some data is retained for years and some only for a few days. For example, data backed up for archival is retained for a longer period than data backed up for operational recovery.

The backup media type or backup target is another consideration, that is driven by RTO and impacts the data recovery time. The time-consuming operation of starting and stopping in a tape-based system affects the backup performance, especially while backing up a large number of small files.

Organizations must also consider the granularity of backups, explained later in section "10.3 Backup Granularity." The development of a backup strategy must include a decision about the most appropriate time for performing a backup to minimize any disruption to production operations. The location, size, number of files, and data compression should also be considered because they might affect the backup process. Location is an important consideration for the data to be backed up. Many organizations have dozens of heterogeneous platforms locally and remotely supporting their business. Consider a data warehouse environment that uses the backup data from many sources. The backup process must address these sources for transactional and content integrity. This process must be coordinated with all heterogeneous platforms at all locations on which the data resides.

The file size and number of files also influence the backup process. Backing up large-size files (for example, ten 1 MB files) takes less time, compared to backing up an equal amount of data composed of small-size files (for example, ten thousand 1 KB files).

Data compression and data deduplication (discussed later in section "10.11 Data Deduplication for Backup") are widely used in the backup environment because these technologies save space on the media. Many backup devices have built-in support for hardware-based data compression. Some data, such as application binaries, do not compress well, whereas text data does compress well.

## 10.3 Backup Granularity

Backup granularity depends on business needs and the required RTO/RPO. Based on the granularity, backups can be categorized as full, incremental and cumulative (differential). Most organizations use a combination of these three backup types to meet their backup and recovery requirements. Figure 10-1 shows the different backup granularity levels.

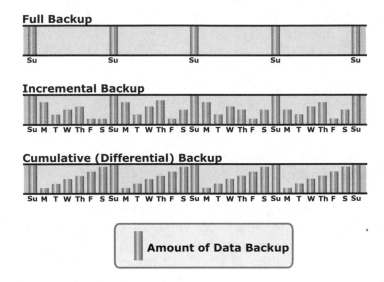

**Figure 10-1:** Backup granularity levels

*Full backup* is a backup of the complete data on the production volumes. A full backup copy is created by copying the data in the production volumes to a backup storage device. It provides a faster recovery but requires more storage space and also takes more time to back up. *Incremental backup* copies the data that has changed since the last full or incremental backup, whichever has occurred more recently. This is much faster than a full backup (because the volume of data backed up is restricted to the changed data only) but takes longer to restore. *Cumulative backup* copies the data that has changed since the last full backup. This method takes longer than an incremental backup but is faster to restore.

## SYNTHETIC FULL BACKUP

Another way to implement a full backup is to use a *synthetic* (or *constructed*) *backup*. This method is used when the production volume resources cannot be exclusively reserved for a backup process for extended periods to perform a full backup. It is usually created from the most recent full backup and all the incremental backups performed after that full backup. This backup is called *synthetic* because the backup is not created directly from production data. A synthetic full backup enables a full backup copy to be created offline without disrupting the I/O operation on the production volume. This also frees up network resources from the backup process, making them available for other production use.

Restore operations vary with the granularity of the backup. A full backup provides a single repository from which the data can be easily restored. The process of restoration from an incremental backup requires the last full backup and all the incremental backups available until the point of restoration. A restore from a cumulative backup requires the last full backup and the most recent cumulative backup.

Figure 10-2 shows an example of restoring data from incremental backup.

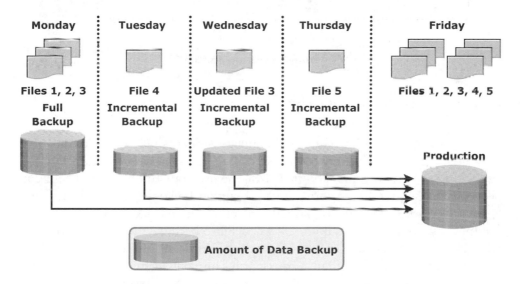

**Figure 10-2:** Restoring from an incremental backup

In this example, a full backup is performed on Monday evening. Each day after that, an incremental backup is performed. On Tuesday, a new file (File 4 in the figure) is added, and no other files have changed. Consequently, only File

4 is copied during the incremental backup performed on Tuesday evening. On Wednesday, no new files are added, but File 3 has been modified. Therefore, only the modified File 3 is copied during the incremental backup on Wednesday evening. Similarly, the incremental backup on Thursday copies only File 5. On Friday morning, there is data corruption, which requires data restoration from the backup. The first step toward data restoration is restoring all data from the full backup of Monday evening. The next step is applying the incremental backups of Tuesday, Wednesday, and Thursday. In this manner, data can be successfully recovered to its previous state, as it existed on Thursday evening.

Figure 10-3 shows an example of restoring data from cumulative backup.

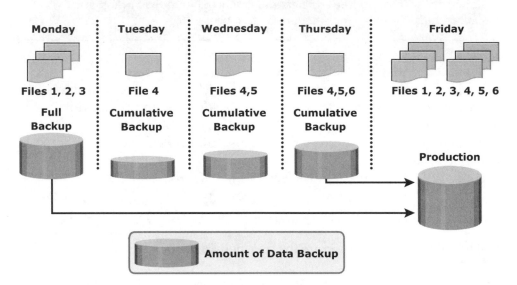

**Figure 10-3:** Restoring a cumulative backup

In this example, a full backup of the business data is taken on Monday evening. Each day after that, a cumulative backup is taken. On Tuesday, File 4 is added and no other data is modified since the previous full backup of Monday evening. Consequently, the cumulative backup on Tuesday evening copies only File 4. On Wednesday, File 5 is added. The cumulative backup taking place on Wednesday evening copies both File 4 and File 5 because these files have been added or modified since the last full backup. Similarly, on Thursday, File 6 is added. Therefore, the cumulative backup on Thursday evening copies all three files: File 4, File 5, and File 6. On Friday morning, data corruption occurs that requires data restoration using backup copies. The first step in restoring data is to restore all the data from the full backup of Monday evening. The next step is to apply only the latest cumulative backup, which is taken on Thursday evening. In this way, the production data can be recovered faster because its needs only two copies of data — the last full backup and the latest cumulative backup.

## 10.4 Recovery Considerations

The retention period is a key consideration for recovery. The retention period for a backup is derived from an RPO. For example, users of an application might request to restore the application data from its backup copy, which was created a month ago. This determines the retention period for the backup. Therefore, the minimum retention period of this application data is one month. However, the organization might choose to retain the backup for a longer period of time because of internal policies or external factors, such as regulatory directives.

If the recovery point is older than the retention period, it might not be possible to recover all the data required for the requested recovery point. Long retention periods can be defined for all backups, making it possible to meet any RPO within the defined retention periods. However, this requires a large storage space, which translates into higher cost. Therefore, while defining the retention period, analyze all the restore requests in the past and the allocated budget.

RTO relates to the time taken by the recovery process. To meet the defined RTO, the business may choose the appropriate backup granularity to minimize recovery time. In a backup environment, RTO influences the type of backup media that should be used. For example, a restore from tapes takes longer to complete than a restore from disks.

## 10.5 Backup Methods

Hot backup and cold backup are the two methods deployed for a backup. They are based on the state of the application when the backup is performed. In a *hot backup*, the application is up-and-running, with users accessing their data during the backup process. This method of backup is also referred to as an *online backup*. A *cold backup* requires the application to be shut down during the backup process. Hence, this method is also referred to as an *offline backup*.

The hot backup of online production data is challenging because data is actively used and changed. If a file is open, it is normally not backed up during the backup process. In such situations, an *open file agent* is required to back up the open file. These agents interact directly with the operating system or application and enable the creation of consistent copies of open files. In database environments, the use of open file agents is not enough, because the agent should also support a consistent backup of all the database components. For example, a database is composed of many files of varying sizes occupying several file systems. To ensure a consistent database backup, all files need to be backed up in the same state. That does not necessarily mean that all files need to be backed up at the same time, but they all must be synchronized so that the database can be restored with consistency. The disadvantage associated with a hot backup is that the agents usually affect the overall application performance.

Consistent backups of databases can also be done by using a cold backup. This requires the database to remain inactive during the backup. Of course, the disadvantage of a cold backup is that the database is inaccessible to users during the backup process.

A *point-in-time* (PIT) copy method is deployed in environments in which the impact of downtime from a cold backup or the performance impact resulting from a hot backup is unacceptable. The PIT copy is created from the production volume and used as the source for the backup. This reduces the impact on the production volume. This technique is detailed in Chapter 11.

To ensure consistency, it is not enough to back up only the production data for recovery. Certain attributes and properties attached to a file, such as permissions, owner, and other metadata, also need to be backed up. These attributes are as important as the data itself and must be backed up for consistency.

In a disaster recovery environment, *bare-metal recovery* (BMR) refers to a backup in which all metadata, system information, and application configurations are appropriately backed up for a full system recovery. BMR builds the base system, which includes partitioning, the file system layout, the operating system, the applications, and all the relevant configurations. BMR recovers the base system first before starting the recovery of data files. Some BMR technologies — for example server configuration backup (SCB) — can recover a server even onto dissimilar hardware.

## SERVER CONFIGURATION BACKUP

Most organizations spend a considerable amount of time and money protecting their application data but give less attention to protecting their server configurations. During disaster recovery, server configurations must be re-created before the application and data are accessible to the user. The process of system recovery involves reinstalling the operating system, applications, and server settings and then recovering the data. During a normal data backup operation, server configurations required for the system restore are not backed up. *Server configuration backup* (SCB) creates and backs up server configuration profiles based on user-defined schedules. The backed up profiles are used to configure the recovery server in case of production-server failure. SCB has the capability to recover a server onto dissimilar hardware.

In a server configuration backup, the process of taking a snapshot of the application server's configuration (both system and application configurations) is known as *profiling*. The profile data includes operating system configurations, network configurations, security configurations, registry settings, application configurations, and so on. Thus, profiling allows recovering the configuration of the failed system to a new server regardless of the underlying hardware.

There are two types of profiles generated in the server configuration backup environment: base profile and extended profile. The base profile contains the key elements of the operating system required to recover the server. The extended profile is typically larger than the base profile and contains all the necessary information to rebuild the application environment.

# 10.6 Backup Architecture

A backup system commonly uses the client-server architecture with a backup server and multiple backup clients. Figure 10-4 illustrates the backup architecture. The backup server manages the backup operations and maintains the backup catalog, which contains information about the backup configuration and backup metadata. Backup configuration contains information about when to run backups, which client data to be backed up, and so on, and the backup metadata contains information about the backed up data. The role of a backup client is to gather the data that is to be backed up and send it to the storage node. It also sends the tracking information to the backup server.

The storage node is responsible for writing the data to the backup device. (In a backup environment, a *storage node* is a host that controls backup devices.) The storage node also sends tracking information to the backup server. In many cases, the storage node is integrated with the backup server, and both are hosted on the same physical platform. A backup device is attached directly or through a network to the storage node's host platform. Some backup architecture refers to the storage node as the *media server* because it manages the storage device.

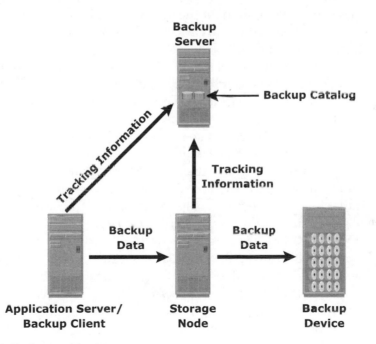

**Figure 10-4:** Backup architecture

Backup software provides reporting capabilities based on the backup catalog and the log files. These reports include information, such as the amount of data backed up, the number of completed and incomplete backups, and the types of errors that might have occurred. Reports can be customized depending on the specific backup software used.

**Protecting backup metadata is an important aspect of backup. If the backup catalog is lost, data recovery will be a challenge. Therefore, an updated copy of the backup catalog should be maintained separately all the time.**

## 10.7 Backup and Restore Operations

When a backup operation is initiated, significant network communication takes place between the different components of a backup infrastructure. The backup operation is typically initiated by a server, but it can also be initiated by a client. The backup server initiates the backup process for different clients based on the backup schedule configured for them. For example, the backup for a group of clients may be scheduled to start at 11:00 p.m. every day.

The backup server coordinates the backup process with all the components in a backup environment (see Figure 10-5). The backup server maintains the information about backup clients to be backed up and storage nodes to be used in a backup operation. The backup server retrieves the backup-related information from the backup catalog and, based on this information, instructs the storage node to load the appropriate backup media into the backup devices. Simultaneously, it instructs the backup clients to gather the data to be backed up and send it over the network to the assigned storage node. After the backup data is sent to the storage node, the client sends some backup metadata (the number of files, name of the files, storage node details, and so on) to the backup server. The storage node receives the client data, organizes it, and sends it to the backup device. The storage node then sends additional backup metadata (location of the data on the backup device, time of backup, and so on) to the backup server. The backup server updates the backup catalog with this information.

After the data is backed up, it can be restored when required. A restore process must be manually initiated from the client. Some backup software has a separate application for restore operations. These restore applications are usually accessible only to the administrators or backup operators. Figure 10-6 shows a restore operation.

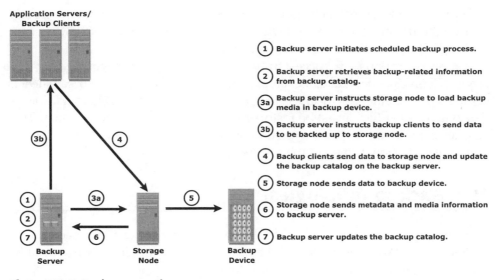

**Figure 10-5:** Backup operation

Upon receiving a restore request, an administrator opens the restore application to view the list of clients that have been backed up. While selecting the client for which a restore request has been made, the administrator also needs to identify the client that will receive the restored data. Data can be restored on the same client for whom the restore request has been made or on any other client. The administrator then selects the data to be restored and the specified point in time to which the data has to be restored based on the RPO. Because all this information comes from the backup catalog, the restore application needs to communicate with the backup server.

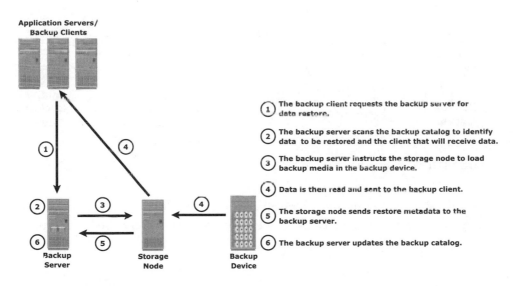

**Figure 10-6:** Restore operation

The backup server instructs the appropriate storage node to mount the specific backup media onto the backup device. Data is then read and sent to the client that has been identified to receive the restored data.

Some restorations are successfully accomplished by recovering only the requested production data. For example, the recovery process of a spreadsheet is completed when the specific file is restored. In database restorations, additional data, such as log files, must be restored along with the production data. This ensures consistency for the restored data. In these cases, the RTO is extended due to the additional steps in the restore operation.

## 10.8 Backup Topologies

Three basic topologies are used in a backup environment: direct-attached backup, LAN-based backup, and SAN-based backup. A mixed topology is also used by combining LAN-based and SAN-based topologies.

In a *direct-attached backup*, the storage node is configured on a backup client, and the backup device is attached directly to the client. Only the metadata is sent to the backup server through the LAN. This configuration frees the LAN from backup traffic. The example in Figure 10-7 shows that the backup device is directly attached and dedicated to the backup client. As the environment grows, there will be a need for centralized management and sharing of backup devices to optimize costs. An appropriate solution is required to share the backup devices among multiple servers. Network-based topologies (LAN-based and SAN-based) provide the solution to optimize the utilization of backup devices.

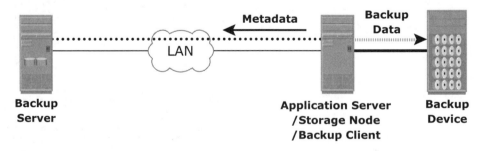

**Figure 10-7:** Direct-attached backup topology

In a *LAN-based backup*, the clients, backup server, storage node, and backup device are connected to the LAN. (see Figure 10-8). The data to be backed up is transferred from the backup client (source) to the backup device (destination) over the LAN, which might affect network performance.

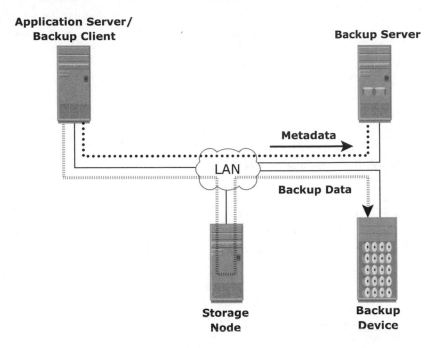

**Figure 10-8:** LAN-based backup topology

This impact can be minimized by adopting a number of measures, such as configuring separate networks for backup and installing dedicated storage nodes for some application servers.

A *SAN-based backup* is also known as a *LAN-free backup*. The SAN-based backup topology is the most appropriate solution when a backup device needs to be shared among clients. In this case, the backup device and clients are attached to the SAN. Figure 10-9 illustrates a SAN-based backup.

In this example, a client sends the data to be backed up to the backup device over the SAN. Therefore, the backup data traffic is restricted to the SAN, and only the backup metadata is transported over the LAN. The volume of metadata is insignificant when compared to the production data; the LAN performance is not degraded in this configuration.

The emergence of low-cost disks as a backup medium has enabled disk arrays to be attached to the SAN and used as backup devices. A tape backup of these data backups on the disks can be created and shipped offsite for disaster recovery and long-term retention.

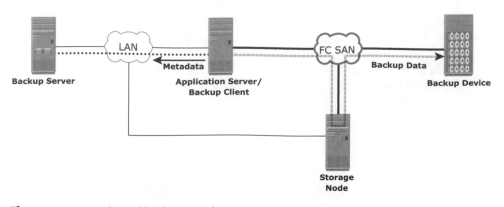

**Figure 10-9:** SAN-based backup topology

The *mixed topology* uses both the LAN-based and SAN-based topologies, as shown in Figure 10-10. This topology might be implemented for several reasons, including cost, server location, reduction in administrative overhead, and performance considerations.

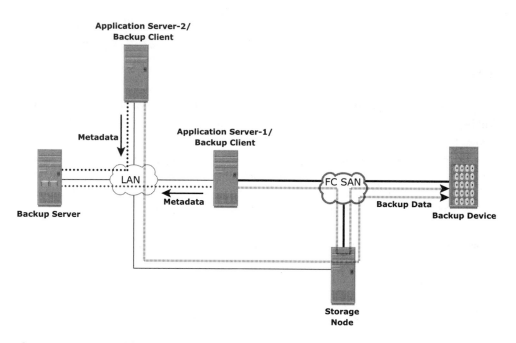

**Figure 10-10:** Mixed backup topology

## 10.9 Backup in NAS Environments

The use of a NAS head imposes a new set of considerations on the backup and recovery strategy in NAS environments. NAS heads use a proprietary operating system and file system structure that supports multiple file-sharing protocols. In the NAS environment, backups can be implemented in different ways: server based, serverless, or using Network Data Management Protocol (NDMP). Common implementations are NDMP 2-way and NDMP 3-way.

### 10.9.1 Server-Based and Serverless Backup

In an *application server-based backup*, the NAS head retrieves data from a storage array over the network and transfers it to the backup client running on the application server. The backup client sends this data to the storage node, which in turn writes the data to the backup device. This results in overloading the network with the backup data and using application server resources to move the backup data. Figure 10-11 illustrates server-based backup in the NAS environment.

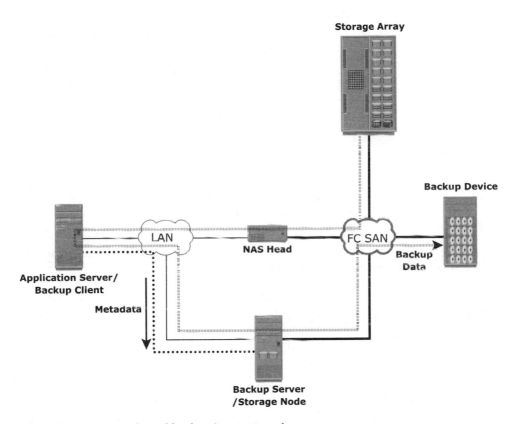

**Figure 10-11:** Server-based backup in a NAS environment

In a *serverless backup*, the network share is mounted directly on the storage node. This avoids overloading the network during the backup process and eliminates the need to use resources on the application server. Figure 10-12 illustrates serverless backup in the NAS environment. In this scenario, the storage node, which is also a backup client, reads the data from the NAS head and writes it to the backup device without involving the application server. Compared to the previous solution, this eliminates one network hop.

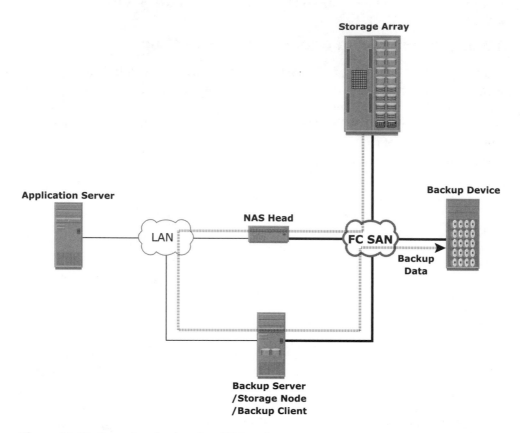

**Figure 10-12:** Serverless backup in a NAS environment

## 10.9.2 NDMP-Based Backup

*NDMP* is an industry-standard TCP/IP-based protocol specifically designed for a backup in a NAS environment. It communicates with several elements in the backup environment (NAS head, backup devices, backup server, and so on) for data transfer and enables vendors to use a common protocol for the backup architecture. Data can be backed up using NDMP regardless of the operating system or platform. Due to its flexibility, it is no longer necessary to transport data through the application server, which reduces the load on the application server and improves the backup speed.

NDMP optimizes backup and restore by leveraging the high-speed connection between the backup devices and the NAS head. In NDMP, backup data is sent directly from the NAS head to the backup device, whereas metadata is sent to the backup server. Figure 10-13 illustrates a backup in the NAS environment using NDMP 2-way. In this model, network traffic is minimized by isolating data movement from the NAS head to the locally attached backup device. Only metadata is transported on the network. The backup device is dedicated to the NAS device, and hence, this method does not support centralized management of all backup devices.

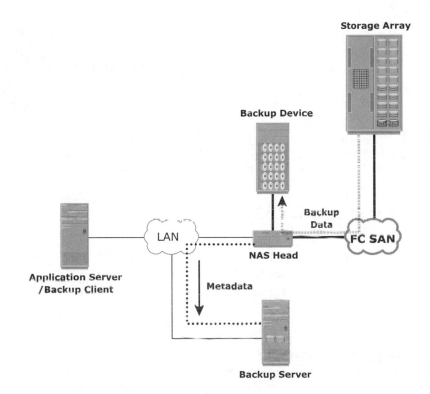

**Figure 10-13:** NDMP 2-way in a NAS environment

In the *NDMP 3-way* method, a separate private backup network must be established between all NAS heads and the NAS head connected to the backup device. Metadata and NDMP control data are still transferred across the public network. Figure 10-14 shows a NDMP 3-way backup.

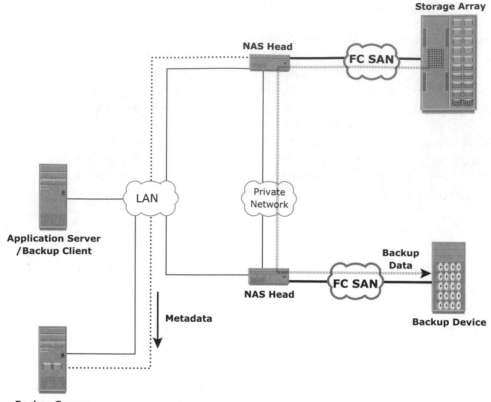

**Figure 10-14:** NDMP 3-way in a NAS environment

An NDMP 3-way is useful when backup devices need to be shared among NAS heads. It enables the NAS head to control the backup device and share it with other NAS heads by receiving the backup data through the NDMP.

## 10.10 Backup Targets

A wide range of technology solutions are currently available for backup targets. Tape and disk libraries are the two most commonly used backup targets. In the past, tape technology was the predominant target for backup due to its low cost. But performance and management limitations associated with tapes and the availability of low-cost disk drives have made the disk a viable backup target. A virtual tape library (VTL) is one of the options that uses disks as a backup medium. VTL emulates tapes and provides enhanced backup and recovery capabilities.

## 10.10.1 Backup to Tape

Tapes, a low-cost solution, are used extensively for backup. Tape drives are used to read/write data from/to a tape cartridge (or cassette). Tape drives are referred to as sequential, or linear, access devices because the data is written or read sequentially. A tape cartridge is composed of magnetic tapes in a plastic enclosure. *Tape mounting* is the process of inserting a tape cartridge into a tape drive. The tape drive has motorized controls to move the magnetic tape around, enabling the head to read or write data.

Several types of tape cartridges are available. They vary in size, capacity, shape, density, tape length, tape thickness, tape tracks, and supported speed.

### *Physical Tape Library*

The physical tape library provides housing and power for a large number of tape drives and tape cartridges, along with a robotic arm or picker mechanism. The backup software has intelligence to manage the robotic arm and entire backup process. Figure 10-15 shows a physical tape library.

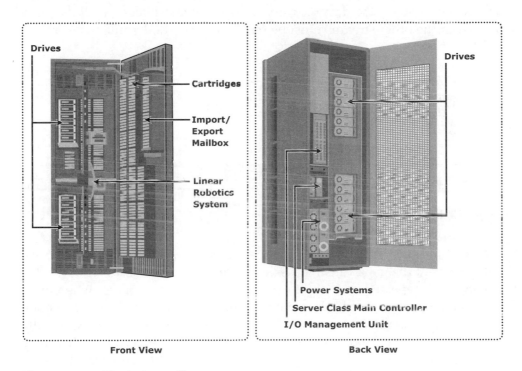

**Figure 10-15:** Physical tape library

*Tape drives* read and write data from and to a tape. Tape *cartridges* are placed in the *slots* when not in use by a tape drive. *Robotic arms* are used to move tapes between cartridge slots and tape drives. *Mail* or *import/export slots* are used to add or remove tapes from the library without opening the access doors (refer to Figure 10-15 Front View).

When a backup process starts, the robotic arm is instructed to load a tape to a tape drive. This process adds delay to a degree depending on the type of hardware used, but it generally takes 5 to 10 seconds to mount a tape. After the tape is mounted, additional time is spent to position the heads and validate header information. This total time is called *load to ready time*, and it can vary from several seconds to minutes. The tape drive receives backup data and stores the data in its internal buffer. This backup data is then written to the tape in blocks. During this process, it is best to ensure that the tape drive is kept busy continuously to prevent gaps between the blocks. This is accomplished by buffering the data on tape drives. The speed of the tape drives can also be adjusted to match data transfer rates.

Tape drive *streaming* or *multiple streaming* writes data from multiple streams on a single tape to keep the drive busy. As shown in Figure 10-16, multiple streaming improves media performance, but it has an associated disadvantage. The backup data is interleaved because data from multiple streams is written on it. Consequently, the data recovery time is increased because all the extra data from the other streams must be read and discarded while recovering a single stream.

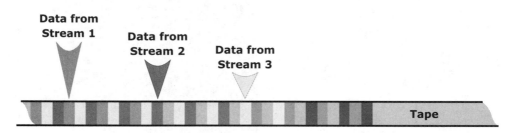

**Figure 10-16:** Multiple streams on tape media

Many times, even the buffering and speed adjustment features of a tape drive fail to prevent the gaps, causing the *"shoe shining effect"* or *"backhitching."* *Shoe shining* is the repeated back and forth motion a tape drive makes when there is an interruption in the backup data stream. For example, if a storage node sends data slower than the tape drive writes it to the tape, the drive periodically stops and waits for the data to catch up. After the drive determines that there is enough data to start writing again, it rewinds to the exact place where the last write took place and continues. This repeated back-and-forth motion not only causes a degradation of service, but also excessive wear and tear to tapes.

When the tape operation finishes, the tape rewinds to the starting position and it is unmounted. The robotic arm is then instructed to move the unmounted tape back to the slot. *Rewind time* can range from several seconds to minutes.

When a *restore* is initiated, the backup software identifies which tapes are required. The robotic arm is instructed to move the tape from its slot to a tape drive. If the required tape is not found in the tape library, the backup software displays a message, instructing the operator to manually insert the required tape in the tape library. When a file or a group of files require restores, the tape must move to that file location sequentially before it can start reading. This process can take a significant amount of time, especially if the required files are recorded at the end of the tape.

Modern tape devices have an indexing mechanism that enables a tape to be fast forwarded to a location near the required data. The tape drive then fine-tunes the tape position to get to the data. However, before adopting a solution that uses this mechanism, one should consider the benefits of data streaming performance versus the cost of writing an index.

### Limitations of Tape

Tapes are primarily used for long-term offsite storage because of their low cost. Tapes must be stored in locations with a controlled environment to ensure preservation of the media and to prevent data corruption. Data access in a tape is sequential, which can slow backup and recovery operations. Tapes are highly susceptible to wear and tear and usually have shorter shelf life. Physical transportation of the tapes to offsite locations also adds to management overhead and increases the possibility of loss of tapes during offsite shipment.

## 10.10.2 Backup to Disk

Because of increased availability, low cost disks have now replaced tapes as the primary device for storing backup data because of their performance advantages. Backup-to-disk systems offer ease of implementation, reduced TCO, and improved quality of service. Apart from performance benefits in terms of data transfer rates, disks also offer faster recovery when compared to tapes.

Backing up to disk storage systems offers clear advantages due to their inherent random access and RAID-protection capabilities. In most backup environments, backup to disk is used as a staging area where the data is copied temporarily before transferring or staging it to tapes. This enhances backup performance. Some backup products allow for backup images to remain on the disk for a period of time even after they have been staged. This enables a much faster restore. Figure 10-17 illustrates a recovery scenario comparing tape versus disk in a Microsoft Exchange environment that supports 800 users with a 75 MB mailbox size and a 60 GB database. As shown in the figure, a restore from the disk took 24 minutes compared to the restore from a tape, which took 108 minutes for the same environment.

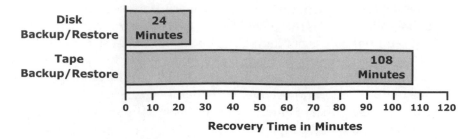

**Figure 10-17:** Tape versus disk restore

Recovering from a full backup copy stored on disk and kept onsite provides the fastest recovery solution. Using a disk enables the creation of full backups more frequently, which in turn improves RPO and RTO.

Backup to disk does not offer any inherent offsite capability and is dependent on other technologies, such as local and remote replication. In addition, some backup products require additional modules and licenses to support backup to disk, which may also require additional configuration steps, including creation of RAID groups and file system tuning. These activities are not usually performed by a backup administrator.

## 10.10.3 Backup to Virtual Tape

*Virtual tapes* are disk drives emulated and presented as tapes to the backup software. The key benefit of using a virtual tape is that it does not require any additional modules, configuration, or changes in the legacy backup software. This preserves the investment made in the backup software.

### Virtual Tape Library

A *virtual tape library* (VTL) has the same components as that of a physical tape library, except that the majority of the components are presented as virtual resources. For the backup software, there is no difference between a physical tape library and a virtual tape library. Figure 10-18 shows a virtual tape library.

Virtual tape libraries use disks as backup media. Emulation software has a database with a list of virtual tapes, and each virtual tape is assigned space on a LUN. A virtual tape can span multiple LUNs if required. File system awareness is not required while backing up because the virtual tape solution typically uses raw devices.

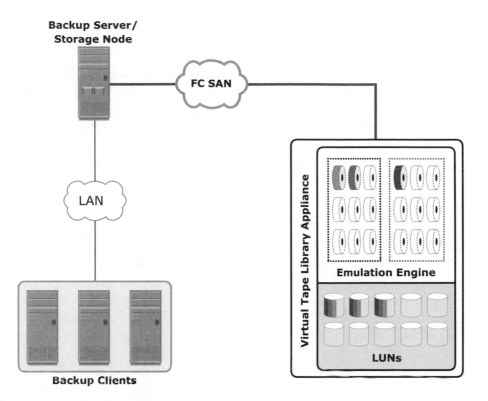

**Figure 10-18:** Virtual tape library

Similar to a physical tape library, a robot mount is virtually performed when a backup process starts in a virtual tape library. However, unlike a physical tape library, where this process involves some mechanical delays, in a virtual tape library it is almost instantaneous. Even the *load to ready* time is much less than in a physical tape library.

After the virtual tape is mounted and the virtual tape drive is positioned, the virtual tape is ready to be used, and backup data can be written to it. In most cases, data is written to the virtual tape immediately. Unlike a physical tape library, the virtual tape library is not constrained by the sequential access and shoe shining effect. When the operation is complete, the backup software issues a rewind command. This rewind is also instantaneous. The virtual tape is then unmounted, and the virtual robotic arm is instructed to move it back to a virtual slot.

The steps to restore data are similar to those in a physical tape library, but the restore operation is nearly instantaneous. Even though virtual tapes are based on disks, which provide random access, they still emulate the tape behavior.

A virtual tape library appliance offers a number of features that are not available with physical tape libraries. Some virtual tape libraries offer *multiple emulation engines* configured in an active cluster configuration. An engine is a dedicated server with a customized operating system that makes physical disks in the VTL appear as tapes to the backup application. With this feature, one engine can pick up the virtual resources from another engine in the event of any failure and enable the clients to continue using their assigned virtual resources transparently.

Data replication over IP is available with most of the virtual tape library appliances. This feature enables virtual tapes to be replicated over an inexpensive IP network to a remote site. As a result, organizations can comply with offsite requirements for backup data. Connecting the engines of a virtual tape library appliance to a physical tape library enables the virtual tapes to be copied onto the physical tapes, which can then be sent to a vault or shipped to an offsite location.

Using virtual tapes offers several advantages over both physical tapes and disks. Compared to physical tapes, virtual tapes offer better single stream performance, better reliability, and random disk access characteristics. Backup and restore operations benefit from the disk's random access characteristics because they are always online and provide faster backup and recovery. A virtual tape drive does not require the usual maintenance tasks associated with a physical tape drive, such as periodic cleaning and drive calibration. Compared to backup-to-disk devices, a virtual tape library offers easy installation and administration because it is preconfigured by the manufacturer. However, a virtual tape library is generally used only for backup purposes. In a backup-to-disk environment, the disk systems are used for both production and backup data.

Table 10-1 shows a comparison between various backup targets.

**Table 10-1:** Backup Targets Comparison

| FEATURES | TAPE | DISK | VIRTUAL TAPE |
|---|---|---|---|
| Offsite Replication Capabilities | No | Yes | Yes |
| Reliability | No inherent protection methods | Yes | Yes |
| Performance | Subject to mechanical operations, loading time | Faster single stream | Faster single stream |
| Use | Backup only | Multiple (backup, production) | Backup only |

# 10.11 Data Deduplication for Backup

Traditional backup solutions do not provide any inherent capability to prevent duplicate data from being backed up. With the growth of information and 24x7 application availability requirements, backup windows are shrinking. Traditional backup processes back up a lot of duplicate data. Backing up duplicate data significantly increases the backup window size requirements and results in unnecessary consumption of resources, such as storage space and network bandwidth.

*Data deduplication* is the process of identifying and eliminating redundant data. When duplicate data is detected during backup, the data is discarded and only the pointer is created to refer the copy of the data that is already backed up. Data deduplication helps to reduce the storage requirement for backup, shorten the backup window, and remove the network burden. It also helps to store more backups on the disk and retain the data on the disk for a longer time.

## 10.11.1 Data Deduplication Methods

There are two methods of deduplication: file level and subfile level. Determining the uniqueness by implementing either method offers benefits; however, results can vary. The differences exist in the amount of data reduction each method produces and the time each approach takes to determine the unique content.

*File-level deduplication* (also called *single-instance storage*) detects and removes redundant copies of identical files. It enables storing only one copy of the file; the subsequent copies are replaced with a pointer that points to the original file. File-level deduplication is simple and fast but does not address the problem of duplicate content inside the files. For example, two 10-MB PowerPoint presentations with a difference in just the title page are not considered as duplicate files, and each file will be stored separately.

*Subfile deduplication* breaks the file into smaller chunks and then uses a specialized algorithm to detect redundant data within and across the file. As a result, subfile deduplication eliminates duplicate data across files. There are two forms of subfile deduplication: fixed-length block and variable-length segment. The *fixed-length block deduplication* divides the files into fixed length blocks and uses a hash algorithm to find the duplicate data. Although simple in design, fixed-length blocks might miss many opportunities to discover redundant data because the block boundary of similar data might be different. Consider the addition of a person's name to a document's title page. This shifts the whole document, and all the blocks appear to have changed, causing the failure of the deduplication method to detect equivalencies. In *variable-length segment deduplication*, if there is a change in the segment, the boundary for only that segment is adjusted, leaving the remaining segments unchanged. This method vastly improves the ability to find duplicate data segments compared to fixed-block.

## 10.11.2 Data Deduplication Implementation

Deduplication for backup can happen at the data source or the backup target.

### Source-Based Data Deduplication

*Source-based data deduplication* eliminates redundant data at the source before it transmits to the backup device. Source-based data deduplication can dramatically reduce the amount of backup data sent over the network during backup processes. It provides the benefits of a shorter backup window and requires less network bandwidth. There is also a substantial reduction in the capacity required to store the backup images. Figure 10-19 shows source-based data deduplication.

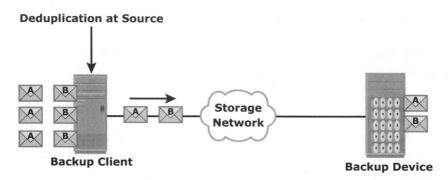

**Figure 10-19:** Source-based data deduplication

Source-based deduplication increases the overhead on the backup client, which impacts the performance of the backup and application running on the client. Source-based deduplication might also require a change of backup software if it is not supported by backup software.

### Target-Based Data Deduplication

*Target-based data deduplication* is an alternative to source-based data deduplication. Target-based data deduplication occurs at the backup device, which offloads the backup client from the deduplication process. Figure 10-20 shows target-based data deduplication.

In this case, the backup client sends the data to the backup device and the data is deduplicated at the backup device, either immediately (inline) or at a scheduled time (post-process). Because deduplication occurs at the target, all the backup data needs to be transferred over the network, which increases network bandwidth requirements. Target-based data deduplication does not require any changes in the existing backup software.

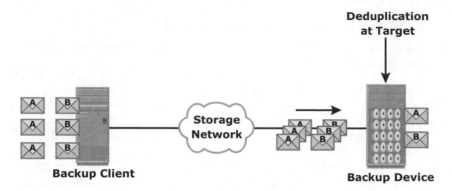

**Figure 10-20:** Target-based data deduplication

*Inline deduplication* performs deduplication on the backup data before it is stored on the backup device. Hence, this method reduces the storage capacity needed for the backup. Inline deduplication introduces overhead in the form of the time required to identify and remove duplication in the data. So, this method is best suited for an environment with a large backup window.

*Post-process deduplication* enables the backup data to be stored or written on the backup device first and then deduplicated later. This method is suitable for situations with tighter backup windows. However, post-process deduplication requires more storage capacity to store the backup images before they are deduplicated.

---

**REMOTE OFFICE/BRANCH OFFICE (ROBO) BACKUP**

Today, businesses have their remote or branch offices spread over multiple locations. Typically, these remote offices have their own local IT infrastructure. This infrastructure includes file, print, web, or e-mail servers, workstations, and desktops, and might also house some applications and databases. Remote offices rely upon these systems to support regional business functions, such as order processing, inventory management, and sales activity.

Too often, business-critical data at remote offices are inadequately protected, exposing the business to the risk of lost data and productivity. As a result, protecting the data of an organization's branch and remote offices across multiple locations is critical for business. Traditionally, remote-office

*(Continued)*

**REMOTE OFFICE/BRANCH OFFICE (ROBO) BACKUP** *(continued)*

data backup was done manually using tapes, which were transported to offsite locations for disaster recovery support. Some of the challenges with this approach follow:

- Lack of skilled onsite technical resources to manage backups
- Risk of sending tapes to offsite locations, which could result in loss or theft of sensitive data

Backing up data from remote offices to a centralized data center was restricted due to the time and cost involved in sending huge volumes of data over the WAN. Therefore, organizations needed an effective solution to address the data backup and recovery challenges of remote and branch offices.

Disk-based backup solutions along with source-based deduplication eliminate the challenges associated with centrally backing up remote-office data. Deduplication considerably reduces the required network bandwidth and enables remote-office data backup using the existing network. Organizations can now centrally manage and automate remote-office backups while reducing the required backup window.

## 10.12 Backup in Virtualized Environments

In a virtualized environment, it is imperative to back up the virtual machine data (OS, application data, and configuration) to prevent its loss or corruption due to human or technical errors. There are two approaches for performing a backup in a virtualized environment: the traditional backup approach and the image-based backup approach.

In the *traditional backup approach*, a backup agent is installed either on the virtual machine (VM) or on the hypervisor. Figure 10-21 shows the traditional VM backup approach. If the backup agent is installed on a VM, the VM appears as a physical server to the agent. The backup agent installed on the VM backs up the VM data to the backup device. The agent does not capture VM files, such as the virtual BIOS file, VM swap file, logs, and configuration files. Therefore, for a VM restore, a user needs to manually re-create the VM and then restore data onto it.

If the backup agent is installed on the hypervisor, the VMs appear as a set of files to the agent. So, VM files can be backed up by performing a file system backup from a hypervisor. This approach is relatively simple because it requires having the agent just on the hypervisor instead of all the VMs. The traditional backup method can cause high CPU utilization on the server being backed up.

**Figure 10-21:** Traditional VM backup

In the traditional approach, the backup should be performed when the server resources are idle or during a low activity period on the network. Also consider allocating enough resources to manage the backup on each server when a large number of VMs are in the environment.

*Image-based backup* operates at the hypervisor level and essentially takes a snapshot of the VM. It creates a copy of the guest OS and all the data associated with it (snapshot of VM disk files), including the VM state and application configurations. The backup is saved as a single file called an "image," and this image is mounted on the separate physical machine–proxy server, which acts as a backup client. The backup software then backs up these image files normally. (see Figure 10-22). This effectively offloads the backup processing from the hypervisor and transfers the load on the proxy server, thereby reducing the impact to VMs running on the hypervisor. Image-based backup enables quick restoration of a VM.

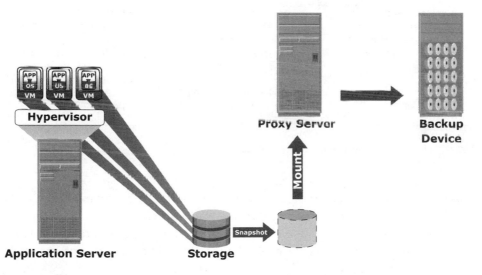

**Figure 10-22:** Image-based backup

The use of deduplication techniques significantly reduces the amount of data to be backed up in a virtualized environment. The effectiveness of deduplication is identified when VMs with similar configurations are deployed in a data center. The deduplication types and methods used in a virtualized environment are the same as in the physical environment.

## 10.13 Data Archive

In the life cycle of information, data is actively created, accessed, and changed. As data ages, it is less likely to be changed and eventually becomes "fixed" but continues to be accessed by applications and users. This data is called *fixed content*. X-rays, e-mails, and multimedia files are examples of fixed content. Figure 10-23 shows some examples of fixed content.

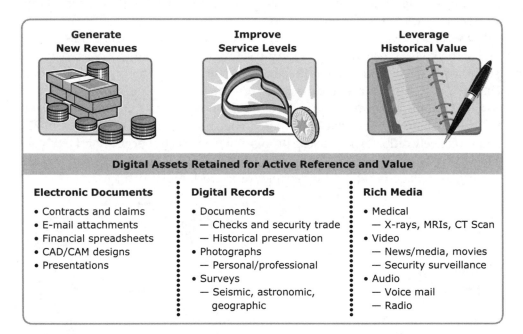

**Figure 10-23:** Examples of fixed content data

All organizations may require retention of their data for an extended period of time due to government regulations and legal/contractual obligations. Organizations also make use of this fixed content to generate new revenue strategies and improve service levels. A repository where fixed content is stored is known as an archive.

An archive can be implemented as an online, nearline, or offline solution:

- **Online archive:** A storage device directly connected to a host that makes the data immediately accessible.

- **Nearline archive:** A storage device connected to a host, but the device where the data is stored must be mounted or loaded to access the data.

- **Offline archive:** A storage device that is not ready to use. Manual intervention is required to connect, mount, or load the storage device before data can be accessed.

Traditionally, optical and tape media were used for archives. Optical media are typically *write once read many* (WORM) devices that protect the original file from being overwritten. Some tape devices also provide this functionality by implementing file-locking capabilities. Although these devices are inexpensive, they involve operational, management, and maintenance overhead. The traditional archival process using optical discs and tapes is not optimized to recognize the content, so the same content could be archived several times. Additional costs are involved in offsite storage of media and media management. Tapes and optical media are also susceptible to wear and tear. Frequent changes in these device technologies lead to the overhead of converting the media into new formats to enable access and retrieval. Government agencies and industry regulators are establishing new laws and regulations to enforce the protection of archives from unauthorized destruction and modification. These regulations and standards have established new requirements for preserving the integrity of information in the archives. These requirements have exposed the shortcomings of the traditional tape and optical media archive solutions.

*Content addressed storage* (CAS) is disk-based storage that has emerged as an alternative to tape and optical solutions. CAS meets the demand to improve data accessibility and to protect, dispose of, and ensure service-level agreements (SLAs) for archive data. CAS is detailed in Chapter 8.

## 10.14 Archiving Solution Architecture

Archiving solution architecture consists of three key components: archiving agent, archiving server, and archiving storage device (see Figure 10-24).

*An archiving agent* is software installed on the application server. The agent is responsible for scanning the data that can be archived based on the policy defined on the archiving server. After the data is identified for archiving, the agent sends the data to the archiving server. Then the original data on the application server is replaced with a stub file. The stub file contains the address of the archived data. The size of this file is small and significantly saves space on primary storage. This stub file is used to retrieve the file from the archive storage device.

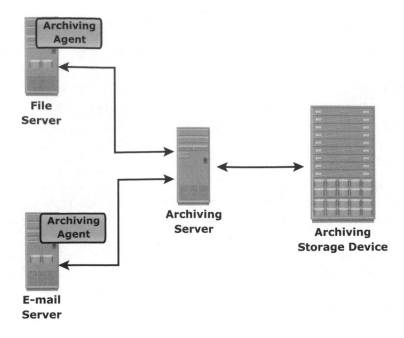

**Figure 10-24:** Archiving solution architecture

*An archiving server* is software installed on a host that enables administrators to configure the policies for archiving data. Policies can be defined based on file size, file type, or creation/modification/access time. The archiving server receives the data to be archived from the agent and sends it to the archive storage device.

*An archiving storage device* stores fixed content. Different types of storage media options such as optical, tapes, and low-cost disk drives are available for archiving.

## 10.14.1 Use Case: E-mail Archiving

E-mail is an example of an application that benefits most by an archival solution. Typically, a system administrator configures small mailboxes that store a limited number of e-mails. This is because large mailboxes with a large number of e-mails can make management difficult, increase primary storage cost, and degrade system performance. When an e-mail server is configured with a large number of mailboxes, the system administrator typically configures a quota on each mailbox to limit its size on that server. Configuring fixed quotas on mailboxes impacts end users. A fixed quota for a mailbox forces users to delete e-mails as they approach the quota size. End users often need to access e-mails that are weeks, months, or even years old.

E-mail archiving provides an excellent solution that overcomes the preceding challenges. Archiving solutions move e-mails that have been identified as candidates for archive from primary storage to the archive storage device based on a policy — for example, "e-mails that are 90 days old should be archived." After the e-mail is archived, it is retained for years based on the retention policy. This considerably saves space on primary storage and enables organizations to meet regulatory requirements. Implementation of an archiving solution gives end users virtually unlimited mailbox space.

## 10.14.2 Use Case: File Archiving

A file sharing environment is another environment that benefits from an archival solution. Typically, users store a large number of files in the shared location. Most of these files are old and rarely accessed. Administrators configure quotas on the file share that forces the users to delete these files. This impacts users because they may require access to files that may be months or even years old. In some cases the user may request an increase in the size of the file share. This in turn increases the cost of primary storage. A file archiving solution archives the files based on the policy such as age of files, size of files, and so on. This considerably reduces the primary storage requirement and also enables users to retain the files in the archive for longer periods.

---

**ARCHIVING DATA TO CLOUD STORAGE**

Today, organizations use cloud storage to archive their data. Cloud storage does not require any upfront capital expenditure (CAPEX) to the organization, such as buying archival hardware and software components. Organizations need to pay only for the cloud resources they consume.

Cloud computing provides infinitely scalable storage to organizations as a service. This enables businesses to expand their storage as required. To use cloud storage for archiving, the archiving application must support the cloud storage APIs.

---

## 10.15 Concepts in Practice: EMC NetWorker, EMC Avamar, and EMC Data Domain

The EMC backup, recovery, and deduplication portfolio consists of a broad range of products for an ever-increasing amount of backup data. This section provides a brief introduction to EMC NetWorker, EMC Avamar, and EMC Data Domain. For the latest information, visit www.emc.com.

## 10.15.1 EMC NetWorker

The EMC NetWorker backup and recovery software centralizes, automates, and accelerates data backup and recovery operations across the enterprise. Following are the features of EMC NetWorker:

- Supports heterogeneous platforms, such as Windows, UNIX, and Linux, and also supports virtual environments
- Supports clustering technologies and open-file backup
- Supports different backup targets: tapes, disks, and virtual tapes
- Supports Multiplexing (or multistreaming) of data
- Provides both source-based and target-based deduplication capabilities by integrating with EMC Avamar and EMC Data Domain respectively
- Uses 256-bit AES (advanced encryption standard) encryption to provide security for the backup data. NetWorker hosts are authenticated using strong authentication based on the Secure Sockets Layer (SSL) protocol.
- The cloud-backup option in NetWorker enables backing up data to both private and public cloud configurations.

NetWorker provides centralized management of the backup environment through a GUI, customizable reporting, and wizard-driven configuration. With the NetWorker Management Console (NMC), backup can be easily administered from any host with a supported web browser. NetWorker also provides many command-line utilities. To facilitate NetWorker administration, several reports are available through the NMC reporting feature. Data maintained in the NMC server database, gathered from any or all of the NetWorker servers, is used to prepare reports on backup statistics and status, events, hosts, users, and devices.

## 10.15.2 EMC Avamar

EMC Avamar is a disk-based backup and recovery solution that provides inherent source-based data deduplication. With its unique global data deduplication feature, Avamar differs from traditional backup and recovery solutions, by identifying and storing only unique subfile data objects. Redundant data is identified at the source, the amount of data that travels across the network is drastically reduced, and the backup storage requirement is also considerably reduced. The three major components of an Avamar system include Avamar server, Avamar backup clients, and Avamar administrator. Avamar server stores client backups and provides the essential processes and services required for client access and remote system administration. The Avamar client software runs on each computer or network server being backed up. Avamar administrator is a user management console application used to remotely administer an Avamar system. Following are the three Avamar server editions:

- **Software only:** The Avamar Software edition is a software-only solution. The server software is installed on customer-supplied, Avamar-qualified hardware platforms.

- **Avamar Data Store:** The Avamar Data Store edition includes both hardware and Avamar server software from EMC.

- **Avamar Virtual Edition:** Avamar Virtual Edition for VMware is Avamar server software deployed as a virtual appliance.

The features of EMC Avamar follows:

- **Data deduplication:** Ensures that data is backed up only once across the backup environment.

- **Systematic fault tolerance:** Uses RAID, RAIN, checkpoints, and replication, which provide data integrity and disaster recovery protection.

- **Standard IP network leveraging:** Optimizes the use of a network for backup; dedicated backup networks are not required. Daily full backups are possible using the existing networks and infrastructure.

- **Scalable server architecture:** Additional storage nodes can be added nondisruptively to an Avamar multinode server in Avamar Data Store to accommodate increased backup storage requirements.

- **Centralized management:** Enables remote management of Avamar servers from a centralized location and through the use of the Avamar Enterprise Manager and Avamar Administrator interfaces.

## 10.15.3 EMC Data Domain

The EMC Data Domain deduplication storage system is a target-based data deduplication solution. Using high-speed, inline deduplication technology, the Data Domain system provides a storage footprint that is signifiacantly smaller on an average than the original data set. It supports various backup and enterprise applications in database, e-mail, content management, and virtual environments. Data Domain systems can scale from small remote office appliances to large data-center systems. These systems are available as integrated appliances or as gateways that use external storage.

Data Domain deduplication storage systems provide the following unique advantages:

- **Data invulnerability architecture:** Provides unprecedented levels of data integrity, data verification, and self-healing capabilities, such as RAID 6 protection. Continuous fault detection, healing, and write verification ensure that the backup is accurately stored, available, and recoverable.

- **Data Domain SISL (Stream-Informed Segment Layout) scaling architecture:** Enables scaling of CPUs to add a direct benefit to the system throughput scalability

- **Support native replication technology:** Enables automatic, secure transfer of compressed data over the wide area network (WAN) with minimum bandwidth requirement

- **Global compression:** Highly efficient deduplication and compression technology, which radically changes storage economics

EMC Data Domain Archiver is a solution for long-term retention of backup and archive data. It is designed with an internal tiering approach to enable cost-effective, long-term retention of data on disk by implementing deduplication technology.

## Summary

Information availability is a critical requirement for information-centric businesses. Backups protect businesses from data loss and also help to meet regulatory and compliance requirements.

Data archiving has further enabled IT organizations to realize cost savings and improve operational efficiency. Data archiving enables meeting regulatory requirements that have helped organizations avoid penalties and issues associated with regulatory compliance.

This chapter detailed backup considerations, methods, technologies, and implementations in a storage networking environment. It also elaborated various backup topologies, architectures, data deduplication, and backup in virtualized environments. In addition, this chapter also detailed archiving solution architecture. Although the selection of a particular backup media is driven by the defined RTO and RPO, disk-based backup has a clear advantage over tape-based backup in terms of performance, availability, faster recovery, and ease of management. These advantages are further supplemented with the use of replication technologies to achieve the highest level of service and availability requirements. Replication technologies are covered in detail in the next two chapters.

**EXERCISES**

1. A customer performs a full backup on the first Sunday of the month followed by a cumulative backup on the other Sundays. They also perform an incremental backup each day Monday through Saturday. Tapes are sent offsite for disaster recovery every morning at 10 a.m. The customer experiences a system crash on the Wednesday of the third week at 3 p.m., requiring a system recovery. How many days worth of tapes need to be retrieved to perform a recovery?

2. There are limited backup devices in a file sharing NAS environment. Suggest a suitable backup implementation that can minimize the network traffic, avoid any congestion, and at the same time not impact the production operations. Justify your answer.

3. What are the various business/technical considerations for implementing a backup solution, and how do these considerations impact the choice of backup solution/implementation?

4. List and explain the considerations in using tape as the backup technology. What are the challenges in this environment?

5. Describe the benefits of using a virtual tape library over a physical tape library.

6. Research and prepare a presentation on the benefits and challenges of using cloud storage for archiving.

# Chapter 11
# Local Replication

In today's business environment, it is imperative for an organization to protect mission-critical data and minimize the risk of business disruption. If a local outage or disaster occurs, fast data restore and restart is essential to ensure business continuity (BC). Replication is one of the ways to ensure BC. It is the process to create an exact copy (replica) of data. These replica copies are used for restore and restart operations if data loss occurs. These replicas can also be assigned to other hosts to perform various business operations, such as backup, reporting, and testing.

Replication can be classified into two major categories: local and remote. Local replication refers to replicating data within the same array or the same data center. Remote replication refers to replicating data at a remote site. This chapter provides details about various local replication technologies, along with restore and restart considerations. This chapter also details local replication in a virtualized environment. Remote replication is covered in Chapter 12.

# 11.1 Replication Terminology

The common terms used to represent various entities and operations in a replication environment are listed here:

- **Source:** A host accessing the production data from one or more LUNs on the storage array is called a *production host*, and these LUNs are known as source LUNs (devices/volumes), production LUNs, or simply the *source*.

- **Target:** A LUN (or LUNs) on which the production data is replicated, is called the target LUN or simply the *target* or replica.

- **Point-in-Time (PIT) and continuous replica:** Replicas can be either a PIT or a continuous copy. The PIT replica is an identical image of the source at some specific timestamp. For example, if a replica of a file system is created at 4:00 p.m. on Monday, this replica is the Monday 4:00 p.m. PIT copy. On the other hand, the continuous replica is in-sync with the production data at all times.

- **Recoverability and restartability:** Recoverability enables restoration of data from the replicas to the source if data loss or corruption occurs. Restartability enables restarting business operations using the replicas. The replica must be consistent with the source so that it is usable for both recovery and restart operations. Replica consistency is detailed in section "11.3 Replica Consistency."

---

**REPLICA VERSUS BACKUP COPY**

 **Replicas are immediately accessible by the applications, but the backup copy must be restored by backup software to make it accessible to applications. Backup is always a point-in-time copy, but a replica can be a point-in-time copy or continuous. Backup is typically used for operational or disaster recovery but replicas can be used for recovery and restart, and also for other business operations, such as backup, reporting, and testing. Replicas typically provide faster RTO compared to recovery from backup.**

---

# 11.2 Uses of Local Replicas

One or more local replicas of the source data may be created for various purposes, including the following:

- **Alternative source for backup:** Under normal backup operations, data is read from the production volumes (LUNs) and written to the backup device. This places an additional burden on the production infrastructure because production LUNs are simultaneously involved in production operations and servicing data for backup operations. The local replica contains an exact point-in-time (PIT) copy of the source data, and therefore can be used as a source to perform backup operations. This alleviates the backup I/O workload on the production volumes. Another benefit of using local replicas for backup is that it reduces the *backup window* to zero.

- **Fast recovery:** If data loss or data corruption occurs on the source, a local replica might be used to recover the lost or corrupted data. If a complete failure of the source occurs, some replication solutions enable a replica to be used to restore data onto a different set of source devices, or production can be restarted on the replica. In either case, this method provides faster recovery and minimal RTO compared to traditional recovery from tape backups. In many instances, business operations can be started using the source device before the data is completely copied from the replica.

- **Decision-support activities, such as reporting or data warehousing:** Running the reports using the data on the replicas greatly reduces the I/O burden placed on the production device. Local replicas are also used for data-warehousing applications. The data-warehouse application may be populated by the data on the replica and thus avoid the impact on the production environment.

- **Testing platform:** Local replicas are also used for testing new applications or upgrades. For example, an organization may use the replica to test the production application upgrade; if the test is successful, the upgrade may be implemented on the production environment.

- **Data migration:** Another use for a local replica is data migration. Data migrations are performed for various reasons, such as migrating from a smaller capacity LUN to one of a larger capacity for newer versions of the application.

## 11.3 Replica Consistency

Most file systems and databases buffer the data in the host before writing it to the disk. A consistent replica ensures that the data buffered in the host is captured on the disk when the replica is created. The data staged in the cache and not yet committed to the disk should be flushed before taking the replica. The storage array operating environment takes care of flushing its cache before the replication operation is initiated. Consistency ensures the usability of a replica and is a primary requirement for all the replication technologies.

### 11.3.1 Consistency of a Replicated File System

File systems buffer the data in the host memory to improve the application response time. The buffered data is periodically written to the disk. In UNIX operating systems, *sync daemon* is the process that flushes the buffers to the disk at set intervals. In some cases, the replica is created between the set intervals, which might result in the creation of an inconsistent replica. Therefore, host memory buffers must be flushed to ensure data consistency on the replica, prior to its creation. Figure 11-1 illustrates how the file system buffer is flushed to the source device before replication. If the host memory buffers are not flushed, the data on the replica will not contain the information that was buffered in the host. If the file system is unmounted before creating the replica, the buffers will be automatically flushed and the data will be consistent on the replica.

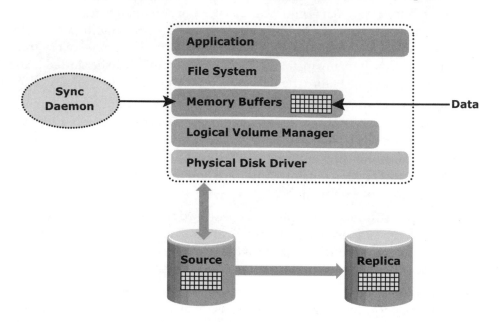

**Figure 11-1:** Flushing the file system buffer

If a mounted file system is replicated, some level of recovery, such as *fsck* or *log replay*, is required on the replicated file system. When the file system replication and check process are completed, the replica file system can be mounted for operational use.

## 11.3.2 Consistency of a Replicated Database

A database may be spread over numerous files, file systems, and devices. All of these must be replicated consistently to ensure that the replica is restorable and restartable. Replication is performed with the database offline or online. If the database is offline during the creation of the replica, it is not available for I/O operations. Because no updates occur on the source, the replica is consistent.

If the database is online, it is available for I/O operations, and transactions to the database update the data continuously. When a database is replicated while it is online, changes made to the database at this time must be applied to the replica to make it consistent. A consistent replica of an online database is created by using the dependent write I/O principle or by holding I/Os momentarily to the source before creating the replica.

A *dependent write I/O* principle is inherent in many applications and database management systems (DBMS) to ensure consistency. According to this principle, a write I/O is not issued by an application until a prior related write I/O has completed. For example, a data write is dependent on the successful completion of the prior log write.

For a transaction to be deemed complete, databases require a series of writes to have occurred in a particular order. These writes will be recorded on the various devices or file systems. Figure 11-2, illustrates the process of flushing the buffer from the host to the source; I/Os 1 to 4 must complete for the transaction to be considered complete. I/O 4 is dependent on I/O 3 and occurs only if I/O 3 is complete. I/O 3 is dependent on I/O 2, which in turn depends on I/O 1. Each I/O completes only after completion of the previous I/O(s).

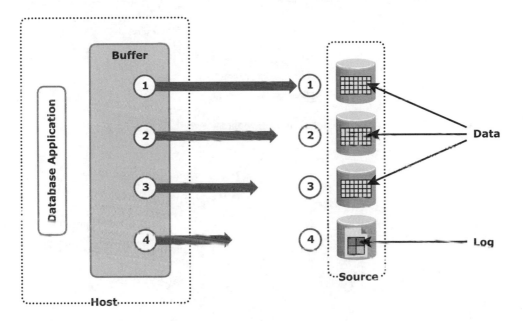

**Figure 11-2:** Dependent write consistency on sources

When the replica is created, all the writes to the source devices must be captured on the replica devices to ensure data consistency. Figure 11-3 illustrates the process of replication from the source to the replica. I/O transactions 1 to 4 must be carried out for the data to be consistent on the replica.

It is possible that I/O transactions 3 and 4 were copied to the replica devices, but I/O transactions 1 and 2 were not copied. Figure 11-4 shows this situation.

In this case, the data on the replica is inconsistent with the data on the source. If a restart were to be performed on the replica devices, I/O 4, which is available on the replica, might indicate that a particular transaction is complete, but all the data associated with the transaction will be unavailable on the replica, making the replica inconsistent.

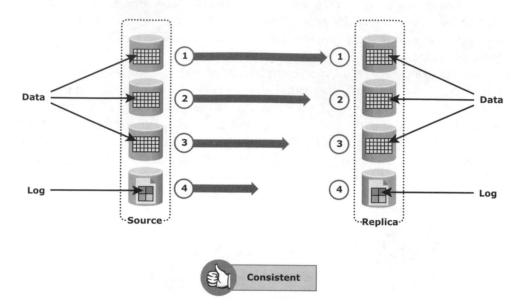

**Figure 11-3:** Dependent write consistency on replica

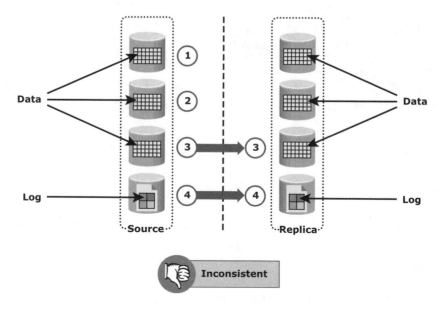

**Figure 11-4:** Inconsistent database replica

Another way to ensure consistency is to make sure that the write I/O to all source devices is held for the duration of creating the replica. This creates a consistent image on the replica. However, databases and applications might time out if the I/O is held for too long.

# 11.4 Local Replication Technologies

Host-based, storage array-based, and network-based replications are the major technologies used for local replication. File system replication and LVM-based replication are examples of host-based local replication. Storage array-based replication can be implemented with distinct solutions, namely, full-volume mirroring, pointer-based full-volume replication, and pointer-based virtual replication. Continuous data protection (CDP) (covered in section "11.4.3 Network-Based Local Replication") is an example of network-based replication.

## 11.4.1 Host-Based Local Replication

LVM-based replication and file system (FS) snapshot are two common methods of host-based local replication.

### LVM-Based Replication

In *LVM-based replication*, the logical volume manager is responsible for creating and controlling the host-level logical volumes. An LVM has three components: physical volumes (physical disk), volume groups, and logical volumes. A *volume group* is created by grouping one or more physical volumes. *Logical volumes* are created within a given volume group. A volume group can have multiple logical volumes.

In LVM-based replication, each *logical block* in a logical volume is mapped to two physical blocks on two different physical volumes, as shown in Figure 11-5. An application write to a logical volume is written to the two physical volumes by the LVM device driver. This is also known as *LVM mirroring*. Mirrors can be split, and the data contained therein can be independently accessed.

### Advantages of LVM-Based Replication

The LVM-based replication technology is not dependent on a vendor-specific storage system. Typically, LVM is part of the operating system, and no additional license is required to deploy LVM mirroring.

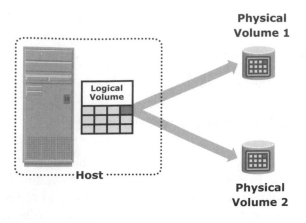

**Figure 11-5:** LVM-based mirroring

## Limitations of LVM-Based Replication

Every write generated by an application translates into two writes on the disk, and thus, an additional burden is placed on the host CPU. This can degrade application performance. Presenting an LVM-based local replica to another host is usually not possible because the replica will still be part of the volume group, which is usually accessed by one host at any given time.

Tracking changes to the mirrors and performing incremental resynchronization operations is also a challenge because all LVMs do not support incremental resynchronization. If the devices are already protected by some level of RAID on the array, then the additional protection that the LVM mirroring provides is unnecessary. This solution does not scale to provide replicas of federated databases and applications. Both the replica and source are stored within the same volume group. Therefore, the replica might become unavailable if there is an error in the volume group. If the server fails, both the source and replica are unavailable until the server is brought back online.

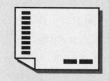

A *federated database* is a collection of databases that work together as a single entity. Each individual database in a federated database is self-contained and fully functional. When a federated database receives a query, it forwards the request to the database entity that contains the requested data. A federated database appears as a unified database to an application. This eliminates the need to send queries to multiple databases and combine the results.

### File System Snapshot

A file system (FS) snapshot is a pointer-based replica that requires a fraction of the space used by the production FS. This snapshot can be implemented by either FS or by LVM. It uses the Copy on First Write (CoFW) principle to create snapshots.

When a snapshot is created, a bitmap and blockmap are created in the metadata of the Snap FS. The bitmap is used to keep track of blocks that are changed on the production FS after the snap creation. The blockmap is used to indicate the exact address from which the data is to be read when the data is accessed from the Snap FS. Immediately after the creation of the FS snapshot, all reads from the snapshot are actually served by reading the production FS. In a CoFW mechanism, if a write I/O is issued to the production FS for the first time after the creation of a snapshot, the I/O is held and the original data of production FS corresponding to that location is moved to the Snap FS. Then, the write is allowed to the production FS. The bitmap and blockmap are updated accordingly. Subsequent writes to the same location do not initiate the CoFW activity. To read from the Snap FS, the bitmap is consulted. If the bit is 0, then the read is directed to the production FS. If the bit is 1, then the block address is obtained from the blockmap, and the data is read from that address on the Snap FS. Read requests from the production FS work as normal.

Figure 11-6 illustrates the write operations to the production file system. For example, a write data "C" occurs on block 3 at the production FS, which currently holds data "c." The snapshot application holds the I/O to the production FS and first copies the old data "c" to an available data block on the Snap FS. The bitmap and blockmap values for block 3 in the production FS are changed in the snap metadata. The bitmap of block 3 is changed to 1, indicating that this block has changed on the production FS. The block map of block 3 is changed and indicates the block number where the data is written in Snap FS, (in this case block 2). After this is done, the I/Os to the production FS are allowed to complete. Any subsequent writes to block 3 on the production FS occur as normal, and it does not initiate the CoFW operation. Similarly, if an I/O is issued to block 4 on the production FS to change the value of data "d" to "D," the snapshot application holds the I/O to the production FS and copies the old data to an available data block on the Snap FS. Then it changes the bitmap of block 4 to 1, indicating that the data block has changed on the production FS. The blockmap for block 4 indicates the block number where the data can be found on the Snap FS, in this case, data block 1 of the Snap FS. After this is done, the I/O to the production FS is allowed to complete.

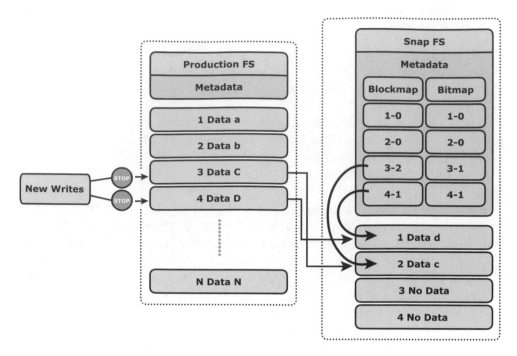

**Figure 11-6:** Write to production FS

## 11.4.2 Storage Array-Based Local Replication

In *storage array-based local replication*, the array-operating environment performs the local replication process. The host resources, such as the CPU and memory, are not used in the replication process. Consequently, the host is not burdened by the replication operations. The replica can be accessed by an alternative host for other business operations.

In this replication, the required number of replica devices should be selected on the same array and then data should be replicated between the source-replica pairs. Figure 11-7 shows a storage array-based local replication, where the source and target are in the same array and accessed by different hosts.

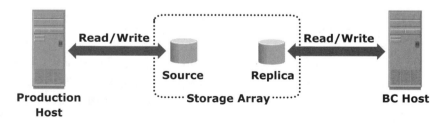

**Figure 11-7:** Storage array-based local replication

Storage array-based local replication is commonly implemented in three ways: full-volume mirroring, pointer-based full-volume replication, and pointer-based virtual replication. Replica devices are also referred as target devices, accessible by other hosts.

## Full-Volume Mirroring

In *full-volume mirroring*, the target is attached to the source and established as a mirror of the source (Figure 11-8 [a]). The data on the source is copied to the target. New updates to the source are also updated on the target. After all the data is copied and both the source and the target contain identical data, the target can be considered as a mirror of the source.

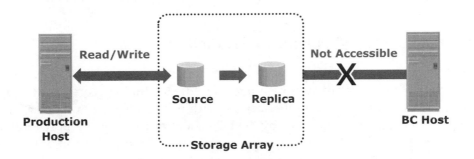

**(a) Full Volume Mirroring with Source Attached to Replica**

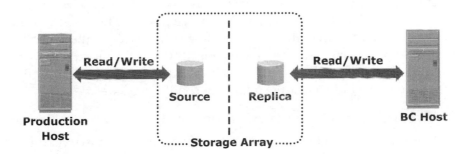

**(b) Full Volume Mirroring with Source Detached from Replica**

**Figure 11-8:** Full-volume mirroring

While the target is attached to the source it remains unavailable to any other host. However, the production host continues to access the source.

After the synchronization is complete, the target can be detached from the source and made available for other business operations. Figure 11-8 (b) shows full-volume mirroring when the target is detached from the source. Both the source and the target can be accessed for read and write operations by the production and business continuity hosts respectively.

After detaching from the source, the target becomes a point-in-time (PIT) copy of the source. The PIT of a replica is determined by the time when the target is detached from the source. For example, if the time of detachment is 4:00 p.m., the PIT for the target is 4:00 p.m.

After detachment, changes made to both the source and replica can be tracked at some predefined granularity. This enables incremental resynchronization (source to target) or incremental restore (target to source). The granularity of the data change can range from 512 byte blocks to 64 KB blocks or higher.

### Pointer-Based, Full-Volume Replication

Another method of array-based local replication is *pointer-based full-volume replication*. Similar to full-volume mirroring, this technology can provide full copies of the source data on the targets. Unlike full-volume mirroring, the target is immediately accessible by the BC host after the replication session is activated. Therefore, data synchronization and detachment of the target is not required to access it. Here, the time of replication session activation defines the PIT copy of the source.

Pointer-based, full-volume replication can be activated in either Copy on First Access (CoFA) mode or Full Copy mode. In either case, at the time of activation, a protection bitmap is created for all data on the source devices. The protection bitmap keeps track of the changes at the source device. The pointers on the target are initialized to map the corresponding data blocks on the source. The data is then copied from the source to the target based on the mode of activation.

In CoFA, after the replication session is initiated, the data is copied from the source to the target only when the following condition occurs:

- A write I/O is issued to a specific address on the source for the first time.

- A read or write I/O is issued to a specific address on the target for the first time.

When a write is issued to the source for the first time after replication session activation, the original data at that address is copied to the target. After this operation, the new data is updated on the source. This ensures that the original data at the point-in-time of activation is preserved on the target (see Figure 11-9).

When a read is issued to the target for the first time after replication session activation, the original data is copied from the source to the target and is made available to the BC host (see Figure 11-10).

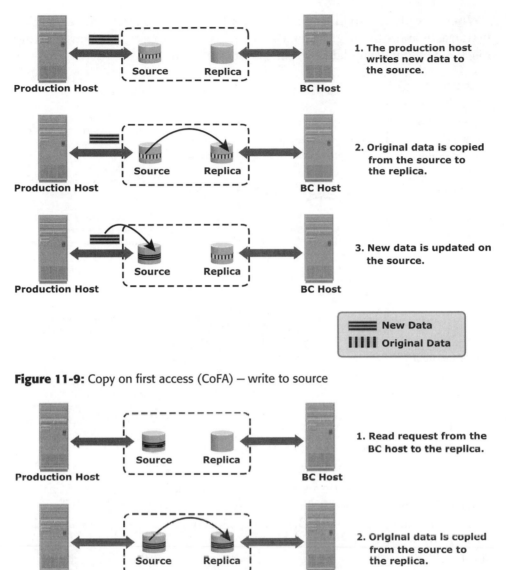

**Figure 11-9:** Copy on first access (CoFA) — write to source

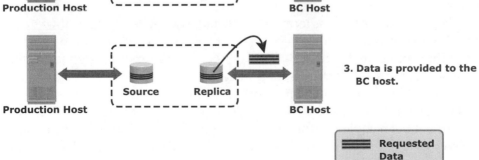

**Figure 11-10:** Copy on first access (CoFA) — read from target

When a write is issued to the target for the first time after the replication session activation, the original data is copied from the source to the target. After this, the new data is updated on the target (see Figure 11-11).

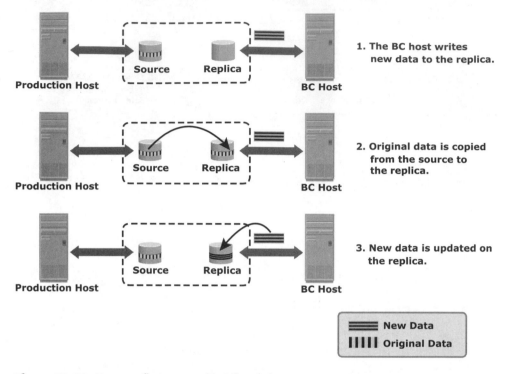

**Figure 11-11:** Copy on first access (CoFA) — write to target

In all cases, the protection bit for the data block on the source is reset to indicate that the original data has been copied over to the target. The pointer to the source data can now be discarded. Subsequent writes to the same data block on the source, and the reads or writes to the same data blocks on the target, do not trigger a copy operation, therefore this method is termed "Copy on First Access."

If the replication session is terminated, then the target device has only the data that was accessed until the termination, not the entire contents of the source at the point-in-time. In this case, the data on the target cannot be used for restore because it is not a full replica of the source.

In a Full Copy mode, all data from the source is copied to the target in the background. Data is copied regardless of access. If access to a block that has not yet been copied to the target is required, this block is preferentially copied to the target. In a complete cycle of the Full Copy mode, all data from the source is copied to the target. If the replication session is terminated now, the target contains all the original data from the source at the point-in-time of activation. This makes the target a viable copy for restore or other business continuity operations.

The key difference between a pointer-based, Full Copy mode and full-volume mirroring is that the target is immediately accessible upon replication session activation in the Full Copy mode. Both the full-volume mirroring and pointer-based full-volume replication technologies require the target devices to be at least as large as the source devices. In addition, full-volume mirroring and pointer-based full-volume replication in the Full Copy mode can provide incremental resynchronization and restore capabilities.

### Pointer-Based Virtual Replication

In *pointer-based virtual replication*, at the time of the replication session activation, the target contains pointers to the location of the data on the source. The target does not contain data at any time. Therefore, the target is known as a *virtual replica*. Similar to pointer-based full-volume replication, the target is immediately accessible after the replication session activation. A protection bitmap is created for all data blocks on the source device. Granularity of data blocks can range from 512 byte blocks to 64 KB blocks or greater.

Pointer-based virtual replication uses the CoFW technology. When a write is issued to the source for the first time after the replication session activation, the original data at that address is copied to a predefined area in the array. This area is generally known as the *save location*. The pointer in the target is updated to point to this data in the save location. After this, the new write is updated on the source. This process is illustrated in Figure 11-12.

When a write is issued to the target for the first time after replication session activation, the data is copied from the source to the save location, and the pointer is updated to the data in the save location. Another copy of the original data is created in the save location before the new write is updated on the save location. Subsequent writes to the same data block on the source or target do not trigger a copy operation. This process is illustrated in Figure 11-13.

When reads are issued to the target, unchanged data blocks since the session activation are read from the source, whereas data blocks that have changed are read from the save location.

Data on the target is a combined view of unchanged data on the source and data on the save location. Unavailability of the source device invalidates the data on the target. The target contains only pointers to the data, and therefore, the physical capacity required for the target is a fraction of the source device. The capacity required for the save location depends on the amount of the expected data change.

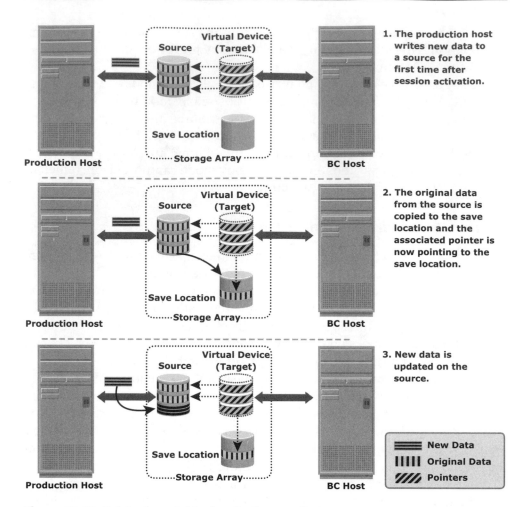

**Figure 11-12:** Pointer-based virtual replication — write to source

## 11.4.3 Network-Based Local Replication

In network-based replication, the replication occurs at the network layer between the hosts and storage arrays. Network-based replication combines the benefits of array-based and host-based replications. By offloading replication from servers and arrays, network-based replication can work across a large number of server platforms and storage arrays, making it ideal for highly heterogeneous environments. *Continuous data protection* (CDP) is a technology used for network-based local and remote replications. CDP for remote replication is detailed in Chapter 12.

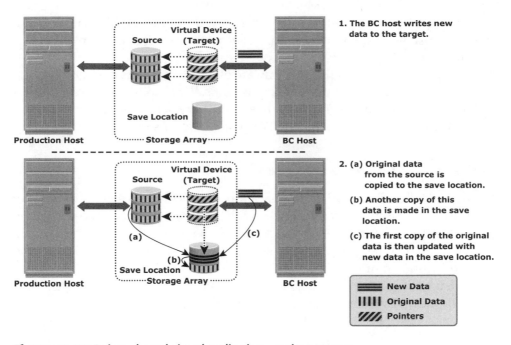

**Figure 11-13:** Pointer-based virtual replication — write to target

## Continuous Data Protection

In a data center environment, mission-critical applications often require instant and unlimited data recovery points. Traditional data protection technologies offer limited recovery points. If data loss occurs, the system can be rolled back only to the last available recovery point. Mirroring offers continuous replication; however, if logical corruption occurs to the production data, the error might propagate to the mirror, which makes the replica unusable. In normal operation, CDP provides the ability to restore data to any previous PIT. It enables this capability by tracking all the changes to the production devices and maintaining consistent point-in-time images.

In CDP, data changes are continuously captured and stored in a separate location from the primary storage. Moreover, RPOs are random and do not need to be defined in advance. With CDP, recovery from data corruption poses no problem because it allows going back to a PIT image prior to the data corruption incident. CDP uses a *journal volume* to store all data changes on the primary storage. The journal volume contains all the data that has changed from the time the replication session started. The amount of space that is configured for the journal determines how far back the recovery points can go. CDP is typically implemented using *CDP appliance* and *write splitters*. CDP implementation may also be host-based, in which CDP software is installed on a separate host machine.

CDP appliance is an intelligent hardware platform that runs the CDP software and manages local and remote data replications. Write splitters intercept writes to the production volume from the host and split each write into two copies. Write splitting can be performed at the host, fabric, or storage array.

### CDP Local Replication Operation

Figure 11-14 describes CDP local replication. In this method, before the start of replication, the replica is synchronized with the source and then the replication process starts. After the replication starts, all the writes to the source are split into two copies. One of the copies is sent to the CDP appliance and the other to the production volume. When the CDP appliance receives a copy of a write, it is written to the journal volume along with its timestamp. As a next step, data from the journal volume is sent to the replica at predefined intervals.

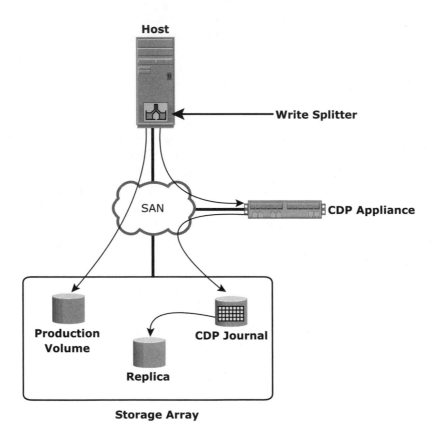

**Figure 11-14:** Continuous data protection – local replication

While recovering data to the source, the CDP appliance restores the data from the replica and applies journal entries up to the point in time chosen for recovery.

# 11.5 Tracking Changes to Source and Replica

Updates can occur on the source device after the creation of PIT local replicas. If the primary purpose of local replication is to have a viable PIT copy for data recovery or restore operations, then the replica devices should not be modified. Changes can occur on the replica device if it is used for other business operations. To enable incremental resynchronization or restore operations, changes to both the source and replica devices after the PIT should be tracked. This is typically done using bitmaps, where each bit represents a block of data. The data block sizes can range from 512 bytes to 64 KB or greater. For example, if the block size is 32 KB, then a 1-GB device would require 32,768 bits (1 GB divided by 32 KB). The size of the bitmap would be 4 KB. If the data in any 32 KB block is changed, the corresponding bit in the bitmap is flagged. If the block size is reduced for tracking purposes, then the bitmap size increases correspondingly.

The bits in the source and target bitmaps are all set to 0 (zero) when the replica is created. Any changes to the source or replica are then flagged by setting the appropriate bits to 1 in the bitmap. When resynchronization or restore is required, a *logical OR* operation between the source bitmap and the target bitmap is performed. The bitmap resulting from this operation references all blocks that have been modified in either the source or replica (see Figure 11-15). This enables an optimized resynchronization or a restore operation because it eliminates the need to copy all the blocks between the source and the replica. The direction of data movement depends on whether a resynchronization or a restore operation is performed.

If resynchronization is required, changes to the replica are overwritten with the corresponding blocks from the source. In this example, that would be blocks labeled 2, 3, and 7 on the replica.

If a restore is required, changes to the source are overwritten with the corresponding blocks from the replica. In this example, that would be blocks labeled 0, 3, and 5 on the source. In either case, changes to both the source and the target cannot be simultaneously preserved.

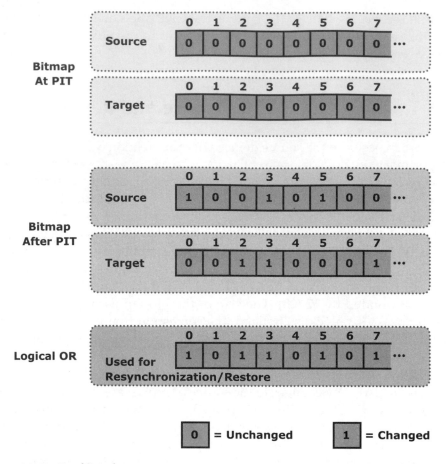

0 = Unchanged    1 = Changed

**Figure 11-15:** Tracking changes

## 11.6 Restore and Restart Considerations

Local replicas are used to restore data to production devices. Alternatively, applications can be restarted using the consistent PIT replicas.

Replicas are used to restore data to the production devices if logical corruption of data on production devices occurs — that is, the devices are available but the data on them is invalid. Examples of logical corruption include accidental deletion of data (tables or entries in a database), incorrect data entry, and incorrect data updates. Restore operations from a replica are incremental and provide a small RTO. In some instances, the applications can be resumed on the production devices prior to the completion of the data copy. Prior to the restore operation, access to production and replica devices should be stopped.

Production devices might also become unavailable due to physical failures, such as the production server or physical drive failure. In this case, applications can be restarted using the data on the latest replica. As a protection against further failures, a Gold Copy (another copy of replica device) of the replica device should be created to preserve a copy of data in the event of failure or corruption of the replica devices. After the issue has been resolved, the data from the replica devices can be restored back to the production devices.

Full-volume replicas (both full-volume mirrors and pointer-based in Full Copy mode) can be restored to the original source devices or to a new set of source devices. Restores to the original source devices can be incremental, but restores to a new set of devices are full-volume copy operations.

In pointer-based virtual and pointer-based full-volume replication in CoFA mode, access to data on the replica is dependent on the health and accessibility of the source volumes. If the source volume is inaccessible for any reason, these replicas cannot be used for a restore or a restart operation.

Table 11-1 presents a comparative analysis of the various storage array-based replication technologies.

**Table 11-1:** Comparison of Local Replication Technologies

| FACTOR | FULL-VOLUME MIRRORING | POINTER-BASED, FULL-VOLUME REPLICATION | POINTER-BASED VIRTUAL REPLICATION |
| --- | --- | --- | --- |
| Performance impact on source due to replica | No impact | CoFA mode — some impact<br><br>Full copy mode — no impact | High impact |
| Size of target | At least the same as the source | At least the same as the source | Small fraction of the source |
| Availability of source for restoration | Not required | CoFA mode — required<br><br>Full copy mode — not required | Required |
| Accessibility to target | Only after synchronization and detachment from the source | Immediately accessible | Immediately accessible |

# 11.7 Creating Multiple Replicas

Most storage array-based replication technologies enable source devices to maintain replication relationships with multiple targets. Changes made to the source and each of the targets can be tracked. This enables incremental resynchronization of the targets. Each PIT copy can be used for different BC activities and as a restore point.

Figure 11-16 shows an example in which a copy is created every 6 hours from the same source.

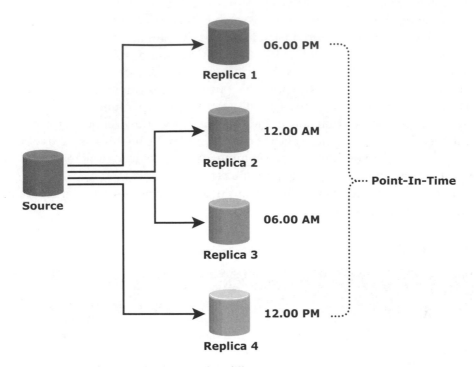

**Figure 11-16:** Multiple replicas created at different PIT

If the source is corrupted, the data can be restored from the latest PIT copy. The maximum RPO in the example shown in Figure 11-16 is 6 hours. More frequent replicas further reduce the RPO.

Array-based local replication technologies also enable the creation of multiple *concurrent* PIT replicas. In this case, all replicas contain identical data. One or more of the replicas can be set aside for restore operations. Decision support activities can be performed using the other replicas.

## 11.8 Local Replication in a Virtualized Environment

The discussion so far has focused on local replication in a physical infrastructure environment. In a virtualized environment, along with replicating storage volumes, virtual machine (VM) replication is also required. Typically, local replication of VMs is performed by the hypervisor at the compute level. However, it can also be performed at the storage level using array-based local replication, similar to the physical environment. In the array-based method, the LUN on which the VMs reside is replicated to another LUN in the same array. For hypervisor-based local replication, two options are available: VM Snapshot and VM Clone.

VM Snapshot captures the state and data of a running virtual machine at a specific point in time. The VM state includes VM files, such as BIOS, network configuration, and its power state (powered-on, powered-off, or suspended). The VM data includes all the files that make up the VM, including virtual disks and memory. A VM Snapshot uses a separate delta file to record all the changes to the virtual disk since the snapshot session is activated. Snapshots are useful when a VM needs to be reverted to the previous state in the event of logical corruptions. Reverting a VM to a previous state causes all settings configured in the guest OS to be reverted to that PIT when that snapshot was created. There are some challenges associated with the VM Snapshot technology. It does not support data replication if a virtual machine accesses the data by using raw disks. Also, using the hypervisor to perform snapshots increases the load on the compute and impacts the compute performance.

VM Clone is another method that creates an identical copy of a virtual machine. When the cloning operation is complete, the clone becomes a separate VM from its parent VM. The clone has its own MAC address, and changes made to a clone do not affect the parent VM. Similarly, changes made to the parent VM do not appear in the clone. VM Clone is a useful method when there is a need to deploy many identical VMs. Installing guest OS and applications on multiple VMs is a time-consuming task; VM Clone helps to simplify this process.

# 11.9 Concepts in Practice: EMC TimeFinder, EMC SnapView, and EMC RecoverPoint

EMC offers a range of storage array-based local replication solutions for different storage arrays. For the Symmetrix array, the EMC TimeFinder family of products is used for full-volume and pointer-based local replication. EMC SnapView is the solution for EMC VNX storage arrays. EMC RecoverPoint is a network-based replication solution. Visit www.emc.com for the latest information.

## 11.9.1 EMC TimeFinder

The TimeFinder family of products consists of two base solutions and four add-on solutions. The base solutions are TimeFinder/Clone and TimeFinder/Snap. The add-on solutions are TimeFinder/Clone Emulation, TimeFinder/Consistency Groups, TimeFinder/Exchange Integration Module, and TimeFinder/SQL Integration Module.

TimeFinder is available for both open systems and mainframes. The base solutions support the different storage array-based local replication technologies discussed in this chapter. The add-on solutions are customizations of the replicas for specific application or database environments.

### TimeFinder/Clone

TimeFinder/Clone creates a PIT copy of the source volume that can be used for backups, decision support, or any other process that requires parallel access to production data. TimeFinder/Clone uses pointer-based full-volume replication technology. TimeFinder/Clone allows creating up to 16 active clones from a single production device, and all the clones are available immediately for read and write access.

### TimeFinder/Snap

TimeFinder/Snap creates space-saving, logical PIT images called snapshots. The snapshots are not full copies but contain pointers to the source data. The target device used by TimeFinder/Snap is called a virtual device (VDEV). It keeps pointers to the source device or SAVE devices. The SAVE devices keep the point-in-time data that has changed on the source after the start of the replication session. TimeFinder/Snap allows creating multiple snapshots, up to 128, from a single source device.

## 11.9.2 EMC SnapView

SnapView is an EMC VNX array-based local replication software that creates a pointer-based virtual copy and full-volume mirror of the source using SnapView snapshot and SnapView clone respectively.

### SnapView Snapshot

A SnapView snapshot is not a full copy of the production volume; it is a logical view of the production volume based on the time at which the snapshot was created. Snapshots are created in seconds and can be retired when no longer needed. A snapshot rollback feature provides instant restore to the source volume. The key terminologies of SnapView snapshot are as follows:

- **SnapView session:** The SnapView snapshot mechanism is activated when a session starts and deactivated when a session stops. A snapshot appears "offline" until there is an active session. Multiple snapshots can be included in a session.

▪ **Reserved LUN pool:** This is a private area, also called a save area, used to contain Copy on First Write (CoFW) data. The "Reserved" part of the name refers to the fact that the LUNs are reserved and therefore cannot be assigned to a host.

### SnapView Clone

SnapView Clones are full-volume copies that require the same disk space as the source. These PIT copies can be used for other business operations, such as backup and testing. SnapView Clone enables incremental resynchronization between the source and replica. Clone fracture is the process of breaking off a clone from its source. After the clone is fractured, it becomes a PIT copy and available for other business operations.

## 11.9.3 EMC RecoverPoint

RecoverPoint is a high-performance, cost-effective, single product that provides local and remote data protection for both physical and virtual environments. It provides faster recovery and unlimited recovery points. RecoverPoint provides continuous data protection and performs replication between the LUNs that reside in one or more arrays at the same site. RecoverPoint uses lightweight splitting technology either at the application server, fabric, or arrays to mirror a write to a RecoverPoint appliance. The RecoverPoint family of products includes RecoverPoint/CL, RecoverPoint/EX, and RecoverPoint/SE.

RecoverPoint/CL is a replication product for a heterogeneous server and storage environment. It supports both EMC and non-EMC storage arrays. This product supports host-based, fabric-based, and array-based write splitters. RecoverPoint/EX supports replication between EMC storage arrays and enables only array-based write splitting. RecoverPoint/SE is a version of RecoverPoint targeted for VNX series arrays and enables only Windows-based host and array-based write splitting.

## Summary

Local replication provides a quick restore to ensure protection against data corruption during major updates to the source data. This technology has become an integral part of day-to-day data center operations.

This chapter looked at the local replication process and described the uses of a local replica. Local replication can be accomplished using various technologies, such as host-based local replication, storage array-based local replication, and network-based local replication. This chapter also described the restore and restart considerations for storage array-based local replication and the creation of multiple replicas. Local replicas of VMs and virtual disks were also covered in the chapter.

Though duplication of data with a local replica ensures high availability, dispersal of the duplicates to different sites is a way to ensure continuous operation for data centers if a disaster occurs that could incapacitate the entire site. Establishing the replicas at the remote site with replication has emerged as a matured technology. Remote replication is covered in detail in the next chapter.

## EXERCISES

1. Research various techniques used to ensure consistency of a local replica.

2. Describe the uses of a local replica in various business operations.

3. Research factors that determine storage capacity requirements for a *save location* in pointer-based virtual replication.

4. Research continuous data protection technology and its benefits over array-based replication technologies.

5. An administrator configures six pointer-based virtual replicas of a source LUN and creates eight full-volume replicas of the same LUN. The administrator then creates four pointer-based virtual replicas for each full-volume replica that was created. How many usable replicas are now available?

# Chapter 12
# Remote Replication

*R*emote replication is the process to create replicas of information assets at remote sites (locations). Remote replication helps organizations mitigate the risks associated with regionally driven outages resulting from natural or human-made disasters. During disasters, the workload can be moved to a remote site to ensure continuous business operation. Similar to local replicas, remote replicas can also be used for other business operations.

This chapter discusses various remote replication technologies, along with three-site replication and data migration applications. This chapter also covers remote replication and VM migration in a virtualized environment.

### KEY CONCEPTS

Synchronous and Asynchronous Replication

LVM-Based Replication

Host-Based Log Shipping

Disk-Buffered Replication

Three-Site Replication

Virtual Machine Migration

## 12.1 Modes of Remote Replication

The two basic modes of remote replication are synchronous and asynchronous. In *synchronous remote replication*, writes must be committed to the source and remote replica (or target), prior to acknowledging "write complete" to the host (see Figure 12-1). Additional writes on the source cannot occur until each preceding write has been completed and acknowledged. This ensures that data is identical on the source and replica at all times. Further, writes are transmitted to the remote site exactly in the order in which they are received at the source. Therefore, write ordering is maintained. If a source-site failure occurs, synchronous remote replication provides zero or near-zero recovery-point objective (RPO).

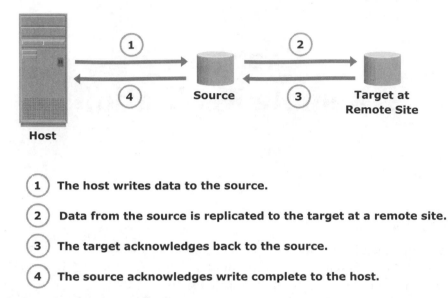

(1) The host writes data to the source.

(2) Data from the source is replicated to the target at a remote site.

(3) The target acknowledges back to the source.

(4) The source acknowledges write complete to the host.

**Figure 12-1:** Synchronous replication

However, application response time is increased with synchronous remote replication because writes must be committed on both the source and target before sending the "write complete" acknowledgment to the host. The degree of impact on response time depends primarily on the distance between sites, bandwidth, and quality of service (QOS) of the network connectivity infrastructure. Figure 12-2 represents the network bandwidth requirement for synchronous replication. If the bandwidth provided for synchronous remote replication is less than the maximum write workload, there will be times during the day when the response time might be excessively elongated, causing applications to time out. The distances over which synchronous replication can be deployed depend on the application's capability to tolerate extensions in response time. Typically, it is deployed for distances less than 200 KM (125 miles) between the two sites.

In *asynchronous remote replication*, a write is committed to the source and immediately acknowledged to the host. In this mode, data is buffered at the source and transmitted to the remote site later (see Figure 12-3).

Asynchronous replication eliminates the impact to the application's response time because the writes are acknowledged immediately to the source host. This enables deployment of asynchronous replication over distances ranging from several hundred to several thousand kilometers between the primary and remote sites. Figure 12-4 shows the network bandwidth requirement for asynchronous replication. In this case, the required bandwidth can be provisioned equal to or greater than the average write workload. Data can be buffered during times when the bandwidth is not enough and moved later to the remote site. Therefore, sufficient buffer capacity should be provisioned.

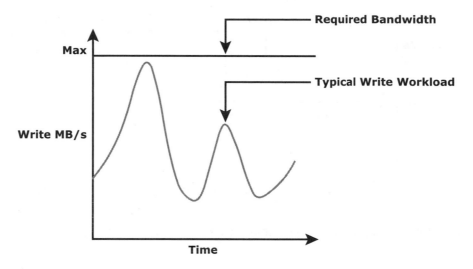

**Figure 12-2:** Bandwidth requirement for synchronous replication

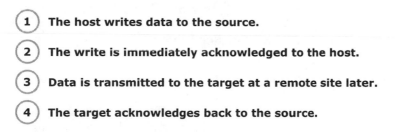

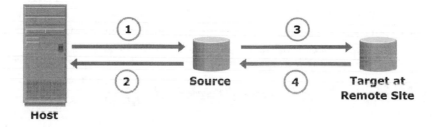

(1) The host writes data to the source.

(2) The write is immediately acknowledged to the host.

(3) Data is transmitted to the target at a remote site later.

(4) The target acknowledges back to the source.

**Figure 12-3:** Asynchronous replication

In asynchronous replication, data at the remote site will be behind the source by at least the size of the buffer. Therefore, asynchronous remote replication provides a finite (nonzero) RPO disaster recovery solution. RPO depends on the size of the buffer, the available network bandwidth, and the write workload to the source.

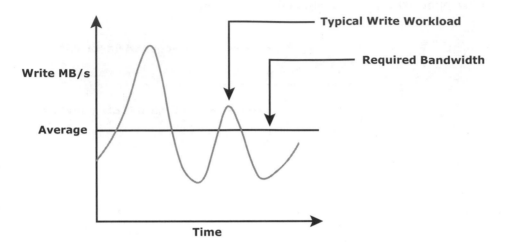

**Figure 12-4:** Bandwidth requirement for asynchronous replication

Asynchronous replication implementation can take advantage of *locality of reference* (repeated writes to the same location). If the same location is written multiple times in the buffer prior to transmission to the remote site, only the final version of the data is transmitted. This feature conserves link bandwidth.

In both synchronous and asynchronous modes of replication, only writes to the source are replicated; reads are still served from the source.

# 12.2 Remote Replication Technologies

Remote replication of data can be handled by the hosts or storage arrays. Other options include specialized network-based appliances to replicate data over the LAN or SAN. An advanced replication option such as three-site replication is discussed in section "12.3 Three-Site Replication."

## 12.2.1. Host-Based Remote Replication

Host-based remote replication uses the host resources to perform and manage the replication operation. There are two basic approaches to host-based remote replication: Logical volume manager (LVM) based replication and database replication via log shipping.

### LVM-Based Remote Replication

*LVM-based remote replication* is performed and managed at the volume group level. Writes to the source volumes are transmitted to the remote host by the LVM. The LVM on the remote host receives the writes and commits them to the remote volume group.

Prior to the start of replication, identical volume groups, logical volumes, and file systems are created at the source and target sites. Initial synchronization of data between the source and replica is performed. One method to perform initial synchronization is to backup the source data and restore the data to the remote replica. Alternatively, it can be performed by replicating over the IP network. Until the completion of the initial synchronization, production work on the source volumes is typically halted. After the initial synchronization, production work can be started on the source volumes and replication of data can be performed over an existing standard IP network (see Figure 12-5).

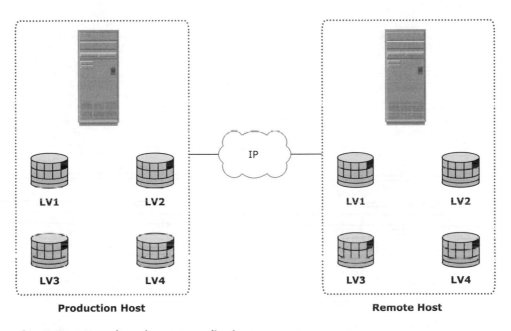

**Figure 12-5:** LVM-based remote replication

LVM-based remote replication supports both synchronous and asynchronous modes of replication. If a failure occurs at the source site, applications can be restarted on the remote host, using the data on the remote replicas.

LVM-based remote replication is independent of the storage arrays and therefore supports replication between heterogeneous storage arrays. Most operating systems are shipped with LVMs, so additional licenses and specialized hardware are not typically required.

The replication process adds overhead on the host CPUs. CPU resources on the source host are shared between replication tasks and applications. This might cause performance degradation to the applications running on the host.

Because the remote host is also involved in the replication process, it must be continuously up and available.

### Host-Based Log Shipping

Database replication via log shipping is a host-based replication technology supported by most databases. Transactions to the source database are captured in logs, which are periodically transmitted by the source host to the remote host (see Figure 12-6). The remote host receives the logs and applies them to the remote database.

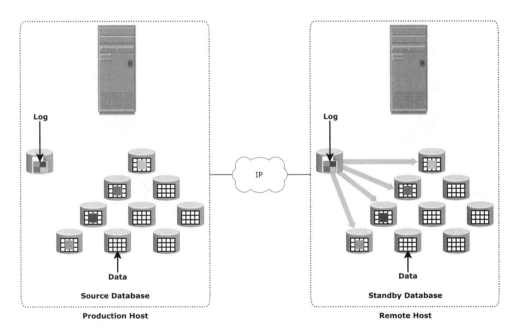

**Figure 12-6:** Host-based log shipping

Prior to starting production work and replication of log files, all relevant components of the source database are replicated to the remote site. This is done while the source database is shut down.

After this step, production work is started on the source database. The remote database is started in a standby mode. Typically, in standby mode, the database is not available for transactions.

All DBMSs switch log files at preconfigured time intervals or when a log file is full. The current log file is closed at the time of log switching, and a new log file is opened. When a log switch occurs, the closed log file is transmitted by the source host to the remote host. The remote host receives the log and updates the standby database.

This process ensures that the standby database is consistent up to the last committed log. RPO at the remote site is finite and depends on the size of the log and the frequency of log switching. Available network bandwidth, latency, rate of updates to the source database, and the frequency of log switching should be considered when determining the optimal size of the log file.

Similar to LVM-based remote replication, the existing standard IP network can be used for replicating log files. Host-based log shipping requires low network bandwidth because it transmits only the log files at regular intervals.

## 12.2.2 Storage Array-Based Remote Replication

In *storage array-based remote replication*, the array-operating environment and resources perform and manage data replication. This relieves the burden on the host CPUs, which can be better used for applications running on the host. A source and its replica device reside on different storage arrays. Data can be transmitted from the source storage array to the target storage array over a shared or a dedicated network.

Replication between arrays may be performed in synchronous, asynchronous, or disk-buffered modes.

### Synchronous Replication Mode

In array-based synchronous remote replication, writes must be committed to the source and the target prior to acknowledging "write complete" to the production host. Additional writes on that source cannot occur until each preceding write has been completed and acknowledged. Figure 12-7 shows the array-based synchronous remote replication process.

In the case of synchronous remote replication, to optimize the replication process and to minimize the impact on application response time, the write is placed on cache of the two arrays. The intelligent storage arrays destage these writes to the appropriate disks later.

If the network links fail, replication is suspended; however, production work can continue uninterrupted on the source storage array. The array operating environment keeps track of the writes that are not transmitted to the remote storage array. When the network links are restored, the accumulated data is transmitted to the remote storage array. During the time of network link outage, if there is a failure at the source site, some data will be lost, and the RPO at the target will not be zero.

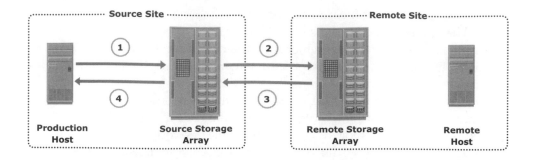

1. Write from the production host is received by the source storage array.

2. Write is then transmitted to the remote storage array.

3. Acknowledgment is sent to the source storage array by the remote storage array.

4. Source storage array signals write-completion to the production host.

**Figure 12-7:** Array-based synchronous remote replication

## Asynchronous Replication Mode

In array-based *asynchronous remote replication mode*, as shown in Figure 12-8, a write is committed to the source and immediately acknowledged to the host. Data is buffered at the source and transmitted to the remote site later. The source and the target devices do not contain identical data at all times. The data on the target device is behind that of the source, so the RPO in this case is not zero.

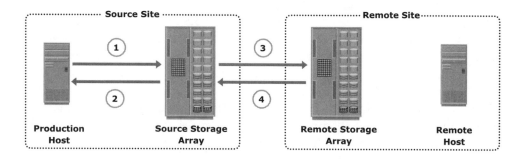

1. The production host writes to the source storage array.

2. The source array immediately acknowledges the production host.

3. These writes are then transmitted to the target array.

4. After the writes are received by the target array, it sends an acknowledgment to the source array.

**Figure 12-8:** Array-based asynchronous remote replication

Similar to synchronous replication, asynchronous replication writes are placed in cache on the two arrays and are later destaged to the appropriate disks.

Some implementations of asynchronous remote replication maintain write ordering. A timestamp and sequence number are attached to each write when it is received by the source. Writes are then transmitted to the remote array, where they are committed to the remote replica in the exact order in which they were buffered at the source. This implicitly guarantees consistency of data on the remote replicas. Other implementations ensure consistency by leveraging the dependent write principle inherent in most DBMSs. In asynchronous remote replication, the writes are buffered for a predefined period of time. At the end of this duration, the buffer is closed, and a new buffer is opened for subsequent writes. All writes in the closed buffer are transmitted together and committed to the remote replica.

Asynchronous remote replication provides network bandwidth cost-savings because the required bandwidth is lower than the peak write workload. During times when the write workload exceeds the average bandwidth, sufficient buffer space must be configured on the source storage array to hold these writes.

## Disk-Buffered Replication Mode

*Disk-buffered replication* is a combination of local and remote replication technologies. A consistent PIT local replica of the source device is first created. This is then replicated to a remote replica on the target array.

Figure 12-9 shows the sequence of operations in a disk-buffered remote replication. At the beginning of the cycle, the network links between the two arrays are suspended, and there is no transmission of data. While production application runs on the source device, a consistent PIT local replica of the source device is created. The network links are enabled, and data on the local replica in the source array transmits to its remote replica in the target array. After synchronization of this pair, the network link is suspended, and the next local replica of the source is created. Optionally, a local PIT replica of the remote device on the target array can be created. The frequency of this cycle of operations depends on the available link bandwidth and the data change rate on the source device. Because disk-buffered technology uses local replication, changes made to the source and its replica are possible to track. Therefore, all the resynchronization operations between the source and target can be done incrementally. When compared to synchronous and asynchronous replications, disk-buffered remote replication requires less bandwidth.

In disk-buffered remote replication, the RPO at the remote site is in the order of hours. For example, a local replica of the source device is created at 10:00 a.m., and this data transmits to the remote replica, which takes 1 hour to complete. Changes made to the source device after 10:00 a.m. are tracked. Another local replica of the source device is created at 11:00 a.m. by applying track changes between the source and local replica (10:00 a.m. copy). During the next cycle of transmission (11:00 a.m. data), the source data has moved to 12:00 p.m. The local replica in the remote array has the 10:00 a.m. data until the 11:00 a.m. data is successfully transmitted to the remote replica. If there is a failure at the source site prior to the completion of transmission, then the worst-case RPO at the remote site would be 2 hours because the remote site has 10:00 a.m. data.

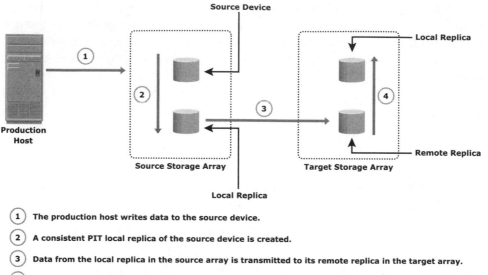

1. The production host writes data to the source device.

2. A consistent PIT local replica of the source device is created.

3. Data from the local replica in the source array is transmitted to its remote replica in the target array.

4. Optionally, a local PIT replica of the remote device on the target array is created.

**Figure 12-9:** Disk-buffered remote replication

## 12.2.3 Network-Based Remote Replication

In network-based remote replication, the replication occurs at the network layer between the host and storage array. Continuous data protection technology, discussed in the previous chapter, also provides solutions for network-based remote replication.

### CDP Remote Replication

In normal operation, CDP remote replication provides any-point-in-time recovery capability, which enables the target LUNs to be rolled back to any previous point in time. Similar to CDP local replication, CDP remote replication typically uses a *journal volume, CDP appliance,* or CDP software installed on a separate host (*host-based CDP*), and a *write splitter* to perform replication between sites. The CDP appliance is maintained at both source and remote sites.

Figure 12-10 describes CDP remote replication. In this method, the replica is synchronized with the source, and then the replication process starts. After the replication starts, all the writes from the host to the source are split into two copies. One of the copies is sent to the local CDP appliance at the source site, and the other copy is sent to the production volume. After receiving the write, the appliance at the source site sends it to the appliance at the remote site. Then, the write is applied to the journal volume at the remote site. For an asynchronous operation, writes at the source CDP appliance are accumulated, and redundant blocks are eliminated. Then, the writes are sequenced and stored with their corresponding timestamp. The data is then compressed, and a checksum is generated. It is then scheduled for delivery across the IP or FC network to the remote CDP appliance. After the data is received, the remote appliance verifies the checksum to ensure the integrity of the data. The data is then uncompressed and written to the remote journal volume. As a next step, data from the journal volume is sent to the replica at predefined intervals.

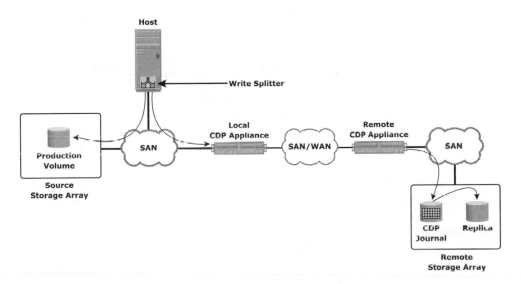

**Figure 12-10:** CDP remote replication

In the asynchronous mode, the local CDP appliance instantly acknowledges a write as soon as it is received. In the synchronous replication mode, the host application waits for an acknowledgment from the CDP appliance at the remote site before initiating the next write. The synchronous replication mode impacts the application's performance under heavy write loads.

For remote replication over extended distances, optical network technologies, such as dense wavelength division multiplexing (DWDM), coarse wavelength division multiplexing (CWDM), and synchronous optical network (SONET) are deployed. For more information about these technologies, refer to Appendix E.

# 12.3 Three-Site Replication

In synchronous replication, the source and target sites are usually within a short distance. Therefore, if a regional disaster occurs, both the source and the target sites might become unavailable. This can lead to extended RPO and RTO because the last known good copy of data would need to come from another source, such as an offsite tape library.

A regional disaster will not affect the target site in asynchronous replication because the sites are typically several hundred or several thousand kilometers apart. If the source site fails, production can be shifted to the target site, but there is no further remote protection of data until the failure is resolved.

*Three-site replication* mitigates the risks identified in two-site replication. In a three-site replication, data from the source site is replicated to two remote sites. Replication can be synchronous to one of the two sites, providing a near zero-RPO solution, and it can be asynchronous or disk buffered to the other remote site, providing a finite RPO. Three-site remote replication can be implemented as a cascade/multihop or a triangle/multitarget solution.

## 12.3.1 Three-Site Replication — Cascade/Multihop

In the *cascade/multihop* three-site replication, data flows from the source to the intermediate storage array, known as a *bunker*, in the first hop, and then from a bunker to a storage array at a remote site in the second hop. Replication between the source and the remote sites can be performed in two ways: synchronous + asynchronous or synchronous + disk buffered. Replication between the source and bunker occurs synchronously, but replication between the bunker and the remote site can be achieved either as disk-buffered mode or asynchronous mode.

### *Synchronous + Asynchronous*

This method employs a combination of synchronous and asynchronous remote replication technologies. Synchronous replication occurs between the source and the bunker. Asynchronous replication occurs between the bunker and the remote site. The remote replica in the bunker acts as the source for asynchronous replication to create a remote replica at the remote site. Figure 12-11 (a) illustrates the synchronous + asynchronous method.

RPO at the remote site is usually in the order of minutes for this implementation. In this method, a minimum of three storage devices are required (including the source). The devices containing a synchronous replica at the bunker and the asynchronous replica at the remote are the other two devices.

If a disaster occurs at the source, production operations are failed over to the bunker site with zero or near-zero data loss. But unlike the synchronous two-site situation, there is still remote protection at the third site. The RPO between the bunker and third site could be in the order of minutes.

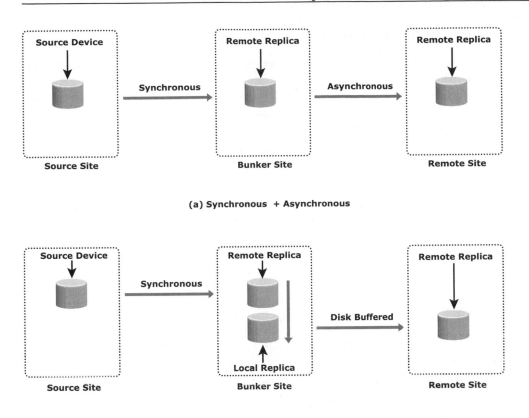

**Figure 12-11:** Three-site remote replication cascade/multihop

If there is a disaster at the bunker site or if there is a network link failure between the source and bunker sites, the source site continues to operate as normal but without any remote replication. This situation is similar to remote site failure in a two-site replication solution. The updates to the remote site cannot occur due to the failure in the bunker site. Therefore, the data at the remote site keeps falling behind, but the advantage here is that if the source fails during this time, operations can be resumed at the remote site. RPO at the remote site depends on the time difference between the bunker site failure and source site failure.

A *regional disaster* in three-site cascade/multihop replication is similar to a source site failure in two-site asynchronous replication. Operations are failover to the remote site with an RPO in the order of minutes. There is no remote protection until the regional disaster is resolved. Local replication technologies could be used at the remote site during this time.

If a disaster occurs at the remote site, or if the network links between the bunker and the remote site fail, the source site continues to work as normal with disaster recovery protection provided at the bunker site.

### Synchronous + Disk Buffered

This method employs a combination of local and remote replication technologies. Synchronous replication occurs between the source and the bunker: a consistent PIT local replica is created at the bunker. Data is transmitted from the local replica at the bunker to the remote replica at the remote site. Optionally, a local replica can be created at the remote site after data is received from the bunker. Figure 12-11 (b) illustrates the synchronous + disk buffered method.

In this method, a minimum of four storage devices are required (including the source) to replicate one storage device. The other three devices are the synchronous remote replica at the bunker, a consistent PIT local replica at the bunker, and the replica at the remote site. RPO at the remote site is usually in the order of hours for this implementation.

The process to create the consistent PIT copy at the bunker and incrementally updating the remote replica occurs continuously in a cycle.

## 12.3.2 Three-Site Replication — Triangle/Multitarget

In *three-site triangle/multitarget replication*, data at the source storage array is concurrently replicated to two different arrays at two different sites, as shown in Figure 12-12. The source-to-bunker site (target 1) replication is synchronous with a near-zero RPO. The source-to-remote site (target 2) replication is asynchronous with an RPO in the order of minutes. The distance between the source and the remote sites could be thousands of miles. This implementation does not depend on the bunker site for updating data on the remote site because data is asynchronously copied to the remote site directly from the source. The triangle/multitarget configuration provides consistent RPO unlike cascade/multihop solutions in which the failure of the bunker site results in the remote site falling behind and the RPO increasing.

The key benefit of three-site triangle/multitarget replication is the ability to failover to either of the two remote sites in the case of source-site failure, with disaster recovery (asynchronous) protection between the bunker and remote sites. Resynchronization between the two surviving target sites is incremental. Disaster recovery protection is always available if any one-site failure occurs.

During normal operations, all three sites are available and the production workload is at the source site. At any given instant, the data at the bunker and the source is identical. The data at the remote site is behind the data at the source and the bunker. The replication network links between the bunker and remote sites will be in place but not in use. Thus, during normal operations, there is no data movement between the bunker and remote arrays. The difference in the data between the bunker and remote sites is tracked so that if a source site disaster occurs, operations can be resumed at the bunker or the remote sites with incremental resynchronization between these two sites.

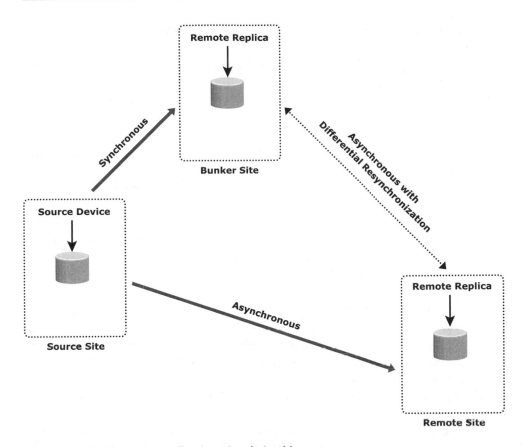

**Figure 12-12:** Three-site replication triangle/multitarget

A *regional disaster* in three-site triangle/multitarget replication is similar to a source site failure in two-site asynchronous replication. If failure occurs, operations failover to the remote site with an RPO within minutes. There is no remote protection until the regional disaster is resolved. Local replication technologies could be used at the remote site during this time.

A failure of the bunker or the remote site is not actually considered a disaster because the operation can continue uninterrupted at the source site while remote disaster recovery protection is still available. A network link failure to either the source-to-bunker or the source-to-remote site does not impact production at the source site while remote disaster recovery protection is still available with the site that can be reached.

## 12.4 Data Migration Solutions

*A data migration and mobility solution* is a specialized replication technique that enables creating remote point-in-time copies. These copies can be used for data mobility, migration, content distribution, and disaster recovery. This solution moves data between heterogeneous storage arrays. Data is moved from one array to the other over the SAN or WAN. This technology is application- and server-operating-system independent because the replication operations are performed by one of the storage arrays.

*Data mobility* refers to moving data between heterogeneous storage arrays for cost, performance, or any other reason. It helps implement a tiered storage strategy. *Data migration* refers to moving data from one storage array to other heterogeneous storage arrays for technology refresh, consolidation, or any other reason. The array performing the replication operations is called the *control array*. Data can be moved from/to devices in the control array to/from a remote array. The devices in the control array that are part of the replication session are called *control devices*. For every control device, there is a counterpart, a *remote device*, on the *remote array*. The terms control or remote do not indicate the direction of data flow; they indicate only the array that is performing the replication operation. The direction of data movement is determined by the replication operation.

The front-end ports of the control array must be zoned to the front-end ports of the remote array. LUN masking should be performed on the remote array to allow access to the remote devices to the front-end port of the control array. In effect, the front-end ports of the control array act as an HBA, initiating data transfer to/from the remote array.

Data migration solutions perform push and pull operations for data movement. These terms are defined from the perspective of the control array. In the *push operation*, data is moved from the control array to the remote array. The control device, therefore, acts like the source, while the remote device is the target.

In the *pull operation*, data is moved from the remote array to the control array. The remote device is the source, and the control device is the target.

When a push or pull operation is initiated, the control array creates a protection bitmap to track the replication process. Each bit in the protection bitmap represents a data chunk on the control device. The chunk size varies with technology implementations. When the replication operation is initiated, all the bits are set to one, indicating that all the contents of the source device need to be copied to the target device. As the replication process copies data, the bits are changed to zero, indicating that a particular chunk has been copied. At the end of the replication process, all the bits become zero.

During the push and pull operations, host access to the remote device is not allowed because the control array has no control over the remote array and cannot track any change on the remote device. Data integrity cannot be guaranteed if changes are made to the remote device during the push and pull operations. The push and pull operations can be either hot or cold. These terms apply to the control devices only. In a *cold operation* the control device is inaccessible to the host during replication. Cold operations guarantee data consistency because both the control and the remote devices are offline. In a *hot operation* the control device is online for host operations. During hot push and pull operations, changes can be made to the control device because the control array can keep track of all changes and thus ensure data integrity.

When the hot push operation is initiated, applications may be up-and-running on the control devices. I/O to the control devices is held while the protection bitmap is created. This ensures a consistent PIT image of the data. The protection bitmap is referred prior to any write to the control devices. If the bit is zero, the write is allowed. If the bit is one, the replication process holds the incoming write, copies the corresponding chunk to the remote device, and then allows the write to complete.

In the hot pull operation, the hosts can access control devices after starting the pull operation. The protection bitmap is referenced for every read or write operation. If the bit is zero, a read or write occurs. If the bit is one, the read or write is held, and the replication process copies the required chunk from the remote device. When the chunk is copied to the control device, the read or write is allowed to complete. The control devices are available for production soon after the pull operation is initiated and the protection bitmap is created.

The control array can keep track of changes made to the control devices, so incremental push operation is possible. A second bitmap, called a *resynchronization bitmap*, is created. All the bits in the resynchronization bitmap are set to zero when a push is initiated, as shown in Figure 12-13 (a). As changes are made to the control device, the bits are flipped from zero to one, indicating that changes have occurred, as shown in Figure 12-13 (b). When resynchronization is required, the push is reinitiated and the resynchronization bitmap becomes the new protection bitmap, as shown in Figure 12-13 (c), and only the modified chunks are transmitted to the remote devices. An incremental pull operation is not possible because tracking changes is not performed at the remote device.

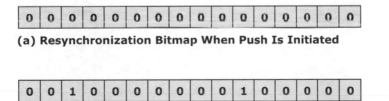

(a) Resynchronization Bitmap When Push Is Initiated

(b) Resynchronization Bitmap When Data Chunks Are Updated

(c) Resynchronization Bitmap Becomes Protection Bitmap

**Figure 12-13:** Bitmap status during push operation

## 12.5 Remote Replication and Migration in a Virtualized Environment

In a virtualized environment, all VM data and VM configuration files residing on the storage array at the primary site are replicated to the storage array at the remote site. This process remains transparent to the VMs. The LUNs are replicated between the two sites using the storage array replication technology. This replication process can be either synchronous (limited distance, near zero RPO) or asynchronous (extended distance, nonzero RPO).

Virtual machine migration is another technique used to ensure business continuity in case of hypervisor failure or scheduled maintenance. VM migration is the process to move VMs from one hypervisor to another without powering off the virtual machines. VM migration also helps in load balancing when multiple virtual machines running on the same hypervisor contend for resources. Two commonly used techniques for VM migration are hypervisor-to-hypervisor and array-to-array migration.

In hypervisor-to-hypervisor VM migration, the entire active state of a VM is moved from one hypervisor to another. Figure 12-14 shows hypervisor-to-hypervisor VM migration. This method involves copying the contents of virtual machine memory from the source hypervisor to the target and then transferring the control of the VM's disk files to the target hypervisor. Because the virtual disks of the VMs are not migrated, this technique requires both source and target hypervisor access to the same storage.

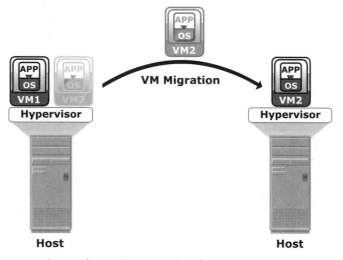

**Figure 12-14:** Hypervisor-to-hypervisor VM migration

In array-to-array VM migration, virtual disks are moved from the source array to the remote array. This approach enables the administrator to move

VMs across dissimilar storage arrays. Figure 12-15 shows array-to-array VM migration. Array-to-array migration starts by copying the metadata about the VM from the source array to the target. The metadata essentially consists of configuration, swap, and log files. After the metadata is copied, the VM disk file is replicated to the new location. During replication, there might be a chance that the source is updated; therefore, it is necessary to track the changes on the source to maintain data integrity. After the replication is complete, the blocks that have changed since the replication started are replicated to the new location. Array-to-array VM migration improves performance and balances the storage capacity by redistributing virtual disks to different storage devices.

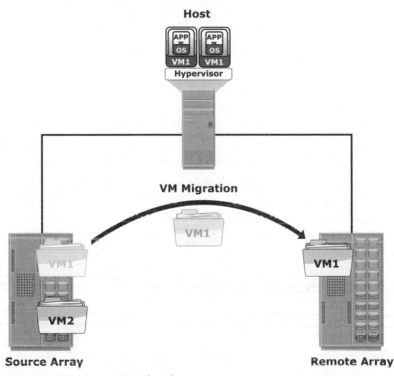

**Figure 12-15:** Array-to-array VM migration

## 12.6 Concepts in Practice: EMC SRDF, EMC MirrorView, and EMC RecoverPoint

This section discusses the EMC products for remote replication. EMC Symmetrix Remote Data Facility (SRDF) and EMC MirrorView are the storage array-based remote application software supported by EMC Symmetrix and VNX, respectively. EMC RecoverPoint is a network-based replication solution. For the latest information, visit www.emc.com.

### 12.6.1 EMC SRDF

SRDF offers a family of technology solutions to implement storage array-based remote replication. The SRDF family of software includes the following:

- **SRDF/Synchronous (SRDF/S):** A remote replication solution that creates a synchronous replica at one or more Symmetrix targets located within campus, metropolitan, or regional distances. SRDF/S provides a no-data-loss solution (near zero RPO) if a local disaster occurs.

- **SRDF/Asynchronous (SRDF/A):** A remote replication solution that enables the source to asynchronously replicate data. It incorporates delta set technology, which enables write ordering by employing a buffering mechanism. SRDF/A provides minimal data loss if a regional disaster occurs.

- **SRDF/DM:** A data migration solution that enables data migration from the source to the target volume over extended distances.

- **SRDF/Automated Replication (SRDF/AR):** A remote replication solution that uses both SRDF and TimeFinder/Mirror to implement disk-buffered replication technology. It is offered as SRDF/AR Single-hop for two-site replication and SRDF/AR Multihop for three-site cascade replication. SRDF/AR provides a long distance solution with RPO in the order of hours.

- **SRDF/Star:** Three-site multitarget remote replication solution that consists of primary (production), secondary (bunker), and tertiary (remote) sites. The replication between the primary and secondary sites is synchronous, whereas the replication between the primary and tertiary sites is asynchronous. If a primary site outage occurs, EMC's SRDF/Star solution enables organizations to quickly move operations and reestablish remote replication between the remaining two sites.

## 12.6.2 EMC MirrorView

The MirrorView software enables EMC VNX storage array-based remote replication. It replicates the contents of a primary volume to a secondary volume that resides on a different VNX storage system. The MirrorView family consists of MirrorView/Synchronous (MirrorView/S) and MirrorView/Asynchronous (MirrorView/A) solutions.

## 12.6.3 EMC RecoverPoint

EMC RecoverPoint Continuous Remote Replication (CRR) is a comprehensive data protection solution that provides bidirectional synchronous and asynchronous replication. In normal operations, RecoverPoint CRR enables users to recover data remotely to any point in time. RecoverPoint dynamically switches between synchronous and asynchronous replication based on the policy for performance and latency.

## Summary

This chapter detailed remote replication technologies. Remote replication provides disaster recovery and disaster restart solutions. It enables business operations to be rapidly restarted at a remote site following an outage, with acceptable data loss.

A remote replica is also used for other business operations, such as backup, reporting, and testing. The segregation of business operations between the source and target protects the source from becoming a performance bottleneck, ensuring improved production performance at the source.

Remote replication also helps in performing data center migrations, and provides the least disturbance to production operations because the applications accessing the source data are not affected.

This chapter also described different types of remote replication solutions. The distance between the primary site and the remote site is a prime consideration when deciding which remote replication technology solution to deploy. Asynchronous replication might adequately meet the RPO and RTO needs, while permitting greater distances between the sites. Three-site remote replication mitigates the risk of two-site failure due to regional disaster. Continuous data protection is a network-based advanced replication solution that provides both local and remote replication with unlimited recovery points. This chapter also discussed remote replication and VM migration in a virtualized environment.

For organizations to be competitive in today's fast-paced, online, and highly interconnected global economy, they must be agile, flexible, and able to respond rapidly to the changing market conditions. The cloud, a next generation style of computing, provides highly scalable and flexible computing available on demand. The next chapter focuses on cloud infrastructure and services.

## EXERCISES

1. What are the considerations for implementing synchronous remote replication?

2. Explain the RPO that can be achieved with synchronous, asynchronous, and disk-buffered remote replication.

3. Discuss the effects of a bunker failure in a three-site replication for the following implementations:

   ▪ Multihop — synchronous + disk buffered

   ▪ Multihop — synchronous + asynchronous

   ▪ Multitarget

4. Discuss the effects of a source failure in a three-site replication for the following implementations and the available recovery options:

   ▪ Multihop — synchronous + disk buffered

   ▪ Multihop — synchronous + asynchronous

   ▪ Multitarget

5. A database is stored on ten 9-GB RAID 1 LUNs. A cascade three-site remote replication solution involving a synchronous and disk-buffered solution has been chosen for disaster recovery. All the LUNs involved in the solution have RAID 1 protection. Calculate the total amount of raw capacity required for this solution.

Section

IV

# Cloud Computing

## In This Section

# Chapter 13
# Cloud Computing

I n today's competitive environment, organizations are under increasing pressure to improve
efficiency and transform their IT processes to
achieve more with less. Businesses need reduced
time-to-market, better agility, higher availability,
and reduced expenditures to meet the changing
business requirements and accelerated pace of
innovation. These business requirements are posing several challenges to IT teams. Some of the
key challenges are serving customers worldwide
around the clock, refreshing technology quickly
and faster provisioning of IT resources — all at reduced costs.

These long-standing challenges are addressed with the emergence of a new
computing style, called *cloud computing*, which enables organizations and individuals to obtain and provision IT resources as a service. With cloud computing,
users can browse and select relevant cloud services, such as compute, software,
storage, or a combination of these resources, via a portal. Cloud computing
automates delivery of selected cloud services to the users. It helps organizations
and individuals deploy IT resources at reduced total cost of ownership with
faster provisioning and compliance adherence.

A widely adopted definition of cloud computing comes from the U.S. National
Institute of Standards and Technology (NIST Special Publication 800-145):

> *Cloud computing is a model for enabling ubiquitous, convenient, on-demand network
> access to a shared pool of configurable computing resources (e.g., networks, servers,
> storage, applications, and services) that can be rapidly provisioned and released with
> minimal management effort or service provider interaction.*

**313**

This chapter covers the enabling technologies, essential characteristics, benefits, services, deployment models, and infrastructure of cloud computing. The chapter also includes the challenges and considerations in adopting cloud computing.

# 13.1 Cloud Enabling Technologies

Grid computing, utility computing, virtualization, and service-oriented architecture are enabling technologies of cloud computing.

- *Grid computing* is a form of distributed computing that enables the resources of numerous heterogeneous computers in a network to work together on a single task at the same time. Grid computing enables parallel computing and is best for large workloads.

- *Utility computing* is a service-provisioning model in which a service provider makes computing resources available to customers, as required, and charges them based on usage. This is analogous to other utility services, such as electricity, where charges are based on the consumption.

- *Virtualization* is a technique that abstracts the physical characteristics of IT resources from resource users. It enables the resources to be viewed and managed as a pool and lets users create virtual resources from the pool. Virtualization provides better flexibility for provisioning of IT resources compared to provisioning in a non-virtualized environment. It helps optimize resource utilization and delivering resources more efficiently.

- *Service Oriented Architecture* (SOA) provides a set of services that can communicate with each other. These services work together to perform some activity or simply pass data among services.

# 13.2 Characteristics of Cloud Computing

A computing infrastructure used for cloud services must have certain capabilities or characteristics. According to NIST, the cloud infrastructure should have five essential characteristics:

- **On-demand self-service:** A consumer can unilaterally provision computing capabilities, such as server time and network storage, as needed, automatically without requiring human interaction with each service provider.

    A cloud service provider publishes a service catalogue, which contains information about all cloud services available to consumers. The service catalogue includes information about service attributes, prices, and request processes. Consumers view the service catalogue via a web-based user interface and use it to request for a service. Consumers can either leverage the "ready-to-use" services or change a few service parameters to customize the services.

▪ **Broad network access:** Capabilities are available over the network and accessed through standard mechanisms that promote use by heterogeneous thin or thick client platforms (for example, mobile phones, tablets, laptops, and workstations).

▪ **Resource pooling:** The provider's computing resources are pooled to serve multiple consumers using a multitenant model, with different physical and virtual resources dynamically assigned and reassigned according to consumer demand. There is a sense of location independence in that the customer generally has no control or knowledge over the exact location of the provided resources but may be able to specify location at a higher level of abstraction (for example, country, state, or data center). Examples of resources include storage, processing, memory, and network bandwidth.

▪ **Rapid elasticity:** Capabilities can be elastically provisioned and released, in some cases automatically, to scale rapidly outward and inward commensurate with demand. To the consumer, the capabilities available for provisioning often appear to be unlimited and can be appropriated in any quantity at any time.

Consumers can leverage rapid elasticity of the cloud when they have a fluctuation in their IT resource requirements. For example, an organization might require double the number of web and application servers for a specific duration to accomplish a specific task. For the remaining period, they might want to release idle server resources to cut down the expenses. The cloud enables consumers to grow and shrink the demand for resources dynamically.

▪ **Measured service:** Cloud systems automatically control and optimize resource use by leveraging a metering capability at some level of abstraction appropriate to the type of service (for example, storage, processing, bandwidth, and active user accounts). Resource usage can be monitored, controlled, and reported, providing transparency for both the provider and consumer of the utilized service.

**MULTITENANCY**

*Multitenancy* **refers to an architecture in which multiple independent consumers (tenants) are serviced using a single set of resources. This lowers the cost of services for consumers. Virtualization enables resource pooling and multitenancy in the cloud. For example, multiple virtual machines from different consumers can run simultaneously on the same physical server that runs the hypervisor.**

# 13.3 Benefits of Cloud Computing

Cloud computing offers the following key benefits:

- **Reduced IT cost:** Cloud services can be purchased based on pay-per-use or subscription pricing. This reduces or eliminates the consumer's IT capital expenditure (CAPEX).

- **Business agility:** Cloud computing provides the capability to allocate and scale computing capacity quickly. Cloud computing can reduce the time required to provision and deploy new applications and services from months to minutes. This enables businesses to respond more quickly to market changes and reduce time-to-market.

- **Flexible scaling:** Cloud computing enables consumers to scale up, scale down, scale out, or scale in the demand for computing resources easily. Consumers can unilaterally and automatically scale computing resources without any interaction with cloud service providers. The flexible service provisioning capability of cloud computing often provides a sense of unlimited scalability to the cloud service consumers.

- **High availability:** Cloud computing has the capability to ensure resource availability at varying levels depending on the consumer's policy and priority. Redundant infrastructure components (servers, network paths, and storage equipment, along with clustered software) enable fault tolerance for cloud deployments. These techniques can encompass multiple data centers located in different geographic regions, which prevents data unavailability due to regional failures.

# 13.4 Cloud Service Models

According to NIST, cloud service offerings are classified primarily into three models: Infrastructure-as-a-Service (IaaS), Platform-as-a-Service (PaaS), and Software-as-a-Service (SaaS).

## 13.4.1 Infrastructure-as-a-Service

The capability provided to the consumer is to provision processing, storage, networks, and other fundamental computing resources where the consumer is able to deploy and run arbitrary software, which can include operating systems and applications. The consumer does not manage or control the underlying cloud infrastructure but has control over operating systems and deployed applications; and possibly limited control of select networking components (for example, host firewalls).

IaaS is the base layer of the cloud services stack (see Figure 13-1 [a]). It serves as the foundation for both the SaaS and PaaS layers.

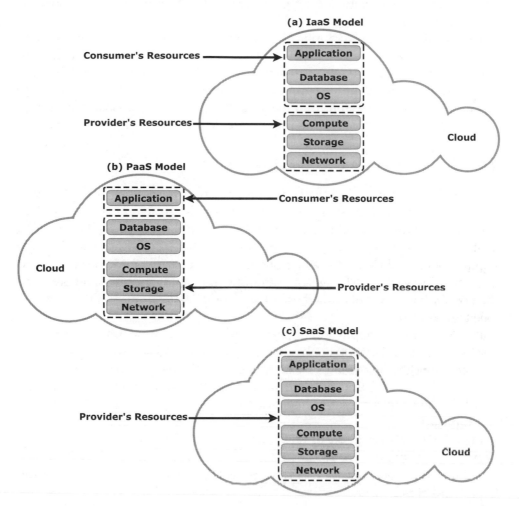

**Figure 13-1:** IaaS, PaaS, and SaaS models

Amazon Elastic Compute Cloud (Amazon EC2) is an example of IaaS that provides scalable compute capacity, on-demand, in the cloud. It enables consumers to leverage Amazon's massive computing infrastructure with no up-front capital investment.

## 13.4.2 Platform-as-a-Service

The capability provided to the consumer is to deploy onto the cloud infrastructure consumer-created or acquired applications created using programming languages, libraries, services, and tools supported by the provider. The consumer does not manage or control the underlying cloud infrastructure including network, servers, operating systems, or storage, but has control over the deployed applications and possibly configuration settings for the application-hosting environment. (See Figure 13-1 [b]).

PaaS is also used as an application development environment, offered as a service by the cloud service provider. The consumer may use these platforms to code their applications and then deploy the applications on the cloud. Because the workload to the deployed applications varies, the scalability of computing resources is usually guaranteed by the computing platform, transparently. Google App Engine and Microsoft Windows Azure Platform are examples of PaaS.

## 13.4.3 Software-as-a-Service

The capability provided to the consumer is to use the provider's applications running on a cloud infrastructure. The applications are accessible from various client devices through either a thin client interface, such as a web browser (for example, web-based e-mail), or a program interface. The consumer does not manage or control the underlying cloud infrastructure including network, servers, operating systems, storage, or even individual application capabilities, with the possible exception of limited user-specific application configuration settings. (See Figure 13-1[c]).

In a SaaS model, applications, such as customer relationship management (CRM), e-mail, and instant messaging (IM), are offered as a service by the cloud service providers. The cloud service providers exclusively manage the required computing infrastructure and software to support these services. The consumers may be allowed to change a few application configuration settings to customize the applications.

EMC Mozy is an example of SaaS. Consumers can leverage the Mozy console to perform automatic, secured, online backup and recovery of their data with ease. Salesforce.com is a provider of SaaS-based CRM applications, such as Sales Cloud and Service Cloud.

# 13.5 Cloud Deployment Models

According to NIST, cloud computing is classified into four deployment models — public, private, community, and hybrid — which provide the basis for how cloud infrastructures are constructed and consumed.

## 13.5.1 Public Cloud

In a *public cloud* model, the cloud infrastructure is provisioned for open use by the general public. It may be owned, managed, and operated by a business, academic, or government organization, or some combination of them. It exists on the premises of the cloud provider.

Consumers use the cloud services offered by the providers via the Internet and pay metered usage charges or subscription fees. An advantage of the public cloud is its low capital cost with enormous scalability. However, for consumers, these benefits come with certain risks: no control over the resources in the cloud, the security of confidential data, network performance, and interoperability issues. Popular public cloud service providers are Amazon, Google, and Salesforce.com. Figure 13-2 shows a public cloud that provides cloud services to organizations and individuals.

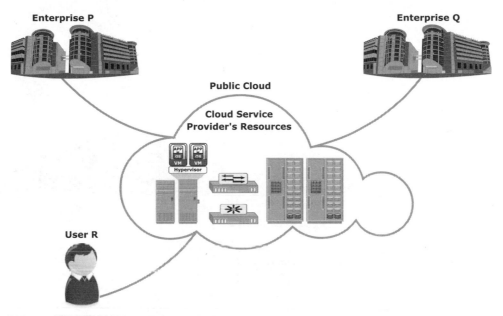

**Figure 13-2:** Public cloud

## 13.5.2 Private Cloud

In a *private cloud* model, the cloud infrastructure is provisioned for exclusive use by a single organization comprising multiple consumers (for example, business units). It may be owned, managed, and operated by the organization, a third party, or some combination of them, and it may exist on or off premises. Following are two variations to the private cloud model:

▪ **On-premise private cloud:** The on-premise private cloud, also known as internal cloud, is hosted by an organization within its own data centers (see Figure 13-3 [a]). This model enables organizations to standardize their cloud service management processes and security, although this model has limitations in terms of size and resource scalability. Organizations would also need to incur the capital and operational costs for the physical resources. This is best suited for organizations that require complete control over their applications, infrastructure configurations, and security mechanisms.

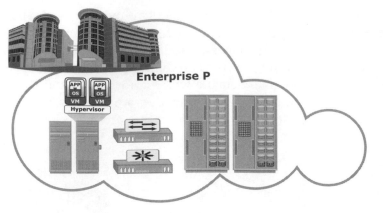

**(a) On-Premise Private Cloud**

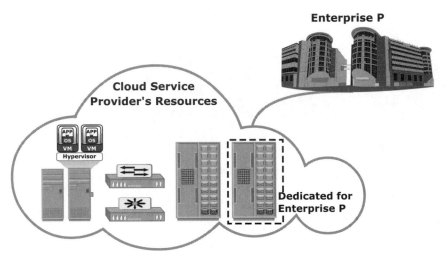

**(b) Externally Hosted Private Cloud**

**Figure 13-3:** On-premise and externally hosted private clouds

- **Externally hosted private cloud:** This type of private cloud is hosted external to an organization (see Figure 13-3 [b]) and is managed by a third-party organization. The third-party organization facilitates an exclusive cloud environment for a specific organization with full guarantee of privacy and confidentiality.

## 13.5.3 Community Cloud

In a *community cloud* model, the cloud infrastructure is provisioned for exclusive use by a specific community of consumers from organizations that have shared concerns (for example, mission, security requirements, policy, and compliance considerations). It may be owned, managed, and operated by one or more of the organizations in the community, a third party, or some combination of them, and it may exist on or off premises. (See Figure 13-4).

In a community cloud, the costs spread over to fewer consumers than a public cloud. Hence, this option is more expensive but might offer a higher level of privacy, security, and compliance. The community cloud also offers organizations access to a vast pool of resources compared to the private cloud. An example in which a community cloud could be useful is government agencies. If various agencies within the government operate under similar guidelines, they could all share the same infrastructure and lower their individual agency's investment.

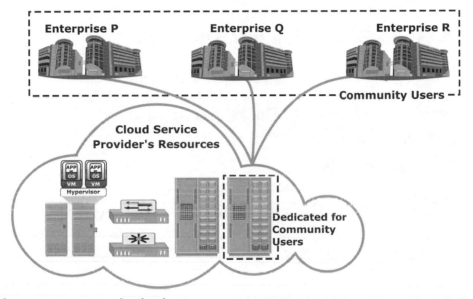

**Figure 13-4:** Community cloud

## 13.5.4 Hybrid Cloud

In a *hybrid cloud* model, the cloud infrastructure is a composition of two or more distinct cloud infrastructures (private, community, or public) that remain unique entities, but are bound together by standardized or proprietary technology that enables data and application portability (for example, cloud bursting for load balancing between clouds).

The hybrid model allows an organization to deploy less critical applications and data to the public cloud, leveraging the scalability and cost-effectiveness of the public cloud. The organization's mission-critical applications and data remain on the private cloud that provides greater security. Figure 13-5 shows an example of a hybrid cloud.

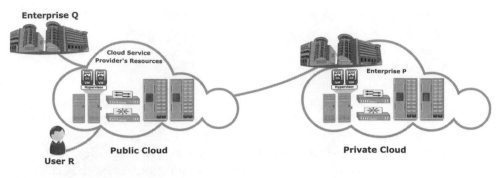

**Figure 13-5:** Hybrid cloud

# 13.6 Cloud Computing Infrastructure

A cloud computing infrastructure is the collection of hardware and software that enables the five essential characteristics of cloud computing. Cloud computing infrastructure usually consists of the following layers:

- Physical infrastructure
- Virtual infrastructure
- Applications and platform software
- Cloud management and service creation tools

The resources of these layers are aggregated and coordinated to provide cloud services to the consumers (see Figure 13-6).

## 13.6.1 Physical Infrastructure

The physical infrastructure consists of physical computing resources, which include physical servers, storage systems, and networks. Physical servers are connected to each other, to the storage systems, and to the clients via networks, such as IP, FC SAN, IP SAN, or FCoE networks.

Cloud service providers may use physical computing resources from one or more data centers to provide services. If the computing resources are distributed across multiple data centers, connectivity must be established among them. The connectivity enables the data centers in different locations to work as a single large data center. This enables migration of business applications and data across data centers and provisioning cloud services using the resources from multiple data centers.

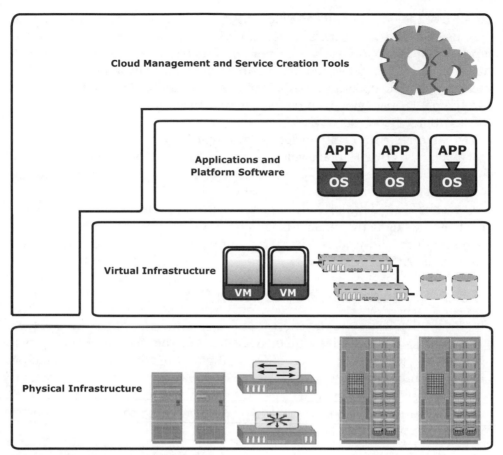

**Figure 13-6:** Cloud infrastructure layers

## 13.6.2 Virtual Infrastructure

Cloud service providers employ virtualization technologies to build a virtual infrastructure layer on the top of the physical infrastructure. Virtualization enables fulfilling some of the cloud characteristics, such as resource pooling and rapid elasticity. It also helps reduce the cost of providing the cloud services. Some cloud service providers may not have completely virtualized their physical infrastructure yet, but they are adopting virtualization for better efficiency and optimization.

Virtualization abstracts physical computing resources and provides a consolidated view of the resource capacity. The consolidated resources are managed as a single entity called a *resource pool*. For example, a resource pool might group CPUs of physical servers within a cluster. The capacity of the resource pool is the sum of the power of all CPUs (for example, 10,000 megahertz) available in the cluster. In addition to the CPU pool, the virtual infrastructure includes other types of resource pools, such as memory pool, network pool, and storage pool. Apart from resource pools, the virtual infrastructure also includes *identity pools*, such as VLAN ID pools and VSAN ID pools. The number of each type of pool and the pool capacity depend on the cloud service provider's requirement to create different cloud services.

Virtual infrastructure also includes virtual computing resources, such as virtual machines, virtual storage volumes, and virtual networks. These resources obtain capacities, such as CPU power, memory, network bandwidth, and storage space from the resource pools. The capacity is allocated to the virtual computing resources easily and flexibly based on the service requirement. Virtual networks are created using network identifiers, such as VLAN IDs and VSAN IDs from the respective identity pools. Virtual computing resources are used for creating cloud infrastructure services.

## 13.6.3 Applications and Platform Software

This layer includes a suite of business applications and platform software, such as the OS and database. Platform software provides the environment on which business applications run. Applications and platform software are hosted on virtual machines to create SaaS and PaaS. For SaaS, both the application and platform software are provided by cloud service providers. In the case of PaaS, only the platform software is provided by cloud service providers; consumers export their applications to the cloud.

## 13.6.4 Cloud Management and Service Creation Tools

The cloud management and service creation tools layer includes three types of software:

- Physical and virtual infrastructure management software
- Unified management software
- User-access management software

This classification is based on the different functions performed by the software. This software interacts with each other to automate provisioning of cloud services.

The physical and virtual infrastructure management software is offered by the vendors of various infrastructure resources and third-party organizations. For example, a storage array has its own management software. Similarly, network and physical servers are managed independently using network and compute management software respectively. This software provides interfaces to construct a virtual infrastructure from the underlying physical infrastructure.

Unified management software interacts with all standalone physical and virtual infrastructure management software. It collects information on the existing physical and virtual infrastructure configurations, connectivity, and utilization. Unified management software compiles this information and provides a consolidated view of infrastructure resources scattered across one or more data centers. It allows an administrator to monitor performance, capacity, and availability of physical and virtual resources centrally. Unified management software also provides a single management interface to configure physical and virtual infrastructure and integrate the compute (both CPU and memory), network, and storage pools. The integration allows a group of compute pools to use the storage and network pools for storing and transferring data respectively. The unified management software passes configuration commands to respective physical and virtual infrastructure management software, which executes the instructions. This eliminates the administration of compute, storage, and network resources separately using native management software.

The key function of the unified management software is to automate the creation of cloud services. It enables administrators to define service attributes such as CPU power, memory, network bandwidth, storage capacity, name and description of applications and platform software, resource location, and backup policy. When the unified management software receives consumer requests for cloud services, it creates the service based on predefined service attributes.

The user-access management software provides a web-based user interface to consumers. Consumers can use the interface to browse the service catalogue and request cloud services. The user-access management software authenticates users before forwarding their request to the unified management software. It also monitors allocation or usage of resources associated to the cloud service instances. Based on the allocation or usage of resources, it generates a chargeback report. The chargeback report is visible to consumers and provides transparency between consumers and providers.

## CLOUD-OPTIMIZED STORAGE

Content-rich applications combined with the growth of user-generated unstructured data is challenging to manage with the traditional approach of storing data at scale. This combination of massive growth, new information types, and the need to serve multiple locations and users around the world, has led to requirements for information storage and management at a global scale. Cloud-optimized storage is a solution to meet these requirements. It delivers scalable and flexible architecture that provides rapid elasticity, global access, and storage capacity on-demand. It also addresses the constraints of rigid, mount-point based interaction between storage and consumer by presenting a singular access point to the entire storage infrastructure.

*(Continued)*

**CLOUD-OPTIMIZED STORAGE** *(continued)*

It leverages a built-in multitenancy model and enables self-service; fully metered access to storage resources thereby delivers storage-as-a-service on a shared infrastructure. Cloud-optimized storage typically leverages object-based storage technology that uses customizable, value-driven metadata to drive storage placement, protection, and life cycle policies. Following are key characteristics of cloud-optimized storage solution:

- Massively scalable infrastructure that supports a large number of objects across a globally distributed infrastructure

- Unified namespace that eliminates capacity, location, and other file system limitations

- Metadata and policy-based information management capabilities that optimize data protection, availability, and cost, based on service levels

- Secure multitenancy that enables multiple applications to be securely served from the same infrastructure. Each application is securely partitioned and data is neither co-mingled nor accessible by other tenants.

- Provides access through REST and SOAP web service APIs and file-based access using a variety of client devices

# 13.7 Cloud Challenges

Although there is growing acceptance of cloud computing, both the cloud service consumers and providers have been facing some challenges.

## 13.7.1 Challenges for Consumers

Business-critical data requires protection and continuous monitoring of its access. If the data moves to a cloud model other than an on-premise private cloud, consumers could lose absolute control of their sensitive data. Although most of the cloud service providers offer enhanced data security, consumers might not be willing to transfer control of their business-critical data to the cloud.

Cloud service providers might use multiple data centers located in different countries to provide cloud services. They might replicate or move data across these data centers to ensure high availability and load distribution. Consumers may or may not know in which country their data is stored. Some cloud service providers allow consumers to select the location for storing their data. Data privacy concerns and regulatory compliance requirements, such as the EU Data Protection Directive and the U.S. Safe Harbor program, create challenges for the consumers in adopting cloud computing.

Cloud services can be accessed from anywhere via a network. However, network latency increases when the cloud infrastructure is not close to the access point. A high network latency can either increase the application response time or cause the application to timeout. This can be addressed by implementing stringent Service Level Agreements (SLAs) with the cloud service providers.

Another challenge is that cloud platform services may not support consumers' desired applications. For example, a service provider might not be able to support highly specialized or proprietary environments, such as compatible OSs and preferred programming languages, required to develop and run the consumer's application. Also, a mismatch between hypervisors could impact migration of virtual machines into or between clouds.

Another challenge is vendor lock-in: the difficulty for consumers to change their cloud service provider. A lack of interoperability between the APIs of different cloud service providers could also create complexity and high migration costs when moving from one service provider to another.

## 13.7.2 Challenges for Providers

Cloud service providers usually publish a service-level agreement (SLA) so that their consumers know about the availability of service, quality of service, downtime compensation, and legal and regulatory clauses. Alternatively, customer-specific SLAs may be signed between a cloud service provider and a consumer. SLAs typically mention a penalty amount if cloud service providers fail to provide the service levels. Therefore, cloud service providers must ensure that they have adequate resources to provide the required levels of services. Because the cloud resources are distributed and service demands fluctuate, it is a challenge for cloud service providers to provision physical resources for peak demand of all consumers and estimate the actual cost of providing the services.

Many software vendors do not have a cloud-ready software licensing model. Some of the software vendors offer standardized cloud licenses at a higher price compared to traditional licensing models. The cloud software licensing complexity has been causing challenges in deploying vendor software in the cloud. This is also a challenge to the consumer.

Cloud service providers usually offer proprietary APIs to access their cloud. However, consumers might want open APIs or standard APIs to become the tenant of multiple clouds. This is a challenge for cloud service providers because this requires agreement among cloud service providers.

# 13.8 Cloud Adoption Considerations

Organizations that decide to adopt cloud computing always face this question: "How does the cloud fit the organization's environment?" Most organizations are not ready to abandon their existing IT investments to move all their business processes to the cloud at once. Instead, they need to consider various factors before moving their business processes to the cloud. Even individuals seeking to use cloud services need to understand some cloud adoption considerations. Following are some key considerations for cloud adoption:

- **Selection of a deployment model:** Risk versus convenience is a key consideration for deciding on a cloud adoption strategy. This consideration also forms the basis for choosing the right cloud deployment model. A public cloud is usually preferred by individuals and start-up businesses. For them, the cost reduction offered by the public cloud outweighs the security or availability risks in the cloud. Small- and medium-sized businesses (SMBs) have a moderate customer base, and any anomaly in customer data and service levels might impact their business. Therefore, they may not be willing to deploy their tier 1 applications, such as Online Transaction Processing (OLTP), in the public cloud. A hybrid cloud model fits in this case. The tier 1applications should run on the private cloud, whereas less critical applications such as backup, archive, and testing can be deployed in the public cloud. Enterprises typically have a strong customer base worldwide. They usually enforce strict security policies to safeguard critical customer data. Because they are financially capable, they might prefer building their own private clouds.

- **Application suitability:** Not all applications are good candidates for a public cloud. This may be due to the incompatibility between the cloud platform software and the consumer applications, or maybe the organization plans to move a legacy application to the cloud. Proprietary and mission-critical applications are core and essential to the business. They are usually designed, developed, and maintained in-house. These applications often provide competitive advantages. Due to high security risk, organizations are unlikely to move these applications to the public cloud. These applications are good candidate for an on-premise private cloud. Nonproprietary and nonmission critical applications are suitable for deployment in the public cloud. If an application workload is network traffic-intensive, its performance might not be optimal if deployed in the public cloud. Also if the application communicates with other data center resources or applications, it might experience performance issues.

- **Financial advantage:** A careful analysis of financial benefits provides a clear picture about the cost-savings in adopting the cloud. The analysis should compare both the Total Cost of Ownership (TCO) and the Return on Investment (ROI) in the cloud and noncloud environment and identify the potential cost benefit. While calculating TCO and ROI, organizations and individuals should consider the expenditure to deploy and maintain their own infrastructure versus cloud-adoption costs. While calculating the expenditures for owning infrastructure resources, organizations should include both the capital expenditure (CAPEX) and operation expenditure

(OPEX). The CAPEX includes the cost of servers, storage, OS, application, network equipment, real estate, and so on. The OPEX includes the cost incurred for power and cooling, personnel, maintenance, backup, and so on. These expenditures should be compared with the operation cost incurred in adopting cloud computing. The cloud adoption cost includes the cost of migrating to the cloud, cost to ensure compliance and security, and usage or subscription fees. Moving applications to the cloud reduces CAPEX, except when the cloud is built on-premise.

▪ **Selection of a cloud service provider:** The selection of the provider is important for a public cloud. Consumers need to find out how long and how well the provider has been delivering the services. They also need to determine how easy it is to add or terminate cloud services with the service provider. The consumer should know how easy it is to move to another provider, when required. They must assess how the provider fulfills the security, legal, and privacy requirements. They should also check whether the provider offers good customer service support.

▪ **Service-level agreement (SLA):** Cloud service providers typically mention quality of service (QoS) attributes such as throughput and uptime, along with cloud services. The QoS attributes are generally part of an SLA, which is the service contract between the provider and the consumers. The SLA serves as the foundation for the expected level of service between the consumer and the provider. Before adopting the cloud services, consumers should check whether the QoS attributes meet their requirements.

# 13.9 Concepts in Practice: Vblock

*Vblock* is a completely integrated cloud infrastructure offering that includes compute, storage, network, and virtualization products. These products are provided by EMC, VMware, and Cisco, who have formed a coalition to deliver Vblocks.

Vblocks enable organizations to build virtualized data centers and cloud infrastructures. Vblocks are pre-architected, preconfigured, pretested and have defined performance and availability attributes. Rather than customers buying and assembling individual cloud infrastructure components, Vblock provides a validated cloud infrastructure solution and is factory-ready for deployment and production. This saves significant cost and deployment time.

EMC Unified Infrastructure Manager (UIM) is the unified management solution for Vblocks. UIM provides a single point of management for Vblocks and manages multiple Vblocks. With UIM, cloud infrastructure services can be provisioned automatically based on provisioning best practices.

For more information on Vblock, visit www.emc.com.

## Summary

Cloud computing, although evolving, is gaining popularity because consumers see a potential cost reduction and service providers see an opportunity to provide new services. Cloud computing has enabled IT organizations and individuals to gain benefits, such as automated and rapid resource provisioning, flexibility, high availability, and faster time to market at a reduced total cost of ownership. Although there are concerns and challenges, the benefits of cloud computing are compelling enough to adopt it.

For organizations that own traditional data centers, cloud adoption is like a journey. The journey begins with the consolidation of computing resources including compute systems, storage, and networks using virtualization technologies. Followed by virtualization of resources, organizations need to take the next step of implementing unified cloud infrastructure management tools and come up with the services catalog. Implementing proper service-management processes is a key to align the delivery of cloud services to the expectations of businesses and consumers.

This chapter detailed cloud characteristics, benefits, services, deployment models, and infrastructure. It also covered cloud challenges and adoption considerations. The next chapter focuses on securing the storage infrastructure, which also includes storage security considerations in virtualized and cloud environments.

---

### EXERCISES

1. **What are the essential characteristics of cloud computing?**
2. **How does cloud computing bring in business agility?**
3. **Research Service Oriented Architecture and its application in cloud computing.**
4. **Research cloud orchestration.**
5. **Research various considerations for selecting a public cloud service provider.**
6. **What are the costs that should be evaluated to determine the financial advantage of cloud?**

# Section

# V

# Securing and Managing
# Storage Infrastructure

## In This Section

# Chapter 14
# Securing the Storage Infrastructure

**KEY CONCEPTS**

Storage Security Framework

The Risk Triad

Denial of Service

Security Domains

Information Rights Management

Access Control

Valuable information, including intellectual property, personal identities, and financial transactions, is routinely processed and stored in storage arrays, which are accessed through the network. As a result, storage is now more exposed to various security threats that can potentially damage business-critical data and disrupt critical services. Securing storage infrastructure has become an integral component of the storage management process in traditional and virtualized data centers. It is an intensive and necessary task, essential to managing and protecting vital information.

Storage security in a public cloud environment is more complex because organizations have less control over the shared IT infrastructure and security measures' enforcement. Further, multitenancy in a cloud environment enables resource sharing, including storage among multiple consumers. Such sharing might pose a threat of commingling data across tenants.

This chapter describes a framework for information security designed to mitigate security threats that may arise and to combat malicious attacks on the storage infrastructure. In addition, this chapter describes basic storage security implementations, such as the security architecture and protection mechanisms in FC-SAN, NAS, and IP-SAN. Further, this chapter describes the additional security considerations in virtualized and cloud environments.

# 14.1 Information Security Framework

The basic information security framework is built to achieve four security goals: confidentiality, integrity, and availability (CIA), along with accountability. This framework incorporates all security standards, procedures, and controls, required to mitigate threats in the storage infrastructure environment.

- **Confidentiality:** Provides the required secrecy of information and ensures that only authorized users have access to data. This requires authentication of users who need to access information.

  Data in transit (data transmitted over cables) and data at rest (data residing on a primary storage, backup media, or in the archives) can be encrypted to maintain its confidentiality. In addition to restricting unauthorized users from accessing information, confidentiality also requires implementing traffic flow protection measures as part of the security protocol. These protection measures generally include hiding source and destination addresses, frequency of data being sent, and amount of data sent.

- **Integrity:** Ensures that the information is unaltered. Ensuring integrity requires detection of and protection against unauthorized alteration or deletion of information. Ensuring integrity stipulates measures such as error detection and correction for both data and systems.

- **Availability:** This ensures that authorized users have reliable and timely access to systems, data, and applications residing on these systems. Availability requires protection against unauthorized deletion of data and denial of service (discussed in section "14.2.2 Threats"). Availability also implies that sufficient resources are available to provide a service.

- **Accountability service:** Refers to accounting for all the events and operations that take place in the data center infrastructure. The accountability service maintains a log of events that can be audited or traced later for the purpose of security.

# 14.2 Risk Triad

Risk triad defines risk in terms of threats, assets, and vulnerabilities. Risk arises when a threat agent (an attacker) uses an existing vulnerability to compromise the security services of an asset, for example, if a sensitive document is transmitted without any protection over an insecure channel, an attacker might get unauthorized access to the document and may violate its confidentiality and integrity. This may, in turn, result in business loss for the organization. In this scenario potential business loss is the risk, which arises because an attacker uses the vulnerability of the unprotected communication to access the document and tamper with it.

To manage risks, organizations primarily focus on vulnerabilities because they cannot eliminate threat agents that appear in various forms and sources to its assets. Organizations can enforce countermeasures to reduce the possibility of occurrence of attacks and the severity of their impact.

Risk assessment is the first step to determine the extent of potential threats and risks in an IT infrastructure. The process assesses risk and helps to identify appropriate controls to mitigate or eliminate risks. Based on the value of assets, risk assessment helps to prioritize investment in and provisioning of security measures. To determine the probability of an adverse event occurring, threats to an IT system must be analyzed with the potential vulnerabilities and the existing security controls.

The severity of an adverse event is estimated by the impact that it may have on critical business activities. Based on this analysis, a relative value of criticality and sensitivity can be assigned to IT assets and resources. For example, a particular IT system component may be assigned a high-criticality value if an attack on this particular component can cause a complete termination of mission-critical services.

The following sections examine the three key elements of the risk triad. Assets, threats, and vulnerabilities are considered from the perspective of risk identification and control analysis.

## 14.2.1 Assets

Information is one of the most important *assets* for any organization. Other assets include hardware, software, and other infrastructure components required to access the information. To protect these assets, organizations must develop a set of parameters to ensure the availability of the resources to authorized users and trusted networks. These parameters apply to storage resources, network infrastructure, and organizational policies.

Security methods have two objectives. The first objective is to ensure that the network is easily accessible to authorized users. It should also be reliable and stable under disparate environmental conditions and volumes of usage. The second objective is to make it difficult for potential attackers to access and compromise the system.

The security methods should provide adequate protection against unauthorized access, viruses, worms, trojans, and other malicious software programs. Security measures should also include options to encrypt critical data and disable unused services to minimize the number of potential security gaps. The security method must ensure that updates to the operating system and other software are installed regularly. At the same time, it must provide adequate redundancy in the form of replication and mirroring of the production data to prevent catastrophic data loss if there is an unexpected data compromise. For the security system to function smoothly, all users are informed about the policies governing the use of the network.

The effectiveness of a storage security methodology can be measured by two key criteria. One, the cost of implementing the system should be a fraction of the value of the protected data. Two, it should cost heavily to a potential attacker, in terms of money, effort, and time.

## 14.2.2 Threats

*Threats* are the potential attacks that can be carried out on an IT infrastructure. These attacks can be classified as active or passive. *Passive attacks* are attempts to gain unauthorized access into the system. They pose threats to confidentiality of information. *Active attacks* include data modification, denial of service (DoS), and repudiation attacks. They pose threats to data integrity, availability, and accountability.

In a data modification attack, the unauthorized user attempts to modify information for malicious purposes. A modification attack can target the data at rest or the data in transit. These attacks pose a threat to data integrity.

*Denial of service* (DoS) attacks prevent legitimate users from accessing resources and services. These attacks generally do not involve access to or modification of information. Instead, they pose a threat to data availability. The intentional flooding of a network or website to prevent legitimate access to authorized users is one example of a DoS attack.

*Repudiation* is an attack against the accountability of information. It attempts to provide false information by either impersonating someone or denying that an event or a transaction has taken place. For example, a repudiation attack may involve performing an action and eliminating any evidence that could prove the identity of the user (attacker) who performed that action. Repudiation attacks include circumventing the logging of security events or tampering with the security log to conceal the identity of the attacker.

---

**EXAMPLES OF PASSIVE ATTACKS**

- **Eavesdropping:** When someone overhears a conversation, the unauthorized access to this information is called eavesdropping.

- **Snooping:** This refers to accessing another user's data in an unauthorized way. In general, snooping and eavesdropping are synonymous.

**Malicious hackers frequently use snooping techniques and equipment such as key loggers to monitor keystrokes and capture passwords and login information, or to intercept e-mail and other private communication and data transmission. Organizations sometimes perform legitimate snooping on employees to monitor their use of business computers and to track Internet usage.**

### 14.2.3 Vulnerability

The paths that provide access to information are often vulnerable to potential attacks. Each of the paths may contain various access points, which provide different levels of access to the storage resources. It is important to implement adequate security controls at all the access points on an access path. Implementing security controls at each access point of every access path is known as *defense in depth*.

Defense in depth recommends using multiple security measures to reduce the risk of security threats if one component of the protection is compromised. It is also known as a "layered approach to security." Because there are multiple measures for security at different levels, defense in depth gives additional time to detect and respond to an attack. This can reduce the scope or impact of a security breach.

*Attack surface, attack vector,* and *work factor* are the three factors to consider when assessing the extent to which an environment is vulnerable to security threats. *Attack surface* refers to the various entry points that an attacker can use to launch an attack. Each component of a storage network is a source of potential vulnerability. An attacker can use all the external interfaces supported by that component, such as the hardware and the management interfaces, to execute various attacks. These interfaces form the attack surface for the attacker. Even unused network services, if enabled, can become a part of the attack surface.

An *attack vector* is a step or a series of steps necessary to complete an attack. For example, an attacker might exploit a bug in the management interface to execute a snoop attack whereby the attacker can modify the configuration of the storage device to allow the traffic to be accessed from one more host. This redirected traffic can be used to snoop the data in transit.

*Work factor* refers to the amount of time and effort required to exploit an attack vector. For example, if attackers attempt to retrieve sensitive information, they consider the time and effort that would be required for executing an attack on a database. This may include determining privileged accounts, determining the database schema, and writing SQL queries. Instead, based on the work factor, they may consider a less effort-intensive way to exploit the storage array by attaching to it directly and reading from the raw disk blocks.

Having assessed the vulnerability of the environment, organizations can deploy specific control measures. Any control measures should involve all the three aspects of infrastructure: people, process, and technology, and the relationships among them. To secure people, the first step is to establish and assure their identity. Based on their identity, selective controls can be implemented for their access to data and resources. The effectiveness of any security measure is primarily governed by processes and policies. The processes should be based on a thorough understanding of risks in the environment and should recognize the relative sensitivity of different types of data and the needs of various stakeholders to access the data. Without an effective process, the deployment of technology is neither cost-effective nor aligned to organizations' priorities. Finally, the technologies or controls that are deployed should ensure compliance with the processes, policies, and people for its effectiveness. These security technologies are directed at reducing vulnerability by minimizing attack surfaces and maximizing the work factors. These controls can be technical or nontechnical. Technical controls are usually implemented through computer systems, whereas nontechnical controls are implemented through administrative and physical controls. Administrative controls include security and personnel policies or standard procedures to direct the safe execution of various operations. Physical controls include setting up physical barriers, such as security guards, fences, or locks.

Based on the roles they play, controls are categorized as preventive, detective, and corrective. The preventive control attempts to prevent an attack; the detective control detects whether an attack is in progress; and after an attack is discovered, the corrective controls are implemented. *Preventive controls* avert the vulnerabilities from being exploited and prevent an attack or reduce its impact. *Corrective controls* reduce the effect of an attack, whereas *detective controls* discover attacks and trigger preventive or corrective controls. For example, an Intrusion Detection/Intrusion Prevention System (IDS/IPS) is a detective control that determines whether an attack is underway and then attempts to stop it by terminating a network connection or invoking a firewall rule to block traffic.

## 14.3 Storage Security Domains

Storage devices connected to a network raise the risk level and are more exposed to security threats via networks. However, with increasing use of networking in storage environments, storage devices are becoming highly exposed to security threats from a variety of sources. Specific controls must be implemented to secure a storage networking environment. This requires a closer look at storage networking security and a clear understanding of the access paths leading to storage resources. If a particular path is unauthorized and needs to be prohibited by technical controls, ensure that these controls are not compromised. If each component within the storage network is considered a potential access point, the attack surface of all these access points must be analyzed to identify the associated vulnerabilities.

To identify the threats that apply to a storage network, access paths to data storage can be categorized into three security domains: *application access, management access,* and *backup, replication, and archive.* Figure 14-1 depicts the three security domains of a storage system environment.

The first security domain involves application access to the stored data through the storage network. The second security domain includes management access to storage and interconnect devices and to the data residing on those devices.

This domain is primarily accessed by storage administrators who configure and manage the environment. The third domain consists of backup, replication, and archive access. Along with the access points in this domain, the backup media also needs to be secured.

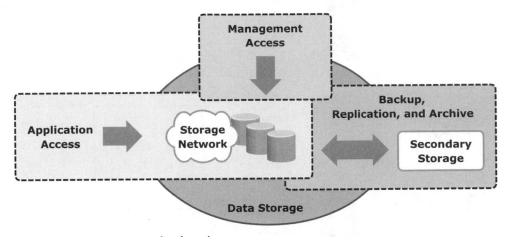

**Figure 14-1:** Storage security domains

To secure the storage networking environment, identify the existing threats within each of the security domains and classify the threats based on the type of security services — availability, confidentiality, integrity, and accountability. The next step is to select and implement various controls as countermeasures to the threats.

## 14.3.1 Securing the Application Access Domain

The *application access domain* may include only those applications that access the data through the file system or a database interface.

An important step to secure the application access domain is to identify the threats in the environment and appropriate controls that should be applied. Implementing physical security is also an important consideration to prevent media theft.

Figure 14-2 shows application access in a storage networking environment. Host A can access all V1 volumes; host B can access all V2 volumes. These volumes are classified according to the access level, such as confidential, restricted, and public. Some of the possible threats in this scenario could be host A spoofing the identity or elevating to the privileges of host B to gain access to host B's resources. Another threat could be that an unauthorized host gains access to the network; the attacker on this host may try to spoof the identity of another host and tamper with the data, snoop the network, or execute a DoS attack. Also any form of media theft could also compromise security. These threats can pose several serious challenges to the network security; therefore, they need to be addressed.

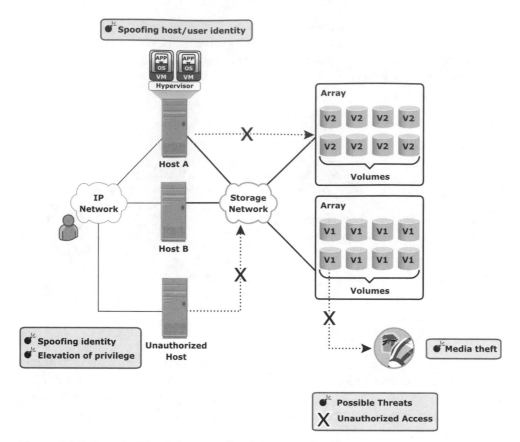

**Figure 14-2:** Security threats in an application access domain

## Controlling User Access to Data

Access control services regulate user access to data. These services mitigate the threats of spoofing host identity and elevating host privileges. Both these threats affect data integrity and confidentiality.

Access control mechanisms used in the application access domain are user and host authentication (technical control) and authorization (administrative control). These mechanisms may lie outside the boundaries of the storage network and require various systems to interconnect with other enterprise identity management and authentication systems, for example, systems that provide strong authentication and authorization to secure user identities against spoofing. NAS devices support the creation of *access control lists* that regulate user access to specific files. The Enterprise Content Management application enforces access to data by using Information Rights Management (IRM) that specifies which users have what rights to a document. Restricting access at the host level starts with authenticating a node when it tries to connect to a network.

Different storage networking technologies, such as iSCSI, FC, and IP-based storage, use various authentication mechanisms, such as Challenge-Handshake Authentication Protocol (CHAP), Fibre Channel Security Protocol (FC-SP), and IPSec, respectively, to authenticate host access.

After a host has been authenticated, the next step is to specify security controls for the storage resources, such as ports, volumes, or storage pools, that the host is authorized to access. *Zoning* is a control mechanism on the switches that segments the network into specific paths to be used for data traffic; *LUN masking* determines which hosts can access which storage devices. Some devices support mapping of a host's WWN to a particular FC port and from there to a particular LUN. This binding of the WWN to a physical port is the most secure.

Finally, it is important to ensure that administrative controls, such as defined security policies and standards, are implemented. Regular auditing is required to ensure proper functioning of administrative controls. This is enabled by logging significant events on all participating devices. Event logs should also be protected from unauthorized access because they may fail to achieve their goals if the logged content is exposed to unauthorized modifications by an attacker.

## Protecting the Storage Infrastructure

Securing the storage infrastructure from unauthorized access involves protecting all the elements of the infrastructure. Security controls for protecting the storage infrastructure address the threats of unauthorized tampering of data in transit that leads to a loss of data integrity, denial of service that compromises availability, and network snooping that may result in loss of confidentiality.

The security controls for protecting the network fall into two general categories: *network infrastructure integrity* and *storage network encryption*. Controls for ensuring the infrastructure integrity include a fabric switch function that ensures fabric integrity. This is achieved by preventing a host from being added to the SAN fabric without proper authorization. Storage network encryption methods include the use of IPSec for protecting IP-based storage networks, and FC-SP for protecting FC networks.

In secure storage environments, root or administrator privileges for a specific device are not granted to every user. Instead, *role-based access control* (RBAC) is deployed to assign necessary privileges to users, enabling them to perform their roles. A role may represent a job function, for example, an administrator. Privileges are associated with the roles and users acquire these privileges based upon their roles.

It is also advisable to consider administrative controls, such as "separation of duties," when defining data center procedures. Clear separation of duties ensures that no single individual can both specify an action and carry it out. For example, the person who authorizes the creation of administrative accounts should not be the person who uses those accounts. Securing management access is covered in detail in the next section.

Management networks for storage systems should be logically separate from other enterprise networks. This segmentation is critical to facilitate ease of management and increase security by allowing access only to the components existing within the same segment. For example, IP network segmentation is enforced with the deployment of filters at Layer 3 by using routers and firewalls, and at Layer 2 by using VLANs and port-level security on Ethernet switches.

Finally, physical access to the device console and the cabling of FC switches must be controlled to ensure protection of the storage infrastructure. All other established security measures fail if a device is physically accessed by an unauthorized user; this access may render the device unreliable.

### Data Encryption

The most important aspect of securing data is protecting data held inside the storage arrays. Threats at this level include tampering with data, which violates data integrity, and media theft, which compromises data availability and confidentiality. To protect against these threats, encrypt the data held on the storage media or encrypt the data prior to being transferred to the disk. It is also critical to decide upon a method for ensuring that data deleted at the end of its life cycle has been completely erased from the disks and cannot be reconstructed for malicious purposes.

Data should be encrypted as close to its origin as possible. If it is not possible to perform encryption on the host device, an encryption appliance can be used for encrypting data at the point of entry into the storage network. Encryption devices can be implemented on the fabric that encrypts data between the host and the storage media. These mechanisms can protect both the data at rest on the destination device and data in transit.

On NAS devices, adding antivirus checks and file extension controls can further enhance data integrity. In the case of CAS, use of MD5 or SHA-256 cryptographic algorithms guarantees data integrity by detecting any change in content bit patterns. In addition, the data erasure service ensures that the data has been completely overwritten by bit sequence before the disk is discarded. An organization's data classification policy determines whether the disk should actually be scrubbed prior to discarding it and the level of erasure needed based on regulatory requirements.

## 14.3.2 Securing the Management Access Domain

Management access, whether monitoring, provisioning, or managing storage resources, is associated with every device within the storage network. Most management software supports some form of CLI, system management console, or a web-based interface. Implementing appropriate controls for securing storage management applications is important because the damage that can be caused by using these applications can be far more extensive.

Figure 14-3 depicts a storage networking environment in which production hosts are connected to a SAN fabric and are accessing production storage array A, which is connected to remote storage array B for replication purposes. Further, this configuration has a storage management platform on Host A. A possible threat in this environment is an unauthorized host spoofing the user or host identity to manage the storage arrays or network. For example, an unauthorized host may gain management access to remote array B.

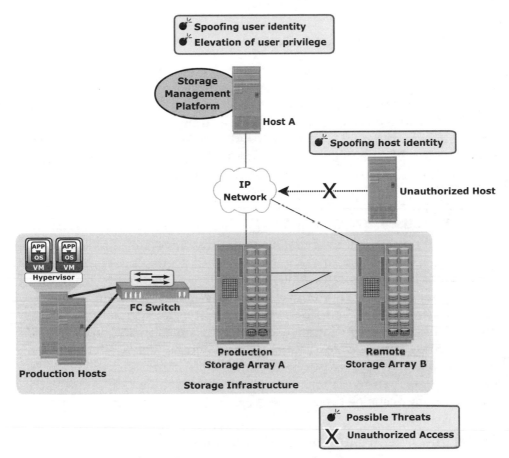

**Figure 14-3:** Security threats in a management access domain

Providing management access through an external network increases the potential for an unauthorized host or switch to connect to that network. In such circumstances, implementing appropriate security measures prevents certain types of remote communication from occurring. Using secure communication channels, such as Secure Shell (SSH) or Secure Sockets Layer (SSL)/Transport Layer Security (TLS), provides effective protection against these threats. Event log monitoring helps to identify unauthorized access and unauthorized changes to the infrastructure. Event logs should be placed outside the shared storage systems where they can be reviewed if the storage is compromised.

The storage management platform must be validated for available security controls and ensures that these controls are adequate to secure the overall storage environment. The administrator's identity and role should be secured against any spoofing attempts so that an attacker cannot manipulate the entire storage array and cause intolerable data loss by reformatting storage media or making data resources unavailable.

### Controlling Administrative Access

Controlling administrative access to storage aims to safeguard against the threats of an attacker spoofing an administrator's identity or elevating privileges to gain administrative access. Both of these threats affect the integrity of data and devices. To protect against these threats, administrative access regulation and various auditing techniques are used to enforce accountability of users and processes. Access control should be enforced for each storage component. In some storage environments, it may be necessary to integrate storage devices with third-party authentication directories, such as Lightweight Directory Access Protocol (LDAP) or Active Directory.

Security best practices stipulate that no single user should have ultimate control over all aspects of the system. If an administrative user is a necessity, the number of activities requiring administrative privileges should be minimized. Instead, it is better to assign various administrative functions by using RBAC. Auditing logged events is a critical control measure to track the activities of an administrator. However, access to administrative log files and their content must be protected. Deploying a reliable Network Time Protocol on each system that can be synchronized to a common time is another important requirement to ensure that activities across systems can be consistently tracked. In addition, having a Security Information Management (SIM) solution supports effective analysis of the event log files.

### Protecting the Management Infrastructure

Mechanisms to protect the management network infrastructure include encrypting management traffic, enforcing management access controls, and applying IP network security best practices. These best practices include the use of IP routers and Ethernet switches to restrict the traffic to certain devices. Restricting network activity and access to a limited set of hosts minimizes the threat of an unauthorized device attaching to the network and gaining access to the management interfaces. Access controls need to be enforced at the storage-array level to specify which host has management access to which array. Some storage devices and switches can restrict management access to particular hosts and limit the commands that can be issued from each host.

A separate private management network is highly recommended for management traffic. If possible, management traffic should not be mixed with either production data traffic or other LAN traffic used in the enterprise. Unused network services must be disabled on every device within the storage network. This decreases the attack surface for that device by minimizing the number of interfaces through which the device can be accessed.

To summarize, security enforcement must focus on the management communication between devices, confidentiality and integrity of management data, and availability of management networks and devices.

## 14.3.3 Securing Backup, Replication, and Archive

Backup, replication, and archive is the third domain that needs to be secured against an attack. As explained in Chapter 10, a backup involves copying the data from a storage array to backup media, such as tapes or disks. Securing backup is complex and is based on the backup software that accesses the storage arrays. It also depends on the configuration of the storage environments at the primary and secondary sites, especially with remote backup solutions performed directly on a remote tape device or using array-based remote replication.

Organizations must ensure that the disaster recovery (DR) site maintains the same level of security for the backed up data. Protecting the backup, replication, and archive infrastructure requires addressing several threats, including spoofing the legitimate identity of a DR site, tampering with data, network snooping, DoS attacks, and media theft. Such threats represent potential violations of integrity, confidentiality, and availability. Figure 14-4 illustrates a generic remote backup design whereby data on a storage array is replicated over a DR network to a secondary storage at the DR site. In a remote backup solution where the storage components are separated by a network, the threats at the transmission layer need to be countered. Otherwise, an attacker can spoof the identity of the backup server and request the host to send its data. The unauthorized host claiming to be the backup server may lead to a remote backup being performed to an unauthorized and unknown site. In addition, attackers can use the DR network connection to tamper with data, snoop the network, and create a DoS attack against the storage devices.

The physical threat of a backup tape being lost, stolen, or misplaced, especially if the tapes contain highly confidential information, is another type of threat. Backup-to-tape applications are vulnerable to severe security implications if they do not encrypt data while backing it up.

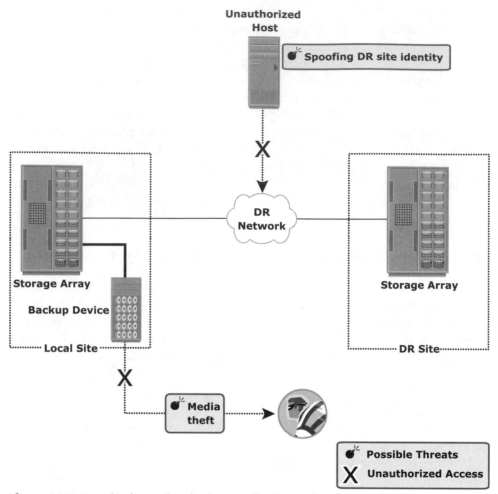

**Figure 14-4:** Security threats in a backup, replication, and archive environment

# 14.4 Security Implementations in Storage Networking

The following discussion details some of the basic security implementations in FC SAN, NAS, and IP-SAN environments.

## 14.4.1 FC SAN

Traditional FC SANs enjoy an inherent security advantage over IP-based networks. An FC SAN is configured as an isolated private environment with fewer nodes than an IP network. Consequently, FC SANs impose fewer security threats. However, this scenario has changed with converged networks and storage consolidation, driving rapid growth and necessitating designs for large, complex SANs that span multiple sites across the enterprise. Today, no single comprehensive security solution is available for FC SANs. Many FC SAN security mechanisms have evolved from their counterpart in IP networking, thereby bringing in matured security solutions.

*Fibre Channel Security Protocol* (FC-SP) standards (T11 standards), published in 2006, align security mechanisms and algorithms between IP and FC interconnects. These standards describe protocols to implement security measures in a FC fabric, among fabric elements and N_Ports within the fabric. They also include guidelines for authenticating FC entities, setting up session keys, negotiating the parameters required to ensure frame-by-frame integrity and confidentiality, and establishing and distributing policies across an FC fabric.

### FC SAN Security Architecture

Storage networking environments are a potential target for unauthorized access, theft, and misuse because of the vastness and complexity of these environments. Therefore, security strategies are based on the *defense in depth* concept, which recommends multiple integrated layers of security. This ensures that the failure of one security control will not compromise the assets under protection. Figure 14-5 illustrates various levels (zones) of a storage networking environment that must be secured and the security measures that can be deployed.

FC SANs not only suffer from certain risks and vulnerabilities that are unique, but also share common security problems associated with physical security and remote administrative access. In addition to implementing SAN specific security measures, organizations must simultaneously leverage other security implementations in the enterprise. Table 14-1 provides a comprehensive list of protection strategies that must be implemented in various security zones. Some of the security mechanisms listed in Table 14-1 are not specific to SAN but are commonly used data center techniques. For example, two-factor authentication is implemented widely; in a simple implementation it requires the use of a username/password and an additional security component such as a smart card for authentication.

### Basic SAN Security Mechanisms

LUN masking and zoning, switch-wide and fabric-wide access control, RBAC, and logical partitioning of a fabric (Virtual SAN) are the most commonly used SAN security methods.

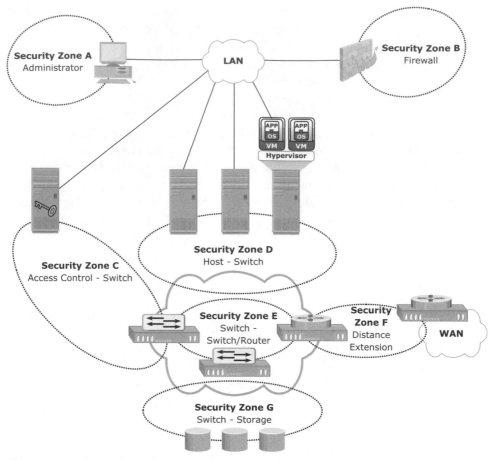

**Figure 14-5:** FC SAN security architecture

**Table 14-1:** Security Zones and Protection Strategies

| SECURITY ZONES | PROTECTION STRATEGIES |
|---|---|
| Zone A (Authentication at the Management Console) | (a) Restrict management LAN access to authorized users (lock down MAC addresses); (b) implement VPN tunneling for secure remote access to the management LAN; and (c) use two-factor authentication for network access. |
| Zone B (Firewall) | Block inappropriate traffic by (a) filtering out addresses that should not be allowed on your LAN; and (b) screening for allowable protocols, block ports that are not in use. |
| Zone C (Access Control-Switch) | Authenticate users/administrators of FC switches using Remote Authentication Dial In User Service (RADIUS), DH-CHAP (Diffie-Hellman Challenge Handshake Authentication Protocol), and so on. |

| SECURITY ZONES | PROTECTION STRATEGIES |
|---|---|
| Zone D (Host to switch) | Restrict Fabric access to legitimate hosts by (a) implementing ACLs: Known HBAs can connect on specific switch ports only; and (b) implementing a secure zoning method, such as port zoning (also known as hard zoning). |
| Zone E (Switch to Switch/Switch to Router) | Protect traffic on fabric by (a) using E_Port authentication; (b) encrypting the traffic in transit; and (c) implementing FC switch controls and port controls. |
| Zone F (Distance Extension) | Implement encryption for in-flight data (a) FC-SP for long-distance FC extension; and (b) IPSec for SAN extension via FCIP. |
| Zone G (Switch to Storage) | Protect the storage arrays on your SAN via (a) WWPN-based LUN masking; and (b) S_ID locking: masking based on source FC address. |

## LUN Masking and Zoning

LUN masking and zoning are the basic SAN security mechanisms used to protect against unauthorized access to storage. LUN masking and zoning are detailed in Chapter 4 and Chapter 5, respectively. The standard implementations of LUN masking on storage arrays mask the LUNs presented to a front-end storage port based on the WWPNs of the source HBAs. A stronger variant of LUN masking may sometimes be offered whereby masking can be done on the basis of source FC addresses. It offers a mechanism to lock down the FC address of a given node port to its WWN. *WWPN zoning* is the preferred choice in security-conscious environments.

## Securing Switch Ports

Apart from zoning and LUN masking, additional security mechanisms, such as port binding, port lockdown, port lockout, and persistent port disable, can be implemented on switch ports. *Port binding* limits the number of devices that can attach to a particular switch port and allows only the corresponding switch port to connect to a node for fabric access. Port binding mitigates but does not eliminate WWPN spoofing. *Port lockdown* and *port lockout* restrict a switch port's type of initialization. Typical variants of port lockout ensure that the switch port cannot function as an E_Port and cannot be used to create an ISL, such as a rogue switch. Some variants ensure that the port role is restricted to only FL_Port, F_Port, E_Port, or a combination of these. *Persistent port disable* prevents a switch port from being enabled even after a switch reboot.

### Switch-Wide and Fabric-Wide Access Control

As organizations grow their SANs locally or over longer distances, there is a greater need to effectively manage SAN security. Network security can be configured on the FC switch by using *access control lists* (ACLs) and on the fabric by using fabric binding.

ACLs incorporate the device connection control and switch connection control policies. The device connection control policy specifies which HBAs and storage ports can be a part of the fabric, preventing unauthorized devices from accessing it. Similarly, the switch connection control policy specifies which switches are allowed to be part of the fabric, preventing unauthorized switches from joining it.

*Fabric binding* prevents an unauthorized switch from joining any existing switch in the fabric. It ensures that authorized membership data exists on every switch and any attempt to connect any switch in the fabric by using an ISL causes the fabric to segment.

Role-based access control provides additional security to a SAN by preventing unauthorized activity on the fabric for management operations. It enables the security administrator to assign roles to users that explicitly specify privileges or access rights after logging into the fabric. For example, the *zone admin* role can modify the zones on the fabric, whereas a basic user may view only fabric-related information, such as port types and logged-in nodes.

### Logical Partitioning of a Fabric: Virtual SAN

VSANs enable the creation of multiple logical SANs over a common physical SAN. They provide the capability to build larger consolidated fabrics and still maintain the required security and isolation between them. Figure 14-6 depicts logical partitioning in a VSAN.

The SAN administrator can create distinct VSANs by populating each of them with switch ports. In the example, the switch ports are distributed over two VSANs: 10 and 20 — for the Engineering and HR divisions, respectively. Although they share physical switching gear with other divisions, they can be managed individually as standalone fabrics. Zoning should be done for each VSAN to secure the entire physical SAN. Each managed VSAN can have only one active zone set at a time.

VSANs minimize the impact of fabricwide disruptive events because management and control traffic on the SAN — which may include RSCNs, zone set activation events, and more — does not traverse VSAN boundaries. Therefore, VSANs are a cost-effective alternative for building isolated physical fabrics. They contribute to information availability and security by isolating fabric events and providing authorization control within a single fabric.

## 14.4.2 NAS

NAS is open to multiple exploits, including viruses, worms, unauthorized access, snooping, and data tampering. Various security mechanisms are implemented in NAS to secure data and the storage networking infrastructure.

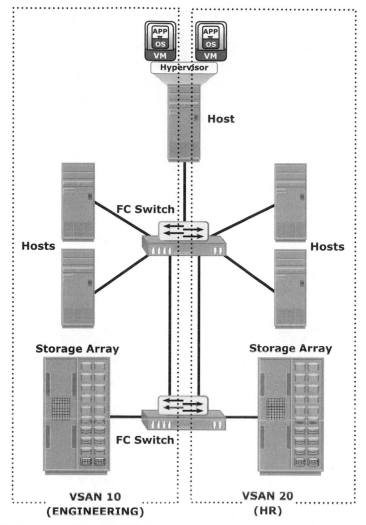

**Figure 14-6:** Securing SAN with VSAN

Permissions and ACLs form the first level of protection to NAS resources by restricting accessibility and sharing. These permissions are deployed over and above the default behaviors and attributes associated with files and folders. In addition, various other authentication and authorization mechanisms, such as Kerberos and directory services, are implemented to verify the identity of network users and define their privileges. Similarly, firewalls protect the storage infrastructure from unauthorized access and malicious attacks.

## NAS File Sharing: Windows ACLs

Windows supports two types of ACLs: *discretionary access control lists* (DACLs) and *system access control lists* (SACLs). The DACL, commonly referred to as the

ACL, that determines access control. The SACL determines what accesses need to be audited if auditing is enabled.

In addition to these ACLs, Windows also supports the concept of object ownership. The owner of an object has hard-coded rights to that object, and these rights do not need to be explicitly granted in the SACL. The owner, SACL, and DACL are all statically held as attributes of each object. Windows also offers the functionality to inherit permissions, which allows the child objects existing within a parent object to automatically inherit the ACLs of the parent object.

ACLs are also applied to directory objects known as security identifiers (SIDs). These are automatically generated by a Windows server or domain when a user or group is created, and they are abstracted from the user. In this way, though a user may identify his login ID as "User1," it is simply a textual representation of the true SID, which is used by the underlying operating system. Internal processes in Windows refer to an account's SID rather than the account's username or group name while granting access to an object. ACLs are set by using the standard Windows Explorer GUI but can also be configured with CLI commands or other third-party tools.

### NAS File Sharing: UNIX Permissions

For the UNIX operating system, a *user* is an abstraction that denotes a logical entity for assignment of ownership and operation privileges for the system. A user can be either a person or a system operation. A UNIX system is only aware of the privileges of the user to perform specific operations on the system and identifies each user by a user ID (UID) and a username, regardless of whether it is a person, a system operation, or a device.

In UNIX, users can be organized into one or more groups. The concept of group serves the purpose to assign sets of privileges for a given resource and sharing them among many users that need them. For example, a group of people working on one project may need the same permissions for a set of files.

UNIX permissions specify the operations that can be performed by any ownership relation with respect to a file. In simpler terms, these permissions specify what the owner can do, what the owner group can do, and what everyone else can do with the file. For any given ownership relation, three bits are used to specify access permissions. The first bit denotes read (r) access, the second bit denotes write (w) access, and the third bit denotes execute (x) access. Because UNIX defines three ownership relations (Owner, Group, and All), a triplet (defining the access permission) is required for each ownership relationship, resulting in nine bits. Each bit can be either set or clear. When displayed, a set bit is marked by its corresponding operation letter (r, w, or x), a clear bit is denoted by a dash (-), and all are put in a row, such as rwxr-xr-x. In this example, the owner can do anything with the file, but group owners and the rest of the world can read or execute only. When displayed, a character denoting the mode of the file may precede this nine-bit pattern. For example, if the file is a directory, it is denoted as "d"; and if it is a link, it is denoted as "l."

## NAS File Sharing: Authentication and Authorization

In a file-sharing environment, NAS devices use standard file-sharing protocols, NFS and CIFS. Therefore, authentication and authorization are implemented and supported on NAS devices in the same way as in a UNIX or Windows file-sharing environment.

Authentication requires verifying the identity of a network user and therefore involves a login credential lookup on a Network Information System (NIS) server in a UNIX environment. Similarly, a Windows client is authenticated by a Windows domain controller that houses the Active Directory. The Active Directory uses LDAP to access information about network objects in the directory and Kerberos for network security. NAS devices use the same authentication techniques to validate network user credentials. Figure 14-7 depicts the authentication process in a NAS environment.

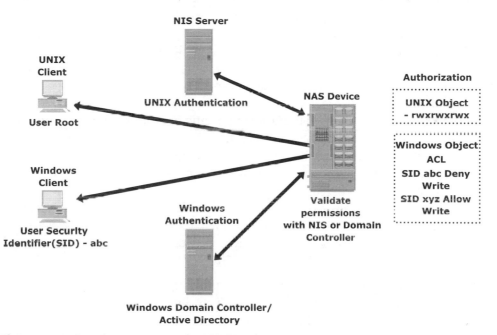

**Figure 14-7:** Securing user access in a NAS environment

Authorization defines user privileges in a network. The authorization techniques for UNIX users and Windows users are quite different. UNIX files use mode bits to define access rights granted to owners, groups, and other users, whereas Windows uses an ACL to allow or deny specific rights to a particular user for a particular file.

Although NAS devices support both of these methodologies for UNIX and Windows users, complexities arise when UNIX and Windows users access and share the same data. If the NAS device supports multiple protocols, the integrity of both permission methodologies must be maintained. NAS device vendors provide a method of mapping UNIX permissions to Windows and vice versa, so a multiprotocol environment can be supported. However, consider these complexities of multiprotocol support when designing a NAS solution. At the same time, validate the domain controller and NIS server connectivity and bandwidth. If multiprotocol access is required, specific vendor access policy implementations need to be considered.

## Kerberos

Kerberos is a network authentication protocol, which is designed to provide strong authentication for client/server applications by using secret-key cryptography. It uses cryptography so that a client and server can prove their identity to each other across an insecure network connection. After the client and server have proven their identities, they can choose to encrypt all their communications to ensure privacy and data integrity.

In Kerberos, authentications occur between clients and servers. The client gets a ticket for a service and the server decrypts this ticket by using its secret key. Any entity, user, or host that gets a service ticket for a Kerberos service is called a *Kerberos client*. The term *Kerberos server* generally refers to the Key Distribution Center (KDC). The KDC implements the Authentication Service (AS) and the Ticket Granting Service (TGS). The KDC has a copy of every password associated with every principal, so it is absolutely vital that the KDC remain secure. In Kerberos, users and servers for which a secret key is stored in the KDC database are known as *principals*.

In a NAS environment, Kerberos is primarily used when authenticating against a Microsoft Active Directory domain, although it can be used to execute security functions in UNIX environments. The Kerberos authentication process shown in Figure 14-8 includes the following steps:

1. The user logs on to the workstation in the Active Directory domain (or forest) using an ID and a password. The client computer sends a request to the AS running on the KDC for a Kerberos ticket. The KDC verifies the user's login information from Active Directory. (This step is not explicitly shown in Figure 14-8.)

2. The KDC responds with an encrypted Ticket Granting Ticket (TGT) and an encrypted session key. TGT has a limited validity period. TGT can be decrypted only by the KDC, and the client can decrypt only the session key.

3. When the client requests a service from a server, it sends a request, consisting of the previously generated TGT, encrypted with the session key and the resource information to the KDC.

4. The KDC checks the permissions in Active Directory and ensures that the user is authorized to use that service.

5. The KDC returns a service ticket to the client. This service ticket contains fields addressed to the client and to the server hosting the service.

6. The client then sends the service ticket to the server that houses the required resources.

7. The server, in this case the NAS device, decrypts the server portion of the ticket and stores the information in a keytab file. As long as the client's Kerberos ticket is valid, this authorization process does not need to be repeated. The server automatically allows the client to access the appropriate resources.

8. A client-server session is now established. The server returns a session ID to the client, which tracks the client activity, such as file locking, as long as the session is active.

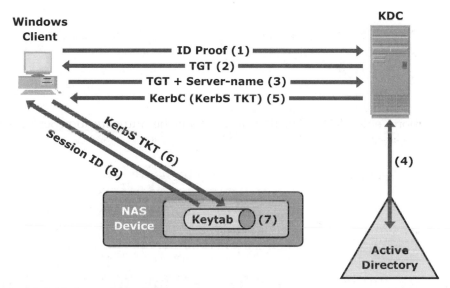

**Figure 14-8:** Kerberos authorization

### Network-Layer Firewalls

Because NAS devices utilize the IP protocol stack, they are vulnerable to various attacks initiated through the public IP network. Network layer firewalls are implemented in NAS environments to protect the NAS devices from these security threats. These network-layer firewalls can examine network packets and compare them to a set of configured security rules. Packets that are not authorized by a security rule are dropped and not allowed to continue to the destination. Rules can be established based on a source address (network or host), a destination address (network or host), a port, or a combination of those factors (source IP, destination IP, and port number). The effectiveness of a firewall depends on how robust and extensive the security rules are. A loosely defined rule set can increase the probability of a security breach.

Figure 14-9 depicts a typical firewall implementation. A demilitarized zone (DMZ) is commonly used in networking environments. A DMZ provides a means to secure internal assets while allowing Internet-based access to various resources. In a DMZ environment, servers that need to be accessed through the Internet are placed between two sets of firewalls. Application-specific ports, such as HTTP or FTP, are allowed through the firewall to the DMZ servers. However, no Internet-based traffic is allowed to penetrate the second set of firewalls and gain access to the internal network.

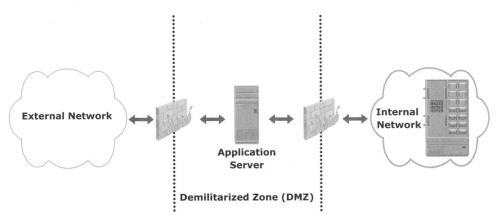

**Figure 14-9:** Securing a NAS environment with a network-layer firewall

The servers in the DMZ may or may not be allowed to communicate with internal resources. In such a setup, the server in the DMZ is an Internet-facing web application accessing data stored on a NAS device, which may be located on the internal private network. A secure design would serve only data to internal and external applications through the DMZ.

**APPLICATION-LAYER FIREWALLS AND XML FIREWALLS**

Application-layer firewalls and XML firewalls are third generation firewalls that control access to an application by filtering out traffic that does not meet the configured firewall policy. Unlike a network-layer firewall, which scans packets based on source address, destination address, and so on, application-layer firewalls provide detailed scanning of a packet's content. An XML firewall is a specialized application-layer firewall that protects applications exposed through XML based interfaces. Typically deployed in an organization's DMZ environment, an XML firewall validates XML traffic, filters XML content, and controls access to XML-based resources.

## 14.4.3 IP SAN

This section describes some of the basic security mechanisms used in IP SAN environments. The *Challenge-Handshake Authentication Protocol* (CHAP) is a basic authentication mechanism that has been widely adopted by network devices and hosts. CHAP provides a method for initiators and targets to authenticate each other by utilizing a secret code or password. CHAP secrets are usually random secrets of 12 to 128 characters. The secret is never exchanged directly over the communication channel; rather, a one-way hash function converts it into a hash value, which is then exchanged. A hash function, using the MD5 algorithm, transforms data in such a way that the result is unique and cannot be changed back to its original form. Figure 14-10 depicts the CHAP authentication process.

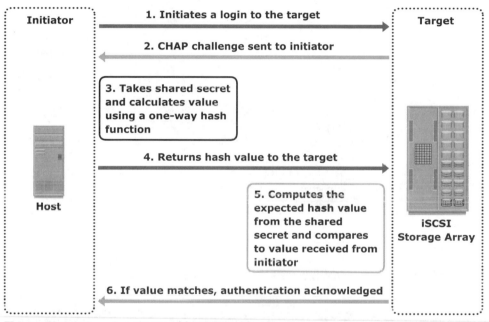

**Figure 14-10:** Securing IPSAN with CHAP authentication

If the initiator requires reverse CHAP authentication, the initiator authenticates the target by using the same procedure. The CHAP secret must be configured on the initiator and the target. A CHAP entry, composed of the name of a node and the secret associated with the node, is maintained by the target and the initiator.

The same steps are executed in a two-way CHAP authentication scenario. After these steps are completed, the initiator authenticates the target. If both authentication steps succeed, then data access is allowed. CHAP is often used because it is a fairly simple protocol to implement and can be implemented across a number of disparate systems.

*iSNS discovery domains* function in the same way as FC zones. Discovery domains provide functional groupings of devices in an IP-SAN. For devices to communicate with one another, they must be configured in the same discovery domain. State change notifications (SCNs) inform the iSNS server when devices are added to or removed from a discovery domain. Figure 14-11 depicts the discovery domains in iSNS.

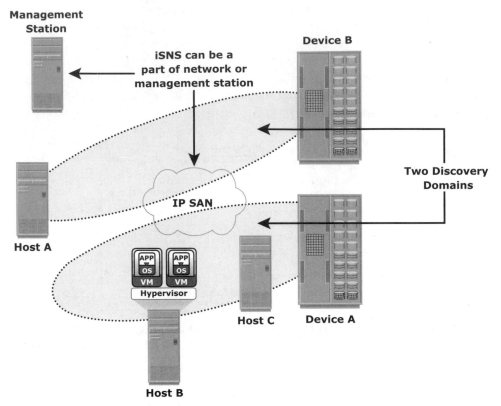

**Figure 14-11:** Securing IPSAN with iSNS discovery domains

## 14.5 Securing Storage Infrastructure in Virtualized and Cloud Environments

This chapter, so far, focused only on the security threats and measures in a traditional data center. These threats and measures are also applicable to information storage in virtualized and cloud environments. However, virtualized and cloud computing environments pose additional threats to an organization's data due to multitenancy and lack of control over the cloud resources. A public cloud has more security concerns compared to a private cloud and demands additional counter measures. This is because in a public cloud, cloud users (consumers) usually have limited control over resources, and therefore, enforcement of security mechanisms by consumers is comparatively difficult.

From a security perspective, both consumers and cloud service providers (CSP) have several security concerns and face multiple threats. Security concerns and security measures are detailed next.

## 14.5.1 Security Concerns

Organizations are rapidly adopting virtualization and cloud computing, however they have some security concerns. These key security concerns are multitenancy, velocity of attack, information assurance, and data privacy.

*Multitenancy*, by virtue of virtualization, enables multiple independent tenants to be serviced using the same set of storage resources. In spite of the benefits offered by multitenancy, it is still a key security concern for users and service providers. Colocation of multiple VMs in a single server and sharing the same resources increase the attack surface. It may happen that business critical data of one tenant is accessed by other competing tenants who run applications using the same resources.

*Velocity-of-attack* refers to a situation in which any existing security threat in the cloud spreads more rapidly and has a larger impact than that in the traditional data center environments. *Information assurance* for users ensures confidentiality, integrity, and availability of data in the cloud. Also the cloud user needs assurance that all the users operating on the cloud are genuine and access the data only with legitimate rights and scope.

*Data privacy* is also a major concern in a virtualized and cloud environment. A CSP needs to ensure that Personally Identifiable Information (PII) about its clients is legally protected from any unauthorized disclosure.

## 14.5.2 Security Measures

Security measures can be implemented at the compute, network, and storage levels. These security measures implemented at three layers mitigate the risks in virtualized and cloud environments.

### Security at the Compute Level

Securing a compute infrastructure includes enforcing the security of the physical server, hypervisor, VM, and guest OS (OS running within a virtual machine).

*Physical server security* involves implementing user authentication and authorization mechanisms. These mechanisms identify users and provide access privileges on the server. To minimize the attack surface on the server, unused hardware components, such as NICs, USB ports, or drives, should be removed or disabled.

A *hypervisor* is a single point of security failure for all the VMs running on it. Rootkits and malware installed on a hypervisor make detection difficult for the antivirus software installed on the guest OS. To protect against attacks, security-critical hypervisor updates should be installed regularly. Further, the hypervisor management system must also be protected. Malicious attacks and infiltration to the management system can impact all the existing VMs and allow attackers to create new VMs. Access to the management system should be restricted to authorized administrators. Furthermore, there must be a separate firewall installed between the management system and the rest of the network.

*VM isolation* and *hardening* are some of the common security mechanisms to effectively safeguard a VM from an attack. VM isolation helps to prevent a compromised guest OS from impacting other guest OSs. VM isolation is implemented at the hypervisor level. Apart from isolation, VMs should be hardened against security threats. Hardening is a process to change the default configuration to achieve greater security.

Apart from the measures to secure a hypervisor and VMs, virtualized and cloud environments also require further measures on the guest OS and application levels.

**TRUSTED NETWORK CONNECT (TNC)**

**TNC is a protocol specification based on the principles of AAA (authentication, authorization and accounting) with the ability to authorize network clients based on hardware configurations, BIOS, kernel versions, updates to OS and anti-virus software, and so on. This protocol is developed by the Trusted Computing Group (TCG) which is an open industry standards organization. TCG creates specifications based on the concept of a hardware root of trust for a variety of devices, applications, and services.**

## Security at the Network Level

The key security measures that minimize vulnerabilities at the network layer are firewall, intrusion detection, demilitarized zone (DMZ), and encryption of data-in-flight.

A *firewall* protects networks from unauthorized access while permitting only legitimate communications. In a virtualized and cloud environment, a firewall can also protect hypervisors and VMs. For example, if remote administration is enabled on a hypervisor, access to all the remote administration interfaces should be restricted by a firewall. A firewall also secures VM-to-VM traffic. This firewall service can be provided using a *Virtual Firewall* (VF). A VF is a firewall service running entirely on the hypervisor. A VF provides packet filtering and monitoring of the VM-to-VM traffic. A VF gives visibility and control over the VM traffic and enforces policies at the VM level.

*Intrusion Detection* (ID) is the process to detect events that can compromise the confidentiality, integrity, or availability of a resource. An ID System (IDS) automatically analyzes events to check whether an event or a sequence of events match a known pattern for anomalous activity, or whether it is (statistically) different from most of the other events in the system. It generates an alert if an irregularity is detected. DMZ and data encryption are also deployed as security measures in the virtualized and cloud environments. However, these deployments work in the same way as in the traditional data center.

### Security at the Storage Level

Major threats to storage systems in virtualized and cloud environments arise due to compromises at compute, network, and physical security levels. This is because access to storage systems is through compute and network infrastructure. Therefore, adequate security measures should be in place at the compute and network levels to ensure storage security. Common security mechanisms that protect storage include the following:

- Access control methods to regulate which users and processes access the data on the storage systems
- Zoning and LUN masking
- Encryption of data-at-rest (on the storage system) and data-in-transit. Data encryption should also include encrypting backups and storing encryption keys separately from the data.
- Data shredding that removes the traces of the deleted data

Apart from these mechanisms, isolation of different types of traffic using VSANs further enhances the security of storage systems. In the case of storage utilized by hypervisors, additional security steps are required to protect the storage. Storage for hypervisors using clustered file systems supporting multiple VMs may require separate LUNs for VM components and VM data.

## 14.6 Concepts in Practice: RSA and VMware Security Products

RSA, the security division of EMC, is the premier provider of security, risk, and compliance solutions, helping organizations to solve their most complex and sensitive security challenges.

VMware offers secure and robust virtualization solutions for virtualized and cloud environments. This section provides a brief introduction to RSA SecureID, RSA Identity and Access Management, RSA Data Protection Manager, and VMware vShield.

## 14.6.1 RSA SecureID

RSA SecurID two-factor authentication provides an added layer of security to ensure that only valid users have access to systems and data. RSA SecurID is based on something a user knows (a password or PIN) and something a user has (an authenticator device). It provides a much more reliable level of user authentication than reusable passwords. It generates a new one-time password code every 60 seconds, making it difficult for anyone other than the genuine user to input the correct token code at any given time. To access their resources, users combine their secret Personal Identification Number (PIN) with the token code that appears on their SecurID authenticator display at that given time. The result is a unique, one-time password to assure a user's identity.

## 14.6.2 RSA Identity and Access Management

The RSA Identity and Access Management product provides identity, security, and access-controls management for physical, virtual, and cloud-based environments through access management. It enables trusted identities to freely and securely interact with systems and access. The RSA Identity and Access Management family has two products: *RSA Access Manager* and *RSA Federated Identity Manager*. RSA Access Manager enables organizations to centrally manage authentication and authorization policies for a large number of users, online web portals, and application resources. Access Manager provides seamless user access with single sign-on (SSO) and preserves identity context for greater security. RSA Federated Identity Manager enables end users to collaborate with business partners, outsourced service providers, and supply-chain partners or across multiple offices or agencies all with a single identity and logon.

## 14.6.3 RSA Data Protection Manager

RSA Data Protection Manager enables deployment of encryption, tokenization, and enterprise key management simply and affordably. The RSA Data Protection Manager family is composed of two products: *Application Encryption and Tokenization* and *Enterprise Key Management*.

- Application Encryption and Tokenization with RSA Data Protection Manager helps to achieve compliance with regulations related to PII by quickly embedding the encryption and tokenization of sensitive data and helping to prevent data loss. It works at the point of creation, ensuring that the data stays encrypted as it is transmitted and stored.

- Enterprise key management is an easy-to-use management tool for encrypting keys at the database, file server, and storage layers. It is designed to simplify the deployment of encryption throughout the enterprise. It also helps to ensure that information is properly secured and fully accessible when needed at any point in its life cycle.

### 14.6.4 VMware vShield

The VMware vShield family includes three products: *vShield App, vShield Edge,* and *vShield Endpoint*.

VMware vShield App is a hypervisor-based application-aware firewall solution. It protects applications in a virtualized environment from network-based threats by providing visibility into network communications and enforcing granular policies with security groups. VMware vShield App observes network activity between virtual machines to define and refine firewall policies and secure business processes through detailed reporting of application traffic.

VMware vShield Edge provides comprehensive perimeter network security for a virtualized environment. It is deployed as a virtual appliance and serves as a network security gateway for all the hosts within the virtualized environment. It provides many services including firewall, VPN, and Dynamic Host Configuration Protocol (DHCP) services.

VMware vShield Endpoint consists of a hardened special security VM with a third party antivirus software. VMware vShield Endpoint streamlines and accelerates antivirus and antimalware deployment because antivirus engine and signature files are updated only within the special security VM. VMware vShield Endpoint improves VM performance by offloading file scanning and other tasks from VMs to the security VM. It prevents antivirus storms and bottlenecks associated with multiple simultaneous antivirus and antimalware scans and updates. It also satisfies audit requirements with detailed logging of antivirus and antimalware activities.

## Summary

The continuing expansion of the storage network has exposed data center resources and storage infrastructures to new vulnerabilities. IP-based storage networking has exposed storage resources to traditional network vulnerabilities. Data aggregation has also increased the potential impact of a security breach. In addition to these security challenges, compliance regulations continue to expand and have become more complex. Data center managers are faced with addressing the threat of security breaches from both within and outside the organization.

Organizations are adopting virtualization and cloud as their new IT model. However, the key concern preventing faster adoption is security. The cloud has more vulnerabilities compared to a traditional or virtualized data center. This is because cloud resources are shared among multiple consumers. Also the consumers have limited control over the cloud resources. Cloud service providers and consumers are facing threat of security breaches in the cloud environment.

This chapter detailed a framework for storage security and provided mitigation methods that can be deployed against identified threats in a storage networking environment. It also detailed the security architecture and protection mechanisms in SAN, NAS, and IP-SAN environments. Further, this chapter touched on the security concerns and measures in a virtualized and cloud environment.

Security has become an integral component of storage management and is the key parameter monitored for all data center components. The following chapter focuses on the management of a storage infrastructure.

## EXERCISES

1. Research the following security mechanisms, and explain how they are used:

   - MD-5 algorithm
   - SHA-256 algorithm
   - RADIUS
   - DH-CHAP

2. A storage array dials a support center automatically whenever an error is detected. The vendor's representative at the support center can log on to the service processor of the storage array through the Internet to perform diagnostics and repair. Discuss the security concerns in this environment and provide security methods that can be implemented to mitigate any malicious attacks through this gateway.

3. Develop a checklist for auditing the security of a storage environment with SAN, NAS, and iSCSI implementations. Explain how you will perform the audit. Research possible security loopholes. List them and provide control mechanisms that should be implemented to eliminate them.

4. Explain various security concerns and measures in the virtualized and cloud environment.

5. Research and prepare a presentation on multifactor authentication security technique.

# Chapter 15
# Managing the Storage Infrastructure

U nprecedented growth of information, proliferation of applications, complexity of business processes, and requirements of 24×7 availability of information have put increasingly higher demands on the storage infrastructure.

Managing storage infrastructure efficiently is a key that enables organizations to address these challenges and ensures continuity of business.

Comprehensive storage infrastructure management requires the implementation of intelligent

tools and robust processes to meet the required service levels. These tools enable performance tuning, data protection, access control, centralized auditing, and meeting compliance requirements. They also ensure the consolidation and better utilization of existing resources, thereby limiting the need for excessive ongoing investment on infrastructure. The management process defines procedures for efficient handling of various operations, such as incident, problem, and change requests. It is imperative to manage not just the individual components, but also the infrastructure end-to-end due to the components' interdependency.

Storage infrastructure management is also composed of strategies, such as *Information Lifecycle Management* (ILM) that optimizes the storage investment while meeting the service levels. ILM helps to manage information based on its value to the business.

Managing the storage infrastructure requires performing various activities, including accessibility, capacity, performance, and security management. All of these activities are interrelated and should be considered to maximize the return on investment. Virtualization technologies have dramatically changed the storage infrastructure management paradigm.

This chapter details the monitoring and management activities of storage infrastructure. It also describes the common standards used for developing storage resource management tools. Further, this chapter also details ILM, its benefits, and storage tiering.

# 15.1 Monitoring the Storage Infrastructure

Monitoring is one of the most important aspects that forms the basis for managing storage infrastructure resources. Monitoring provides the performance and accessibility status of various components. It also enables administrators to perform essential management activities. Monitoring also helps to analyze the utilization and consumption of various storage infrastructure resources. This analysis facilitates capacity planning, forecasting, and optimal use of these resources. Storage infrastructure environment parameters such as heating and power supplies are also monitored.

## 15.1.1 Monitoring Parameters

Storage infrastructure components should be monitored for accessibility, capacity, performance, and security. *Accessibility* refers to the availability of a component to perform its desired operation during a specified time period. Monitoring the accessibility of hardware components (for example, a port, an HBA, or a disk drive) or software component (for example, a database) involves checking their availability status by reviewing the alerts generated from the system. For example, a port failure might result in a chain of availability alerts.

A storage infrastructure uses redundant components to avoid a single point of failure. Failure of a component might cause an outage that affects application availability, or it might cause performance degradation even though accessibility is not compromised. Continuously monitoring for expected accessibility of each component and reporting any deviation helps the administrator to identify failing components and plan corrective action to maintain SLA requirements.

*Capacity* refers to the amount of storage infrastructure resources available. Examples of capacity monitoring include examining the free space available on a file system or a RAID group, the mailbox quota allocated to users, or the numbers of ports available on a switch. Inadequate capacity leads to degraded performance or even application/service unavailability. *Capacity monitoring* ensures uninterrupted data availability and scalability by averting outages before they occur. For example, if 90 percent of the ports are utilized in a particular

SAN fabric, this could indicate that a new switch might be required if more arrays and servers need to be installed on the same fabric. Capacity monitoring usually leverages analytical tools to perform trend analysis. These trends help to understand future resource requirements and provide an estimation on the time line to deploy them.

*Performance monitoring* evaluates how efficiently different storage infrastructure components are performing and helps to identify bottlenecks. Performance monitoring measures and analyzes behavior in terms of response time or the ability to perform at a certain predefined level. It also deals with the utilization of resources, which affects the way resources behave and respond. Performance measurement is a complex task that involves assessing various components on several interrelated parameters. The number of I/Os performed by a disk, application response time, network utilization, and server-CPU utilization are examples of performance parameters that are monitored.

Monitoring a storage infrastructure for security helps to track and prevent unauthorized access, whether accidental or malicious. *Security monitoring* helps to track unauthorized configuration changes to storage infrastructure resources. For example, security monitoring tracks and reports the initial zoning configuration performed and all the subsequent changes. Security monitoring also detects unavailability of information to authorized users due to a security breach. Physical security of a storage infrastructure can also be continuously monitored using badge readers, biometric scans, or video cameras.

## 15.1.2 Components Monitored

Hosts, networks, and storage are the components within the storage environment that should be monitored for accessibility, capacity, performance, and security. These components can be physical or virtualized.

### Hosts

The accessibility of a host depends on the availability status of the hardware components and the software processes running on it. For example, a host's NIC failure might cause inaccessibility of the host to its user. Server clustering is a mechanism that provides high availability if a server failure occurs.

Monitoring the file system capacity utilization of a host is important to ensure that sufficient storage capacity is available to the applications. Running out of file system space disrupts application availability. Monitoring helps estimate the file system's growth rate and predict when it will reach 100 percent. Accordingly, the administrator can extend (manually or automatically) the file system's space proactively to prevent application outage. Use of virtual provisioning technology enables efficient management of storage capacity requirements but is highly dependent on capacity monitoring.

Host performance monitoring mainly involves a status check on the utilization of various server resources, such as CPU and memory. For example, if a server running an application is experiencing 80 percent of CPU utilization continuously, it indicates that the server may be running out of processing power, which can lead to degraded performance and slower response time. Administrators can take several actions to correct the problem, such as upgrading or adding more processors and shifting the workload to different servers. In a virtualized environment, additional CPU and memory may be allocated to VMs dynamically from the pool, if available, to meet performance requirements.

Security monitoring on servers involves tracking of login failures and execution of unauthorized applications or software processes. Proactive measures against unauthorized access to the servers are based on the threat identified. For example, an administrator can block user access if multiple login failures are logged.

### Storage Network

Storage networks need to be monitored to ensure uninterrupted communication between the server and the storage array. Uninterrupted access to data over the storage network depends on the accessibility of the physical and logical components of the storage network. The physical components of a storage network include switches, ports, and cables. The logical components include constructs, such as zones. Any failure in the physical or logical components causes data unavailability. For example, errors in zoning, such as specifying the wrong WWN of a port, result in failure to access that port, which potentially prevents access from a host to its storage.

Capacity monitoring in a storage network involves monitoring the number of available ports in the fabric, the utilization of the interswitch links, or individual ports, and each interconnect device in the fabric. Capacity monitoring provides all the required inputs for future planning and optimization of fabric resources.

Monitoring the performance of the storage network enables assessing individual component performance and helps to identify network bottlenecks. For example, monitoring port performance involves measuring the receive or transmit link utilization metrics, which indicates how busy the switch port is. Heavily used ports can cause queuing of I/Os on the server, which results in poor performance.

For IP networks, monitoring the performance includes monitoring network latency, packet loss, bandwidth utilization for I/O, network errors, packet retransmission rates, and collisions.

Storage network security monitoring provides information about any unauthorized change to the configuration of the fabric — for example, changes to the zone policies that can affect data security. Login failures and unauthorized access to switches for performing administrative changes should be logged and monitored continuously.

### *Storage*

The accessibility of the storage array should be monitored for its hardware components and various processes. Storage arrays are typically configured with redundant components, and therefore individual component failure does not usually affect their accessibility. However, failure of any process in the storage array might disrupt or compromise business operations. For example, the failure of a replication task affects disaster recovery capabilities. Some storage arrays provide the capability to send messages to the vendor's support center if hardware or process failures occur, referred to as a *call home*.

Capacity monitoring of a storage array enables the administrator to respond to storage needs preemptively based on capacity utilization and consumption trends. Information about unconfigured and unallocated storage space enables the administrator to decide whether a new server can be allocated storage capacity from the storage array.

A storage array can be monitored using a number of performance metrics, such as utilization rates of the various storage array components, I/O response time, and cache utilization. For example, an over utilized storage array component might lead to performance degradation.

A storage array is usually a shared resource, which may be exposed to security threats. Monitoring security helps to track unauthorized configuration of the storage array and ensures that only authorized users are allowed to access it.

## 15.1.3 Monitoring Examples

A storage infrastructure requires implementation of an end-to-end solution to actively monitor all the parameters of its components. Early detection and preemptive alerting ensure uninterrupted services from critical assets. In addition, the monitoring tool should analyze the impact of a failure and deduce the root cause of symptoms.

### *Accessibility Monitoring*

Failure of any component might affect the accessibility of one or more components due to their interconnections and dependencies. Consider an implementation in a storage infrastructure with three servers: H1, H2, and H3. All the servers are configured with two HBAs, each connected to the production storage array through two switches, SW1 and SW2, as shown in Figure 15-1. All the servers share two storage ports on the storage array and multipathing software is installed on all the servers.

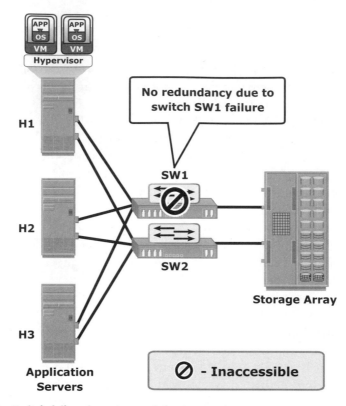

**Figure 15-1:** Switch failure in a storage infrastructure

If one of the switches (SW1) fails, the multipathing software initiates a path failover, and all the servers continue to access data through the other switch, SW2. However, due to the absence of a redundant switch, a second switch failure could result in inaccessibility of the array. Monitoring for accessibility enables detecting the switch failure and helps an administrator to take corrective action before another failure occurs.

In most cases, the administrator receives symptom alerts for a failing component and can initiate actions before the component fails.

## *Capacity Monitoring*

In the scenario shown in Figure 15-2, servers H1, H2, and H3 are connected to the production array through two switches, SW1 and SW2. Each of the servers is allocated storage on the storage array. When a new server is deployed in this configuration, the applications on the new server need to be given storage capacity from the production storage array. Monitoring the available capacity (configurable and unallocated) on the array helps to proactively decide whether the array can provide the required storage to the new server. Also, monitoring the available number of ports on SW1 and SW2 helps to decide whether the new server can be connected to the switches.

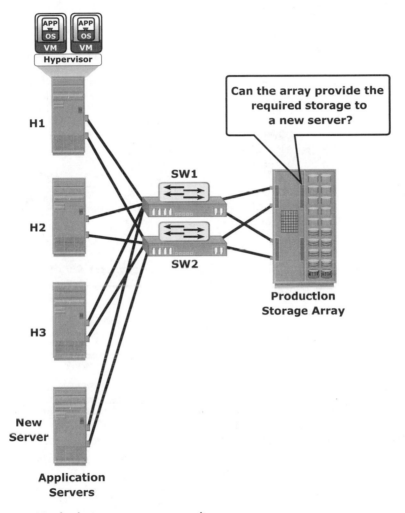

**Figure 15-2:** Monitoring storage array capacity

The following example illustrates the importance of monitoring the file system capacity on file servers. Figure 15-3 (a) illustrates the environment of a file system when full and that results in application outage when no capacity monitoring is implemented. Monitoring can be configured to issue a message when thresholds are reached on the file system capacity. For example, when the file system reaches 66 percent of its capacity, a warning message is issued, and a critical message is issued when the file system reaches 80 percent of its capacity (see Figure 15-3 [b]). This enables the administrator to take action to extend the file system before it runs out of capacity. Proactively monitoring the file system can prevent application outages caused due to lack of file system space.

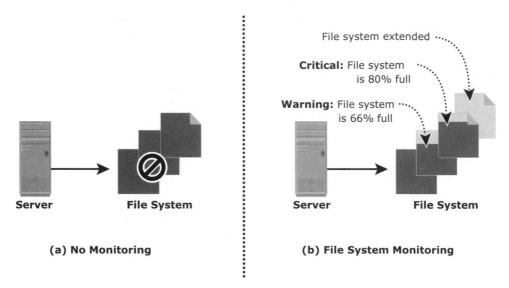

**Figure 15-3:** Monitoring server file system space

## Performance Monitoring

The example shown in Figure 15-4 illustrates the importance of monitoring performance on storage arrays. In this example, servers H1, H2, and H3 (with two HBAs each) are connected to the storage array through switch SW1 and SW2. The three servers share the same storage ports on the storage array to access LUNs. A new server running an application with a high work load must be deployed to share the same storage port as H1, H2, and H3.

Monitoring array port utilization ensures that the new server does not adversely affect the performance of the other servers. In this example, utilization of the shared storage port is shown by the solid and dotted lines in the graph. If the port utilization prior to deploying the new server is close to 100 percent, then deploying the new server is not recommended because it might impact the performance of the other servers. However, if the utilization of the port prior to deploying the new server is closer to the dotted line, then there is room to add a new server.

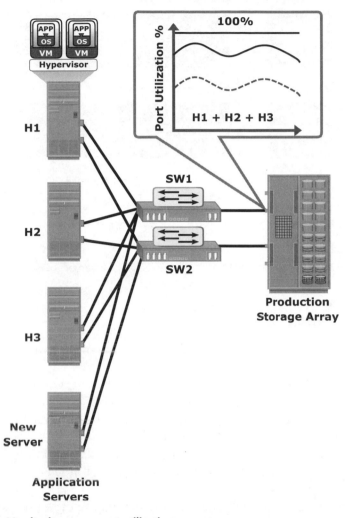

**Figure 15-4:** Monitoring array port utilization

Most servers offer tools that enable monitoring of server CPU usage. For example, Windows Task Manager displays CPU and memory usage, as shown in Figure 15-5. However, these tools are inefficient at monitoring hundreds of servers running in a data-center environment. A data-center environment requires intelligent performance monitoring tools that are capable of monitoring many servers simultaneously.

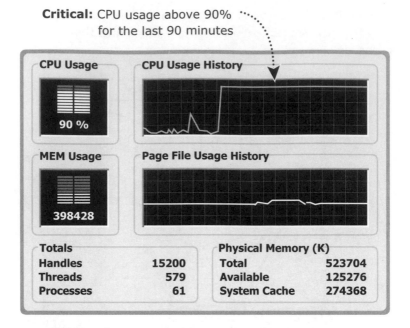

**Critical:** CPU usage above 90%
for the last 90 minutes

**Figure 15-5:** Monitoring the CPU and memory usage of a server

### Security Monitoring

The example shown in Figure 15-6 illustrates the importance of monitoring security in a storage array.

In this example, the storage array is shared between two workgroups, WG1 and WG2. The data of WG1 should not be accessible to WG2 and vice versa. A user from WG1 might try to make a local replica of the data that belongs to WG2. If this action is not monitored or recorded, it is difficult to track such a violation of information security. Conversely, if this action is monitored, a warning message can be sent to prompt a corrective action or at least enable discovery as part of regular auditing operations.

An example of host security monitoring is tracking of login attempts at the host. The login is authorized if the login ID and password entered are correct; or the login attempt fails. These login failures might be accidental (mistyping) or a deliberate attempt to access a server. Many servers usually allow a fixed number of successive login failures, prohibiting any additional attempts after these login failures. In a monitored environment, the login information is recorded in a system log file, and three successive login failures trigger a message, warning of a possible security threat.

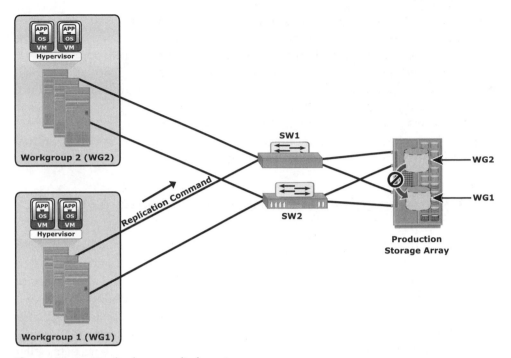

**Figure 15-6:** Monitoring security in a storage array

## 15.1.4 Alerts

Alerting of events is an integral part of monitoring. Alerting keeps administrators informed about the status of various components and processes — for example, conditions such as failure of power, disks, memory, or switches, which can impact the availability of services and require immediate administrative attention. Other conditions, such as a file system reaching a capacity threshold or a soft media error on disks, are considered warning signs and may also require administrative attention.

Monitoring tools enable administrators to assign different severity levels based on the impact of the alerted condition. Whenever a condition with a particular severity level occurs, an alert is sent to the administrator, a script is triggered, or an incident ticket is opened to initiate a corrective action. Alert classifications can range from information alerts to fatal alerts. *Information alerts* provide useful information but do not require any intervention by the administrator. The creation of a zone or LUN is an example of an information alert. *Warning alerts* require administrative attention so that the alerted condition is contained and does not affect accessibility. For example, if an alert indicates that the number of soft media errors on a disk is approaching a predefined threshold value, the administrator can decide whether the disk needs to be replaced. *Fatal alerts* require immediate attention because the condition might affect overall performance, security, or availability. For example, if a disk fails, the administrator must ensure that it is replaced quickly.

Continuous monitoring, with automated alerting, enables administrators to respond to failures quickly and proactively. Alerting provides information that helps administrators prioritize their response to events.

# 15.2 Storage Infrastructure Management Activities

The pace of information growth, proliferation of applications, heterogeneous infrastructure, and stringent service-level requirements have resulted in increased complexity of managing storage infrastructures. However, the emergence of storage virtualization and other technologies, such as data deduplication and compression, virtual provisioning, federated storage access, and storage tiering, have enabled administrators to efficiently manage storage resources.

The key storage infrastructure management activities performed in a data center can be broadly categorized into availability management, capacity management, performance management, security management, and reporting.

## 15.2.1 Availability Management

A critical task in availability management is establishing a proper guideline based on defined service levels to ensure availability. *Availability management* involves all availability-related issues for components or services to ensure that service levels are met. A key activity in availability management is to provision redundancy at all levels, including components, data, or even sites. For example, when a server is deployed to support a critical business function, it requires high availability. This is generally accomplished by deploying two or more HBAs, multipathing software, and server clustering. The server must be connected to the storage array using at least two independent fabrics and switches that have built-in redundancy. In addition, the storage arrays should have built-in redundancy for various components and should support local and remote replication.

## 15.2.2 Capacity Management

The goal of *capacity management* is to ensure adequate availability of resources based on their service level requirements. Capacity management also involves optimization of capacity based on the cost and future needs. Capacity management provides capacity analysis that compares allocated storage to forecasted storage on a regular basis. It also provides trend analysis based on the rate of consumption, which must be rationalized against storage acquisition and deployment timetables. Storage provisioning is an example of capacity management. It involves activities, such as creating RAID sets and LUNs, and allocating them to the host. Enforcing capacity quotas for users is another example of capacity management. Provisioning a fixed amount of user quotas restricts users from exceeding the allocated capacity.

Technologies, such as data deduplication and compression, have reduced the amount of data to be backed up and thereby reduced the amount of storage capacity to be managed.

## 15.2.3 Performance Management

*Performance management* ensures the optimal operational efficiency of all components. Performance analysis is an important activity that helps to identify the performance of storage infrastructure components. This analysis provides information on whether a component meets expected performance levels.

Several performance management activities need to be performed when deploying a new application or server in the existing storage infrastructure. Every component must be validated for adequate performance capabilities as defined by the service levels. For example, to optimize the expected performance levels, activities on the server, such as the volume configuration, database design or application layout, configuration of multiple HBAs, and intelligent multipathing software, must be fine-tuned. The performance management tasks on a SAN include designing and implementing sufficient ISLs in a multiswitch fabric with adequate bandwidth to support the required performance levels. The storage array configuration tasks include selecting the appropriate RAID type, LUN layout, front-end ports, back-end ports, and cache configuration, when considering the end-to-end performance.

## 15.2.4 Security Management

The key objective of the *security management* activity is to ensure confidentiality, integrity, and availability of information in both virtualized and nonvirtualized environments. Security management prevents unauthorized access and configuration of storage infrastructure components. For example, while deploying an application or a server, the security management tasks include managing the user accounts and access policies that authorize users to perform role-based activities. The security management tasks in a SAN environment include configuration of zoning to restrict an unauthorized HBA from accessing specific storage array ports. Similarly, the security management task on a storage array includes LUN masking that restricts a host's access to intended LUNs only.

## 15.2.5 Reporting

*Reporting* on a storage infrastructure involves keeping track and gathering information from various components and processes. This information is compiled to generate reports for trend analysis, capacity planning, chargeback, and performance. Capacity planning reports contain current and historic information about the utilization of storage, file systems, database tablespace, ports, and so on. Configuration and asset management reports include details about device allocation, local or remote replicas, and fabric configuration. This report also lists all the equipment, with details, such as their purchase date, lease status, and maintenance records. Chargeback reports contain information about the allocation or utilization of storage infrastructure components by various departments or user groups. Performance reports provide details about the performance of various storage infrastructure components.

## 15.2.6 Storage Infrastructure Management in a Virtualized Environment

Virtualization technology has dramatically changed the complexity of storage infrastructure management. In fact, flexibility and ease of management are key drivers for wide adoption of virtualization at all layers of the IT infrastructure.

Storage virtualization has enabled dynamic migration of data and extension of storage volumes. Due to dynamic extension, storage volumes can be expanded nondisruptively to meet both capacity and performance requirements. Because virtualization breaks the bond between the storage volumes presented to the host and its physical storage, data can be migrated both within and across data centers without any downtime. This has made the administrator's tasks easier while reconfiguring the physical environment.

Virtual storage provisioning is another tool that has changed the infrastructure management cost and complexity scenario. In conventional provisioning, storage capacity is provisioned upfront in anticipation of future growth. Because growth is uneven, some users or applications find themselves running out of capacity, whereas others have excess capacity that remains underutilized. Use of virtual provisioning can address this challenge and make capacity management less challenging. In virtual provisioning, storage is allocated from the shared pool to hosts on-demand. This improves the storage capacity utilization, and thereby reduces capacity management complexities.

Virtualization has also contributed to network management efficiency. VSANs and VLANs made the administrator's job easier by isolating different networks logically using management tools rather than physically separating them. Disparate virtual networks can be created on a single physical network, and reconfiguration of nodes can be done quickly without any physical changes. It has also addressed some of the security issues that might exist in a conventional environment.

On the host side, compute virtualization has made host deployment, reconfiguration, and migration easier than physical environment. Compute, application, and memory virtualization have not only improved provisioning, but also contributed to the high availability of resources.

## STORAGE MULTITENANCY

Multiple tenants sharing the same resources provided by a single landlord (resource provider) is called multitenancy. Two common examples of multitenancy are multiple virtual machines sharing the same server hardware through the use of a hypervisor running on the server, and multiple user applications using the same storage platform. Multitenancy is not a new concept; however, it has become a topic of much discussion due to the rise in popularity of cloud deployments, because shared infrastructure is a core component of any cloud strategy.

As with any shared services, security and service level assurance are a key concerns in a multitenant storage environment. Secure multitenancy means that no tenant can access another tenant's data. To achieve this, any storage deployment should follow the four pillars of multitenancy:

- **Secure separation:** This enables data path separation across various tenants in a multitenant environment. At the storage layer, this pillar can be divided into four basic requirements: separation of data at rest, address space separation, authentication and name service separation, and separation of data access.

- **Service assurance:** Consistent and reliable service levels are integral to storage multitenancy. Service assurance plays an important role in providing service levels that can be unique to each tenant.

- **Availability:** High availability ensures a resilient architecture that provides fault tolerance and redundancy. This is even more critical when storage infrastructure is shared by multiple tenants, because the impact of any outage is magnified.

- **Management:** This includes provisions that allow a landlord to manage basic infrastructure while delegating management responsibilities to tenants for the resources that they interact with day to day. This concept is known as balancing the provider (landlord) in-control with the tenant in-control capabilities.

## 15.2.7 Storage Management Examples

The following section provides examples of various storage management activities.

### Example 1: Storage Allocation to a New Server/Host

Consider the deployment of a new RDBMS server to the existing nonvirtualized storage infrastructure. As a part of storage management activities, first, the administrator needs to install and configure the HBAs and device drivers on the server before it is physically connected to the SAN. Optionally, multipathing software can be installed on the server, which might require additional configuration. Further, storage array ports should be connected to the SAN.

As the next step, the administrator needs to perform zoning on the SAN switches to allow the new server access to the storage array ports via its HBAs. To ensure redundant paths between the server and the storage array, the HBAs of the new server should be connected to different switches and zoned with different array ports.

Further, the administrator needs to configure LUNs on the array and assign these LUNs to the storage array front-end ports. In addition, LUN masking configuration is performed on the storage array, which restricts access to LUNs by a specific server.

The server then discovers the LUNs assigned to it by either a *bus rescan* process or sometimes through a server reboot, depending upon the operating system installed. A volume manager may be used to configure the logical volumes and file systems on the host. The number of logical volumes or file systems to be created depends on how a database or an application is expected to use the storage. The administrator's task also includes installation of a database or an application on the logical volumes or file systems that were created.

The last step is to make the database or application capable of using the new file system space. Figure 15-7 illustrates the activities performed on a server, a SAN, and a storage array for the allocation of storage to a new server.

In a virtualized environment, provisioning storage to a VM that runs an RDBMS requires different administrative tasks.

Similar to a nonvirtualized environment, a physical connection must be established between the physical server, which hosts the VMs, and the storage array through the SAN. At the SAN level, a VSAN can be configured to transfer data between the physical server and the storage array. The VSAN isolates this storage traffic from any other traffic in the SAN. Further, the administrator can configure zoning within the VSAN.

At the storage side, administrators need to create thin LUNs from the shared storage pool and assign these thin LUNs to the storage array front-end ports. Similar to a physical environment, LUN masking needs to be carried out on the storage array.

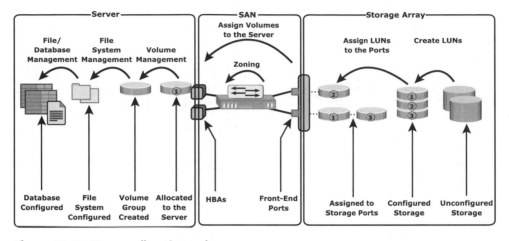

**Figure 15-7:** Storage allocation tasks

At the physical server side, the hypervisor discovers the assigned LUNs. The hypervisor creates a logical volume and file system to store and manage VM files. Then, the administrator creates a VM and installs the OS and RDBMS on the VM. While creating the VM, the hypervisor creates a virtual disk file and other VM files in the hypervisor file system. The virtual disk file appears to the VM as a SCSI disk and is used to store the RDBMS data. Alternatively, the hypervisor enables virtual provisioning to create a thin virtual disk and assigns it to the VM. Hypervisors usually have native multipathing capabilities. Optionally, a third-party multipathing software may be installed on the hypervisor.

## Example 2: File System Space Management

To prevent a file system from running out of space, administrators need to perform tasks to offload data from the existing file system. This includes deleting unwanted files or archiving data that is not accessed for a long time.

Alternatively, an administrator can extend the file system to increase its size and avoid an application outage. The dynamic extension of file systems or a logical volume depends on the operating system or the logical volume manager (LVM) in use. Figure 15-8 shows the steps and considerations for the extension of file systems in the flow chart.

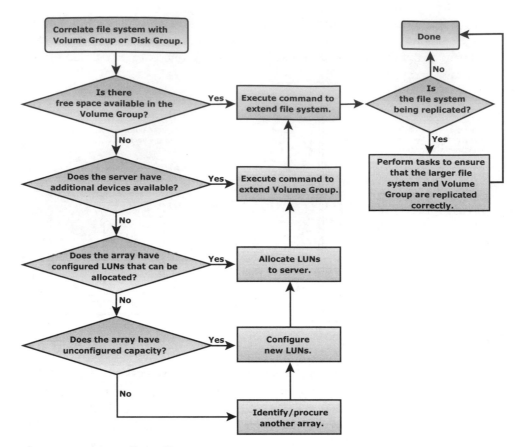

**Figure 15-8:** Extending a file system

## Example 3: Chargeback Report

This example explores the storage infrastructure management tasks necessary to create a chargeback report.

Figure 15-9 shows a configuration deployed in a storage infrastructure. Three servers with two HBAs each connect to a storage array via two switches, SW1 and SW2. Individual departmental applications run on each of the servers. Array replication technology is used to create local and remote replicas. The production device is represented as A, the local replica device as B, and the remote replica device as C.

A report documenting the exact amount of storage resources used by each application is created using a chargeback analysis for each department. If the unit for billing is based on the amount of raw storage (usable capacity plus protection provided) configured for an application used by a department, the exact amount of raw space configured must be reported for each application. Figure 15-9 shows a sample report. The report shows the information for two applications, Payroll_1 and Engineering_1.

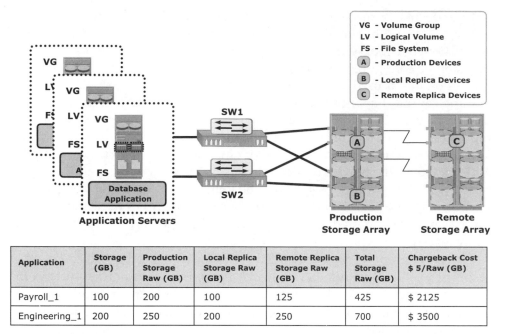

**Figure 15-9:** Chargeback report

| Application | Storage (GB) | Production Storage Raw (GB) | Local Replica Storage Raw (GB) | Remote Replica Storage Raw (GB) | Total Storage Raw (GB) | Chargeback Cost $ 5/Raw (GB) |
|---|---|---|---|---|---|---|
| Payroll_1 | 100 | 200 | 100 | 125 | 425 | $ 2125 |
| Engineering_1 | 200 | 250 | 200 | 250 | 700 | $ 3500 |

The first step to determine chargeback costs is to correlate the application with the exact amount of raw storage configured for that application.

As indicated in Figure 15-10, the Payroll_1 application storage space is traced from file systems to logical volumes to volume groups and to the LUNs on the array. When the applications are replicated, the storage space used for local replication and remote replication is also identified. In the example shown, the application is using Source Vol 1 and Vol 2 (in the production array). The replication volumes are Local Replica Vol 1 and Vol 2 (in the production array) and Remote Replica Vol 1 and Vol 2 (in the remote array).

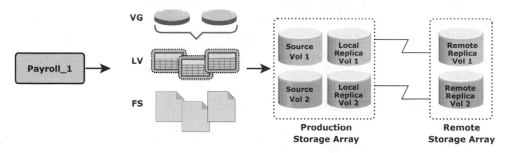

**Figure 15-10:** Correlation of capacity configured for an application

The amount of storage allocated to the application can be easily computed after the array devices are identified. In this example, consider that Source

Vol 1 and Vol 2 are each 50 GB in size, the storage allocated to the application is 100 GB (50 + 50). The allocated storage for replication is 100 GB for local replication and 100 GB for remote replication. From the allocated storage, the raw storage configured for the application is determined based on the RAID protection that is used for various array devices.

If the Payroll_1 application's production volumes are RAID 1-protected, the raw space used by the production volumes is 200 GB. Assume that the local replicas are on unprotected volumes, and the remote replicas are protected with a RAID 5 configuration, then 100 GB of raw space is used by the local replica and 125 GB by the remote replica. Therefore, the total raw capacity used by the Payroll_1 application is 425 GB. The total cost of storage provisioned for Payroll_1 application will be $2,125 (assume cost per GB of storage is $5). This exercise must be repeated for each application in the enterprise to generate the chargeback report.

Chargeback reports can be extended to include a pre-established cost of other resources, such as the number of switch ports, HBAs, and array ports in the configuration. Chargeback reports are used by data center administrators to ensure that storage consumers are well aware of the costs of the services that they have requested.

## 15.3 Storage Infrastructure Management Challenges

Monitoring and managing today's complex storage infrastructure is challenging. This is due to the heterogeneity of storage arrays, networks, servers, databases, and applications in the environment. For example, heterogeneous storage arrays vary in their capacity, performance, protection, and architectures.

Each of the components in a data center typically comes with vendor-specific tools for management. An environment with multiple tools makes understanding the overall status of the environment challenging because the tools may not be interoperable. Ideally, management tools should correlate information from all components in one place. Such tools provide an end-to-end view of the environment, and a quicker root cause analysis for faster resolution to alerts.

## 15.4 Developing an Ideal Solution

An ideal solution should offer meaningful insight into the status of the overall infrastructure and provide root cause analysis for each failure. This solution should also provide central monitoring and management in a multivendor storage environment and create an end-to-end view of the storage infrastructure.

The benefit of end-to-end monitoring is the ability to correlate one component's behavior with the other. In many cases, looking at each component individually may not be sufficient to reveal the actual cause of the problem. The central monitoring and management system should gather information from all the components and manage them through a single-user interface. In addition, it must provide a mechanism to notify administrators about various events using methods, such as e-mail and Simple Network Management Protocol (SNMP) traps. It should also have the capability to generate monitoring reports and run automated scripts for task automation.

The ideal solution must be based on industry standards, by leveraging common APIs, data model terminology, and taxonomy. This enables the implementation of policy-based management across heterogeneous devices, services, applications, and deployed topologies.

Traditionally, SNMP protocol was the standard used to manage multivendor SAN environments. However, SNMP was inadequate for providing the detailed information required to manage the SAN environment. The unavailability of automatic discovery functions and weak modeling constructs are some inadequacies of SNMP in a SAN environment. Even with these limitations, SNMP still holds a predominant role in SAN management, although newer open storage SAN management standards have emerged to monitor and manage storage environments more effectively.

## 15.4.1 Storage Management Initiative

The Storage Networking Industry Association (SNIA) has been engaged in an initiative to develop a common storage management interface. SNIA has developed a specification called Storage Management Initiative-Specification (SMI-S). This specification is based on the Web-Based Enterprise Management (WBEM) technology, and Distributed Management Task Force's (DMTF) Common Information Model (CIM). The initiative was formally created to enable broad interoperability and management among heterogeneous storage and SAN components. For more information, see www.snia.org.

SMI-S offers substantial benefits to users and vendors. It forms a normalized, abstracted model to which a storage infrastructure's physical and logical components can be mapped. This model is used by management applications, such as storage resource management, device management, and data management, for standardized, end-to-end control of storage resources.

Using SMI-S, device software developers have a unified object model with details about managing the breadth of storage and SAN components. SMI-S-compliant products lead to easier, faster deployment and accelerated adoption of policy-based storage management frameworks. Moreover, SMI-S eliminates the need for the development of vendor-proprietary management interfaces and enables vendors to focus on value-added features.

## 15.4.2 Enterprise Management Platform

An enterprise management platform (EMP) is a suite of applications that provides an integrated solution for managing and monitoring an enterprise storage infrastructure. These applications have powerful, flexible, unified frameworks that provide end-to-end management of both physical and virtual resources. EMP provides a centrally managed, single point of control for resources throughout the storage environment.

These applications can proactively monitor storage infrastructure components and alert users about events. These alerts are either shown on a console depicting the faulty component in a different color, or they can be configured to send the alert by e-mail. In addition to monitoring, an EMP provides the necessary management functionality, which can be natively implemented into the EMP or can launch the proprietary management utility supplied by the component manufacturer.

An EMP also enables easy scheduling of operations that must be performed regularly, such as the provisioning of resources, configuration management, and fault investigation. These platforms also provide extensive analytical, remedial, and reporting capabilities to ease storage infrastructure management. EMC ControlCenter and EMC Prosphere, described in section 15.7 "Concepts in Practice," are examples of an EMP.

# 15.5 Information Lifecycle Management

In both traditional data center and virtualized environments, managing information can be expensive if not managed appropriately. Along with the tools, an effective management strategy is also required to manage information efficiently. This strategy should address the following key challenges that exist in today's data centers:

- **Exploding digital universe:** The rate of information growth is increasing exponentially. Creating copies of data to ensure high availability and repurposing has contributed to the multifold increase of information growth.

- **Increasing dependency on information:** The strategic use of information plays an important role in determining the success of a business and provides competitive advantages in the marketplace.

- **Changing value of information**: Information that is valuable today might become less important tomorrow. The value of information often changes over time.

Framing a strategy to meet these challenges involves understanding the value of information over its life cycle. When information is first created, it often has the highest value and is accessed frequently. As the information ages, it is accessed less frequently and is of less value to the organization. Understanding the value of information helps to deploy the appropriate infrastructure according to the changing value of information.

For example, in a sales order application, the value of the information (customer data) changes from the time the order is placed until the time that the warranty becomes void (see Figure 15-11). The value of the information is highest when a company receives a new sales order and processes it to deliver the product. After the order fulfillment, the customer data does not need to be available for real-time access. The company can transfer this data to less expensive secondary storage with lower performance until a warranty claim or another event triggers its need. After the warranty becomes void, the company can dispose of the information.

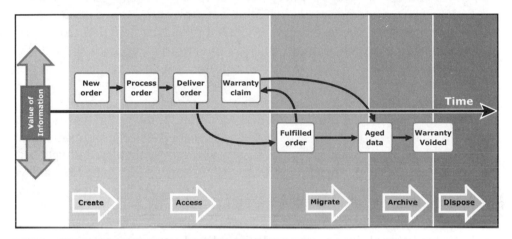

**Figure 15-11:** Changing value of sales order information

*Information Lifecycle Management* (ILM) is a proactive strategy that enables an IT organization to effectively manage information throughout its life cycle based on predefined business policies. From data creation to data deletion, ILM aligns the business requirements and processes with service levels in an automated fashion. This allows an IT organization to optimize the storage infrastructure for maximum return on investment. Implementing an ILM strategy has the following key benefits that directly address the challenges of information management:

- **Lower Total Cost of Ownership (TCO):** By aligning the infrastructure and management costs with information value. As a result, resources are not wasted, and complexity is not introduced by managing low-value data at the expense of high-value data.

- **Simplified management:** By integrating process steps and interfaces with individual tools and by increasing automation

- **Maintaining compliance:** By knowing what data needs to be protected for what length of time

- **Optimized utilization:** By deploying storage tiering

# 15.6 Storage Tiering

*Storage tiering* is a technique of establishing a hierarchy of different storage types (tiers). This enables storing the right data to the right tier, based on service level requirements, at a minimal cost. Each tier has different levels of protection, performance, and cost. For example, high performance solid-state drives (SSDs) or FC drives can be configured as tier 1 storage to keep frequently accessed data, and low cost SATA drives as tier 2 storage to keep the less frequently accessed data. Keeping frequently used data in SSD or FC improves application performance. Moving less-frequently accessed data to SATA can free up storage capacity in high performance drives and reduce the cost of storage. This movement of data happens based on defined tiering policies. The tiering policy might be based on parameters, such as file type, size, frequency of access, and so on. For example, if a policy states "Move the files that are not accessed for the last 30 days to the lower tier," then all the files matching this condition are moved to the lower tier.

Storage tiering can be implemented as a manual or an automated process. *Manual storage tiering* is the traditional method where the storage administrator monitors the storage workloads periodically and moves the data between the tiers. Manual storage tiering is complex and time-consuming. *Automated storage tiering* automates the storage tiering process, in which data movement between the tiers is performed nondisruptively. In automated storage tiering, the application workload is proactively monitored; the active data is automatically moved to a higher performance tier and the inactive data to a higher capacity, lower performance tier. Data movements between various tiers can happen within (intra-array) or between (inter-array) storage arrays.

## 15.6.1 Intra-Array Storage Tiering

The process of storage tiering within a storage array is called *intra-array storage tiering*. It enables the efficient use of SSD, FC, and SATA drives within an array and provides performance and cost optimization. The goal is to keep the SSDs busy by storing the most frequently accessed data on them, while moving out the less frequently accessed data to the SATA drives. Data movements executed between tiers can be performed at the LUN level or at the sub-LUN level. The performance can be further improved by implementing tiered cache. LUN tiering, sub-LUN tiering, and cache tiering are detailed next.

Traditionally, storage tiering is operated at the LUN level that moves an entire LUN from one tier of storage to another (see Figure 15-12 [a]). This movement includes both active and inactive data in that LUN. This method does not give effective cost and performance benefits. Today, storage tiering can be implemented at the sub-LUN level (see Figure 15-12 [b]). In sub-LUN level tiering, a LUN is broken down into smaller segments and tiered at that level. Movement of data with much finer granularity, for example 8 MB, greatly enhances the value proposition of automated storage tiering. Tiering at the sub-LUN level effectively moves active data to faster drives and less active data to slower drives.

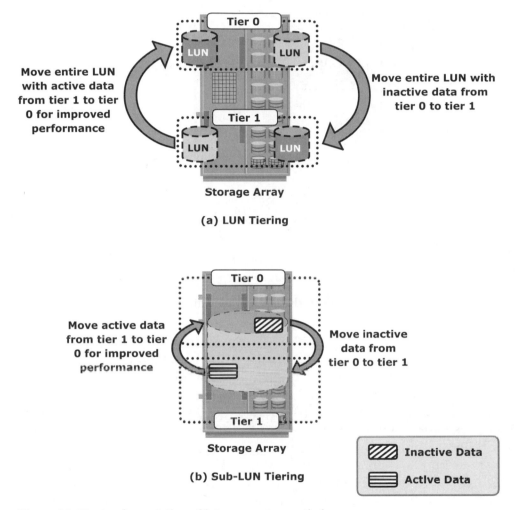

**Figure 15-12:** Implementation of intra-array storage tiering

Tiering is also be implemented at the cache level, as shown in Figure 15-13. A large cache in a storage array improves performance by retaining a large amount of frequently accessed data in a cache, so most reads are served directly from the cache. However, configuring a large cache in the storage array involves more cost. An alternative way to increase the size of the cache is by utilizing the SSDs on the storage array. In cache tiering, SSDs are used as a large capacity secondary cache to enable tiering between DRAM (primary cache) and SSDs (secondary cache). Server flash-caching is another tier of cache in which a flash-cache card is installed in the server to further enhance the application's performance.

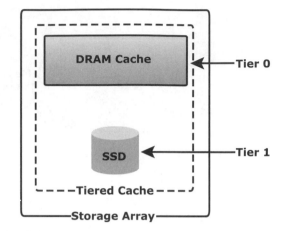

**Figure 15-13:** Cache tiering

## 15.6.2 Inter-Array Storage Tiering

The process of storage tiering between storage arrays is called *inter-array storage tiering*. Inter-array storage tiering automates the identification of active or inactive data to relocate them to different performance or capacity tiers between the arrays. Figure 15-14 illustrates an example of a two-tiered storage environment. This environment optimizes the primary storage for performance and the secondary storage for capacity and cost. The policy engine, which can be software or hardware where policies are configured, facilitates moving inactive or infrequently accessed data from the primary to the secondary storage. Some prevalent reasons to tier data across arrays is archival or to meet compliance requirements. As an example, the policy engine might be configured to relocate all the files in the primary storage that have not been accessed in one month and archive those files to the secondary storage. For each archived file, the policy engine creates a small space-saving stub file in the primary storage that points to the data on the secondary storage. When a user tries to access the file at its original location on the primary storage, the user is transparently provided with the actual file from the secondary storage.

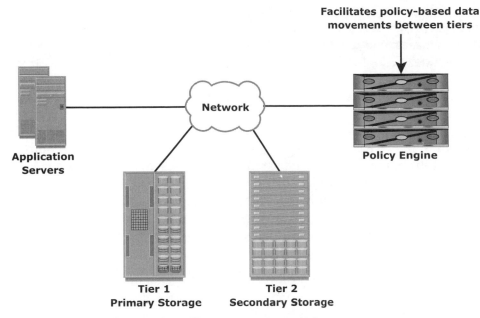

**Figure 15-14:** Implementation of inter-array storage tiering

## 15.7 Concepts in Practice: EMC Infrastructure Management Tools

Businesses today face challenges in managing their IT infrastructure due to the large number of heterogeneous resources in their environment. These resources may be physical resources, virtualized resources, or cloud resources. EMC offers different tools that satisfy different requirements of the business. EMC ControlCenter and ProSphere are suites of software that can perform end-to-end management of storage infrastructure, while EMC Unisphere is software that manages EMC storage arrays, such as VNX and VNXe. EMC Unified Infrastructure Manager (UIM) is software that manages the Vblock infrastructure (cloud resources). For more information, visit www.emc.com/.

### 15.7.1 EMC ControlCenter and Prosphere

EMC ControlCenter is a family of storage resource management (SRM) applications that provide a unified solution to manage a multivendor storage infrastructure. It helps address the challenges to manage a large, complex storage environment that includes hosts, storage networks, storage, and virtualization across all the layers. ControlCenter provides capabilities, such as storage planning, provisioning, monitoring, and reporting. It enables implementing an ILM strategy by providing comprehensive management of tiered storage infrastructure. It also provides an end-to-end view of the entire networked storage infrastructure that includes SAN, NAS, and host storage resources, including a virtualized environment. It provides a central administrative console, discovery of new components, quota management, event management, root cause analysis, and chargeback. ControlCenter comes with built-in security features that provide access control, data confidentiality, data integrity, logging, and auditing. It offers an intuitive, easy-to-use interface that provides insight into the complex relationships of the environment. ControlCenter uses an agent to discover the components in the environment.

EMC ProSphere is also storage resource management software built to meet the demands of the new cloud computing era. EMC ProSphere improves productivity and service levels in the virtualized and cloud environment. ProSphere includes the following key capabilities:

- **End-to-end visibility:** It offers an intuitive, easy-to-use interface that provides insight into the complex relationships between objects in large, virtualized environments.

- **Multi-site management:** From a single console, ProSphere's federated architecture aggregates information from across sites and simplifies information management between data centers. ProSphere is managed from a web browser to allow easy access over the Internet for remote management.

- **Improved productivity in growing virtualized environments:** ProSphere introduces an innovative technology called Smart Groups, which groups objects with similar characteristics into a user-defined group for performing management tasks. This enables IT to take a policy-based approach to manage objects or to set data collection policies.

- **Fast, easy, and efficient deployment:** Agent-less discovery eliminates the burden of deploying and managing host agents. ProSphere is packaged as a virtual appliance that can be installed in a short time.

- **Delivery of IT as a service:** With ProSphere, service levels can now be monitored from host-to-storage layers. This allows organizations to maintain consistent service levels at an optimal price-performance ratio to meet business objectives to delivering IT-as-a-service.

## 15.7.2 EMC Unisphere

EMC Unisphere is a unified storage management platform that provides intuitive user interfaces for managing EMC VNX and EMC VNXe storage arrays. Unisphere is web-enabled and supports remote management of storage arrays. Some of the key capabilities offered by Unisphere follow:

- Provides unified management for file, block, and object storage
- Provides single sign-on for all devices in a management domain
- Supports automated storage tiering and ensures that data is stored in the correct tier to meet performance and cost
- Provides management of both physical and virtual components

### 15.7.3 EMC Unified Infrastructure Manager (UIM)

EMC Unified Infrastructure Manager is a unified management solution for Vblocks. (Vblock is covered in Chapter 13.) It enables configuring the Vblock infrastructure resources and activating cloud services. It provides a single user interface to manage multiple Vblocks and eliminates the need for configuring compute, network, and storage separately using different virtual infrastructure management tools.

UIM provides a dashboard that shows how the Vblock infrastructure is configured and how the resources are used. This enables an administrator to monitor the configuration and utilization of the Vblock infrastructure resources and to plan for capacity requirements. UIM also provides a topology or a map view of the Vblock infrastructure, which enables an administrator to quickly locate and understand the interconnections of the Vblock infrastructure components and services. It provides an alerts console, which allows an administrator to see the alerts against the Vblock infrastructure resources and the associated services affected by problems. UIM performs a compliance check during resource configuration. It validates compliance with configuration best practices. It also prevents conflicting resource identity assignments, for example, accidentally assigning a MAC address to more than one virtual NIC.

## Summary

The explosion of data, its criticality, and increasing dependency of businesses on digital information is leading to larger, complex storage infrastructures. These infrastructures are increasingly challenging to manage. Poorly managed storage infrastructures can put the entire business at risk if a catastrophic failure occurs.

This chapter detailed monitoring and managing the storage infrastructure activities. Further, this chapter detailed Information Lifecycle Management and its benefits and storage tiering.

For more information and additional reading on information storage and management, virtualization, and the cloud, visit `http://education.emc.com/ismbook`.

## EXERCISES

1. Research and prepare a presentation on SMI-S.

2. Research management of cloud infrastructure and services.

3. Research storage multitenancy and its advantages and disadvantages.

4. An engineering design department of a large company maintains more than 600,000 engineering drawings that its designers access and reuse, modify, or update as required. The design team wants instant access to the drawings for its current projects but is currently constrained by an infrastructure that cannot scale to meet the response time requirements. The team has classified the drawings as Most Frequently Accessed, Frequently Accessed, and Occasionally Accessed.

   ▪ Suggest a strategy for the engineering design department that optimizes the storage infrastructure by using ILM.

   ▪ Explain how you can use tiered storage based on access frequency.

   ▪ Detail the hardware and software components you need to implement your strategy.

   ▪ Research the products and solutions currently available to meet the solution you propose.

5. Research management of object-based storage and scale-out NAS.

# Appendix A
# Application I/O Characteristics

Application I/O characteristics influence the overall performance of storage system and storage solution design. This appendix describes key application I/O characteristics.

## Random and Sequential

I/O is characterized as either random or sequential. *Random I/O* refers to successive read/write operations from noncontiguous addresses — accesses that are spread across the addressable capacity of the LUN. Examples of applications that largely generate random I/O include messaging, OLTP (online transaction processing) applications.

*Sequential I/O* refers to successive read/write operations from contiguous addresses — one logical block address after another. In sequential I/O access, disk seek time is reduced because the read/write head moves little to access the next block. Examples of sequential I/O include data backup.

## Reads and Writes

Another aspect of the I/O workload is the ratio of read I/Os to write I/Os generated by an application. The sum of the read rate and the write rate is the *I/O rate* (the number of I/O operations per second). The application's I/O rate is one of the important factors that determine the minimum number of disks required for the application. In storage systems, cache plays an important role to improve the system performance. Table A-1 summarizes how read I/O and write I/O interact with the cache.

**Table A-1:** Read/Write Interactions with Cache

| I/O TYPE | READ | WRITE |
|---|---|---|
| Random | Hard to effectively cache (difficult to predict prefetch); requires multiple fast disks for good performance. | Caching is effective, resulting in a response time better than disk response time. |
| Sequential | Caching is extremely effective (predicting prefetch is easy); reads are done at cache speeds. | Caching is effective; cache is flushed quickly because entire disk stripe can be written. |

Typical read versus write ratio for common business applications are as follows:

- **Online transaction processing (OLTP):** 67 percent reads and 33 percent writes.

- **Decision support system (DSS):** Also referred to as data warehouse or business intelligence. I/O load is 80 percent to 90 percent reads to data tables including frequent table scans (sequential reads).

- **Backup:** As long as the file system is not fragmented, file-based backups are sequential.

# I/O Request Size

The size of I/O generated by an application may vary depending upon the type of the application. Some of the overhead to execute an I/O is fixed. If data exists in large chunks, it is more efficient to transmit larger blocks because a host can move data faster by using larger I/Os than smaller I/Os. The response time of each large transaction is longer than the response time for a single small transaction, but the combined service time of many smaller transactions is greater than a single transaction that contains the same amount of data. Table A-2 shows typical applications and their characteristics.

**Table A-2:** Application Characteristics

| APPLICATION | SEEK TYPE | I/O REQUEST SIZES | PROPORTION OF I/O AS WRITES |
| --- | --- | --- | --- |
| Microsoft Exchange | Random | 32 KB | Moderate to high |
| SAP/Oracle applications | Random | ~8 KB | Depends on application |
| RDBMS: Data entry/ OLTP | Random | Database or file system page size | Moderate to high |
| RDBMS: Online (transaction) logs | Sequential | 512 byte+ | High, except for archiving process |
| RDBMS: Temp space | Random | Database or file system page size | Very high |

# Appendix B
# Parallel SCSI

Shugart Associates and NCR developed a system interface in 1981 and named it Shugart Associates System Interface (SASI). SASI was developed to build a proprietary, high-performance standard, primarily for use by these two companies. However, to increase the acceptance of SASI in the industry, the standard was updated to a more robust interface and renamed SCSI. In 1986, the American National Standards Institution (ANSI) acknowledged the new SCSI as an industry standard.

SCSI, first developed for hard disks, is often compared to IDE/ATA. SCSI offers improved performance, scalability, and compatibility options, making it suitable for high-end computers. However, the high cost associated with SCSI limits its popularity among home or business desktop users.

Prior to the development of SCSI, the interfaces used for communication between devices varied with each device. For example, an HDD interface could be used only with a hard disk drive. SCSI was developed to provide a device-independent mechanism for attaching to and accessing host computers. SCSI also provided an efficient peer-to-peer I/O bus that supported multiple devices. Today, SCSI is commonly used as a hard disk interface. However, SCSI can be used for connecting devices, such as tape drives, printers, and optical media drives, to the host computer without modifying the system hardware or software. Over the years, SCSI has undergone radical changes and has evolved into a robust industry standard.

Along with the evolving SCSI standards, SCSI interfaces underwent several improvements. Parallel SCSI, or SCSI parallel interface (SPI), was the original SCSI interface. The SCSI design is now making a transition into Serial Attached SCSI (SAS), which is based on a serial point-to-point design, while retaining the other aspects of the SCSI technology.

# SCSI Standards Family

The SCSI standard defines a reference model that specifies common behaviors for SCSI devices and an abstract structure that is generic to all SCSI I/O system implementations. The set of SCSI standards specifies the interfaces, functions, and operations necessary to ensure interoperability between conforming SCSI implementations. For more information, read the Technical Committee T10 "SCSI Architecture Model-4 (SAM-4)" document from www.t10.org. Figure B-1 shows the relationship of this standard to the other standards and related projects in the SCSI family of standards.

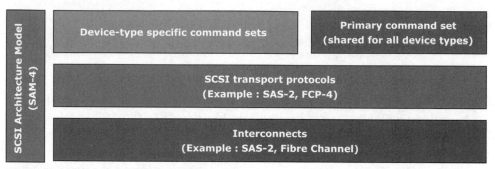

**Figure B-1:** The SCSI standards family

The following list describes the components of the SCSI standards family:

- **SCSI Architecture Model:** Defines the SCSI systems model, the functional partitioning of the SCSI standard set, and the requirements applicable to all SCSI implementations and implementation standards

- **Device-Type Specific Command Sets:** Implementation standards that define specific device types including a device model for each device type. These standards specify the required commands and behaviors specific to a given device type and prescribe the requirements to be followed by a SCSI initiator device when sending commands to a SCSI target device having the specific device type. The commands and behaviors for a specific device type may include reference commands and behaviors shared by all SCSI devices.

- **Shared Command Set:** An implementation standard that defines a model for all SCSI device types. This standard specifies the required commands and behavior common to all SCSI devices, regardless of the device type, and prescribes the requirements to be followed by a SCSI initiator device when sending commands to any SCSI target device.

- **SCSI Transport Protocols:** Implementation standards that define the requirements for exchanging information so that different SCSI devices can communicate

▪ **Interconnects:** Implementation standards that define the communication mechanism employed by the SCSI transport protocols. These standards may describe the electrical and signaling requirements essential for SCSI devices to interoperate over a given interconnect. Interconnect standards may allow the interconnection of devices other than SCSI devices in ways that are outside the scope of this standard.

## SCSI Client-Server Model

In a SCSI environment, an initiator-target concept represents the client-server model. In a SCSI client-server model, a particular SCSI device acts as a SCSI target device, a SCSI initiator device, or a SCSI target/initiator device. Each device performs the following functions:

▪ **SCSI initiator device:** Issues a command to the SCSI target device to perform a task. A SCSI host adapter is an example of an initiator.

▪ **SCSI target device:** Executes commands to perform the task received from a SCSI initiator. Typically, a SCSI peripheral device acts as a target device; however, in certain implementations, the host adapter can also be a target device.

Figure B-2 displays the SCSI client-server model, in which a SCSI initiator, or a client, sends a request to a SCSI target, or a server. The target performs the tasks requested and sends the output to the initiator, using the protocol service interface.

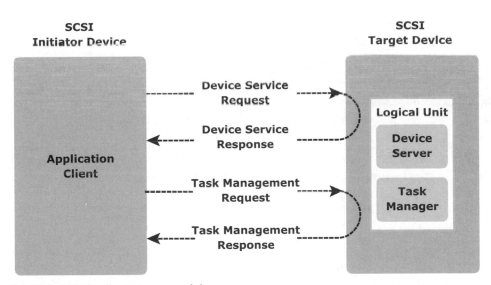

**Figure B-2:** SCSI client-server model

A SCSI target device contains one or more logical units. A logical unit is an object that implements one of the device functional models as described in the SCSI command standards. The logical unit processes the commands sent by a SCSI initiator. A logical unit has two components, a device server and a task manager. The *device server* addresses client requests, and the *task manager* performs management functions.

The SCSI initiator device composed of an application client and task management function initiates device service and task management requests. Each device service request contains a *Command Descriptor Block* (CDB), which defines the command to be executed and lists command-specific inputs and other parameters specifying how to process the command. The application client also creates tasks, objects within the logical unit, representing the work associated with a command or a series of linked commands. A task persists until either the Task Complete Response is sent or the task management function or exception condition ends it.

The SCSI devices are identified by a specific number called a SCSI ID. In narrow SCSI (bus width = 8), the devices are numbered 0 through 7; in wide (bus width = 16) SCSI, the devices are numbered 0 through 15. These ID numbers set the device priorities on the SCSI bus. In narrow SCSI, 7 has the highest priority and 0 has the lowest priority. In wide SCSI, the device IDs from 8 through 15 have the highest priority, but the entire sequence of wide SCSI IDs has a lower priority than narrow SCSI IDs. Therefore, the overall priority sequence for a wide SCSI is 7, 6, 5, 4, 3, 2, 1, 0, 15, 14, 13, 12, 11, 10, 9, and 8.

When a device is initialized, SCSI enables automatic assignment of device IDs on the bus, which prevents two or more devices from using the same SCSI ID.

## Parallel SCSI Addressing

In the parallel SCSI initiator-target communication (see Figure B-3), an initiator ID uniquely identifies the initiator and is used as an originating address. This ID is in the range of 0 through 15, with the range 0 through 7 being the most common. A target ID uniquely identifies a target and is used as the address for exchanging commands and status information with initiators. The target ID is in the range of 0 through 15.

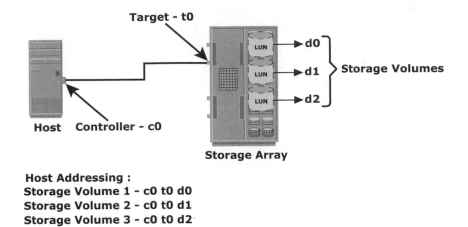

Host Addressing :
Storage Volume 1 - c0 t0 d0
Storage Volume 2 - c0 t0 d1
Storage Volume 3 - c0 t0 d2

**Figure B-3:** SCSI Initiator-Target communication

SCSI addressing uses the UNIX naming convention to identify a disk. It uses three identifiers — initiator ID, target ID, and a LUN — in the $cn|tn|dn$ format, which is also referred as *ctd addressing*. Here, cn is the initiator ID, commonly referred to as the *controller ID*; tn is the target ID of the device, such as t0, t1, t2, and so on; and dn is the device number reflecting the actual address of the device unit, such as d0, d1, and d2. A device identifies a specific logical unit in a target. The implementation of SCSI addressing may differ from one vendor to another.

# Appendix C
# SAN Design Exercises

## Exercise 1

An organization wants to implement a full mesh FC SAN. Following is the specification of servers, storage systems, and switches involved in the design:

- Number of hosts = 30. Each host has two single-port HBAs.
- Number of storage arrays = 4. Each array has eight front-end ports.
- Available switching elements:

  - Modular FC switches with minimum 16 ports. The number of ports in a switch can be increased up to 32 ports by adding additional port cards. Each port card includes 8 ports.
  - At least two interswitch links (ISLs) must exist between any two switches to ensure high availability.

At a minimum, how many switches are required to meet the given requirements? Justify the number of ports in each FC switch considering cost optimization.

### Solution

Total number of host ports = 30 hosts × 2 ports = 60 ports
Total number of storage array ports = 4 arrays × 8 ports = 32 ports
Total number of node ports = 60 + 32 = 92 ports

Each FC switch can provide a maximum of 32 ports. Considering 32 ports per switch, four switches provide a total of 128 ports. In four 32-port switch full mesh topology, 24 switch ports are used for ISLs, and the remaining 104 ports can be used for node connectivity. However, the fabric requires 92 ports for node connectivity. Therefore, to optimize the cost, the organization should deploy three 32-port switches and one 24-port switch. In this implementation, the number of switch ports available for node connectivity is 96, of which 92 ports can be used to connect nodes and the remaining 4 ports are available for future growth.

# Exercise 2

The IT infrastructure of an organization consists of three storage arrays direct-attached to a heterogeneous mix of 45 servers. All servers are dual-attached to the arrays for high availability. Because each storage array has 32 front-end ports, each could support a maximum of 16 servers. However, each existing storage array has the disk capacity to support a maximum of 32 servers. The organization plans to purchase 45 more servers to meet its growth requirements.

If it continues using direct-attached storage, the organization needs to purchase additional storage arrays to connect these new servers. The organization realizes that its existing storage arrays are poorly utilized; therefore, it plans to implement FC SAN to overcome the scalability and utilization challenges. The organization uses high-performance applications; therefore, it wants to minimize the hop count for the server's access to storage.

Propose a switched fabric topology to address the organization's challenges and requirements. Justify your choice of the fabric topology. If 72-port switches are available for FC SAN implementation, determine the minimum number of switches required in the fabric.

## Solution

Full mesh topology is not suitable for an environment that requires high scalability. Partial mesh, although, provides more scalability than full mesh, but several hops or ISLs may be required for the network traffic to reach its destination. Therefore, the recommended solution is core-edge topology. The core-edge topology provides higher scalability than mesh topology and provides one-hop storage access to all servers in the environment. Because of the deterministic pattern (from the edge to the core) of FC traffic movement, it is easy to calculate traffic load distribution across ISLs.

Total number of server ports = 90 servers × 2 ports = 180 ports
Total number of array ports = 3 arrays × 32 ports = 96 array ports
Number of switches at the core = 96 array ports/72 ports per switch ≈ 2 switches

The core switches provide 144 ports of which 96 ports will be used for array connectivity. The remaining 48 ports can be used for ISLs and future growth.

Number of switches at the edge = 180 server ports/72 ports per switch ≈ 3 switches

The edge switches provide 216 ports of which 180 ports will be used for server connectivity. The remaining 36 ports can be used for ISLs and future growth.

Number of edge switch ports used for connecting to core switches = 6

This is less than the remaining edge switch ports.

Number of core switch ports used for connecting to edge switches = 6

This is less than the remaining core switch ports.

So, at minimum, two core switches and three edge switches are required to implement the core-edge fabric.

# Appendix D
# Information Availability
# Exercises

## Exercise 1

A system has three components and requires all three components to be operational 24 hours, Monday through Friday. Failure of component 1 occurs as follows:

- Monday = No failure.
- Tuesday = 5 a.m. to 7 a.m.
- Wednesday = No failure.
- Thursday = 4 p.m. to 8 p.m.
- Friday = 8 a.m. to 11 a.m.

Calculate the MTBF and MTTR of component 1.

## Solution

The formula for MTBF is

(total operational time/number of failures).

Therefore,

MTBF = (24 hours * 5 days)/3 = 120 hours/3 = 40 hours

The formula for MTTR is

(total downtime/number of failures).

Therefore,

Total downtime = 2 hours on Tuesday + 4 hours on Thursday + 3 hours on Friday

So,

MTTR = (9 hours/3) = 3 hours

# Exercise 2

A system has three components and requires all three components to be operational during 8 a.m. through 5 p.m. business hours, Monday through Friday. Failure of component 2 occurs as follows:

- Monday = 8 a.m. to 11 a.m.
- Tuesday = No failure.
- Wednesday = 4 p.m. to 7 p.m.
- Thursday = 5 p.m. to 8 p.m.
- Friday = 1 p.m. to 2 p.m.

Calculate the availability of component 2.

## Solution

Availability (%) = system uptime/(system uptime + system downtime)

System downtime = 3 hours on Monday + 1 hour on Wednesday + 1 hour on Friday = 5 hours

System uptime = total operational time – system downtime = 45 hours – 5 hours = 40 hours

Availability (%) = 40/45 = 88.9%

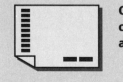 **Operational hours are 8 a.m. through 5 p.m., so any failure of a component outside these hours will not be considered as downtime.**

# Appendix E
# Network Technologies for
# Remote Replication

For remote replication over extended distances, various optical network technologies are deployed such as dense wavelength division multiplexing (DWDM), coarse wavelength division multiplexing (CWDM), and synchronous optical network (SONET).

## DWDM

Dense wavelength division multiplexing (DWDM) is an optical technology by which different data from different channels are transported at different wavelengths over a fiber-optic link at the same time. This is in contrast with a conventional fibre-optic system in which just one channel is carried over a single wavelength traveling through a single fiber. DWDM is a fiber-optic transmission technique, and several separate wavelengths (or channels) of data can be multiplexed into a multicolored light stream transmitted on a single optical fiber. Using DWDM, different data formats at different data rates can be transmitted together. Specifically, IP, ESCON, FC, SONET, and ATM data can all travel at the same time within the optical fiber (see Figure E-1).

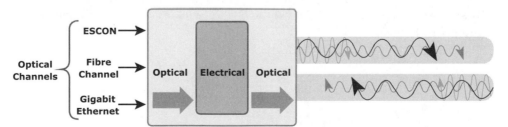

**Figure E-1:** Dense wavelength division multiplexing (DWDM)

DWDM can multiplex and demultiplex a large amount of channels. Each channel is allocated its own specific wavelength (lambda) band. Each wavelength band is generally separated by 10 nm spacing. As optical technologies improve, separations between each channel may be further reduced enabling more channels to be packed (tighter) onto a single fiber.

## CWDM

Coarse wavelength division multiplexing (CWDM), like DWDM, enables different data from different channels to transport at different wavelengths over a fiber-optic link at the same time. Compared to DWDM, CWDM consolidates environments containing a low number of channels at a reduced cost. CWDM contains 20 nm separations between each assigned channel wavelength. With CWDM technology the number of channel wavelengths to be packed onto a single fiber is greatly reduced. A CWDM system supports 16 channels or below, whereas DWDM supports channels ranging from 16 channels or above.

## SONET

Synchronous optical network (SONET) is a network technology that involves transferring a large payload through an optical fiber over long distances and operates at the physical layer level. SONET multiplexes data streams of different speeds into a frame and sends them across the network. The European variation of SONET is synchronous digital hierarchy (SDH).

SONET/SDH uses generic framing procedure (GFP) and supports the transport of both packet-oriented (Ethernet, IP) and character-oriented (FC) data. SONET defines optical carrier (OC) and electrically equivalent synchronous transport signal (STS) for the fiber-optic based transmission.

SONET transfers data at a high speed. (For example, OC-768 provides line rates up to 40 Gbps.) The basic SONET/SDH signal operates at 51.84 Mbps and is designated synchronous transport signal level one (STS-1) or OC-1. The STS-1 frame is the basic unit of transmission in SONET/SDH. For example, multiple STS-1 circuits can be aggregated to form higher-speed links. STS-3 (155.52 Mb/s) is equivalent to SONET level OC-3 and SDH level STM-1 (Synchronous Transport Module).

# Appendix F
# Acronyms and Abbreviations

**ACC**   Accept

**ACL**   Access Control List

**AD**   Active Directory

**AES**   Advanced Encryption Standard

**AL-PA**   Arbitrated Loop Physical Address

**ALU**   Arithmetic Logic Unit

**Amazon EC2**   Amazon Elastic Compute Cloud

**Amazon S3**   Amazon Simple Storage Service

**ANSI**   American National Standards Institute

**API**   Application Programming Interface

**AR**   Automated Replication

**ARB**   Arbitration Frame

**AS**   Authentication Service

**ASCII**   American Standard Code for Information Interchange

**ASIC**   Application-Specific Integrated Circuit

**ATAPI**   Advanced Technology Attachment Packet Interface

**ATM**   Asynchronous Transfer Mode

**AUI**   Application User Interface

**AVM**   Automatic Volume Management

**BB_Credit**   Buffer to Buffer Credit

**BBU**   Battery Backup Unit

**BC**   Business Continuity

**BCP**   Business Continuity Planning

**BCV**   Business Continuance Volume

**BIA**   Business Impact Analysis

**BIOS**   Basic Input/Output System

**BLOB**   Binary Large Object

**BMR**   Bare Metal Recovery

**CA**   Content Address

**CAPEX**   Capital Expenditure

**CAS**   Content-Addressed Storage

**CCS**   Common Command Set

**CD**   Compact Disc

**CDB**   Command Descriptor Block

**CDF**   Content Descriptor File

**CDP**   Continuous Data Protection

**CD-R**   Compact Disc-Recordable

**CD-ROM**   Compact Disc Read-Only Memory

**CD-RW**   Compact Disc Rewritable

**CE+**   Compliance Edition Plus

**CEE**   Converged Enhanced Ethernet

**CG**   Consistency Group

**CHAP**   Challenge-Handshake Authentication Protocol

**CHS**   Cylinder, Head, and Sector

**CID**   Connection ID

**CIFS**   Common Internet File System

**CIM**   Common Information Model

**CKD**   Count Key Data

**CLI**   Command-Line Interface

**CmdSN**   Command Sequence Number

**CMIP**   Common Management Information Protocol

**CMIS**   Common Management Information Service

**CN**   Congestion Notification

**CNA**   Converged Network Adapter

**COFA**   Copy on First Access

**COFW**   Copy on First Write

**CPM**   Content Protection Mirrored

**CPP**   Content Protection Parity

**CPU**   Central Processing Unit

**CRC**   Cyclic Redundancy Check

**CRM**   Customer Relationship Management

**CRR**   Continuous Remote Replication

**CS_CTL**   Class-Specific Control

**CSMA/CD**   Carrier Sense Multiple Access/Collision Detection

**CSP**   Cloud Service Provider

**CWDM**   Coarse Wave Division Multiplexing

**DAC**   Discretionary Access Control

**DACL**   Discretionary Access Control List

**DAE**   Disk Array Enclosure

**DART**   Data Access in Real Time

**DAS**   Direct-Attached Storage

**DataSN**   Data Sequence Number

**DBA**   Database Administrator

**DBMS**   Database Management System

**DCB**   Data Center Bridging

**DCBX**   Data Center Bridging Exchange Protocol

**DCP**   Data Collection Policy

**DDoS**   Distributed Denial of Service

**DDR SDRAM**   Double Data Rate Synchronous Dynamic Random Access Memory

**DF-CTL**   Data Field Control

**DFS**   Distributed File System

**DH-CHAP**   Diffie-Hellman Challenge Handshake Authentication Protocol

**DHCP**   Dynamic Host Configuration Protocol

**D_ID**   Destination ID

**DMTF**   Distributed Management Task Force

**DMX**   Direct Matrix

**DMZ**   Demilitarized Zone

**DNS**   Domain Name System

**DoS**   Denial of Service

**DPE**   Disk Processor Enclosure

**DR**   Disaster Recovery

**DRM**   Digital Rights Management

**DSA**   Directory System Agent

**DSS**   Decision Support System

**DVD**   Digital Versatile Disc or Digital Video Disc

**DVD-ROM**   Digital Versatile Disc Read-Only Memory

**DWDM**   Dense Wave Division Multiplexing

**ECA**   Enginuity Consistency Assist

**ECC**   Error Correction Code

**E_D_TOV**   Error Detect Time Out Value

**EE_Credit**   End-to-End Credit

**EIDE**   Enhanced Integrated Drive Electronics

**EMP**   Enterprise Management Platform

**EOF**   End of Frame

**E_Port**   Expansion Port

**ERP**   Enterprise Resource Planning

**ESCON**   Enterprise Systems Connection

**ETL**   Extract, Transform, and Load

**ETS**   Enhanced Transmission Selection

**EUI**   Extended Unique Identifier

**EXT 2/3**   Extended File System

**FAT**   File Allocation Table

**FBA**   Fixed-Block Architecture

**FC**   Fibre Channel

**FC-AL**   Fibre Channel Arbitrated Loop

**F_CTL**   Frame Control

**FCF**   Fibre Channel Forwarder

**FCIP**   Fibre Channel over IP

**FCoE**   Fibre Channel over Ethernet

**FCP**   Fibre Channel Protocol

**FC-PH**   Fibre Channel Physical and Signaling Interface

**FC-PI**   Fibre Channel Physical Interface

**FCS**   Frame Check Sequence

**FC-SAN**   Fibre Channel Storage Area Network

**FC-SP**   Fibre Channel Security Protocol

**FC-SW**   Fibre Channel Switched Fabric

**FCWG**   Fibre Channel Working Group

**FDDI**   Fibre Distributed Data Interface

**FICON**   Fibre Connection

**FIFO**   First In First Out

**FLOGI**   Fabric Login

**FL_Port**   Fabric Loop Port

**F_Port**   Fabric Port

**FRU**   Field Replaceable Unit

**FS**   File System

**FSPF**   Fabric Shortest Path First

**FTP**   File Transfer Protocol

**GB**   Gigabyte

**GBIC**   Gigabit Interface Converter

**GB/s**   Gigabyte per Second

**Gb/s**   Gigabit per Second

**GFP**   Generic Framing Procedure

**GHz**   Gigahertz

**GigE**   Gigabit Ethernet

**G_Port**    Generic Port

**GUI**    Graphical User Interface

**HBA**    Host Bus Adapter

**HDA**    Head Disk Assembly

**HDD**    Hard Disk Drive

**HIPAA**    Health Insurance Portability and Accountability Act

**HIPPI**    High Performance Parallel Interface

**HSM**    Hierarchical Storage Management

**HTTP**    Hypertext Transfer Protocol

**HWM**    High Watermark

**IA**    Information Availability

**IaaS**    Infrastructure-as-a-Service

**ID**    Intrusion Detection

**IDE/ATA**    Integrated Device Electronics/Advanced Technology Attachment

**IDS/IPS**    Intrusion Detection/Intrusion Prevention System

**IEEE**    Institute of Electrical and Electronics Engineers

**IETF**    Internet Engineering Task Force

**iFCP**    Internet Fibre Channel Protocol

**ILM**    Information Lifecycle Management

**IM**    Instant Messaging

**INCITS**    Inter National Committee for Information Technology Standards

**I/O**    Input/Output

**IOPS**    Input Output Per Second

**IP**    Internet Protocol

**IPC**    Inter Process Communication

**IP-SAN**    Internet Protocol Storage Area Network

**IPSec**    Internet Protocol Security

**iQN**    iSCSI Qualified Name

**IRM**    Information Rights Management

**iSCSI**    Internet Small Computer Systems Interface

**iSCSI PDU**   ISCSI Protocol Data Unit

**ISL**   Interswitch link

**iSNS**   Internet Storage Name Server

**ISO**   International Organization for Standardization

**ITU**   International Telecommunication Union

**JBOD**   Just a Bunch of Disks

**KDC**   Key Distribution Center

**KVM**   Keyboard, Video, and Mouse

**LACP**   Link Aggregation Control Protocol

**LAN**   Local Area Network

**Lb**   Least Blocks

**LBA**   Logical Block Addressing

**LC**   Lucent Connector

**LCA**   Link Capacity Adjustment

**LCAS**   Link Capacity Adjustment Scheme

**LCC**   Link Control Card

**LDAP**   Lightweight Directory Access Protocol

**LEP**   Link End Point

**Lo**   Least I/Os

**LR**   Link Reset

**LRR**   Link Reset Response

**LRU**   Least Recently Used

**LUN**   Logical Unit Number

**LV**   Logical Volume

**LVDS**   Low-Voltage Differential Signaling

**LVM**   Logical Volume Management

**LWM**   Low Watermark

**MAC**   Media Access Control

**MAID**   Massive Array of Idle Disks

**MAN**   Metropolitan Area Network

**MD5**   Message-Digest Algorithm

**MHz**   Megahertz

**MIB**   Management Information Base

**MIBE**   Matrix Interface Board Enclosure

**MirrorView/A**   MirrorView / Asynchronous

**MirrorView/S**   MirrorView / Synchronous

**MLC**   Multi-Level Cell

**MMF**   Multimode Fiber

**MPFS**   Multi-Path File System

**MPP**   Massively Parallel Processing

**MRU**   Most Recently Used

**MSS**   Maximum Segment Size

**MTBF**   Mean Time Between Failure

**MTTR**   Mean Time to Repair

**MTU**   Maximum Transfer Unit

**NAA**   Network Address Authority

**NACA**   Normal Auto Contingent Allegiance

**NAND**   Negated AND

**NAS**   Network-Attached Storage

**NDMP**   Network Data Management Protocol

**NFS**   Network File System

**NIC**   Network Interface Card

**NIS**   Network Information Services

**NIST**   National Institute of Standards and Technology

**NL_Port**   Node Loop Port

**NMC**   NetWorker Management Console

**NPIV**   N_Port ID Virtualization

**N_Port**   Node Port

**NTFS**   New Technology File System

**NTP**   Network Time Protocol

**OID**   Object ID

**OLTP**   Online Transaction Processing

**OPEX**   Operational Expenditure

**OS**   Operating System

**OSD**   Object-based Storage Device

**OSI**   Open System Interconnection

**OTF**   Open Tape Format

**OXID**   Originator Exchange Identifier

**P2P**   Peer-to-Peer

**PaaS**   Platform-as-a-Service

**PAgP**   Port Aggregation Protocol

**PATA**   Parallel Advanced Technology Attachment

**PCI**   Peripheral Component Interconnect

**PCIe**   Peripheral Component Interconnect Express

**PDU**   Protocol Data Unit

**PFC**   Priority-based Flow Control

**PII**   Personally Identifiable Information

**PIT**   Point in Time

**PKI**   Public Key Infrastructure

**PLOGI**   Port Login

**pNFS**   Parallel Network File System

**PRLI**   Process Login

**PV**   Physical Volume

**PVID**   Physical Volume Identifier

**QoS**   Quality of Service

**R2T**   Request to Transfer

**RADIUS**   Remote Authentication Dial-In User Service

**RAID**   Redundant Array of Independent Disks

**RAIN**   Redundant Array of Independent Nodes

**RAM**   Random Access Memory

**R_A_TOV**   Resource Allocation Time-Out Value

**RBAC**   Role-Based Access Control

**R_CTL**   Routing Control

**RDBMS**   Relational Database Management System

**REST**   Representational State Transfer

**RFC**   Requests for Comments

**RLP**   Reserved LUN Pool

**ROBO**   Remote Office/Branch Office

**ROI**   Return on Investment/Information

**ROM**   Read-Only Memory

**RPC**   Remote Procedure Call

**RPO**   Recovery Point Objective

**RR**   Round-Robin

**R_RDY**   Receiver Ready

**RSCN**   Registered State Change Notification

**RTD**   Round-Trip Delay

**RTO**   Recovery Time Objective

**R/W**   Read/Write

**Rx**   Receiver

**SaaS**   Software-as-a-Service

**SACK**   Selective Acknowledge

**SACL**   System Access Control List

**SAL**   SCSI Application Layer

**SAN**   Storage Area Network

**SAS**   Serial Attached SCSI

**SASI**   Shugart Associate System Interface

**SATA**   Serial Advanced Technology Attachment

**SC**   Standard Connector

**SCA**   Side Channel Attacks

**SCN**   State Change Notification

**SCSI**   Small Computer System Interface

**SDH**   Synchronous Digital Hierarchy

**SEC**   Securities and Exchange Commission

**SFP+**   Small Form Factor Pluggable Plus

**SHA**   Secure Hash Algorithm

**SID**   Security Identifier

**SIM**   Security Information Management

**SIS**   Single-Instance Storage

**SISL**   Stream-Informed Segment Layout

**SLA**   Service Level Agreement

**SLC**   Single-Level Cell

**SLED**  Single Large Expensive Drive

**SLP**  Service Location Protocol

**SMB**  Server Message Block

**SMF**  Single-Mode Fiber

**SMI**  Storage Management Initiative

**SMI-S**  Storage Management Initiative – Specification

**SMTP**  Simple Mail Transfer Protocol

**SNIA**  Storage Networking Industry Association

**SNMP**  Simple Network Management Protocol

**SNS**  Simple Name Server

**SOA**  Service Oriented Architecture

**SOAP**  Simple Object Access Protocol

**SOF**  Start of Frame

**SONET**  Synchronous Optical Networking

**SP**  Storage Processor

**SPE**  Storage Processor Enclosure

**SPI**  SCSI Parallel Interface

**SPOF**  Single Point of Failure

**SPS**  Standby Power Supply

**SRDF**  Symmetrix Remote Data Facility

**SRDF/A**  SRDF/Asynchronous

**SRDF/AR**  SRDF/Automated Replication

**SRDF/CE**  SRDF/Cluster Enabler

**SRDF/CG**  SRDF/Consistency Groups

**SRDF/DM**  SRDF/Data Mobility

**SRDF/S**  SRDF/Synchronous

**SRM**  Storage Resource Management

**SSD**  Solid-State Drive

**SSH**  Secure Shell

**SSID**  Session ID

**SSL**  Secure Sockets Layer

**ST**   Straight Tip

**StatSN**   Status Sequence Number

**STPL**   SCSI Transport Protocol Layer

**STS**   Synchronous Transport Signal

**SW-RSCN**   Switch Registered State Change Notification

**TB**   Terabyte

**TCO**   Total Cost of Ownership

**TCP**   Transmission Control Protocol

**TGS**   Ticket Granting Service

**TGT**   Ticket Granting Ticket

**TLS**   Transport Layer Security

**TLU**   Tape Library Unit

**TOE**   TCP/IP Offload Engine

**TPI**   Tracks per Inch

**Tx**   Transmitter

**UDP**   User Datagram Protocol

**UFS**   UNIX File System

**UID**   User Identifier

**UIM**   Unified Infrastructure Manager

**ULP**   Upper-Layer Protocol

**URI**   Universal Resource Identifier

**URL**   Uniform Resource Locator

**USB**   Universal Serial Bus

**VC**   Virtual Circuit

**VCAT**   Virtual Concatenation

**VDC**   Virtualized Data Center

**VDEV**   Virtual Device

**VE_Port**   Virtual E_port

**VF**   Virtual Firewall

**VF_Port**   Virtual F_port

**VG**   Volume Group

**VLAN**   Virtual LAN

**VM**   Virtual Machine

**VMM**   Virtual Memory Manager

**VN_Port**   Virtual N_port

**VPN**   Virtual Private Network

**VSAN**   Virtual Storage Area Network

**VTL**   Virtual Tape Library

**WAN**   Wide Area Network

**WBEM**   Web-Based Enterprise Management

**WDM**   Wavelength-Division Multiplexing

**WORM**   Write Once, Read Many

**WORO**   Write Once, Read Occasionally

**WWN**   World Wide Name

**WWNN**   World Wide Node Name

**WWPN**   World Wide Port Name

**XCM**   Environmental Control Module

**XML**   Extensible Markup Language

# Glossary

**8b/10b encoding** — An algorithm that converts 8-bit data into 10-bit transmission characters.

**64b/66b encoding** — An algorithm that converts 64-bit data into 66-bit transmission characters.

**Access control** — Services to regulate user access to resources.

**Access Control List (ACL)** — A list of permissions that specifies who can access a resource and with what privileges.

**Accessibility** — Capability to access required information at the right place by the authorized user.

**Accountability services** — A service that enables administrators to track activities performed on a system and link them back to individuals in such a way that there is little possibility for individuals to deny responsibility for their activities.

**Active archive** — Category of data that is not likely to change or cannot be changed—often referred to as fixed content data.

**Active attack** — Unauthorized alteration of information that may pose a threat to data integrity and availability.

**Active changeable** — A category of data that is subject to change and can be changed is referred to as "changeable" data.

**Active Directory (AD)** — Microsoft implementation used to provide central authentication and authorization services.

**Active path** — A path currently available and actively used for I/O transmission.

**Active/active** — An architecture designed for high availability in which all the components are active and available to perform a task if another component fails.

**Active/passive** — An architecture designed for high availability in which the redundant components are idle and are waiting to perform a task if an active component fails.

**Actuator arm assembly** — An assembly to which all R/W heads are attached.

**Advanced Encryption Standard (AES)** — A block cipher (cryptographic algorithm) designated by the National Institute of Standards and Technology.

**Alert** — Notification of an event that may or may not need attention/ action, depending on the type of alert.

**American National Standards Institute (ANSI)** — A nonprofitable organization that coordinates the development and use of voluntary consensus standards for products, services, processes, and systems in the United States.

**Application** — A computer program that provides the logic for computing operations.

**Application Programming Interface (API)** — A set of function calls that enables communication between applications or between an application and an operating system.

**Application specific integrated circuit (ASIC)** — An integrated circuit designed to perform a specific function.

**Application virtualization** — A method for packaging applications to be portable.

**Arbitrated Loop** — A shared Fibre Channel loop whereby each device contends with other devices to perform I/O operations; it is analogous to a token ring.

**Arbitration** — A technique to determine which node gets control of the loop in FC-AL when one or more nodes attempt to transmit data.

**Archive** — A repository where fixed content is placed for long-term retention.

**Array/disk array/storage array** — A group of hard disk drives that work together as a unit.

**Asynchronous replication** — A write complete is acknowledged immediately to the source host. These writes are queued in the log, transmitted in the same order, and updated to the source.

**Attack surface** — Various ways in which an attacker can launch an attack.

**Attack vector** — A series of steps necessary to complete an attack.

**Authentication** — A process to verify the identity claimed by a sender in a communication.

**Authorization** — A process to identify a requestor's access rights to resources.

**Automatic path failover** — A seamless failover in the event of a path failure whereby I/O failover occurs on an available alternative path without disrupting application operations.

**Availability** — An extent to which a component is available and functions according to business expectations during its specified time of operations.

**Availability services** — Services that ensure reliable and timely access to data for authorized users.

**Average queue size** — An average number of requests in a queue.

**Average rotational latency** — One-half of the time taken for a full rotation of the disk drive platter.

**Back up to disk** — Use of disks to store backup data.

**Backup** — A copy of production data.

**Backup catalog** — A database that holds information about backup processes and meta data.

**Backup client** — A software that retrieves data from a production host and sends it to a storage node for backup.

**Backup server** — A server that manages a backup operation and maintains the backup catalog.

**Backup window** — A period of time for which a source is available to perform a backup procedure.

**Bandwidth (network)** — Maximum amount of data that can be transferred over a network in one second; expressed in Mbits/second (Mb/s).

**Bare metal hypervisor** — A virtualization platform that runs on the hardware without needing a separate host OS.

**Bare-metal recovery (BMR)** — A backup in which all meta data, system information, and application configuration is appropriately backed up for a full system recovery.

**Battery Backup Unit (BBU)** — A battery-operated power supply used as an auxiliary source in the event of power failure.

**BB_Credit** — Defines the maximum number of frames that can be present over the link at any given point in time.

**BC Planning (BCP)** — A disciplined approach enabling an organization's business functions to operate during and after a disruption.

**Big data** — Data sets so large that they are ungainly to manipulate using traditional tools.

**Binary Large Object (BLOB)** — A bit sequence of user data representing the actual content of a file. It is independent of the name and physical location of the file.

**Bit** — A basic unit of information in computing that can exist in one of two possible distinct states. The unit symbol of the bit is lowercase character b.

**Block** — A unit of contiguous fixed-size space on a disk drive.

**Block-level virtualization** — Provides an abstraction layer in the SAN between the hosts and the storage arrays.

**Block size** — An application's basic unit of data storage and retrieval.

**Bridged topology** — A topology that provides connectivity between an FC and IP network.

**Broad network access** — Capabilities available over the network and accessed through standard mechanisms that promote use by heterogeneous thin or thick client platforms.

**Broadcast** — A simultaneous transmission of a message to all the receivers.

**Buffer** — A temporary storage area, usually in RAM.

**Bunker site** — An intermediate site between production and remote that is used in cascaded/multihop three-site replication to mitigate the risks associated with two-site replication.

**Bus** — A collection of paths that facilitates data transmission from one part of the computer to another.

**Business continuity (BC)** — Preparing for, responding to, and recovering from an outage that may adversely affect business operations.

**Business Impact Analysis (BIA)** — A process to evaluate the effects of not performing a business function for a time period.

**Byte** — A unit of information that is 8 binary digits. The unit symbol for the byte is uppercase character B.

**Cache** — A semiconductor memory where data is placed temporarily to reduce the time required to service I/O requests from the host.

**Cache Coherency** — Copies of the same data in two different cache addresses is maintained identical at all times.

**Cache mirroring** — Each write to cache is held in two different memory addresses on two independent memory boards.

**Cache vaulting** — The process of dumping the contents of cache into a dedicated set of physical disks during a power failure.

**Call home** — Sends a message to the vendor's support center in the event of hardware or process failures.

**Capacity management** — Ensures the adequate allocation of resources for all services based on their service level requirements.

**Capital Expenditure (CAPEX)** — Money spent on physical assets.

**Carrier Sense Multiple Access/Collision Detection (CSMA/CD)** — A set of rules specifying how network devices respond when two devices attempt to use a data channel simultaneously (called a *collision*).

**Cascade/Multihop** — Replication whereby data flows from the source to the intermediate storage array, known as a *bunker*, in the first hop and then to a storage array at a remote site in the second hop.

**Challenge-Handshake Authentication Protocol (CHAP)** — Basic authentication used by initiator and target to authenticate each other via the exchange of a secret code or password.

**Channel** — A high-bandwidth connection between a processor and other processors or devices.

**Chargeback report** — A report that enables storage administrators to identify storage usage by an application/business unit to appropriately distribute storage costs across applications/business unit.

**Checksum** — A redundancy check to verify data integrity by detecting errors in the data during transmission.

**C-H-S addressing** — Use of physical addresses, consisting of the cylinder, head, and sector (CHS) number, for specific locations on the disk.

**Cipher** — A method in which arbitrary symbols represent units of plain text.

**Class of Service (CoS)** — FC standards that differentiate between the quality of network services, treating each type as a class with its own level of service priority.

**Client-initiated backup** — A manual/automatic backup process initiated by a client.

**Client-server model** — A model in which a client requests and uses the services provided by a server capable of serving multiple clients at the same time.

**Cloud** — A model for enabling convenient, on-demand network access to a shared pool of configurable computing resources (for example, networks, servers, storage, applications, and services) that can be rapidly provisioned and released with minimal management effort or service provider interaction.

**Cloud scale** — The concept that the cloud may have the potential to provide infinite scale for end-user needs.

**Cloud service provider** — The person, organization, or entity responsible for making a service available to cloud consumers.

**Cold backup** — A backup that requires the application to be shut down.

**Cold site** — A site where an enterprise's operations can be moved if a disaster occurs — one with minimum IT infrastructure and environmental facilities in place, but not active.

**Command-line interface (CLI)** — An application user interface that accepts typed commands "one line" at a time in a command prompt window.

**Command queuing** — An algorithm that optimizes the order in which received commands are executed.

**Common Information Model (CIM)** — An object-oriented description of the entities and relationships in a business' management environment maintained by the Distributed Management Task Force.

**Common Internet File System (CIFS)** — A Microsoft client-server application protocol that enables client programs to make requests for files and services on remote computers over TCP/IP.

**Common Management Information Protocol (CMIP)** — A network management protocol built on the Open Systems Interconnection (OSI) communication model.

**Common Management Information Service (CMIS)** — A service used by network elements for network management.

**Community cloud** — The cloud infrastructure is shared by several organizations and supports a specific community that has shared concerns (for example, mission, security requirements, policy, and compliance considerations). It may be managed by the organizations or a third party and may exist on-premise or off-premise.

**Compliance** — To adhere to government/industry regulations.

**Compute (Host or Server)** — A computing platform that runs applications and databases.

**Concatenation** — The process of logically joining address spaces of disks and presenting the result as a single large address space.

**Confidentiality** — Providing the required secrecy for information.

**Configuration Management Database (CMDB)** — A database that contains information about the components of an information system.

**Congestion Notification (CN)** — A mechanism for detecting congestion and notifying the source to move the traffic flow away from the congested links.

**Consistency group** — A group of logical devices located on a single or multiple storage arrays that need to be managed as a single entity.

**Console** — The primary interface to view, manage, configure, and handle reporting of various components (managed objects).

**Content Address (CA)** — An identifier that uniquely addresses the content of a file and not its location.

**Content Addressed Storage (CAS)** — An object-oriented system for storing fixed-content data. It provides a cost-effective networked storage solution.

**Content authenticity** — Achieved at two levels: by generating a unique content address and by automating the process of continuously checking and recalculating the content address.

**Content Protection Mirrored (CPM)** — The data object is mirrored for the total protection of data against failure.

**Content Protection Parity (CPP)** — Data is transformed into segments, with an additional parity segment for the total protection of data against failure.

**Continuous Data Protection (CDP)** — A technology whereby the recovery points or checkpoints are set with fine granularity so that data can be recovered without significant loss.

**Control Station** — Provides dedicated processing capabilities to control, manage, and configure a NAS solution.

**Converged Enhanced Ethernet (CEE)** — A specification for the existing Ethernet standard that eliminates the lossy nature of Ethernet.

**Converged network adapter (CNA)** — A technology that supports data networking (TCP/IP) and storage networking (Fibre Channel) traffic on a single I/O adapter.

**Copy on First Access (CoFA)** — A pointer-based full volume replication method that copies the data from source to target only when the write operation is issued on the source or a read/write operation is performed on the target for the first time. The replica is immediately available when the session starts.

**Copy on First Write (CoFW)** — A pointer-based virtual replication method whereby data is copied to a predefined area in the array when a write occurs to the source or target for the first time.

**Cryptography** — A technique for hiding information for the purpose of security.

**Cumulative backup (differential backup)** — Copies the data that has changed since last full backup.

**Cyclic redundancy check (CRC)** — A technique for detecting errors in digital data for verifying data integrity. In this method, a certain number of check bits, often called a checksum, are appended to the message being transmitted.

**Cylinder** — A set of concentric, hollow, cylindrical slices through the platters in a disk drive.

**Data** — A piece of recorded information.

**Data Access in Real Time (DART)** — Celerra's specialized operating system, which runs on the Data Mover.

**Data center** — Provides centralized data processing capabilities to businesses. Its core elements are applications, databases, operating systems, networks, and storage.

**Data Center Bridging (DCB)** — A suite of Ethernet protocol extensions defined for reliable storage transports.

**Data Center Bridging eXchange Protocol (DCBX)** — A discovery and capability exchange protocol, which helps Converged Enhanced Ethernet (CEE) devices to convey and configure their features with the other CEE devices in the network.

**Data compression** — The process of encoding information using fewer bits.

**Data consistency** — The usability, validity, and integrity of related data components.

**Data Encryption Standard (DES)** — A cryptographic algorithm published by the National Institute of Standards and Technology (NIST).

**Data integrity** — The assurance that data is not modified unintentionally.

**Data security** — The means to ensure both that data is safe from corruption and that its access is suitably controlled.

**Data shedding** — A process for deleting data and making it unrecoverable.

**Data store** — The part of the cache that holds the data.

**Data tampering** — Deliberate altering of data.

**Data transfer rate** — The amount of data per second that a drive can deliver to the controller.

**Database Management System (DBMS)** — A program that provides a structured way to store data in logically organized tables that are interrelated.

**Defense in depth** — Implementing security controls at each access point of every access path.

**Delta set** — Implementation of asynchronous replication uses a large storage cache for temporarily buffering the outstanding writes assigned for the target. The buffered data represents the difference, or delta set, between the source and the target writes.

**Demilitarized zone (DMZ)** — A host or network used as a buffer between an organization's private network and the outside public network.

**Denial-of-Service (DoS) attack** — An attack that denies the use of resources to legitimate users.

**Dense wavelength Division Multiplexing (DWDM)** — A technology that carries data from different sources together on an optical fiber, with each signal carried on its own separate wavelength.

**Desktop-as-a-Service (DaaS)** — Outsourcing a virtual desktop infrastructure (VDI) to a third-party service provider. Typically, DaaS has a multitenancy architecture and the service is purchased on a subscription basis. In this delivery model, the service provider manages the back-end responsibilities of data storage, backup, security, and upgrades. The customer's personal data is copied to and from the virtual desktop during logon/logoff and access to the desktop is device, location, and network independent.

**Desktop virtualization** — The remote display, hosting, or manipulation of a graphical computer environment (desktop).

**Device driver** — Special software that permits the operating system and computer hardware device to interact with each other.

**Diffie-Hellman Challenge Handshake Authentication Protocol (DH-CHAP)** — A secure key exchange authentication protocol that provides authentication between a Fibre Channel initiator and responder.

**Direct-attached backup** — A backup device attached directly to the backup client.

**Direct-attached storage (DAS)** — Storage directly attached to a server or workstation.

**Director (Switch)** — Class of interconnection device that has a large port count and redundant components for enterprise class connectivity requirements.

**Directory** — A container in a file system that contains pointers to multiple files.

**Directory service (DS)** — An application or a set of applications that stores and organizes information about a computer network's users and network resources. This enables network administrators to manage user access to the resources.

**Directory System Agent (DSA)** — An LDAP directory that can be distributed among many LDAP servers. Each DSA has a replicated version of the full directory that is synchronized periodically.

**Disaster recovery** — The process, policies, and procedures for restoring operations critical to the resumption of business, including regaining access to data.

**Disaster recovery plan (DRP)** — A plan for coping with the unexpected or sudden loss of data access with a focus on data protection. A part of business continuity planning.

**Disaster restart** — The process of restarting business operations with consistent copies of data.

**Discovery domain** — Provides a functional grouping of devices in an IP-SAN. For devices to communicate with one another, they must be configured in the same discovery domain.

**Discretionary Access Control (DAC)** — An access policy determined by the owner of an object.

**Disk-buffered replication** — A combination of local and remote replication technologies; it creates a local PIT replica first and then a remote replica of the local PIT replica.

**Disk drive** — A nonvolatile storage device that stores data using rapidly rotating platters with magnetic surfaces.

**Disk image backup** — A backup consisting of a copy of each of the blocks comprising a disk's usable storage area.

**Disk partitioning** — The creation of logical divisions on a hard disk.

**Distributed computing** — Any computing that involves multiple computers remote from each other that each have a role in a computation problem or information processing.

**Distributed file system (DFS)** — A file system distributed across several computer nodes.

**Distributed Management Task Force (DMTF)** — An organization that develops management standards for computer systems and enterprise environments.

**Domain ID** — A Domain ID is the unique identifier assigned to every switch (domain) in a fabric.

**Domain Name System (DNS)** — Helps to translate human-readable hostnames into IP addresses.

**Downtime** — The amount of time during which a system is in an inaccessible state.

**Dynamic Host Configuration Protocol (DHCP)** — An approach to dynamically assigning an IP address to a host.

**Elasticity** — Fast and graceful response to changing resource requirements.

**Encryption** — The process to transform information using an algorithm (called a *cipher*) to make it unreadable to unauthorized users.

**End-to-End Credit (EE-Credit)** — A mechanism that controls the data flow for class 1 and class 2 traffic using buffers.

**Enterprise management platform (EMP)** — Integrated applications or suites of applications that manage and monitor the data center environment.

**Enterprise Resource Management (ERM)** — Software that manages all aspects of an organization's assets, services, and functions.

**Enterprise Systems Connection (ESCON)** — An optical serial interface between IBM mainframe computers and peripheral devices.

**Error-correction coding** — An encoding method that detects and corrects errors at the receiving end of data transmission.

**Expansion port (E_Port)** — A port used to connect two FC switches through an interswitch link (ISL)

**Export** — Publishes the file system to UNIX clients that can mount or access the remote file system.

**eXtensible Markup Language (XML)** — A universal format for structured documents and data on the World Wide Web.

**Extent** — A set of consecutively addressed disk blocks that is part of a single virtual disk-to-member disk array mapping.

**External transfer rate** — The rate at which data can be moved through the interface to the HBA.

**Fabric** — A Fibre Channel topology with one or more switching devices.

**Fabric Login (FLOGI)** — Login performed between an N_Port and an F_Port.

**Fabric Loop port (FL_Port)** — A port on a switch that connects to an FC arbitrated loop.

**Fabric port (F_Port)** — A port on the switch that connects to an N_Port.

**Fabric Shortest Path First (FSPF)** — Used in an FC network, a routing protocol that calculates the shortest path between nodes.

**Failback** — This operation enables the resumption of normal business operations at the source site. Failback is invoked after a failover has been initiated.

**Failover** — Automatic switching of a function to a redundant component upon failure of an active component.

**Fan-in** — Qualified number of storage ports that can be accessed by a single initiator through a SAN.

**Fan-out** — Qualified number of initiators that can access a single storage port through a SAN.

**Fatal alert** — A warning about a condition requiring immediate attention because the condition may affect the overall performance or availability of the system.

**Fault tolerance** — Describes a system or component designed in such a way that if a failure occurs, a backup component or procedure can immediately take its place with no loss of service.

**FCoE Forwarder (FCF)** — A Fibre Channel switching element that encapsulates the FC frames, received from the FC port, into the FCoE frames and also de-encapsulates the FCoE frames received from the Ethernet Bridge to the FC frames.

**Federated database** — A collection of databases treated as one entity and viewed through a single user interface.

**Federation** — Disparate data stores in other locations that enable organizations to seamlessly move workloads.

**Fibre Channel (FC)** — An interconnect that supports multiple protocols and topologies. Data is transferred serially on a variety of copper and optical links at a high speed.

**Fibre Channel Industry Association (FCIA)** — A mutual benefit nonprofit international organization of manufacturers, system integrators, developers, vendors, industry professionals, and end users. It delivers a broad base of Fibre Channel infrastructure technology to support a wide array of applications within the mass storage and IT-based arenas.

**Fibre Channel over Ethernet (FCoE)** — A standard for using the Fibre Channel protocol over Ethernet networks.

**Fibre Channel over IP protocol (FCIP)** — TCP/IP-based tunneling protocol for connecting Fibre Channel SANs over IP.

**Fibre Channel Protocol (FCP)** — A transport protocol that transports SCSI commands over a Fibre Channel network.

**Fibre Channel Security Protocol (FCSP)** — An ANSI standard that describes the protocols used to implement security in a Fibre Channel fabric.

**Fibre Connect (FICON)** — High speed input/output interface for mainframe computer connections to storage devices.

**Fiber Distributed Data Interface (FDDI)** — An ANSI standard for token ring MANs, based on the use of optical fiber cable to transmit data at a rate of 100 Mbps.

**Field-Replaceable Unit (FRU)** — A component of a system that can be replaced only by a vendor engineer.

**File-level access** — An abstraction of block-level access that hides the complexities of logical block addressing to the applications.

**File-level virtualization** — Provides the independency between the data accessed at the file level and the location where the files are physically stored.

**File server** — A server used to address file-sharing requirements.

**File system** — A structured way to store and organize data in the form of files that represent a block of information.

**File Transfer Protocol (FTP)** — A network protocol that enables the transfer of files between computers over the Internet.

**Firewall** — A dedicated appliance, or software, that inspects network traffic passing through it and denies or permits passage based on a set of rules.

**Firmware** — Software primed or embedded in a device.

**Fixed content** — Data that does not change over its life cycle.

**Flash drives** — Storage device that uses semiconductor-based memory to store data.

**Flow control** — Enables network traffic organization to match the sending and receiving device throughput.

**Flushing** — The process of committing data from cache to disk.

**Formatting** — A process to prepare a disk drive for data storage by writing required information on the disk.

**Force flushing** — In case of a large I/O burst, this process forcibly flushes dirty pages onto the disk.

**Frame** — A data stream that has been encoded by a data link layer for digital transmission over a node-to-node link.

**Front-end controller** — Receives and processes I/O requests from the host and communicates with cache or the back end.

**Front-end Port** — Provides the interface between the storage system and the host or interconnect devices (switch or director).

**Full backup** — Copying of all data from a source to a backup device.

**Full duplex** — Simultaneous transmission and reception of data on a single link.

**Full restore** — Entire data from the target is copied to the source. All data at the source is overwritten by the target data.

**Full stroke** — The time taken by the read/write head to move across the entire width of the disk, from the innermost track to the outermost track.

**Full virtualization** — Sufficiently complete simulation of the underlying hardware to allow software, typically a guest operating system, to run unmodified. A hypervisor mediates between host OS and guest OS.

**Full-volume mirroring** — The target is attached to the source and established as the mirror of the source. This is accomplished by copying all the existing data and synchronously updating the target for each write on the source.

**Gateway NAS** — A device consisting of an independent NAS head and one or more storage arrays.

**Generic framing procedure (GFP)** — A multiplexing technique that enables the mapping of variable-length payloads into synchronous-payload envelopes.

**Gigabit Ethernet (GbE)** — A group of Ethernet standards in which data is transmitted at a rate of 1 Gbit per second.

**Gigabit Interface Converter (GBIC)** — A transceiver that can convert electrical signals to optical signals and vice versa.

**Global namespace** — Maps logical pathnames to physical locations.

**Gold copy** — A copy of the replica device created prior to restarting applications using the replica device.

**Governance** — Rules, processes, or laws by which businesses are operated and regulated.

**Governance, Risk, and Compliance (GRC)** — Rules and regulations for government/business compliance and associated risk assessment.

**Graphical User Interface (GUI)** — An interface for issuing commands to a computer utilizing a pointing device, such as a mouse, that manipulates and activates graphical images on a monitor.

**Grid computing** — Applying the resources of many computers in a network at the same time to process a single problem.

**Guest operating system** — An operating system that has been installed on a virtual machine (VM).

**Hard Disk Assembly (HDA)** — A set of rotating platters and heads sealed in a case.

**Hardware assist virtualization** — A virtualization technique that enables the computer's processor to virtualize instructions to offload to system hardware.

**Heartbeat** — A messaging mechanism used by MirrorView software to determine whether a secondary device is available after it is determined unreachable.

**Heterogeneous** — Compilation and coordination of different hardware and software systems for a unified presence.

**Hierarchical Storage Management (HSM)** — Policy-based management that enables moving data from high-cost storage media to low-cost storage media.

**High availability** — Ensures that no data is lost if a disaster occurs at the source.

**High Performance Computing (HPC)** — The use of parallel processing for running advanced application programs efficiently, reliably, and quickly.

**High Performance Parallel Interface (HIPPI)** — A high-speed computer bus used to connect to a storage device.

**High watermark** — The cache utilization level at which the storage system starts high-speed flushing of cache data.

**Host** — A client or server computer that runs applications.

**Host bus adapter (HBA)** — Hardware that connects a host computer to a storage area network or directly to a storage device.

**Hot backup** — Backing up data when the application is up-and-running, with users accessing it.

**Hot site** — A computer room with the required hardware, operating system, application, and network support to perform business operations in case of a disaster or nonavailability of an application.

**Hot spare** — An idle disk drive that replaces a failed drive in any protected RAID group.

**Hot swap** — The replacement of a hardware component with a similar one while the computer system using it remains in operation.

**Hub** — An interconnectivity device that connects nodes in a logical loop whereby the nodes must share the bandwidth.

**Hybrid cloud** — The cloud infrastructure is a composition of two or more clouds (private, community, or public) that remain unique entities but are bound together by standardized or proprietary technology that enables data and application portability (for example, cloud bursting for load-balancing between clouds).

**HyperText Markup Language (HTML)** — A computer language consisting of a set of tags that describes how a document is displayed by a web browser.

**HyperText Transfer Protocol (HTTP)** — An application level protocol typically run over TCP/IP that enables the exchange of files via the World Wide Web.

**Hypervisor** — A virtualization platform that enables multiple operating systems to run concurrently on a physical host computer. The hypervisor is responsible for interacting directly with the physical resources of the host computer.

**Idle flushing** — Continuous destaging of data from cache to disk when the cache utilization level is between the high and low watermark.

**In-band** — An implementation in which the virtualized environment configurations reside internal to the data path.

**Incremental backup** — Copy of data that has changed since the last full or incremental backup, whichever has occurred more recently.

**Information** — The knowledge derived from data.

**Information Lifecycle Management (ILM)** — A proactive and dynamic strategy that helps businesses to manage the growth of information based on its business value.

**Information Rights Management (IRM)** — A technology that protects sensitive information from unauthorized access; sometimes referred to as Enterprise Digital Rights Management.

**Information Technology Infrastructure Library (ITIL)** — Collection of best practices for IT service management.

**Infrastructure-as-a-Service** — The capability provided to the consumer is to provision processing, storage, networks, and other fundamental computing resources where the consumer can deploy and run arbitrary software, which can include operating systems and applications. The consumer does not manage or control the underlying cloud infrastructure but has control over operating systems, storage, deployed applications, and possibly limited control of select networking components (for example, host firewalls).

**Initiator** — A device that starts a data request.

**Inode** — A data structure that contains information and is associated with every file and directory.

**I/O burst** — A large number of writes that occur within a very short duration.

**I/O controller** — Component that processes I/O requests one at a time.

**Input/Output channel (I/O channel)** — Provides the communication between the I/O bus and the CPU.

**Input Output per Second (IOPS)** — Number of reads and writes performed per second.

**In-sync** — Implies that the primary logical device and secondary logical device contain identical data.

**Integrated Device Electronics/Advanced Technology Attachment (IDE/ ATA)** — Standard interface protocol used for connecting storage devices, such as disk drives and CD-ROM drives inside in a personal compute system.

**Integrity checking** — Ensures that the content of a file matches the digital signature (hashed output or CA).

**Interface** — A communication boundary between two elements, such as software, a hardware device, or a user.

**Internal transfer rate** — The speed at which data moves from the disk surface to the read/write heads.

**International Committee for Information Technology Standards (INCITS)** — A forum for information technology developers, producers, and users for the creation and maintenance of formal IT standards. INCITS is accredited by, and operates under rules approved by, the American National Standards Institute (ANSI).

**Internet Engineering Task Force (IETF)** — The body that defines standard Internet operating protocols such as TCP/IP.

**Internet Protocol (IP)** — A protocol used for communicating data across a packet-switched network.

**Internet Protocol Security (IPSec)** — A suite of algorithms, protocols, and procedures used for securing IP communications by authenticating and/or encrypting each packet in a data stream.

**Internet Protocol storage area network (IP SAN)** — Hybrid storage networking solutions that leverage IP networks.

**Internet Small Computer System Interface protocol (iSCSI)** — An IP-based protocol built on SCSI. It carries block-level data over traditional IP networks.

**Internet Storage Name Service (iSNS)** — A protocol that enables the automated discovery of storage devices on an IP network.

**Interswitch link (ISL)** — A link that connects two switches/fabrics through E_Ports.

**Intrusion Detection (IDS)** — A detection control that identifies intrusion in the IT systems and attempts to stop attacks by terminating a network connection or invoking a firewall rule to block traffic.

**IP Storage** — Storage networking over TCP/IP networks.

**IT-as-a-Service** — Complete end-to-end services to present and provide information technology infrastructure as an on-demand and scalable service.

**Jitter** — Unwanted variation in signal characteristics.

**Journal file system** — A file system that uses a separate area called log or journal to track all the changes to a file system, enabling easy recovery in the event of a file system crash.

**Jukebox** — Collections of optical disks in an "array" used to store and access fixed content.

**Jumbo frames** — Large IP frames used in high-performance networks to increase performance over long distances.

**Just a bunch of disks (JBOD)** — A collection of disks without the coordinated control of control software.

**k28.5** — A special 10-bit character used to indicate the beginning of a Fibre Channel command.

**Kerberos** — A network authentication protocol that enables individuals communicating over a nonsecure network to prove their identity to one another in a secure manner.

**Key Distribution Center (KDC)** — A Kerberos server that implements the authentication and ticket-granting services.

**LAN-based backup** — Data to be backed up is transferred from the application server to the storage node over the LAN.

**Landing zone** — The area of a hard disk where the R/W head rests on the platter near the spindle.

**Latency** — Time delay between an I/O request and completion of that I/O.

**Least Recently Used (LRU)** — A cache algorithm whereby addresses that have not been accessed for a long time are freed up or marked for reuse.

**Level 1 (L1) cache** — An additional cache that is associated with the CPU. It holds data and program instructions that are likely to be needed by the CPU in the near future.

**Lightweight Directory Access Protocol (LDAP)** — An application protocol for accessing an information directory over TCP/IP.

**Link aggregation** — A technique for network high availability configuration. It enables multiple active Ethernet connections to the same switch to appear as a single link.

**Link Aggregation Control Protocol (LACP)** — An IEEE standard for combining two or more physical data channels into one logical data channel for high availability.

**Load balancing** — A method of evenly distributing the workload across multiple computer systems, network links, CPUs, hard drives, or other resources to get optimal resource utilization.

**Local area network (LAN)** — An IP-based communication infrastructure that shares a common link to connect a large number of interconnecting nodes within a small geographic area (typically a building or campus).

**Local bus or I/O bus** — A high-speed pathway that connects CPU and peripheral devices for data transfer.

**Local replication** — The process to create a copy of a production volume, within the same storage array (in the case of array-based local replication) or within the same data center (in the case of host-based local replication).

**Log shipping** — A host-based replication method whereby all activities at the source are captured into a "log" file and periodically shipped and applied to the remote site.

**Logical arrays** — A subset of disks within an array that can be grouped to form logical associations — for example, a RAID set.

**Logical Block Addressing (LBA)** — A method to address the location of a predefined storage space (block) using running numbers (ex: 1 to 65536) instead of cylinder-head-sector numbers.

**Logical Unit Number (LUN)** — An identifier of a logical storage unit presented to a host for storing and accessing data on those units.

**Logical volume** — Virtual disk partition created within a volume group.

**Logical volume manager (LVM)** — Host-resident software that creates and controls host-level logical volumes.

**Lossless Ethernet network** — An Ethernet network composed only of full duplex links, Lossless Ethernet MACs, and Lossless Ethernet bridging elements.

**Low watermark** — The point at which the storage system stops the forced flushing and returns to idle flush behavior.

**LUN binding** — The process to create LUNs within a RAID set.

**LUN masking** — A process that provides data access control so that the host can see only the LUNs it is intended to access.

**Magnetic tape** — A sequential storage medium used for data storage, backup, and archiving.

**Mail or import/export slot** — A slot used to add or remove tapes from the tape-library without opening the access doors.

**Malware** — A malicious software designed with the intent of compromising confidentiality, integrity, or availability.

**Management Information Base (MIB)** — A collection of objects in a (virtual) database used to manage entities (such as routers and switches) in a network.

**Maximum Transmission Unit (MTU)** — A setting that determines the size of the largest packet that can be transmitted without data fragmentation.

**MD5** — A message-digest algorithm that produces a 128-bit digest.

**Mean Time Between Failure (MTBF)** — A measure (in hours) of the average life expectancy of an individual component.

**Mean Time To Repair (MTTR)** — The average time required to repair a faulty component.

**Measured service** — Cloud systems automatically control and optimize resource use by leveraging a metering capability at some level of abstraction appropriate to the type of service (for example, storage, processing, bandwidth, and active user accounts). Resource usage can be monitored, controlled, and reported, providing transparency for both the provider and consumer of the utilized service.

**Media Access Control (MAC)** — A mechanism to control physical media in a shared media network.

**Memory virtualization** — A technique that gives an application program the impression that it has its own contiguous logical memory independent of available physical memory.

**Meta data** — Data about data that describes the characteristics of data such as content, quality, and condition.

**MetaLUN** — A logical unit expanded by aggregating multiple logical units.

**Metering** — Monitoring cloud usage for resource provisioning and costing.

**Metropolitan area network (MAN)** — A large computer network, usually spanning a geographical area no longer than 20 km.

**Mirroring** — A data redundancy technique whereby all the data is written to two disk drives simultaneously to provide protection against single-disk failure.

**Mixed topology** — A backup topology that uses both LAN-based and SAN-based backup topologies.

**Mixed zoning** — A combination of the WWN and port zoning technique.

**Modification attack** — An unauthorized attempt to modify information for malicious purposes.

**Monitoring** — The process of continuous collection of information and review of the entire storage infrastructure.

**Most Recently Used (MRU)** — A cache algorithm whereby the addresses that have been accessed most recently are freed up or marked for reuse.

**Mounting** — The process to make a file system usable by creating a mount point. The process of inserting a tape cartridge into a tape drive is also referred to as mounting.

**Multicast** — Delivers frames to multiple destination ports at the same time.

**Multi-Level Cell (MLC)** — A memory element in flash memory capable of storing more than one bit of data.

**Multimode Fiber (MMF)** — A fiber optic cable carrying multiple data streams in the form of light beams.

**Multipath I/O (MPIO)** — A fault-tolerant mechanism for a host to direct I/O requests to a storage device on more than one access path.

**Multipathing** — Enables two or more data paths to be simultaneously used for read/write operations.

**Multiplexing** — Transmitting multiple signals over a single communications line or channel.

**Multi-tenancy** — Many applications coexisting on the same infrastructure.

**Name server** — A host that implements a name service protocol.

**Namespace** — An abstract container that provides context for the items it holds (for example, names, technical terms, and words).

**National Institute of Standards and Technology (NIST)** — A nonregulatory federal agency within the U.S. Commerce Department's Technology Administration. NIST's mission is to develop and promote measurement, standards, and technology to enhance productivity, facilitate trade, and improve the quality of life.

**Network** — A set of interconnected devices for resource sharing.

**Network-attached storage (NAS)** — A dedicated file-serving device (with integrated or shared storage) attached to a local area network.

**Network Data Management Protocol (NDMP)** — An open protocol used to control data backup and recovery communications between primary and secondary storage in a heterogeneous network environment.

**Network File System (NFS)** — A common file-sharing method in a UNIX environment.

**Network Information System (NIS)** — Helps users identify and access a unique resource over the network.

**Network Interface Card (NIC)** — Computer hardware designed for computers to communicate over an IP network.

**Network latency** — Time taken for a packet to move from source to destination.

**Network layer firewalls** — A firewall implemented at the network layer to examine network packets and compare them to a set of configured security rules.

**Network portal** — A port to access any iSCSI node within a device.

**Network Time Protocol (NTP)** — A protocol for synchronizing the clocks of computer systems over packet-switched, variable-latency data networks.

**Network topology** — A schematic description of a network arrangement, including its nodes and connecting lines.

**Network virtualization** — A technique for creating virtual networks, independent of the physical network.

**Node** — A device or element connected in the network, such as a host or storage.

**Node loop port (NL-Port)** — A node port that supports the arbitrated loop topology.

**Node port (N-port)** — An end point in the fabric — typically a host port (HBA) or a storage array port connected to a switch in a switched fabric.

**Nonprotected restore** — A restore process in which the target remains attached to the source after the restore operation is complete and all the writes to the source are mirrored onto the target.

**Nonrepudiation** — Assurance that a subject cannot later deny having performed an action. Proof of delivery is provided in a communication for nonrepudiation.

**Non-Volatile Random Access Memory (NVRAM)** — Random access memory that has been made impervious to data loss due to power failure through the use of batteries or implementation technology such as flash memory.

**N_Port_ID virtualization (NPIV)** — A Fibre Channel configuration that enables multiple N_port IDs to share a single physical N_port.

**Object-based storage device (OSD)** — A disk-based storage system that stores data in a container called objects.

**Offline backup** — The database is not available for an I/O operation when replication takes place.

**On-demand self-service** — A consumer can unilaterally provision computing capabilities, such as server time and network storage, as needed automatically without requiring human interaction with each service's provider.

**Online backup** — A form of backup in which the data being backed up may be accessed by applications.

**Online Transaction Processing (OLTP)** — A system that processes transactions the instant the computer receives them and updates master files immediately.

**Open file agents** — These agents interact directly with the operating system and enable the consistent backup of open files.

**Operating environment** — A term used to refer an operating system of a storage array.

**Operational backup** — Collection of data for the eventual purpose of restoring, at some point in the future, data that has become lost or corrupted.

**Operational expenditure (OPEX)** — The expenses associated with transacting normal business operations.

**Optical Disc Drive (ODD)** — A disk drive that uses laser light or electromagnetic waves near the light spectrum as part of the process of reading and writing data. It is a computer's peripheral device that stores data on optical discs.

**Orchestration** — Coordination of disparate resources to make events happen within the system.

**Ordered set** — The low-level Fibre Channel (FC-1 layer) functions, such as frame demarcation and signaling, used for data transmission.

**Out-of-band** — An implementation in which the virtualized environment configurations reside externally to the data path.

**Out-of-sync** — Implies that the target data is not in a consistent state and requires full synchronization.

**Over commitment** — Allocating more resources (such as memory and CPU) than physically available.

**P2V (physical to virtual)** — Virtualization of physical application servers to virtual VMs.

**Packet loss** — When one or more packets of data traveling across a computer network fail to reach their destination.

**Page** — A small unit of cache memory allocation.

**Para-virtualization** — Virtualization environments that require modifications to guest operating systems in exchange for higher efficiency. Guest OS is tailored to run on a hypervisor.

**Parity** — A mathematical construct that enables re-creation of the missing segment of data.

**Parity bit** — An extra bit used in checking for errors in data bits during transmission. In modem communications, it is used to check the accuracy of each transmitted character.

**Partition** — A logical division of the capacity of a physical or logical disk.

**Partitioning** — Dividing a larger-capacity disk into virtual, smaller-capacity volumes.

**Passive attack** — An attempt to gain unauthorized access to information without altering it. Passive attacks may threaten the confidentiality of information.

**Passive path** — A path that is configured and ready but just not used at the moment. Usually available if a failure occurs.

**Password** — A form of secret authentication data used to control access to a resource.

**Payload** — Part of a data stream that represents user information and overhead, if any.

**Peripheral Component Interconnect (PCI)** — A standard bus for connecting I/O devices to a personal computer.

**Personally Identifiable Information (PII)** — Any data about an individual that could potentially identify that person.

**Platform-as-a-Service** — The capability provided to the consumer is to use the provider's applications running on a cloud infrastructure. The applications are accessible from various client devices through a thin client interface such as a web browser (for example, web-based e-mail). The consumer does not manage or control the underlying cloud infrastructure including network, servers, operating systems, storage, or even individual application capabilities, with the possible exception of limited user-specific application configuration settings.

**Platter** — One or more flat, circular disks found on a typical disk drive. It is a rigid disk coated with magnetic material on both surfaces.

**PLOGI (Port login)** — Performed between one N_port (initiator) and another N_port (target storage port) to establish a session.

**Point-in-time (PIT) copy** — A copy of data that contains a consistent image of the data as it appeared at a given point in time.

**Port** — A physical connecting point to which a device is attached.

**Port zoning** — Access to data is determined by the physical port to which a node is connected.

**Portal group** — A group of network portals that can collectively support a multiple-connection session.

**Prefetch (read ahead)** — In a sequential read request, a contiguous set of associated disk blocks that have not yet been requested by the host is read from the disk, and placed in cache in advance.

**Primitive sequence** — An ordered set transmitted continually until a specified response is received, as defined in an FC-1 layer.

**Private cloud** — Virtualized resources available as a service within one organization. It may, however, be managed by a third party.

**Private Key** — A cryptographic key in an asymmetric cryptosystem that is not made public.

**Process login (PRLI)** — N_port to N_port login used to exchange service parameters. The PRLI verification process is dependent on the ULP.

**Production data** — Data generated by an application hosted on a server.

**Propagation** — Transmission (spreading) of signals through any medium from one place to other.

**Propagation delay** — Amount of time taken by a packet to travel from its source to destination.

**Protocol** — A set of rules or standards that enable systems or devices to communicate.

**Protocol data unit (PDU)** — A message transmitted between two nodes on a network for communication.

**Public cloud** — A provider's service offering available to the public via a contractual agreement.

**Public Key** — A cryptographic key made public for purposes of using asymmetric encryption with an entity that has the private key.

**Public Key Infrastructure (PKI)** — Software, hardware, people, and procedures used to facilitate the secure creation and management of digital certificates.

**Quality of Service (QoS)** — A defined measure of performance in a data communication system.

**Queue** — Location where an I/O request waits before it is processed by the I/O controller.

**Quiescent state** — An application or device state in which the data is consistent. Processing is suspended, and tasks are either completed or not started.

**Quota** — Restrictions specified at the user level about the maximum capacity allocated (for example, the mailbox quota and the file system quota).

**RAID controller** — Specialized hardware that performs all RAID calculations and presents disk volumes to host.

**Random access memory (RAM)** — Volatile memory that allows direct access to any memory location.

**Random I/O** — Consecutive I/O requests that do not access adjacent data locations in a storage system.

**Rapid elasticity** — Capabilities can be rapidly and elastically provisioned, in some cases automatically, to quickly scale out and rapidly released to quickly scale in. To the consumer, the capabilities available for provisioning often appear to be unlimited and can be purchased in any quantity at any time.

**Raw capacity** — The total amount of addressable capacity of the storage devices in a storage system.

**Raw partition** — A disk partition not managed by the volume manager.

**Read-only memory (ROM)** — Nonvolatile memory type in which data can be read but not written.

**Read/write heads** — Components of the hard drive that read and write the data from or onto a disk drive. Most drives have two read/write heads per platter, one for each surface of the platter.

**Recoverability** — Ability of a replica to enable data restoration to resume business operations, with a predefined RPO and RTO, if a data loss or corruption occurs.

**Recovery-point objective (RPO)** — Point in time at which systems and data must be recovered after an outage. It defines the amount of data loss that a business can endure.

**Recovery-time objective (RTO)** — Time within which systems, applications, or functions must be recovered after an outage. It defines the amount of downtime that a business can endure and survive.

**Redundancy** — An inclusion of extra components (for example, disk drive, HBA, link, or data) that enables continued operation if any of the working components fail.

**Redundant Array of Independent Disks (RAID)** — Inclusion of a set of multiple independent disk drives in an array of disk drives, which yields performance exceeding that of a single large expensive drive.

**Redundant Array of Inexpensive Nodes (RAIN)** — Data is replicated to multiple independent nodes to provide redundancy in CAS.

**Registered State Change Notification (RSCN)** — Used to propagate information about changes in the state of one node to all other nodes in the fabric.

**Reliability** — Assurance that a system can continue its normal business operations for a specific period under the given conditions.

**Remote Authentication Dial-in User Service (RADIUS)** — An authentication, authorization, and accounting protocol for controlling access to network resources.

**Remote backup** — A copy from the primary storage is performed directly to the backup media, which is located at another site.

**Remote Procedure Call (RPC)** — A technology that enables a computer program to cause a subroutine or procedure to execute in another computer without the programmer explicitly coding the details for the remote interaction.

**Remote replication** — Process of copying source data stored in a local storage array to an array located at a remote site.

**Replica** — An image/copy of data usable by another application.

**Representational State Transfer (REST)** — An approach for getting information content from a website by reading a designated web page that contains an eXtensible Markup Language (XML) file that describes and includes the wanted content.

**Repudiation attack** — An attack that denies or obfuscates the authorship of something.

**Resource pooling** — The provider's computing resources are pooled to serve multiple consumers using a multitenant model, with different physical and virtual resources dynamically assigned and reassigned according to consumer demand. There is a sense of location independence in that the customer generally has no control or knowledge over the exact location of the provided resources but may specify location at a higher level of abstraction (for example, country, state, or data center). Examples of resources include storage, processing, memory, network bandwidth, and virtual machines.

**Response time** — Amount of time a system or functional unit takes to react to a given input.

**Restartability** — Determines the validity and usability of replicated data to restart business operations if a disaster occurs.

**Restore** — To return data to its original or usable and functioning condition.

**Resynchronization** — Process to restore only the data blocks that are updated after the PIT is copied to the target.

**Retention period** — Duration for which a business needs to retain the backup copies of data.

**Return on Investment (ROI)** — A calculation of the financial benefits gained from investing money on developing/modifying a system.

**Rewind time** — Time taken to rewind the tape to the starting position.

**Risk analysis** — An analysis performed as part of the BC process that considers the component failure rate and average repair time, which are measured by MTTR and MTBF.

**Robotic arms** — Component of a tape library used for moving tapes from its slots to a drive and back.

**Role-based access control (RBAC)** — An approach to restricting system access to authorized users based on their respective roles.

**Roll back** — Reverting a secondary replica to a previous point-in-time copy.

**Rolling Disaster** — Disasters marked by different beginning and end points that might be several milliseconds or minutes apart.

**Rotation speed** — Speed at which a hard drive platter rotates.

**Rotational latency** — Time taken by the platter to rotate and position the data location under the read/write head.

**Round-robin** — I/O requests are assigned to each available path in rotation.

**Round-trip delay (RTD)** — Delay between when data is sent and the acknowledgment is received from the remote site.

**Router** — An internetworking device that enables the routing of information between different networks.

**SAN-based backup** — A method of backing up data over a SAN.

**Save location** — A set of private LUNs that preserves PIT data just before it is updated at the source or the target by hosts.

**Scale out** — Scaling across or adding resources in a horizontal fashion to meet wide-spread or copious amounts of demand. The opposite is scale-up, which is to scale upwardly to meet performance expectations and demands.

**SCSI Application Layer (SAL)** — An uppermost layer in the SCSI communication model that contains both client and server applications that initiate and process SCSI I/O operations by using a SCSI application protocol.

**SCSI Transport Protocol Layer (STPL)** — Contains the services and protocols that enable communication between an initiator and targets.

**Sector** — Smallest individually addressable units of a disk drive on which data is physically stored.

**Secure Shell (SSH)** — A network protocol that enables data to be exchanged over a secure channel between two computers.

**Secure Sockets Layer (SSL)** — A cryptographic protocol that provides secure communications between a client and a server over the Internet using public key cryptography.

**Securities and Exchange Commission (SEC)** — A United States government agency that has the primary responsibility to enforce the federal securities laws and to regulate the securities industry/stock market.

**Security information management** — A collection of data, such as an event log in a central repository, used for effective analysis.

**Seek time** — The time required for the read/write heads in a disk drive to move between tracks of the disk.

**Seek time optimization** — Commands are executed based on optimizing read/write head movements, which may result in improved response time.

**Selective Acknowledge (SACK)** — With SACK, the data receiver can inform the sender about all segments that have arrived successfully, enabling the sender to retransmit only those segments that are actually lost.

**SendTargetDiscovery** — A command issued by an initiator to begin the discovery process. The target responds with the names and addresses of the targets available to the host.

**SEQ_ID** — An identifier of the frame as a component of a specific sequence and exchange as defined in an FC-2 layer.

**Sequence** — A contiguous set of frames sent from one port to another.

**Serial Advanced Technology Attachment (SATA)** — A serial version of IDE/ATA, designed for serial transfer of data.

**Serial attached SCSI (SAS)** — A point-to-point serial protocol that provides an alternative to parallel SCSI.

**Server-based virtualization** — A technique for masking or abstracting the physical hardware from the operating system. It enables multiple operating systems to run concurrently on single or clustered physical machines.

**Server/host/compute virtualization** — Enables multiple operating systems and applications to run simultaneously on different virtual machines created on a single or groups of physical servers.

**Serverless backup** — A backup methodology that uses a device other than the server to copy data to a backup device.

**Server Message Block (SMB)** — A network file system access protocol designed for Windows clients to communicate file access requests to Windows servers.

**Service catalog** — A catalog, listing services, components, attributes of services and associated prices.

**Service-Oriented Architecture (SOA)** — An architecture specifically created to support a particular service and its set of expectations.

**Service Set Identifier (SSID)** — A 32-character unique identifier attached to the header of packets sent over a WLAN that acts as a password when a mobile device tries to connect to the BSS.

**Shared secret** — A preshared key known only to the parties involved in a secure communication.

**Simple Mail Transfer Protocol (SMTP)** — The standard Internet e-mail protocol used for sending e-mail messages.

**Service-level agreement (SLA)** — An agreement between a provider and the consumer of a service.

**Service location protocol (SLP or srvloc)** — A service discovery protocol that enables computers and other devices to find services in a local area network without prior configuration.

**Simple Network Management Protocol (SNMP)** — A network management protocol that monitors the health and performance of network-attached devices.

**Simple Object Access Protocol (SOAP)** — A packaging protocol that packages XML messages for communication between the web services and the client.

**Single-instance Storage (SiS)** — Enables a system to avoid keeping multiple copies of user data by identifying each object using its unique object ID.

**Single Large Expensive Drive (SLED)** — A single high-capacity, and generally more expensive, drive attached to a computer.

**Single-Level Cell (SLC)** — A memory technology used in solid state drives that stores one bit on each memory cell, resulting in faster transfer speeds, lower power consumption, and higher cell endurance.

**Single-mode fiber (SMF)** — A type of optical fiber that carries data in a form of a single ray of light projected at the center of the core.

**Single point of failure** — Failure of a component that can terminate the availability of the entire system or IT service.

**Small Computer System Interface (SCSI)** — A popular storage interface used to connect a peripheral device to a computer and to transfer data between them.

**Snapshot** — A point-in-time copy of data.

**Sniffer** — A software tool that can identify network traffic packets.

**Snooping** — Unauthorized access to the data of another user or organization.

**Software-as-a-Service** — A capability provided to the consumer to use the provider's applications running on a cloud infrastructure. The applications are accessible from various client devices through a thin client interface such as a web browser (for example, web-based e-mail). The consumer does not manage or control the underlying cloud infrastructure including network, servers, operating systems, storage, or even individual application capabilities, with the possible exception of limited user-specific application configuration settings.

**Solid-state drive (SSD)/Flash drive** — A data storage device that uses solid-state memory to store data persistently.

**Source ID (S_ID)** — The standard FC address for the source port.

**Spindle** — The part of the hard disk assembly that connects all platters and is connected to a motor.

**Spoofing** — A practice whereby one person or program successfully masquerades as another by falsifying data, thereby gaining an illegitimate advantage.

**Standby power supply (SPS)** — A power supply that maintains power to cache for long enough to enable the content in cache to be copied to the vault.

**State Change Notification (SCN)** — The notification sent to an iSNS server when devices are added or removed from a discovery domain.

**Storage area network (SAN)** — A high-speed, dedicated network of shared storage devices and servers.

**Storage array–based remote replication** — Replication that is initiated and terminated at the storage array.

**Storage controller** — A device that processes storage requests and directs them to storage devices.

**Storage Management Initiative (SMI)** — A storage standard used to enable broad interoperability among heterogeneous storage vendor systems.

**Storage network** — A network whose primary purpose is the transfer of data between compute systems and storage and among storage.

**Storage Networking Industry Association (SNIA)** — A nonprofit organization to lead the industry in developing and promoting standards, technologies, and educational services to empower organizations in the management of information.

**Storage Node (Backup/Recovery)** — A part of the backup package that controls one or more backup devices (a tape drive, a tape library, or a backup to disk device) and receives backup data from backup clients.

**Storage Resource Management (SRM)** — Management of storage resources (physical and logical) that includes storage elements, storage devices, appliances, virtual devices, disk volumes, and file resources.

**Storage virtualization** — The act of abstracting the internal function of a storage system from applications, compute servers, or general network resources for the purpose of enabling application and network independent management of storage or data.

**Store** — Receives data from agents, processes the data, and updates the repository.

**Strip** — A group of contiguously addressed blocks within each disk of a RAID set.

**Stripe** — A set of aligned strips that spans all the disks within a RAID set.

**Stripe width** — Equal to the number of disk drives in the RAID array.

**Striping** — The splitting and distribution of data across multiple disk drives.

**Structured data** — Data that can be organized into rows and columns, and usually stored in a database or spreadsheet.

**Stub file** — A small file, typically 8 KB, which contains meta data from the original file.

**Superblock** — Contains important information about the file system, such as its type, creation and modification dates, size and layout of the file system, count of available resources, and a flag indicating the mount status of the file system.

**Swap file** — Also known as a page file or a swap space, this is a portion of the physical disk made to look like physical memory to the operating system.

**Switched fabric** — A Fibre Channel topology whereby each device has a unique, dedicated I/O path to the device it communicates with.

**Switches** — More intelligent devices than hubs, switches directly route data from one physical port to another.

**Switching** — A process of connecting network segments by using a hardware device called a switch.

**Symmetrix Enginuity** — Symmetrix Enginuity is the operating environment for EMC Symmetrix.

**Symmetrix Remote Data Facility (SRDF)** — Storage array-based remote replication software products supported by EMC Symmetrix.

**Synchronous Digital Hierarchy (SDH)** — A standard developed by the International Telecommunication Union (ITU), documented in standard G.707 and its extension, G.708.

**Synchronous optical network (SONET)** — A standard for optical telecommunications transport whereby traffic from multiple subscribers is multiplexed together and sent out onto a ring as an optical signal.

**System bus** — The bus that carries data between the processor and memory.

**Tag RAM** — An integrated part of the cache that tracks the location of data in the data store; it is where the data is found in memory and where the data belongs on the disk.

**Tampering** — An unauthorized modification that alters the proper functioning of a device, system, or communications path in a manner that degrades the security or functionality it provides.

**Tape cartridges** — A device that contains magnetic tapes used for data storage.

**Tape drive** — A data storage device that reads and writes data stored on a magnetic tape.

**Target** — A SCSI device that executes a command to perform the task received from a SCSI initiator.

**Target ID** — Uniquely identifies a target and is used as the address for exchanging commands and status information with initiators.

**TCP Offload Engine (TOE)** — A technology for improving TCP/IP performance by offloading TCP/IP processing to a network interface card.

**TCP/IP Offload Engine (TOE) card** — A TOE card offloads the TCP management functions from the host.

**Thin provisioning** — Presenting desired capacity of a LUN while masking total capacity.

**Threats** — Attacks that can be carried out on the IT infrastructure.

**Throughput** — Measurement of the amount of data that can be successfully transferred within a set time period.

**Tiered storage** — An environment that classifies storage into two or more tiers, based on differences in price, performance, capacity, and functionality.

**Total Cost of Ownership (TCO)** — A financial estimate of direct and indirect costs for owning software or hardware.

**Tracks** — The logical concentric rings on a disk drive platter.

**Transmission code** — Used in FC primarily to improve the transmission characteristic of information across the fiber.

**Transmission Control Protocol (TCP)** — A connection-based protocol that establishes a virtual session before information is sent from the source to the destination.

**Transmission word** — A data transmission unit in FC-1 whereby each transmission word contains a string of four contiguous transmission characters or bytes.

**Triangle/Multitarget** — A three-site remote replication process whereby data at the source site is replicated to an intermediate storage array (bunker) in the first hop and then to the remote storage array in the second hop.

**Trusted Computing Base (TCB)** — A set of all components in a computing environment that provides a secure environment.

**Tunneling protocol** — A protocol that encapsulates the payload to a different delivery protocol to provide secure communication.

**Universal Serial Bus (USB)** — A widely used serial bus interface to communicate with peripheral devices.

**Unstructured data** — Data that has no inherent structure and is usually stored as different types of files.

**Upper Layer Protocol (ULP)** — Refers to a more abstract protocol when performing encapsulation.

**User Datagram Protocol (UDP)** — A connectionless transport layer protocol used in IP.

**User identifier (UID)** — Each user in a UNIX environment is identified using a unique UID.

**Virtual Concatenation (VCAT)** — An inverse multiplexing technique to split the bandwidth equally into logical groups, which may be transported or routed independently.

**Virtual Data Center (VDC)** — A virtualized representation of a physical infrastructure and the services that it may provide.

**Virtual Desktop Infrastructure (VDI)** — A desktop virtualization technique that enables desktop operating systems to run on a virtual machine (virtual desktop) residing on servers in a data center. Users can remotely access these desktops from a variety of client devices, such as laptops, desktops, and mobile devices.

**Virtual E_Port (VE_Port)** — Virtual Extension Port in an FCoE Switch for ISLs.

**Virtual F_Port (VF_Port)** — Virtual Fabric Port in an FCoE Switch.

**Virtual Fabric (VF)** — A Fabric identified by a VF_ID composed of partitions of switches and N_Ports having a single fabric management and an independent address space.

**Virtual LAN (VLAN)** — A switched network logically segmented by functions, project teams, or applications, regardless of the physical location of network users.

**Virtual machine (VM)** — A software image of a computer that behaves like a physical machine. It also appears to the network to be a separate physical machine. Multiple VMs can run on the same physical machine.

**Virtual pools** — A logical group or cluster of resources.

**Virtual private network (VPN)** — A secured dedicated communication network tunneled through another network.

**Virtual storage area network (VSAN)** — A collection of ports from a set of connected Fibre Channel switches that form a virtual fabric.

**Virtual tape library (VTL)** — Disk storage that is logically presented as tape libraries or tape drives to the application thorough emulation software.

**Virtualization** — A technique of masking or abstracting physical resources by presenting a logical view of them.

**Virus** — A malicious computer program that can infect a computer without permission or knowledge of the user.

**VLAN tagging** — Process that inserts a marker (tag) into the Ethernet frame. Tag contains VLAN ID.

**Volume group (VG)** — A group of physical volumes (disk) from which a logical volume (essentially a partition) can be created.

**Vulnerability** — A defect in data protection mechanisms that could be exploited by a threat.

**Warning alert** — Conditions that require administrative attention to prevent the condition from becoming an event that affects accessibility.

**Wavelength-Division Multiplexing (WDM)** — A technology that multiplexes multiple optical carrier signals on a single optical fiber by using different wavelengths of laser light to carry different signals.

**Web-Based Enterprise Management (WBEM)** — A set of management and Internet standard architectures developed by the Distributed Management Task Force that leverages emerging web-based technologies.

**Web console** — A web-based interface that enables remote and local network monitoring of the SAN.

**Wide area network (WAN)** — Internetwork of computers that spans across geographical area (crossing metropolitan or even national boundaries); also used to interconnect multiple LANs.

**World Wide Name (WWN)** — A vendor-supplied, 64-bit globally unique identifier number assigned to nodes and ports in a fabric.

**World Wide Node Name (WWNN)** — A 64-bit node WWN used during fabric login.

**World Wide Port Name (WWPN)** — A 64-bit port WWN used during fabric login.

**Write aside size** — If an I/O request exceeds this predefined size, writes are directly sent to the disk, instead of written to cache. This reduces the impact of large writes consuming a large area of cache.

**Write-back cache** — Data is placed in the cache and an acknowledgment is sent to the host immediately. Later, data from cache is committed (destaged) to the disk.

**Write cache** — A portion of a cache set aside for temporarily storing data from a write operation before writing it to the disk for persistent storage.

**Write Once Read Many (WORM)** — An ability of the storage device (such as optical disks) to write once and read many times.

**Write penalty** — The I/O overhead in both mirrored and parity RAID configurations whereby every single write operation is manifested into additional write I/Os to the disks.

**Write splitting** — A process to capture writes and redirect them—one to the source and one to the journal.

**Write-through cache** — Data is placed in cache, written to the disk, and then acknowledged to the host.

**ZIP** — A popular data compression and archival format.

**Zone bit recording** — A method to record data that takes advantage of the disk's geometry by storing more sectors per track on outer tracks than on inner tracks.

**Zone set** — A group of zones that can be activated or deactivated as a single entity in a fabric. Zone sets are also referred to as *zone configurations*.

**Zoning** — A fabric-level process that enables nodes within the fabric to be logically segmented into groups. Members of the zone can communicate only with each other.

Index

# Index

## A

access control, 340–341, 361, 427

access control list (ACL), 169, 340, 349, 350, 351–352, 427

Access Manager, 362

access nodes, 197

access time. *See* seek time

accessibility, 202, 427

accountability service, 334, 427

ACL. *See* access control list

active archive, 427

active attack, 336, 427

active changeable, 427

Active Directory (AD), 171, 353, 354, 355, 427

active path, 427

active/active, 85–86, 218–219, 428

active/passive, 86–87, 219–220, 428

actuator arm assembly, 33, 428

AD. *See* Active Directory

administrative access, 344

advanced encryption standard (AES), 258, 428

Advanced Technology Attachment (ATA), 30, 82

AES. *See* advanced encryption standard

alert, 428

American National Standards Institute (ANSI), 96, 399, 428

ANSI. *See* American National Standards Institute

API. *See* Application Programming Interface

applications, 11, 17, 18, 43–45, 47, 428
cloud computing, 327
firewall, 356
I/O, 395–397
security, 338–342

Application Encryption and Tokenization, 362

Application Programming Interface (API), 20, 327, 428

application server-based backup, 239

application-specific integrated circuit (ASIC), 27, 101, 428

arbitrated loop, 102–103, 428

arbitration, 428

archive, 225, 226, 254–257, 345–346, 428

array/disk array/storage array, 428

arrival time, 39

AS. *See* Authentication Service